Freelance Graphics for Windows
The Art of Presentation

Other Prima Computer Books

Available Now

WINDOWS Magazine Presents: Access from the Ground Up
Advanced PageMaker 4.0 for Windows
DESQview: Everything You Need to Know
DOS 6: Everything You Need to Know
WINDOWS Magazine Presents: Encyclopedia for Windows
Excel 4 for Windows: Everything You Need to Know
Excel 4 for Windows: The Visual Learning Guide
Harvard Graphics for Windows: The Art of Presentation
LotusWorks 3: Everything You Need to Know
Microsoft Works for Windows By Example
NetWare 3.x: A Do-It-Yourself Guide
Novell Netware Lite: Simplified Network Solutions
PageMaker 4.0 for Windows: Your Complete Guide
PageMaker 4.2 for the Mac: Everything You Need to Know
WINDOWS Magazine Presents: The Power of Windows and DOS Together,
   2nd Edition
Quattro Pro 4: Everything You Need to Know
QuickTime: Making Movies with Your Macintosh
Smalltalk Programming for Windows (with 3½" disk)
Superbase Revealed!
SuperPaint 3: Everything You Need to Know
Windows 3.1: The Visual Learning Guide
Word for Windows 2: Desktop Publishing By Example
WordPerfect 5.1 for Windows By Example
WordPerfect 5.1 for Windows: Desktop Publishing By Example

Upcoming Books

CorelDRAW! 4 Revealed!
Improv for Windows Revealed! (with 3½" disk)
PageMaker 5 for Windows: Everything You Need to Know
WordPerfect 6 for DOS: The Visual Learning Guide

How to Order:

Individual orders and quantity discounts are available from the publisher, Prima Publishing, P.O. Box 1260BK, Rocklin, CA 95677-1260; telephone (916) 786-0426; fax (916) 786-0488. If you are seeking a discount, include information on your letterhead concerning the intended use of the books and the number of books you wish to purchase.

WINDOWS MAGAZINE

Freelance Graphics for Windows
The Art of Presentation

Gerald E. Jones

Prima Publishing
P.O. Box 1260BK
Rocklin, CA 95677-1260
(916) 786-0426

Prima Computer Books is an imprint of Prima Publishing, Rocklin, California 95677

Executive Editor: Roger Stewart
Managing Editor: Neweleen Trebnik
Production Coordinator: Linda Beatty
Technical Reviewer: Nick Dargahi
Cover Design: Page Design, Inc.

Project Editor: Stefan Grünwedel
Copyeditor: Janna Hecker Clark
Production: Professional Book Center
Color Insert Layout: Marian Hartsough
Associates, Ocean Quigley

Freelance Graphics is a registered trademark of Lotus Development Corporation. If you have problems installing or running the software, notify the software manufacturer at 800-265-6887. Prima Publishing cannot provide software support.

Windows is a trademark of Microsoft Corporation.

Prima Publishing and the author have attempted throughout this book to distinguish proprietary trademarks from descriptive terms by following the capitalization style used by the manufacturer.

Reasonable efforts have been made to verify the accuracy of representations about products, services, and applications described in this book. Inclusion of such descriptions in the book should not be construed as endorsement by the author or by contributors or subject organizations. The author makes no claim as to the fitness of any product, service, or application described herein for any purpose whatsoever. The author further disclaims any liability for representations made about products, services, or applications described herein or for any damages, consequential or otherwise arising from such representations.

Library of Congress Cataloging-in-Publication Data
Jones, Gerald E.
    Freelance Graphics for Windows : the Art of Presentation / Gerald
    E. Jones.
        p.   cm.
        ISBN 1-55958-306-1 (pbk.) : $27.95
        1. Computer graphics. 2. Freelance graphics for Windows.
    I. Title.
    T385.J673   1993
    006.'869–dc20   92-46889
                                                                   CIP

Printed in the United States of America

93 94 95 96 RRD 10 9 8 7 6 5 4 3 2

Contents at a Glance

CONTENTS

9 Making Organization Charts and Diagrams   327

13   Preparing a Presentation   493

PREFACE

This is actually a book within a book. The tutorial chapters (4 through 10) constitute a software user's guide for the widely popular Freelance Graphics for Windows program. But beyond that, this is also a casebook in business graphics design and applications. The larger book encompasses all aspects of developing and presenting visual information in business. Although examples are given using Freelance Graphics for Windows, the principles apply to any method of charting—whether done by computer or by hand.

In the case and application material, there's a viewpoint you seldom find in tutorial software texts. That is, you become acquainted with the full range of problems (and solutions) that come with using business graphics software—including problems that have little to do with the software or even with computers. For example, you'll find out why:

- Different color palettes are needed for slides and overhead transparencies
- Colors and fonts can look very different on the screen and on output such as paper and film
- Certain graph formats can have inherently misleading aspects
- Middle-level managers have a compelling reason to prefer slides on film to electronic screen shows

- The biggest challenge in producing a major corporate meeting can be not generating the slides but keeping track of changes
- Converting spreadsheet files to charts isn't just a matter of identifying cells and ranges.

Much of this information is drawn from my experience as creative director for a computer-graphics production house. From that job, I went on to develop business-graphics systems and software, and there's some of that perspective here, also. This book is offered in the hope that my advice based on this experience will make your own work life easier.

BOOK ORGANIZATION

This book is divided into four major parts:

I. Designing an Effective Presentation
II. Learning Freelance Graphics for Windows
III. Gaining the Professional Edge
IV. Applying Freelance Graphics for Windows

Part I: Designing an Effective Presentation

The first three chapters cover the principles of graphic information display and design. Even though you can generate graphics using Freelance Graphics without this background, the material will become increasingly valuable as you begin to use the program to create effective business communications.

Part II: Learning Freelance Graphics for Windows

Chapters 4 through 10 amount to a quick course in hands-on usage of Freelance Graphics for Windows. Through examples, you will learn to generate all the chart types. The program is exceptionally easy to learn, just by working with it and following the on-screen prompts and menus. What pitfalls I've found, I'll share with you.

Part III: Gaining the Professional Edge

The third part of the book gives you a professional perspective on using business graphics as an essential part of your regular work. This is valuable information whether you are a graphic arts professional, support staff member, information analyst, or presenter.

Chapter 11 provides technical background in computer graphics, which can give you insight into the capabilities and limitations of the Freelance Graphics package and its use with other types of information and graphics systems.

Chapter 12 deals with the crucial topic of color—both as an element of design and as a tool within Freelance Graphics for Windows. The approach is from the viewpoint of the graphic arts professional.

Chapter 13 describes how presentations can be designed to suit the specific technical characteristics of different visual display media, including paper handouts, overhead transparencies, color slides, and video. Also covered are power production techniques in Freelance Graphics for Windows, including styles and custom page layouts, as well as Screen Shows and SmartShows.

Chapter 14 covers all of the issues surrounding sharing graphic information generated by Freelance Graphics for Windows with other computer systems, such as exporting files to other programs, computer networks, outside slide and graphics services, multimedia, and electronic conferencing.

The discussion in Chapter 15 sets Freelance Graphics in the environment of professional graphic arts by covering the effective management of major productions.

Part IV: Applying Freelance Graphics for Windows

Chapters 16 through 20 present case histories and examples of output produced for specific business situations. Covered are reports and newsletters, financial briefings, speeches, interactive shows, and large annual meetings.

Installation notes and a suggested hardware configuration for Freelance Graphics for Windows are presented in the appendix.

ACKNOWLEDGMENTS

I wish to thank Allison Parker and Candace Clemens at Lotus Development Corporation (Cambridge, Massachusetts) for providing software and documentation. Many queries were also fielded by the public relations staff at McGlinchey & Paul (Lexington, Massachusetts), including Constance Mazelsky and Barbara Ewen.

Special thanks to Nick Dargahi for his in-depth review of the manuscript and helpful suggestions.

Cliff Leach and Dallas Wright at Autographix (Burlington, Massachusetts) provided imaging services for color slides.

Jack Reed of Lloyd & Clark Marketing Communications (Encino, California) and Debbie Parisi of Prima Publishing handled publicity for the book.

Information on film and television aspect ratios was kindly provided by my friend and colleague Sherwin Becker of the Society of Motion Picture and Television Engineers (White Plains, New York).

I am grateful to Amy Davis for first seeing potential in this material and to Roger Stewart and Stefan Grünwedel at Prima Publishing for helping me carry this book through to completion.

Thanks to Laurie Stewart of Prima and the staff at Professional Book Center (Denver, Colorado) for an outstanding production job.

Thank you, Georja Oumano Jones, for your persistent belief that such minor literary miracles will someday make us rich.

REFERENCES

Much of the information in this book that does not concern the specifics of software products was published originally as *Looking Good with Harvard Graphics* and *Harvard Graphics for Windows: The Art of Presentation*. For purposes of permissions, this book is a derivation of those works.

The concept of peer, presentation, and publication levels was suggested to me by John Cool in his paper "Redefining Business Graphics" (1984).

Figure 3-6 and the accompanying quotation first appeared in "As the World Turns," reported by Scott Morris, in the July 1988 issue of *Omni* magazine. This material is reprinted by permission (©1988 Omni Publications International, Ltd.).

The survey of American movie audiences cited in Chapter 12 is taken from "Practical Motion Picture Photography," by Russell Campbell (New York: A.S. Barnes & Co., 1970).

The quotation about storyboard preparation in Chapter 13 is from "Audiovisual Notes from Kodak," Kodak Periodical No. T-91-2-1, Rochester, New York, 1982.

Portions of this text first appeared as a series of articles I wrote for the Business Graphics column of *Computer Graphics World* and are reprinted here by permission:

"Graphics Teleconferencing," August, 1983

"Desk-Top Film Recorders," October, 1983

"Can Creativity Be Automated?", April, 1985

"Dealing with Graphic Arts Service Bureaus," June, 1985

"Inside Graphic Arts Service Bureaus," July, 1985

"Elements of Visual Style," September, 1985

"Prospects for HDTV as a Presentation Medium," October, 1985

"Color Use, Abuse in Presentations," May, 1986

Other observations on business graphics software first appeared in my article "Picture Processors: A Look at Business Graphics Software," *Interface Age*, November, 1983.

I N T R O D U C T I O N

HOW TO MAKE A CHART
WITHOUT READING THIS BOOK

No matter what your age, getting a new software product can be like unwrapping a marvelous new toy—even if it has a serious business purpose. And why shouldn't it be fun? After all, that's the purpose of technology—to make work easier and more enjoyable.

If you have already installed Freelance Graphics for Windows, you can be productive almost immediately. You do not need to pore over volumes of information simply to make charts or drawings. The product is specifically designed to be used in offices by people who have no formal training in the graphic arts. The program is quick and easy to learn. And it is also easy to *relearn*—an important consideration, since you might not necessarily use the program every day. (In fact, if you're like most people, you concentrate on making graphics about once a month, usually when you are preparing reports.)

A major reason why this program is easy to use is the Windows environment itself. In Windows, applications have similar sets of drawing and editing tools, using the same scheme of mouse actions and menu selections. Windows also makes it easy to exchange data and pictures among the applications it supports.

CREATING A PRESENTATION

Now, put this promised ease of use to the test. You can create a new presentation by following these steps:

1. Start Freelance Graphics for Windows.

    In Windows Program Manager, double-click on the Lotus Applications group icon. (Use the mouse to move the pointer to the icon, and press twice in rapid succession on the left mouse button.)

    Then, double-click on the icon labeled Freelance Graphics.

2. Start a new presentation.

    The Welcome to Freelance Graphics dialog box will appear, as shown in Figure I-1. The option Create a New Presentation is preselected, so just click on OK to begin.

3. Select a SmartMaster set.

    A dialog box called Choose a Look for Your Presentation will appear, as shown in Figure I-2. Looks, or presentation styles, in Freelance Graphics for Windows are called SmartMaster sets. For now, to use the preselected set, simply click on OK.

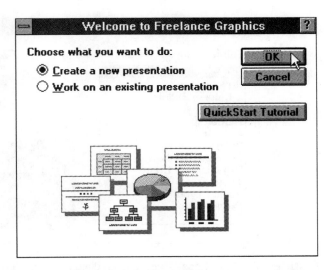

FIGURE I-1. Starting the program opens this dialog box, which is preset for beginning a new presentation.

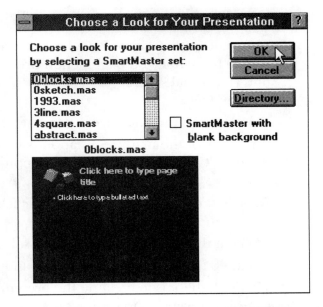

FIGURE I-2. In the Choose a Look for Your Presentation dialog box, the currently selected SmartMaster set is previewed below the file listing.

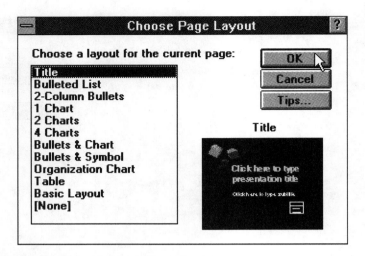

FIGURE I-3. The Choose Page Layout dialog box lists the predesigned layouts in the SmartMaster set. The currently selected layout is previewed in the lower-right corner of the box.

4. Start with the title page.

   The dialog box Choose Page Layout will appear, as shown in Figure I-3. When you begin a new presentation, the Title layout, your usual starting place, is preselected. Once again, just click on OK.

5. Enter text on the title page.

   A preview of the first presentation page will appear. Click on the text "Click here to type presentation title."

   A text box will open, as shown in Figure I-4. Type **Sales Report** and complete your entry by clicking on OK. (Do not press Enter after typing the text.)

   Click on the text "Click here to type subtitle."

   A text box will open. Type **Year End** and then click on OK.

   That's all there is to creating the presentation title page. The completed page is shown in Figure I-5.

FIGURE I-4.   The page title is entered through this text box.

When you click on OK in a text box, the title first appears surrounded by handles, or small squares, a method of selecting the text for editing. It is not necessary here, but you can click anywhere outside the text area to release the handles.

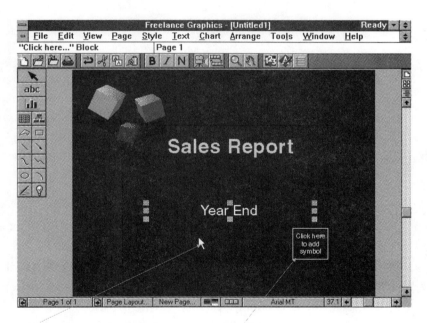

Click here to release the handles   This prompt will not appear on
surrounding the subtitle   Screen Shows or printouts

FIGURE I-5.   Completed title page

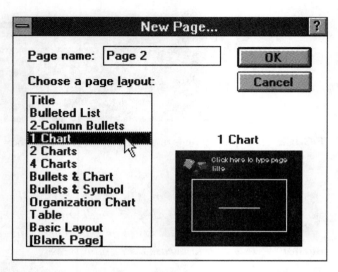

FIGURE I-6. The New Page dialog box. Select from the page layouts in the SmartMaster set.

Now, add a vertical bar chart to your new presentation.

6. Start a new page for the bar chart.

Click on the New Page button at the bottom of the screen:

The New Page dialog box will open, as shown in Figure I-6. In its Choose a Page Layout box, click on 1 Chart (for a single chart on the page), then on OK.

A page layout for a data chart will appear. Click on the text "Click here to create a chart."

7. Select a chart type.

The New Chart Gallery dialog box will appear (Figure I-7), from which you can select among many different plot types and styles. Click on 3D Bar (XYZ).

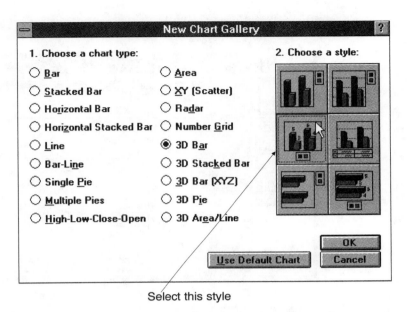

Select this style

FIGURE I-7. The New Chart Gallery dialog box. When you select any of the option buttons on the left, alternate styles for that chart type appear as buttons at the right.

Six different styles of 3-D bar graphs will appear in the dialog box as buttons under the caption Choose a Style. Click on the first button in the second row, then on OK.

8. Enter the data for the chart.

The Chart Data & Titles window will open. It is laid out like a spreadsheet, with lettered columns and numbered rows.

Refer to Figure I-8 as you enter the data. Click on the first cell beneath the column A heading.

Type **East**, press the Right Arrow key to move to the next cell in the row, and type **West**.

Click on cell A1 (at the intersection of column A and row 1).

Type the following data items, pressing Enter after each one to drop down to the next-lower cell: **235, 248, 354, 287.**

Click on cell B1 and type the data items, pressing Enter after each: **369, 388, 415, 334.**

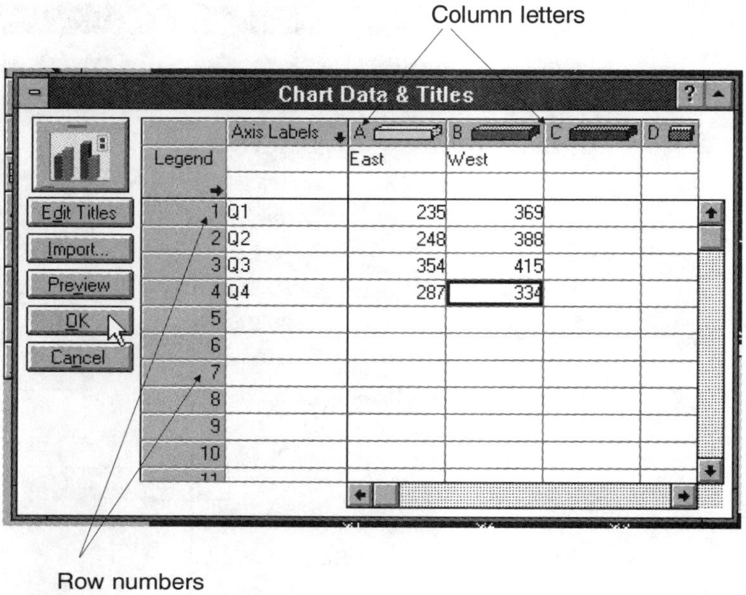

Column letters

Row numbers

FIGURE I-8. The Chart Data & Titles window will hold entries for data charts. It is laid out like a spreadsheet, with lettered columns and numbered rows. (Although it is not necessary here, you can drag the borders of this window and its scroll bars to resize it and adjust the view.)

Click on the first cell in row 1 (first numbered cell in the Axis Labels column). Here you will enter text labels for each major increment of the *x* axis. Type the following labels, pressing Enter after each: **Q1, Q2, Q3, Q4**.

Click on the OK button located at the left edge of the data-entry window.

The bar chart will appear in the middle of the page layout. Notice how the program automatically took care of all the details of composition.

9. Add a title to the page.

Click on the text "Click here to type page title." A text box will open. Type **Quarterly Results**, then click on OK. The completed graph is shown in Figure I-9. (Again, click outside the text area to release the handles.)

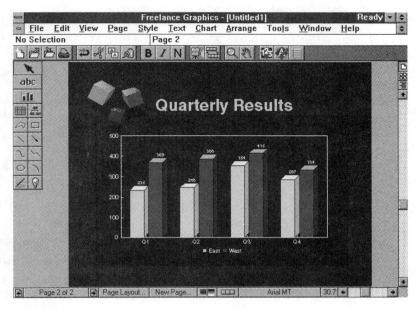

FIGURE I-9. Completed 3-D bar chart. This example may be attractive, but can you tell which of its elements might be confusing or misleading to an audience? (There's a solution in Chapter 2.)

10. Print the presentation.

   From the main menu bar, select File, then Print. (Or, press Ctrl-P.) The Print File dialog box will appear. If your printer is properly installed and configured for Windows, select the Print button to start printing.

11. Save your work in the file SAMPLE.PRE.

   Always end a session by saving your work to disk. Select File➤Save (or press Ctrl-S). Type the filename **sample** (you can omit the extension), then select OK. (This procedure saves an entire presentation, or sequence of pages. In Freelance Graphics for Windows, a presentation file ends with the extension .PRE.)

   In these few steps, you can observe a number of things about Freelance Graphics for Windows:

   • Creating new presentation pages involves a combination of selecting commands from menus and typing entries for data.

Selections, or sequences of program commands, can be made with the mouse from pull-down menus. For some frequently used commands, there are also shortcut key combinations called *accelerator keys* (Ctrl-P, for example, is an alternative way of selecting File➤Print).

- Once you have entered the data for a chart, it is displayed much as it will appear on output, or on-screen in WYSIWYG (What You See Is What You Get) mode. Colors, hatches, patterns, and text fonts are rendered realistically throughout your work session.

- Program options are presented to you in dialog boxes. Option buttons and check boxes are examples of controls used for option settings. Default options are preselected but can be changed. When you select the OK button, you accept the entries and close the dialog box. Or, you can abort the entries and return to the previous menu selection by selecting the Cancel button.

YOU'LL WANT TO READ THIS BOOK ANYWAY

Getting a new software product *and trying it immediately* is tempting—like eating one of those tiny morsels that's offered as a free sample from a bakery or candy store. If you want more, you've come to the right place.

You'll want to read the rest of this book if after this short introduction you have questions, such as:

- What does this bar chart communicate? How can I make it reinforce a business message? (See Chapters 1 through 3.)

- How can I take full advantage of Windows? Work on several tasks at a time? Exchange data, graphics, pictures, and sound recording with other programs? (See Chapters 4 and 14.)

- How can I generate different types of charts and drawings? Edit pages to suit my requirements? Generate title pages and bulleted lists automatically from a speech outline? Organize an entire presentation at a glance? (Work through the examples in Chapters 5 through 10.)

- How can I become a productive user of computer and network services? A proficient producer of computer graphics? An accomplished presenter? (See Chapters 11 through 15.)

- How can I adapt the techniques in Freelance Graphics for Windows to specific business applications, such as desktop publishing, financial analysis, market briefings, and interactive training? (Read the case studies in Chapters 16 through 20.)

YES, BUT WHAT DOES THE CHART SAY?

Returning to the sample bar chart, note that the example is purposely lacking in several important respects. You were given the data, but you don't have a clue about its correct interpretation. For example, are the results expressed in thousands of dollars or millions of units sold? As it is, there is no way to tell. And that's just one of several problems with this chart. Not only do you need to supply meaningful data, you must also decide what visual techniques, such as chart options, will help you succeed in interpreting those data for a business audience.

The discussion under "What's Wrong with This Picture" (at the conclusion of Chapter 2) reviews this chart from the viewpoint of effective business communication and presents pointers for improving it.

If you'd like to learn more than the basic procedures for creating and giving presentations, read on. The objective of this book is to help you become a more persuasive communicator.

Designing an Effective Presentation

C hapters 1 through 3 cover the principles of graphic information display and design. Before you immerse yourself in the details of learning to use Freelance Graphics for Windows, here's an opportunity to think about effective business communications—and the results you want to achieve.

P
A
R
T

I

C H A P T E R   1

THE IMPORTANCE
OF LOOKING GOOD

A good-looking presentation goes a long way.
— Donald Trump, *The Art of the Deal*

hen you're trying to make a good impression, the manner of presentation is as important as the content.

In business, making effective presentations is an essential job skill. It's just as important as knowing how to write a concise, persuasive letter, how to handle yourself on the telephone, or how to dress for meetings with customers or clients. For you to be successful in whatever you're doing, you must be able to convey confidence in your ideas to people whose decisions will affect you, your job, your company. The accepted vocabulary for making presentations, especially at top management levels, is graphics. Even if you prepare presentation materials on behalf of others, you need to understand how messages can be conveyed effectively through graphics.

This book is all about harnessing the power of graphics to highlight and stimulate business presentations—and to motivate decisions. Freelance Graphics for Windows is covered here as a primary tool for composing presentation graphics for two reasons. First, this graphics software program is designed specifically for businesspeople who must produce high-quality charts in a hurry. You need not be concerned with details of graphic layout and design. The expertise of graphic designers, in effect, is built into the program. Second, the Windows environment enhances this ease of use and increases the flexibility of Freelance Graphics, particularly when it is combined with other applications, such as word-processing, spreadsheet, and database systems.

When creating charts with Freelance Graphics, your primary task usually is to supply the data, which can be numbers to be plotted or explanatory text, such as labels. The challenge to you, therefore, has more to do with making judgments about the content and message of your charts rather than with the method of creating them. You must select data that carry a meaningful business message, then you must be able to assess the effectiveness of the charts the program generates from those data.

Some of the cases and examples that I'll share with you are drawn from my personal experiences as a creative director and show producer working in the computer graphics field, years before microcomputer graphics software appeared on the market—back when you needed a roomful of equipment costing half a million dollars just to make a color slide!

A main difference between then and now is that the personal computer has greatly simplified the whole process of generating graphics for business presentations. The principles of building effective presentations, however, haven't changed. This book covers both the underlying principles of good presentation and the mechanics of using Freelance Graphics for Windows.

FREELANCE GRAPHICS PRESENTATIONS, PAGES, AND CHARTS

In Freelance Graphics for Windows, the primary document, or unit of information storage, is called a *presentation*. The storage scheme for these files is diagrammed in Figure 1-1. In computer terms, a presentation is a type of document file. In turn, a presentation is a

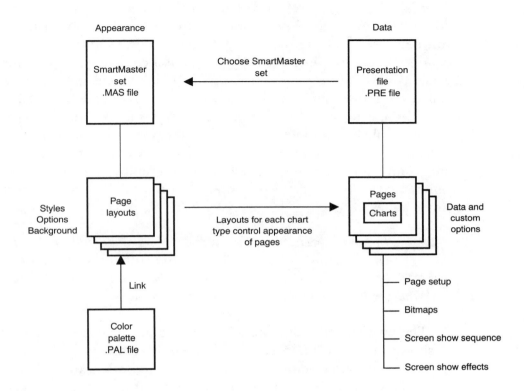

FIGURE 1-1. Relationship of SmartMaster sets of page layouts and presentation files

collection of visual images called *pages,* arranged in sequence. The term *page* is used in Freelance Graphics for Windows to describe a single sheet or frame of any output medium that will be used for the final presentation. For example, a page can be a printed sheet of paper that will be bound in a report. Or a page can be a piece of photographic film that will be mounted in a frame as an overhead transparency or as a slide. Pages can also be shown sequentially as computer-screen displays in a *screen show.*

Other types of output from a presentation file are called *handouts* and *speaker notes,* which are reference materials—usually printouts—that can contain one or more pages with optional comments.

A handy feature of Freelance Graphics for Windows is that both color pages for projection and monochrome handouts for printing can be produced from the same presentation, without making any changes to the graphics themselves. This is a change from previous versions of Freelance Graphics, in which individual graphics are called *charts* or *drawings* and are stored in separate data files (.CH1 and .DRW extensions). In Freelance Graphics for Windows, a presentation file holds an entire sequence of pages, and each page can be composed of several charts or drawings. If you ever need to create a stand-alone graphic, such as a single graph to be bound with report text, you would need to create a presentation that holds a single page.

In previous versions of Freelance Graphics and Freelance Plus for DOS, separate files contain sequential listings of the chart or drawing files that make up a screen show. In Freelance Graphics for Windows, however, the presentation file is the show.

The program supports the following broad categories of charts, as shown in Figure 1-2: text charts, which are composed of words; graphs, which show numeric relationships; and organization charts, which show job and reporting relationships within a department or company. (In Freelance Graphics, all other types of free-form graphics are called *drawings*.)

For a presenter, these chart types can be the basic elements of a visual vocabulary. Many business messages can be visualized very effectively using only these elements. But to round out its own presentation, this book also covers other elements you might want to use, including diagrams, photographs, and drawings.

Typical business functions that make use of charts include finance, marketing, and administration. However, these same graphic techniques can be used to great effect in other disciplines, such as engineering and project management, scientific data analysis and reporting, and training.

A.

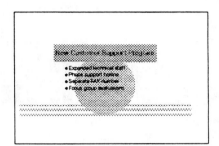

B.

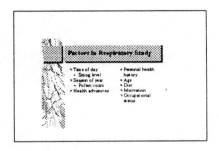

C.

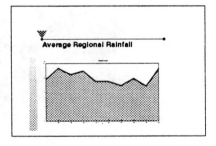

D.

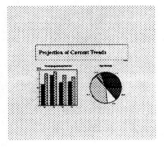

E.

FIGURE 1-2. Various page layouts are available in each SmartMaster set: A. Title, B. Bulleted List, C. 2-Column Bullets, D. 1 Chart, E. 2 Charts (continued next page)

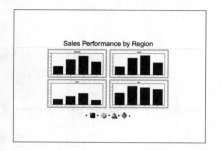

F.

G.

H.

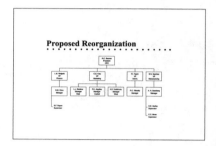

I.

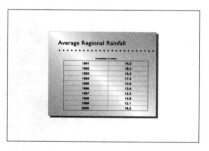

J.

FIGURE 1-2. Various page layouts are available in each SmartMaster set:
F. 4 Charts, G. Bullets & Chart, H. Bullets & Symbol, I. Organization
Chart, and J. Table.

FREELANCE GRAPHICS: AN EVERYDAY TOOL?

Freelance Graphics for Windows should become one of your every-day work tools, as useful as word-processing or spreadsheet pro-grams, the two microcomputer software products most commonly used in business. However, until applications could be coordinated within the Windows environment, graphics traditionally had been far less popular than these other applications. If presentations are so important and graphics so fundamental, why aren't people as comfortable making charts and drawings as they are creating a memo or budget?

An Answer to Graphics Phobia?

I believe that there are two basic reasons graphics have not been used more frequently—even by people who are otherwise comfort-able using computers for word processing or spreadsheet analysis. First, for all our sophistication as users of graphics and video, busi-ness organizations still use printed documents as the primary medium of information. If you were to survey middle managers who routinely use microcomputers, you would probably find that typically charts are made *after* a tentative management decision has been reached. In other words, a manager might first make a deci-sion by looking at the numbers on a printout or spreadsheet, and only later use a graph to communicate the basis for the decision.

An alternative is to generate a graph as a decision support tool. The graph can provide a means for seeing the effects of different decisions or strategies, the chart serving as a reporting or display format for *what-if* analyses (Figure 1-3).

Users of Windows spreadsheet software for what-if analysis will be pleased to learn that Freelance Graphics for Windows not only can exchange data with spreadsheet applications, but also can link a graph to the data source so that a change in the spreadsheet will trigger an automatic update of the graph.

But the benefits of what-if graphic analysis are often missed—not so much for lack of technical capability within the software, but

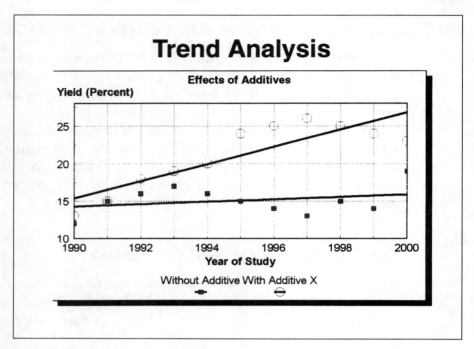

FIGURE 1-3. A comparison graph can be an effective tool for *what-if* analysis.

because some people have never become comfortable with a primarily visual vocabulary and work style. There is evidently a perception that the process of generating a graph will somehow get in the way of the analysis, and there's always the temptation to double-check the numbers, no matter what the graph shows.

This isn't true for all disciplines. Engineers, for example, depend daily on graphic analysis techniques such as process diagrams, schematics, and flowcharts. In particular, engineers and architects who have been trained in drafting have been eager recipients of computer-aided design (CAD) technology. Perhaps it comes down to the fact that making pictures is a mainstream activity in the engineering world, but it's a support service in the management areas of finance, marketing, and administration.

A second, more obvious reason for reluctance about graphics is the perception that specialized technical skills are required. Executives believe that they can write, but don't necessarily think that they can draw. This was a real barrier to graphics literacy when the primary means of using a computer was through its keyboard. The computer keyboard is comfortable in an office setting because it is so similar to familiar equipment—the typewriter and the calculator.

Specialized graphic systems such as CAD have relied less on the keyboard than on a stylus and digitizer tablet, the electronic analog of pen and paper. This is a comfortable input device for people who are used to working at a drawing board. In fact, the tablet can be considerably smaller and more convenient. But on office desks, tablets have never caught on; they seem to be in the way. Because business charting uses the keyboard somewhat more, switching between the keys and the stylus can be annoying.

The Windows environment builds on the popularity of the mouse as a pointing and input device. The mouse takes up much less space than a tablet on a desk top, and it has become a more accepted companion to the keyboard. With a mouse or electronic pen and a graphical user interface such as Windows, the idea of drawing at a computer somehow seems more natural, less intimidating.

However, some people feel that they work faster and more efficiently using the keyboard alone. It can also be cumbersome to use a mouse with a portable computer (although some models have built-in trackballs or pens that serve the same purpose). Windows and Freelance Graphics for Windows both permit you to use keystrokes instead of mouse selections. To further speed the chart creation process, you can create custom page layouts, or templates, for charts that you prepare routinely so that you can generate a new page with just a few keystrokes.

As for any assumed difficulties of drawing with a computer, a few key entries are sufficient to generate most charts. Actions analogous to drawing simply aren't needed to create any of the chart types. But, you almost certainly will prefer to work with some type of pointing device—such as a mouse, stylus, or pen—to draw and manipulate graphic objects such as lines and shapes.

If you wish, you can learn to use the software with the keyboard alone. You can then add a mouse or pen after you have gained familiarity with the system, particularly if you want to increase your speed and productivity.

This book assumes that you are using both a mouse and a keyboard. Where keystrokes are quicker and more efficient, such as accelerator-key combinations, these alternatives are pointed out.

Trade-Offs

To say that Freelance Graphics for Windows is easy to use is not to imply that it's uncomplicated. It is a very sophisticated software product, with many advanced features. Like some other well-designed programs, the program appears straightforward and deceptively simple to the first-time user. However, if you probe deeper to uncover some of its inner workings, there is a wealth of capabilities to discover—and complexities to learn and master.

The ease of use designed into Freelance Graphics for Windows is what software designers call a trade-off. That is, to achieve this benefit, something else was sacrificed. To achieve simplicity of operation, or ease of use, the software designers deliberately restricted your initial options. Preselected values, or defaults, have been set for variables such as color, type style, layout and composition, line width, and so on. In short, most of the elements that an art director or graphic designer would worry about have been predefined for you.

This approach—placing ease of use above all other considerations—has been the main reason for the success of Freelance Graphics for Windows as a commercial software product. The program is not intimidating, it requires very little training and no specialized knowledge, and it produces attractive results. In short, Freelance Graphics overcomes the typical objections and misperceptions about the difficulty of using graphics in a business setting.

To more advanced users, and particularly to graphic arts professionals, such an easy way out may seem limiting. However, many of the limitations that the program seems to impose can be removed

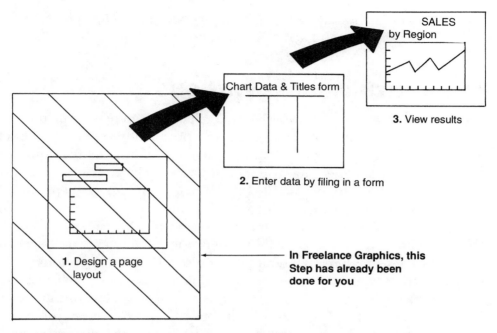

FIGURE 1-4. Creating presentation pages can be as simple as filling in the data on a form.

by interacting with it at deeper levels. This book explores those levels, as well as covering the fundamentals of learning the program for the first time.

Speed is another benefit that comes with ease of use and simplicity. Another reason for the popularity of Freelance Graphics for Windows is that business people are in a hurry. With this program, you can get good results quickly and consistently. To perhaps a majority of users, these advantages are more important than flexibility of graphic design. Indeed, for people without formal training in graphic design, such flexibility provides too many choices and can be downright bewildering.

Another way of looking at the differences in approach between Freelance Graphics for Windows and some other business graphics software packages is to regard chart generation as a two-step process, as shown in Figure 1-4. In the first step you select a chart or presentation design, and in the second step you produce it by entering the data and actually generating the output.

CUSTOMIZING PRESENTATIONS

The philosophy underlying Freelance Graphics for Windows is to keep the steps of formatting and production separate. The important design steps have already been done for the first-time user: If you enter the data, you can produce a chart. The program stores option settings that affect the appearance of pages separately from individual presentations. Text fonts, colors, layout, and other options are derived from a separate *SmartMaster* page layout file. A SmartMaster is actually a collection of masters for page layout. These masters are templates, or sets of default options, for each chart type. Many predefined sets of layout masters are provided with the program, and you can modify them or create new ones. To change the appearance of all pages in a presentation, you need only choose a different SmartMaster set. (This technique is similar to the use of style sheets in some word-processing applications.)

In effect, a SmartMaster set is an empty presentation file; a presentation is a set of page layouts into which data have been entered. When you create a new presentation, all the options from the associated SmartMaster file are loaded into it and are subsequently stored with your data in the presentation file.

In Freelance Graphics for Windows, you can make design changes to a page after the data have been input, but this is not the most productive way to work. Instead, you can specify design changes initially in a modified, or custom, page layout that is included in the SmartMaster set. Having made these selections, you can then produce new pages rapidly simply by entering the data. Some adjustments may be required, but the assumption is that data will be used to drive preselected layouts with little or no subsequent modification. Again, just by applying a different SmartMaster set, you can change the look of an entire presentation very quickly. In this respect, a SmartMaster can be regarded as a set of *global* options, or settings that affect all pages in a presentation.

The separation of design and production in Freelance Graphics for Windows (as separate SmartMaster sets and presentation files) also makes it possible for nontechnical people to handle volume production work. For custom presentations, a set of modified page layouts, or design guidelines, can be stored in a separate SmartMaster file. Separate customized styles with different design choices can be stored for different presentations, clients, or departments. Each set of custom layouts, then, can reflect the preferences of one group of end users.

Screen Shows and SmartShows

It's important to think of Freelance Graphics for Windows as a tool for creating and managing entire presentations rather than individual graphics. Besides its charting and drawing functions, the program includes tools for organizing presentations.

In Freelance Graphics terminology, a presentation that is displayed in page sequence on the computer screen is a screen show. As mentioned previously, in Freelance Graphics for Windows a presentation file contains all pages, or screens, arranged sequentially in a show. You can also specify various kinds of transition effects between pages. (The show order is also the sequence in which pages will be printed.)

The program also gives you the ability to create interactive shows, or *SmartShows*. A SmartShow is a screen show for which the display sequence is controlled by user selections. Selections can be embedded within slides as *Buttons,* or special graphic objects that change the show sequence when clicked. When the operator of the show clicks on a Button with the mouse, an event that you define is triggered, such as jumping (branching) to a specific page number or pausing. It is also possible to launch other applications, or trigger startup of other programs, from within SmartShows.

Alternate Views

Freelance Graphics for Windows is actually a collection of three different program modules, each of which presents a different view of the data in a presentation. The modules are the Current Page view (also called the Freelance Graphics window), the Outliner, and the Page Sorter. Charting and drawing functions comparable to those in previous versions of the program are available in the Current Page view. The Outliner and Page Sorter are capabilities unique to the Windows version.

The Current Page view and the Page Sorter provide WYSIWYG (What You See Is What You Get) displays that resemble actual output. One page at a time is shown in Current Page view, and you can view the entire presentation with the Page Sorter.

The Outliner shows a text view of the entire presentation. It is a word-processing utility that permits you to build presentation content as text in outline form. Text entered through the Outliner is converted automatically to title or bullet charts. The process works in reverse, as well: Text entered in the Current Page view automatically appears in the Outliner, arranged in page sequence. (The Outliner shows text data only, without charts or drawings.)

The Page Sorter module is a tool for viewing and arranging the page sequence in a presentation. Pages are shown as *thumbnail,* or miniaturized, views that can be rearranged with the mouse, much as you would shuffle photographic slides on a light table.

A TOOL FOR BUSINESS COMMUNICATION

A couple of generalizations can be drawn here. First, Freelance Graphics for Windows is intended primarily for nontechnical users who have no formal training in graphic arts. Second, the program imposes some limitations, but perhaps not as many as you would think. You will never realize the full potential of this remarkable software if you are always content to accept its default settings. In this respect, ease of use can be a pitfall: What you see (at first) isn't all you can get!

Another important objective of this book, then, is to peel back the top layer of the program and let you have a look at the seemingly hidden potential of Freelance Graphics for Windows.

COMPUTER GRAPHICS: A MULTIDISCIPLINARY ACTIVITY

Another reason for the apparent complexity of computer graphics in business applications is that it can involve multiple disciplines, many of them highly technical. One of the virtues of Freelance Graphics for Windows is that much of this technical expertise is designed into the software—and hidden from view. But knowing about these technical areas can help you later when you begin to penetrate the top layer and explore all the options that Freelance Graphics offers.

Of course, knowing who the players are can tell you who to call when you have a problem. Key players in the business graphics arena include:

- Information users
- Data processors
- System administrators
- Artists and designers
- Computer graphics technicians
- Photographic laboratory technicians
- Video engineers
- Reprographic technicians

Technical issues in each of these areas of responsibility are covered in later chapters.

Information Users

If you are making a presentation, your audience is composed of information users. These are the people who make decisions based on the information you present. (If you are using graphics for decision support, you are the information user.) Information users are concerned mainly with the content of your presentation. However, your audience will certainly be affected and perhaps influenced by the medium, manner, and style of your presentation, including the design of its visual material. For any presentation, it's important to identify the information users because to achieve the best results you must tailor the presentation to the expectations—conscious or otherwise—of your audience. This topic is explored in depth in Chapter 3.

Data Processors

People who develop the content that will ultimately be shown in your presentation are data processors. For example, you may need statistics on consumer demographics and buying preferences for a market briefing. The data processors in this case would be the research department that prepared a market survey in which you found the statistics. It's important to identify the data processors because you may have to talk to them—or to their computer systems—to extract the data you need.

System Administrators

If your computer is connected to a local area network (LAN), an individual will be designated to oversee use and maintenance of shared resources, such as scanners and printers, as well as disk storage on file servers. This person may also be responsible for maintaining your computer or workstation, including setup of new software. In the Windows environment, this level of technical help might be needed to assure that the memory and disk capacities of your computer are being used at peak efficiency.

Artists and Designers

A graphic arts professional may consult with you in designing and producing your presentation. Increasingly, artists and designers in the audiovisual field have special expertise in computer graphics. Resources available to you may include an art department or computer graphics operation within your organization, or a commercial art house or production agency.

There's a common perception that creating business graphics is a lot like cooking—you either do it yourself or you go out. Today, with the advent of standardized file formats for exchanging graphics among systems and applications, there may be situations in which it is feasible (and preferable) to do *both* on the same project, and still achieve seamless results. For example, graphic designers can create custom page layouts that will be used subsequently by presenters in building their presentations. This is an excellent way to encourage adherence to corporate design guidelines, as well as to increase productivity.

Or you might generate charts for a presentation with Freelance Graphics for Windows, then transmit the output electronically to a production facility for enhancement or matching with such related visuals as product photography or designer graphics. This approach is useful for coordinating major business meetings, such as dealer shows and sales rallies. Since Freelance Graphics can produce output files that are compatible with other computer graphics systems, it is now feasible for client organizations to collaborate electronically with production houses.

Computer Graphics Technicians

People in this category include professionals familiar with the special requirements of generating images with the aid of computers. Within the world of Freelance Graphics, these are the people who support the system you are using. Support resources available to you may include computer-systems consulting firms, software dealers, corporate *management information systems* (MIS) departments, and, of course, the customer service department at Lotus Development Corporation, the makers and distributors of Freelance Graphics for Windows. (An important aspect of support involves helping you match computer hardware and software components to your needs, which is covered briefly in the Appendix.)

Photographic Laboratory Technicians

If your output requirements include color slides, you'll depend on the expertise of photographic laboratory technicians. If you record pages on film as slides or transparencies with a desktop film recorder, you'll be sending the exposed film to a lab for processing. If you submit files electronically to a service bureau for film recording and processing, the lab people will be behind the scenes, but just as essential. In this technical area, you need to be aware that the color generated by computer systems is consistent, but the chemical processes involved in developing color film are subject to considerable variation.

Computer graphics generally require extremely close tolerances in photo lab work, so you may not want to send your computer-generated slide film to the same lab that does your vacation pictures. In particular, you must be concerned about whether the colors in a set of revised slides will match the rest of the presentation. Also, if you require multiple copies of a slide presentation, you will need to understand how copying inevitably affects color and sharpness. There can be differences that will be obvious to you and to your supervisor, manager, or client. Some of the technical considerations imposed by photographic technology are covered in Chapters 11–13.

Video Engineers

Just as demanding in its own respect, and with a completely different set of rules, is video technology. Video engineers will assist you when you use slides for broadcast graphics or when you use projection video to present charts directly from a computer system. Be aware particularly that conventional video and videotape systems can handle only a narrow range of the colors generated by your computer graphics system.

Reprographic Technicians

Handling output media, such as overhead transparencies, and printed documents, such as reports, is the job of reprographic technicians. Techniques include black-and-white or color photocopying, as well as conventional printing methods such as offset lithography. Reprographic technologies are needed primarily when output must be produced in quantity. As with film and video, producing output for print media may require some planning to allow for the differences in reproduction characteristics.

The key players described above can assist you in preparing, producing, and presenting visual materials that are truly professional in design and quality. As you gain familiarity with Freelance Graphics for Windows, you will know when it might be appropriate to take some of these matters into your own hands and when to seek some technical assistance.

THE BUSINESS SITUATION AND THE AUDIENCE

Technical issues aside, there is one area in which you must be the expert: It's up to you, whether you're the presenter or the presentation producer, to understand the business situation (the presentation opportunity), to identify the audience, and to anticipate its expectations. This doesn't mean that you must tell people only what they want to hear. Rather, to design an effective presentation, you must be aware of the unspoken assumptions and preconceived notions that members of your audience bring with them to the meeting room.

The business situation, the reason for the presentation, will shape much of your strategy. Is this an informal meeting within your own work group or department to explore alternative approaches to a problem? Is it a formal review of your group's performance by top management? Is it an industrial theatrical show for your company's dealers or stockholders? The answer gives you a feeling for what's appropriate. Just as there are different expectations and unspoken rules for picnics and for dinner parties, there are different expectations for each type and level of meeting. Using visual materials that are not appropriate to your business audience can make as bad an impression as showing up at a formal dinner party in your Bermuda shorts with a sack of paper plates and hot dogs.

He Needed a New Plant. . .Yesterday

If you think I'm exaggerating, consider the following true story about the general manager of a manufacturing division of a large industrial conglomerate who found himself in a desperate situation.

The manufacturing division had closed a large, long-term order for an essential drive-train subcomponent just at a time when automakers had retooled to produce front-wheel-drive cars. The order meant hundreds of thousands of units annually for years to come, and many millions of dollars in sales for the division. The problem was that the division did not have sufficient manufacturing capacity to meet the order. After assessing existing plant capacity with engineering staff, the general manager concluded that what was needed was not plant expansion, but a totally new facility. The cost of such a project was estimated at $40 million, requiring a major commitment from the company's board of directors.

Over a period of months, the general manager worked with his director of finance to develop a proposal for financing and building the plant. When they were finished, they had a detailed plan for using state tax subsidies and a corporate bond issue, along with attractive return-on-investment projections.

The general manager planned to fly to company headquarters with the director of finance to present the proposal to the board of directors. With the meeting less than a week away, the general manager's secretary phoned headquarters to confirm the arrangements. It came as something of a shock when the chairman's assistant mentioned, almost in passing, that the general manager might want to ship his slide presentation ahead so that it could be set up properly for the projection system in the boardroom.

They Want *Slides?*

The general manager had planned to simply have a dozen copies of his report run off and bound in black imitation leather. This, he assumed, would be an appropriate, and suitably conservative, presentation format. Instead, he learned that the board expected to see all major presentations on slides. Further, the format was quite specific: two-screen rear projection, with text on the left screen and charts on the right (Figure 1-5). Slides were to be executed according to a company style book that specified black backgrounds and strict adherence to a color scheme of red, white, and blue!

The general manager made a panic call to his advertising agency, and the next day the agency account executive, a professional speech writer, the general manager, and his director of finance walked in on my colleagues and me at a computer graphics production house. An assistant at the agency had phoned ahead to warn us only that this group had an urgent project, that they would meet with us through the day and into the night if necessary, and to ask that we please order lunch and dinner in.

After a short briefing on the situation, the general manager asked me, "So what do we put on slide one?" It went that way for several hours, and I sketched a *storyboard,* or sequence of slide layouts,

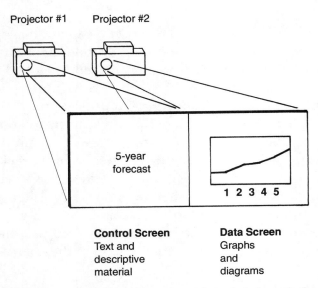

Projector #1   Projector #2

5-year
forecast

1 2 3 4 5

Control Screen
Text and
descriptive
material

Data Screen
Graphs
and
diagrams

FIGURE 1-5. Two-screen rear projection is a common executive presentation
method.

as the group decided which of the key points in the presentation
would be visualized. An example is presented in Figure 1-6.

After several hours, the meeting broke up; the writer went away
to write the speech, the general manager and the finance director
checked into a local hotel, and the computer artists started to work

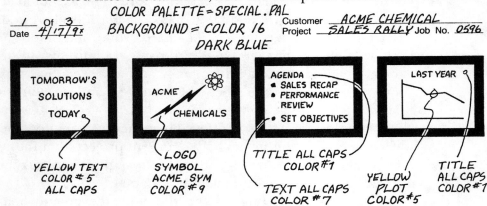

FIGURE 1-6. Storyboard sketches help you visualize a presentation and document the preliminary design.

on the slides. Two days later, the general manager flew to company headquarters to make the slide presentation.

And he got his plant.

The Lesson for You?

Understand the business situation and all its nuances. Know the audience and their expectations and preferences.

Levels of Presentation: Knowing Your Needs

Computer graphics consultant John Cool has proposed three broad categories for analyzing the business situation and audience requirements. These categories imply the use of different presentation strategies and media (Figure 1-7). The categories are:

- Peer level
- Presentation level
- Publication level

Peer Level

Presentations at peer level are informal meetings within or among work groups. Typical purposes are to analyze data, to discuss alternative ways of tackling problems, to divide the work load into individual assignments, and so on.

A peer-level meeting usually has just a few participants. An appropriate display medium is often the computer screen itself. What-if analyses can be particularly useful in these situations for exploring all the options available. Other media can include overhead transparencies—or perhaps just a blank flip chart or board and a marker.

A peer-level meeting is informal, with lots of give and take. Compared with other meeting situations, there is not as much concern about exploring options that might prove to be false leads, dead

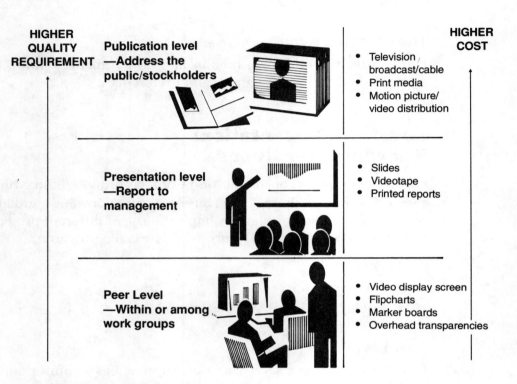

FIGURE 1-7.   Prepare material appropriate to the level of presentation.

ends, or downright mistakes. It's a time to experiment. There is also apt to be less concern about the details of appearance.

Some training sessions, particularly those in which colleagues help one another during actual assignments, fall into the peer category.

Presentation Level

Meetings at the presentation level represent a step up in formality. In business, this situation typically involves reporting to management. The focus can be accounting for expenditures, evaluating performance, or forecasting and setting goals. The presentation is relatively structured, and you may speak from a prepared text or from notes. It is usually not a time to be exploring options.

Advocates of computer graphics have expected that electronic projection and real-time computer analysis would become popular media for management presentations. (The term *war-room graphics* has been coined to describe these wall-sized interactive displays.) However, presenters are understandably reluctant to engage in all-out what-if analysis with their managers. The situation can be just too open-ended. Using electronic graphics at the presentation level introduces some of the informality and uncertainty that is more appropriate to the peer level. Like trial lawyers who avoid asking questions in court for which they don't know the answers, presenters at the management level wish to control the situation.

The appropriate medium at this level is usually color slides, perhaps along with printed handouts. In some cases, overhead transparencies may be used, particularly if the room must remain lit.

Publication Level

Presentation to a company's stockholders, to its dealers, or to the general public takes place at the publication level. The term implies printed matter, such as newsletters, corporate magazines, and brochures. It can also include broadcast video, programmed multi-image slide presentations, and industrial theatrical shows.

At this level, the presentation is entirely canned, or prepared in advance. Months of production work and considerable expense may go into the effort. The corporate image in the community, after all, is at stake.

Levels of Presentation: Quality and Cost

The levels of peer, presentation, and publication also correspond roughly to expected levels of quality and cost of visual materials. For example, there may be no special requirement for image quality at the peer level. A chalk-talk is an inexpensive way to present information graphically. At the other extreme, graphics for a major industrial show must be of the highest quality; the public exposure of the organization justifies the expense.

This rule of thumb doesn't always hold, however. For example, physicians often need to analyze computer-generated imagery in peer-level conferences. The highest possible quality (at a cost premium) is needed for medical diagnostic applications such as computerized axial tomography (CAT) scans and magnetic resonance imaging. High-quality display requirements at the peer level are apparently more common in science and engineering disciplines, and for purposes of this book are outside the realm of business graphics.

In the middle ground of the presentation level, quality and cost issues are less clearly defined. Presenting high-quality visuals, such as slides, respects the formality of the occasion and conveys a sense of propriety, effort, and attention to detail. However, your audience also may be concerned that you've spent too much! Now that microcomputer software like Freelance Graphics for Windows has greatly reduced the expense of preparing and generating high-quality graphics, the expense issue may have receded somewhat. Audiences are coming to expect even low-cost graphics to look good, and with tools like Freelance Graphics for Windows, there's really no excuse for not having professional-looking charts and drawings.

CHAPTER 2

COMMUNICATING WITH CHARTS

I think presentation by computer is a branch of show biz and writing, not of psychology, engineering, or pedagogy.
—Ted Nelson, *Computer Lib/Dream Machines*

G raphics is a language of its own. Conceived and designed skillfully, a graphic image can deliver a powerful message in a single glance.

The fundamentals of graphic design and visual presentation do not depend on any specific tools. Certainly, with a tool like Freelance Graphics for Windows, you should never again have to lay out a chart with a pencil and graph paper. The program will generate clean lines, true right angles, sharp fonts, uniformly spaced grids, correctly plotted data points, vivid colors—in short, high-quality images that are mechanically correct.

But before you immerse yourself in the details of learning to use the program, you should develop some critical judgment about whether the results you produce with it will communicate your ideas. Put another way, there is no built-in capability in any graphics software package that can prevent you from creating a chart that is misleading or confusing to your audience. This chapter and the one that follows focus on the principles of design for business graphics.

USING CHARTS EFFECTIVELY

Charting conventions are accepted formats for representing data. Related to, but more basic than, chart type is the communication purpose of a chart in a presentation. In the most general terms, the purpose of a chart or drawing is to convey an idea. The most effective chart has a single purpose or conveys a single idea. Purposes of charts in business presentations can be to show:

- Data reduction
- Quantity versus time
- Proportion and comparison
- Flow and relationships
- Tables and spreadsheets
- Signposts and leaders
- Illustration of a concept or process

Data Reduction

Most types of graphs are a form of data reduction, summarizing results to aid understanding. A mathematical average is a kind of data reduction. If my average bowling score is 100, you don't need to look at all my individual game scores to know that I'm not very good at it.

Data reduction can have its perils, however. In many cases, you would be correct in assuming that a bowler whose average score is 100 is just a beginner. But it's also possible that the bowler usually scores higher and suffered a thumb injury during the final games of a tournament, so some exceptionally low scores distorted the average. In other words, simplicity of presentation isn't always a virtue. You, as the presenter, have the responsibility of judging when a particular presentation format distorts the data.

Like other methods of data reduction, charts and graphs should be concise and simple—snapshots, in effect, of some body of data.

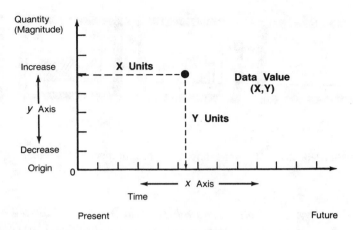

FIGURE 2-1. XY plotting for quantity versus time presentation

Quantity-versus-Time Graphs

Perhaps the most common scheme for graphs used in business is a plot of quantity versus time, as shown in Figure 2-1. The magnitude, or amount, of the quantity being measured increases along the *y* axis, or along the vertical scale. Time progresses from left to right along the *x* axis, or horizontal scale. (This scheme is derived from the Cartesian coordinate system, which is covered in Chapter 11 in relation to the way pictures are represented in computer graphics.)

A sequence of data items is plotted as a series of points on the graph in left-to-right order. (This usually corresponds to the order of data entry.) In Freelance Graphics, such a sequence of points is called a *data set*. Lines or shapes are drawn to link the points, according to the plotting style chosen. As shown in Figure 2-2, data points can be indicated by the height of separate bars (bar graph), connected to form a line (line graph), or connected and the area underneath shaded (area graph). Or data points may be shown as dots or symbols in what's called a *scatter graph*, or point chart. All these types, and many variations on them, are supported by Freelance Graphics for Windows. Appropriate uses of each of these chart types are covered below, as well as in the discussion on making data charts in Chapters 7 and 8.

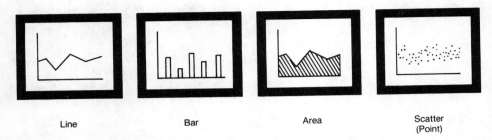

| Line | Bar | Area | Scatter (Point) |

FIGURE 2-2. XY types: line, bar, area, and scatter charts

In Lotus terminology, used in both Freelance Graphics and 1-2-3, the term XY *graph* can refer specifically to scatter charts. In this book, XY *data chart* often is used to describe any of several chart types that have x and y axes, and XY (Scatter) chart *refers to the more specialized point-chart format.*

Charts that show quantity versus time can be understood readily by your audience because the graphing scheme plays to deep cultural biases, as discussed in Chapter 3. Time proceeds from left to right because in Western cultures we read that way and share the notion that rightward movement means progress. Similarly, upward movement usually implies increase or gain.

Most important from the standpoint of design, quantity-time graphs that depart from this scheme may have less impact because they show relationships in ways that are counter to the expectations of the audience.

Variations on XY data chart types include:

- Cumulative plots
- Special formats

Cumulative Plotting: Line, Bar, and Area Charts

In conventional graphing, sets of data can be built on one another in two different ways:

- A data set can use the previous set as its baseline, with each y value being added to the maximum y value of the previous set: Where one set peaks, the next begins. Refer to Figure 2-3.

- Each y value in a set can be a running total of all its preceding values in the *same* set, as shown in Figure 2-4.

In Freelance Graphics, the first option is available, though the term *cumulative* is not used. With this option, called *stacked,* data sets in bar or area charts are "layered" on one another (Figure 2-3); that is, the data sets accumulate on one another. In this stacked chart, the y-axis values of each of the data points of the second set are added to the corresponding y values of the first set, creating a layered effect.

The second option represents the more common usage of the term *cumulative,* in which data accumulate *within each set.* As shown in Figure 2-4, within the same data set, the second y data point is

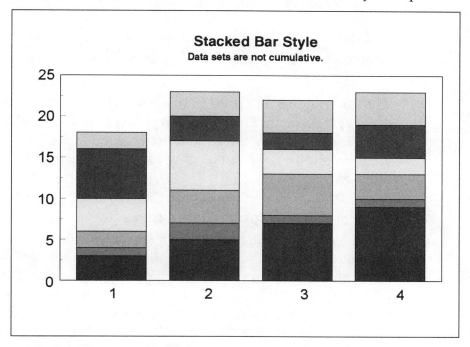

FIGURE 2-3. Data sets can be built on one another, as shown in this stacked chart.

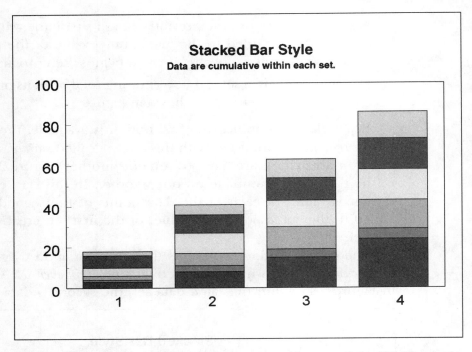

FIGURE 2-4. A running total of data is represented in a cumulative XY data chart.

added to the first, the third to the first two, and so on to the end of the set. There is no built-in feature in Freelance Graphics for Windows for generating such cumulative data. However, cumulative totals might be generated in a spreadsheet program and then imported.

Special Formats for XY Data Charts

XY data charts include variations used for specific applications. For example, stock prices are typically shown as *floating bars,* and seemingly random or empirically collected data may be shown as discrete dots in scatter graphs. In Freelance Graphics for Windows, a special chart type is provided for plotting stock prices: High-Low-Close-Open (HLCO). There is also a separate chart type for scatter graphs: XY (Scatter).

Proportion and Comparison

Another type of chart compares two or more quantities. The comparison usually is represented as proportional shapes. A pie chart, in which proportions are shown as slices, or sectors, of a circle, is an example. Pie charts can be created readily with Freelance Graphics for Windows.

Note that, unlike quantity-time graphs, a pie chart shows quantities and proportions in strictly *relative* terms. A pie slice represents some percentage of, or ratio to, the whole. With this scheme, there is no way of showing graphically what the absolute quantities, or magnitudes, of the pieces are. You can, of course, include descriptive labels, but it's the graphic elements—the shapes and sizes, in this case—that should carry the primary message.

Consider the example of a pie chart that shows your company's market share as a percentage of total sales in the industry, as presented in Figure 2-5. Given this pie alone (without any other labels), the audience cannot tell what the sales volumes are. In some cases, the actual volumes may be irrelevant to your message, but discussions of market share often center on how much share has been gained or lost during some time period.

Consider the example in Figure 2-6. This graph shows two pies, one for last year's sales results and one for this year's. The comparison seems straightforward enough: In a one-year interval, the company's share declined by four percent.

Look at the difference in impact—and meaning—of the same comparison, but with the relative sizes of the pies adjusted to show the increase in overall sales volume from one year to the next (Figure 2-7). This comparison shows that the company now has a smaller share of a much larger pie. In this respect, this graph gives a more accurate impression than the comparison of same-size pies.

TIP *Freelance Graphics for Windows does not include an option for proportionally sizing multiple pies. However, you can achieve this effect by creating separate single pie charts, adding them to the same page, and sizing the pies by dragging their handles.*

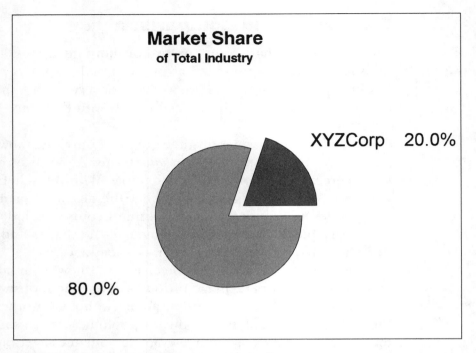

FIGURE 2-5. A pie chart can convey an overall summary.

Making the pies different sizes does not necessarily remove all the ambiguity from the comparison. How do you show the overall increase from one year to the next? In Figure 2-7, the increase is shown as the ratio between the areas of the circles. But comparing the pies *by area* may be misleading.

Figure 2-8 shows why comparing pie sizes by area doesn't fit the commonsense expectations of the audience. If the sales volume doubled from one year to the next, the audience might expect to see next year's circle twice as "tall" as this year's. However, when you enlarge a circle in one direction, it also grows in the other. A circle that is twice the diameter of another actually is *four times larger* in area.

One way to resolve this dilemma is to return to the quantity-versus-time concept. An alternate way to show market share, with the added information of absolute quantity and time, is as a stacked bar

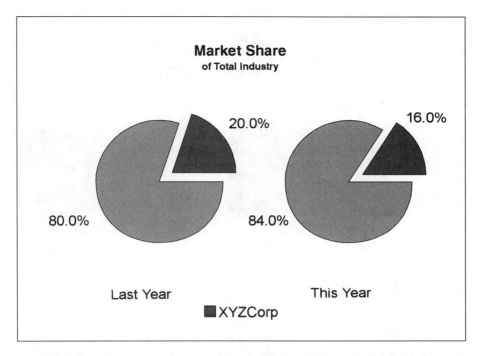

FIGURE 2-6. These two pie charts show that the market share this year is four percent less than last year.

chart, as shown in Figure 2-9. Much the same effect is achieved by an area chart, as shown in Figure 2-10. Both the bar and the area charts show clearly that XYZCorp dollar volume actually increased only slightly, while its market share declined because the total volume of the market was growing even faster.

Another type of distortion can be introduced when you attempt to mix proportional representation with quantity-time. In the example in Figure 2-11, the designer of the graph apparently thought it would add a creative touch to use symbols of people instead of bars. The distortion arises from the visual comparison of areas, just as with the two pie charts in the prior example. Even though the projected increase from this year to next is just 20 percent, the actual area of the symbol representing next year is approximately twice as large. In other words, the increase is made to look much bigger than it really is—200 percent instead of 20!

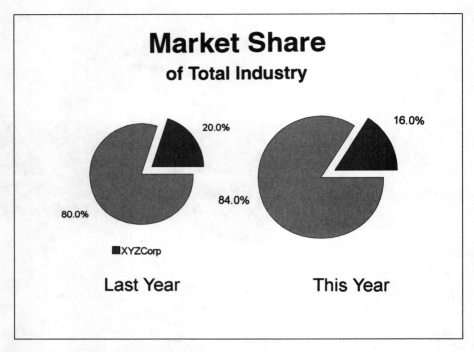

FIGURE 2-7. Pies sized proportionally

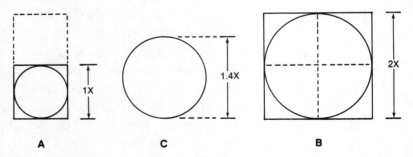

FIGURE 2-8. Circle (or square) B, which is twice as tall as A, is actually four times larger by area. Circle C, which is twice as large by area, somehow doesn't give the visual impression of twofold growth, since it is only 1.4 times taller.

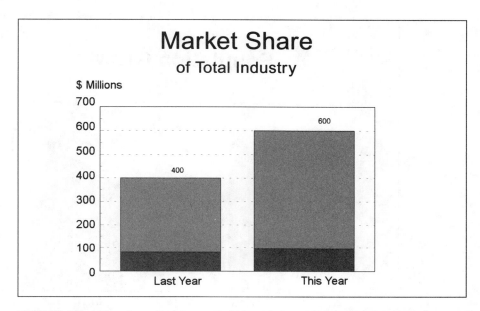

FIGURE 2-9. The data used to create Figure 2-6 are shown here as stacked bars.

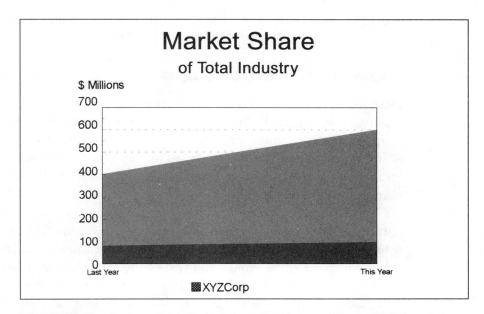

FIGURE 2-10. An area chart displays the same data used to create Figure 2-6.

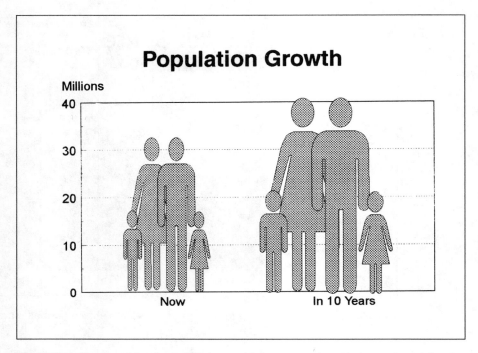

FIGURE 2-11.   In a bar chart, differences in the areas of symbols can be misleading; only the height (*y* value) is relevant.

Flow and Relationships

Another category of visual presentation includes all types of diagrams. These usually depict the flow of a process or the relationships among entities. Examples of diagrams include flowcharts, schematics, organization charts, structure charts (or hierarchy diagrams), various types of conceptual models such as Venn diagrams, and engineering drawings.

One type of diagram that can be produced with Freelance Graphics for Windows is the organization chart (Figure 2-12), which shows reporting relationships in an organizational hierarchy. (To save space and to make the rest of the chart bigger, the last level is shown here as a *laddered list*.) Organization-style charts also can be adapted to build other types of flow or hierarchic diagrams. For example, a structure chart, a specific type of diagram used in com-

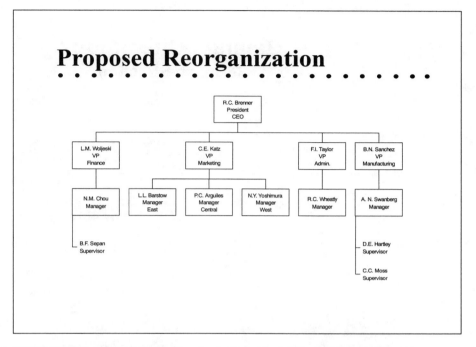

Proposed Reorganization

FIGURE 2-12. The organization chart is a type of diagram supported by Free-lance Graphics for Windows.

puter programming, uses the same hierarchic organization (see Figure 2-13).

Some other types of diagrams can be produced in Freelance Graphics for Windows by manipulating symbols in the library DIA-GRAM.SYM.

As a general rule, diagrams should be used sparingly in presentations. Perhaps the best application of diagrams is in peer-level meetings, where the analysis of the diagram (and the system or process it depicts) is the main purpose of the meeting.

Unlike charts and graphs that show data reduction, diagrams document the complexity or details of a process. It may even require some technical skill to understand the charting conventions

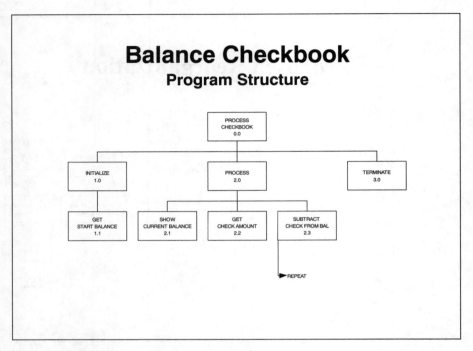

FIGURE 2-13. The organization chart can be adapted for a programming structure chart.

and symbols and to interpret the diagram. There are usually many different ways to "read" a diagram, whereas there are usually only a few ways—ideally, only *one* way—to read a graph. Therefore, diagrams may be more suitable for reference and analysis than for presentation.

So, if you are tempted to use a diagram in a presentation-level meeting or in a publication, consider either simplifying it or highlighting a specific area of interest. If you must cover the diagram in detail, break the presentation into several frames, highlighting only one process step or discussion point in each frame, as shown in Figure 2-14. Use the overall view of the diagram as a means of orienting the audience for the close-up views that follow, returning as necessary to the overall view to reorient them.

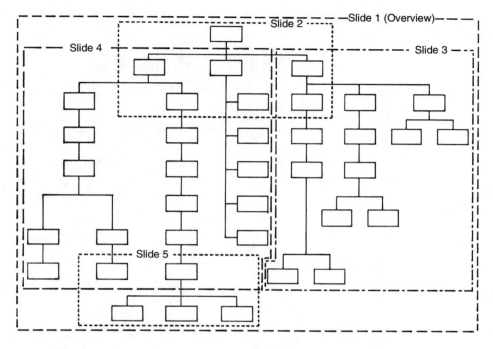

FIGURE 2-14. A complex diagram can be broken into several frames for presentation.

Simplified diagrams can be created with the drawing tools of Freelance Graphics for Windows. For example, you can create and position shapes such as circles, various kinds of curves and arcs, ellipses (ovals), and rectangles and then connect them with lines or arrows, as shown in Figure 2-15. However, the precision of these drawings is somewhat limited. For example, to create engineering drawings, you'd need a computer-aided design (CAD) system. In a practical sense, the drawing limitations may help you keep your diagrams simple.

If you must incorporate complex diagrams into a presentation, the diagrams may be created with other graphics software, such as AutoCAD, and then imported to Freelance Graphics for Windows (or passed through the Windows Clipboard). The diagrams then may be annotated within Freelance Graphics and output along with

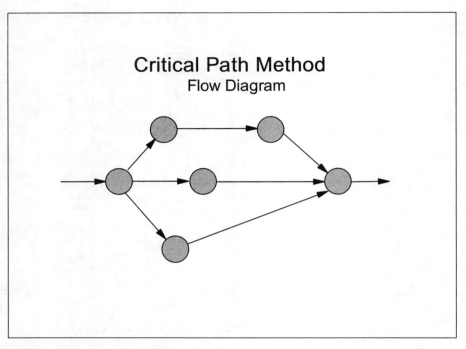

FIGURE 2-15. This simple *Critical Path Method* (CPM) chart was made with the Arrow and Ellipse tools of Freelance Graphics for Windows.

the other visuals in your presentation, allowing for consistency of design and color. Exchanging drawings with other computer graphic systems is covered in Chapter 14.

Tables and Spreadsheets

A table is an array of text, which may be alphabetic, numeric, or both (alphanumeric), arranged in vertical columns and horizontal rows. A particular tabular format is the spreadsheet, which has its roots in financial accounting. In the terminology of Freelance Graphics for Windows, text that is arranged in columns is a *table chart*.

In the conventional spreadsheet format used in accounting, the body of the table contains numeric data. Alphanumeric text may be used as labels or captions at the top of columns or to the left of rows. For example, labels might include sales periods, units of measure, account classifications, and so on. The bottom row of the spreadsheet usually shows subtotals for each column (adding down the column). The rightmost column shows subtotals for each row (adding across the row). In accounting terminology, these subtotals are called *footings*.

At the intersection of the two sets of subtotals, or at the bottom right corner of the spreadsheet, is a *grand total*. Originally, a primary purpose for manual spreadsheets was to provide an arithmetic check of the totals. The same grand total should result from adding down the rightmost column or adding across the bottom row; to put it in accounting terms, a correctly calculated spreadsheet should *cross-foot*. If an error has been made in any of the totals, it will show up as a mismatch between the footings.

Journals of daily transactions, balance sheets of assets and liabilities, and general ledgers showing debits and credits by account classifications are other standardized accounting tables that can be regarded as specialized versions of the spreadsheet format.

One of the most popular microcomputer tools for business applications is electronic spreadsheet software. Popular packages include Lotus 1-2-3, Microsoft Excel, and Borland Quattro Pro, all of which are available in versions for Windows. Electronic spreadsheets offer several major enhancements over manual calculation methods:

- The value stored at any location (or *cell*) on the spreadsheet may be calculated by a user-defined formula. For example, you could embed a formula for converting percentage values or fractions to decimals, yen to dollars, or months to years. Formulas can also include input from calculations elsewhere in the spreadsheet.

- Specific types of math transformations are predefined within the program and can be specified simply as keywords or functions within formulas. Examples include regression curves, moving averages, statistical functions, and financial calculations.

- The software can recalculate or update the entire spreadsheet after any change is entered.

Chart Data & Titles windows in Freelance Graphics for Windows are laid out as spreadsheets, with lettered columns and numbered rows. Through this form you can enter or import data for XY, pie, radar, and numeric grid (table) charts.

In relation to graphs that show data reduction, tables and spreadsheets can be regarded as data in raw form. As a presentation format, a table is not easily grasped by the audience. Even though the values contained in it may represent considerable reduction of actual or empirical data, relationships are not immediately apparent. In this respect, spreadsheets are like diagrams—more appropriate for detailed analysis and peer-level meetings than for summary and presentation.

Herein lies one of the most common of the presenter's pitfalls. To many professionals, particularly those with backgrounds in accounting and finance, working with spreadsheets is second nature. Anyone who has ever designed business presentations for a living has encountered the client who approaches you with a sheet of computer printout and asks, "Can you make me a slide of this?"

Yes, I can make a slide of that. Of course, anyone who is sitting farther than three feet from the screen won't be able to read it, much less understand what you're trying to tell them by showing it all. Just because you do your analysis or get your reports in spreadsheets, you don't necessarily want to present information to others this way.

Instead, I can make perhaps a dozen table charts from it by showing selected sections of the spreadsheet.

Even better—I can show each of those sections as a meaningful graph. The spreadsheet section and the graph in Figures 2-16 and 2-17 show identical data. Unquestionably, the graph communicates better.

So, here's another rule of thumb: Use tabular or spreadsheet formats in presentations only when you are sure that your audience is already very familiar with the format and prefers or expects to see

	X-Values	A	B	C	D
Legend					
			Regression		
1	25	300	283.3456		
2	30	325	297.4412		
3	35	310	311.5367		
4	40	300	325.6323		
5	45	320	339.7279		
6	50	330	353.8235		
7	55	375	367.9191		
8	60	390	382.0147		
9	65	380	396.1103		
10	70	425	410.2059		
11	75	405	424.3015		
12	80	440	438.397		
13	85	460	452.4926		
14	90	510	466.5882		
15	95	505	480.6838		
16	100	450	494.7794		

Buttons: Edit Titles, Import.., Preview, OK, Cancel. Window title: Chart Data & Titles

FIGURE 2-16. Spreadsheet data, including regression calculations, have been pasted into the Chart Data & Titles window, which has the same arrangement of lettered columns and numbered rows.

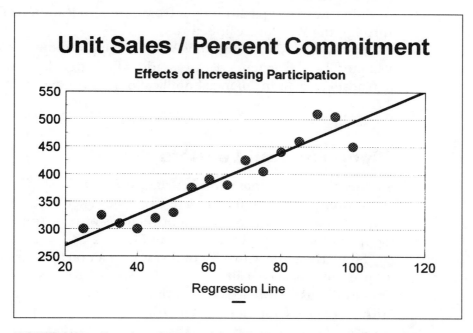

FIGURE 2-17. Data from the spreadsheet in Figure 2-16 imported to Freelance Graphics for Windows (actually, pasted from the Windows Clipboard)

the data displayed this way. There may be no alternative to displaying a company's balance sheet, for example. However, once the data have been presented in the expected format, graphs of the key account classifications might support the discussion that follows.

As with diagrams, if you must present data in tabular form, keep the tables concise. This is necessary both for readability and for comprehension. In cases where a large table must be shown, show a bird's-eye view and then come in closer in subsequent frames to highlight your discussion points. If the discussion is lengthy, return to the overall view occasionally to reorient the audience before showing the next detail frame.

Spreadsheets, especially in electronic form, provide a perfect marriage for Freelance Graphics for Windows. Spreadsheet data files can be converted automatically into graphs such as bar, line, and pie charts by reading the data into a Chart Data & Titles window in Freelance Graphics for Windows. The most convenient way of doing this is to pass the data from one application to the other through the Windows Clipboard.

Exchanging data with other Windows applications is covered in Chapter 14. An extended case study, which details conversion of spreadsheet data in financial applications, is presented in Chapter 17.

Signposts and Leaders

Besides the visuals that show key data and relationships, other visuals in your presentation can serve to give it structure.

Title pages can precede major sections of your presentation as signposts for each topic, as shown in Figure 2-18.

Similarly, a title with a list of text items can recap your key discussion points, as shown in Figure 2-19. Speech writers call such text frames discussion *leaders*. Both titles and lists can be created easily with Freelance Graphics for Windows.

FIGURE 2-18.   Text signpost, or title page

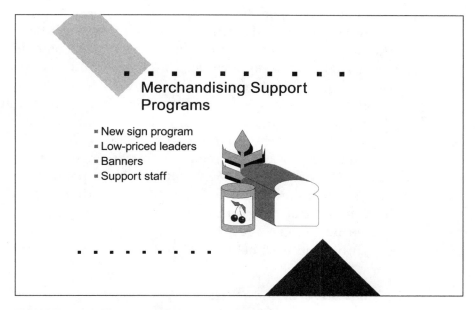

FIGURE 2-19.   Text discussion leader: a list of topics

Signpost and leader pages can correspond directly to the main topic headings in your speech outline. The signposts and leaders visualize the outline structure for your audience for greater clarity of presentation.

Highlighting your discussion topics with signposts and leaders adheres to that time-honored advice for public speakers:

- Tell 'em what you're gonna tell 'em.
- Tell 'em.
- Tell 'em what you told 'em.

You can structure two-screen presentations visually by using the left screen for signposts and leaders and the right screen for charts, graphs, diagrams, and illustrations. In this approach, the left screen is called the *control screen* because it tells the audience what to expect on the right screen and how to interpret it. Departing from this left-right division is potentially confusing and a relatively poor use of an otherwise effective medium. Remember that many corporate boardrooms are equipped for two-screen projection.

A frequent mistake of novice speech writers is to ignore timing the appearance of the visual image so that it coincides with the speech copy that supports it. This correspondence, called *visual cuing,* is particularly noticeable with text frames. For example, if slides are being shown in sequence, the audio message must match the visual image at the moment a slide is cued, or first appears. In short, the audience should see what you say, when you say it.

Cuing errors can be seen sometimes on television news programs. Copywriters and artists often work in parallel (and without apparent communication) to meet close deadlines. At air time the juxtaposition of the picture and the news copy can be odd, even humorous (Figure 2-20). For example, a picture of a huge, growling grizzly bear appears behind the newscaster, who reads the following copy:

Secretary of the Interior Hugo Hollow announced today that more public attention should be focused on the plight of the North American grizzly bear. . . .

FIGURE 2-20. An example of improper visual cuing

As a result of this unfortunate juxtaposition, many viewers will have the initial impression that the hairy face on the screen belongs to Secretary Hollow. One solution would be to rewrite the news copy so that it begins:

The plight of the North American grizzly bear. . . .

The effect of incorrect visual cuing is a jarring distraction from your intended message. Some careful speech writers go so far as to avoid differences in verb tense and word order between visual and spoken copy, even if this makes the text on the screen less concise. A related problem stems from the tendency of audiences to read ahead of you. If you show a leader frame that lists your discussion points, the audience can read much faster than you can talk. Since you're trying to focus their attention according to *your* agenda, you want to minimize opportunities to read ahead.

A solution to this read-ahead problem is to present the topics as a *buildup sequence,* or *text build,* as shown in Figure 2-21. You cue each buildup step as you reach that topic in your presentation. As shown

TEXT BUILD

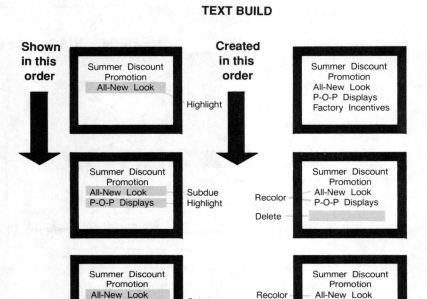

FIGURE 2-21. Text buildup sequences can be created in reverse order.

in the figure, you can create a pleasing effect by highlighting the current topic and subduing the previous topics as the text frame builds.

TIP *Buildup frames can be generated with Freelance Graphics for Windows by creating and storing the last frame first, then deleting (and possibly recoloring) each topic and storing the result, until the entire sequence has been created. That is, you create a buildup sequence in reverse order. Make sure that the layout of the SmartMaster being used will not cause the program to recompose the image with each deletion. This technique is covered further in Chapters 5, 6, and 10. The program also can generate buildups of bulleted lists automatically.*

Illustration

A final category of visual formats is the illustration, which can include pictures of objects or scenes. Free-form drawings also come under this category, as distinct from schematic drawings, or diagrams. For example, a political cartoon is an illustrative drawing.

In business presentations, photographs—especially product photographs—are commonly used for illustrative support. The term *table-top photography* covers close-up pictures of business forms, brochures, small objects, and so on.

As shown in Figure 2-22, photography can be enhanced for your presentation with computer graphic techniques. Text for titles and *callouts* (labels and pointers) can be generated and then combined with bitmap images (including digitized photography)—all within Freelance Graphics for Windows. (A *bitmap* is a mosaic of picture elements, or *pixels*.) Computer-generated background colors, frames, and borders also can be added to photography in order to create a look consistent with the rest of the presentation. Similar

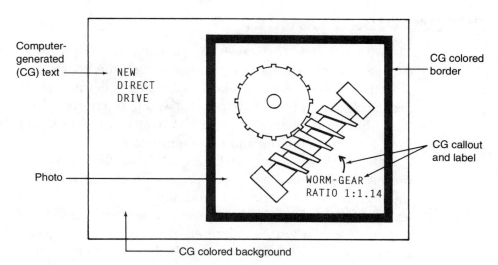

FIGURE 2-22. Photographic composites can be created in Freelance Graphics for Windows by filling a rectangle with a bitmap image.

techniques can be used for video presentations. (Photographs can be scanned digitally for importation to Freelance Graphics or combined with computer-generated slides using photo-optic techniques in the film laboratory.) Techniques for enhancing photography with computer graphics are covered in Chapter 13.

You can also use illustrations to embellish and add visual interest to the charts in your presentation. Freelance Graphics for Windows comes with an extensive set of *symbol libraries* from which previously created illustrations can be recalled and added to any page. Symbol libraries are the electronic equivalent of *clip art,* or catalogs of pre-drawn generic illustrations, a mainstay of graphic production shops.

Electronic clip art can be sized, colored, and positioned in Freelance Graphics for Windows to produce the desired composition. But remember that the illustration should reinforce the main idea of the visual. Adding symbols purely for decoration may make the presentation prettier, but it may actually diminish its effectiveness.

XY GRAPHING CONCEPTS

The discussion here focuses on charting techniques for XY data chart types, including bar, line, area, and scatter charts.

The emphasis is not on how to actually generate the charts with Freelance Graphics for Windows, which is covered later in this book, but on how manipulating characteristics of a graph can reinforce—or distort—your intended message.

The message conveyed by an XY data chart can be changed merely by manipulating its *axis ranges* (Figure 2-23). Axis ranges are the bounds of the vertical or horizontal scales. In Freelance Graphics for Windows, manipulating the axis ranges is called *scaling.* The appearance of a graph—whether it seems to have marked fluctuations or whether it seems essentially flat—is an impression created by scaling.

Freelance Graphics for Windows calculates axis ranges for you, based on the minimum and maximum values of the data sets you

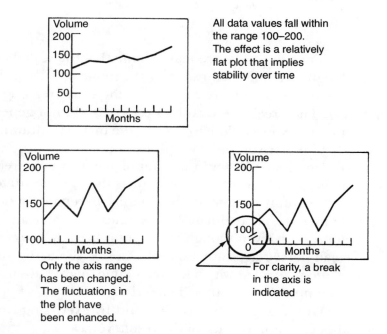

FIGURE 2-23. Manipulation of axis ranges, or scaling, controls the impression given by a plot.

have entered. You may wish to edit the axis ranges to change the overall impression of a graph. For example, assume the data are plotted on a vertical scale of 0 to 100. The same plot will be smoothed considerably by plotting it instead on a scale of 0 to 200.

An important consideration is whether to begin the axis range somewhere other than 0, which might be the expected starting point. If all plot data fall within the range of 100 to 150, starting the scale at 0 would cause a relatively flat plot. But if you wanted to emphasize the fluctuations in the plot, you might reset the starting point to 100.

Use the command Chart➤Scale to reset minimum and maximum scale values. For best results, if you reset one bound manually, reset the other also.

Since the audience may assume that the scale begins at 0, some designers recommend starting the range at 0, then showing a break in the axis line before continuing the scale (refer again to Figure 2-23). The Freelance Graphics program will not generate the break, however; you would have to edit the image by drawing over it.

Whether you use a graph just the way the program generates it or you alter it in some way, ultimately you must rely on your own judgment about whether it depicts the data accurately. Even creating a graph automatically—merely by entering data into a pre-defined graph template—sometimes will yield an incorrect visual impression, even though the input is literally correct. Pie wedges of small percentages, for example, can be so narrow that they cannot be seen. Or a bar with a low data value might have negligible height, as compared with others in a series.

With considerable caution and by exercising careful judgment about the appearance of the result, you can solve these problems by fudging the data to a higher value to create a slightly larger result, then adding a text label (perhaps as a special callout) showing the actual data value. For example, in Figure 2-24, the actual data value of the All Others slice is so small that it would be plotted as a thin line. The value was increased to make the slice more visible, but its accompanying label shows the true number.

Other options for creating XY data charts include:

- Dual *y* axes
- Multiple plot areas
- Multiple graph types

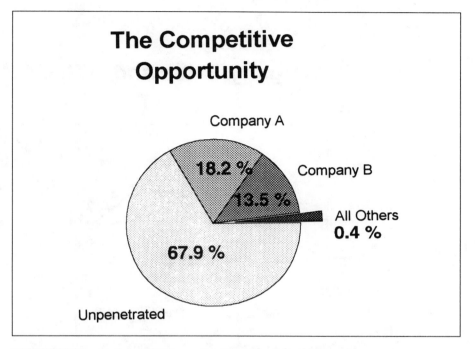

The Competitive Opportunity

Company A

18.2 %

Company B

13.5 %

All Others
0.4 %

67.9 %

Unpenetrated

FIGURE 2-24.   Fudged pie slice with data label. The size of the slice is much larger than its actual data value.

Dual Y Axes

It is sometimes desirable to superimpose two graphs that are plotted with different vertical axes. Given a typical horizontal axis—say the months of the year—it might be necessary to plot sales volume on one vertical axis and the number of salespeople in the field on another vertical axis. This can be done by having a right vertical axis, as well as one on the left. For clarity, of course, it is best to color-code the plots to their respective vertical axes. Freelance Graphics for Windows allows you to specify right as well as left vertical axes, designated Y (left) and $2Y$ (right). (In mathematics, these two axes often are termed y_1 and y_2.)

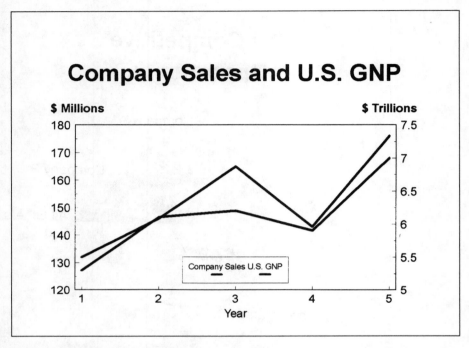

FIGURE 2-25. Dual *y* axes offer flexibility for plotting dissimilar sets of values.

Dual axes are particularly useful when you are trying to show a basic relationship between two plots that have different orders of magnitude. For example, you may wish to show your company's annual sales volume (measured in millions, say) superimposed on a plot of the Gross National Product (measured in trillions). One way to solve the discrepancy in magnitude is to plot your sales volume against a scale on the left and the GNP against a different scale on the right (Figure 2-25).

Multiple Plot Areas

Sometimes it is necessary to show more than one plot on the same page, but not superimposed. Freelance Graphics for Windows permits multiple charts of any type on a page.

Multiple Chart Types

Especially for what-if analysis, you may want to look at the same data in different graph types, but would prefer to avoid the inconvenience of reentering the data. Freelance Graphics for Windows can convert the same set of data readily into any of the XY types (line, bar, area, etc.). Conversion between XY and pie types is also possible, but less straightforward, since a pie graph is limited to four data sets, each shown as a different pie.

WHAT'S WRONG WITH THIS PICTURE?

Look again at the sample XY data chart presented in the Introduction (the chart is shown here as Figure 2-26). As a tool for communicating information, there are several things wrong with it:

- The units of the y data values are not identified. This is an essential key to interpreting the graph. The problem can be corrected by adding the y axis title: Sales ($ Millions).

- In the example, you were instructed to select three-dimensional bars. This is a popular and aesthetically attractive technique, but the result can be misleading. Specifically, because of the three-dimensional effect at the tops of the bars, it can be difficult for the audience to measure the heights against the y axis. A two-dimensional graph would be easier to interpret.

- Finally, what is the purpose of showing this graph? Apparently, the performance of both sales regions followed the same overall trend, peaking in the third quarter. Is the conclusion justified, then, that the fluctuations are due largely to seasonal variations rather than other factors? To clarify this point, it might be helpful to make a comparison with last year's results. Also, sales volumes were generally higher in the West than in the East. Is this a result of better management, or is the market in the West simply larger? Again, a comparison with the prior year might be helpful.

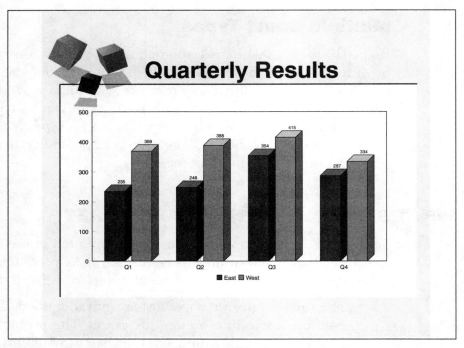

FIGURE 2-26. The sample chart described in the introduction has several inherent flaws.

A chart that attempts to resolve some of these problems is presented in Figure 2-27.

Flexibility in Chart Creation

As I mentioned in the first chapter, Freelance Graphics for Windows is fast and easy to use, with some trade-offs in flexibility. To gain speed, you can handle routine graph production as a two-step process of *layout definition* and *data update*. The layout definition process has already been done for you: A layout for each major graph type is included in each SmartMaster set. If you wish, you can redesign these layouts, or templates, so that later it can be just as fast and efficient to create custom charts. However, designing efficient templates that will require little or no editing is not all that easy; the

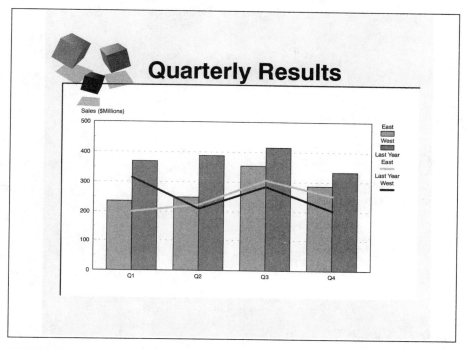

FIGURE 2-27. Revised sample chart. Some of the more obvious problems have been corrected.

software part is easy enough, but thinking ahead about your business situation can be challenging. For example, guessing probable data ranges can be like trying to predict next week's weather. It's the kind of task that seems simple enough in theory but can become complex in practice.

It is quite true that you can create charts very quickly with Freelance Graphics for Windows just by entering the data and accepting the program's default settings. But this chapter has attempted to point out that, while these charts may appear quite attractive, it takes a critical eye—and probably some editing—to produce charts that carry the intended message.

The following chapter takes a broader perspective, covering general principles of graphic design for visual communication—regardless of the technical aspects of computer graphic systems.

CHAPTER 3

GRAPHIC DESIGN: MAKING IDEAS VISIBLE

The artist's job is not to render the visible, but to make visible.
— Paul Klee

W hen you design a graphic presentation for a business meeting, you're not so much a fine artist as an image engineer. An image engineer is someone whose job it is, as Klee says, literally to make ideas visible.

In graphic design as in so many other disciplines, ideas are more important than tools. Klee was trying to counsel artists that they are not just practitioners of the technical skills of copying forms from one medium to another. Rather, artists should be able to perceive and think about the world primarily in visual terms. As an image engineer, you are a visualizer, not just a person who has become skilled at using a pencil, airbrush—or Freelance Graphics software.

It's helpful to think of yourself as an image engineer for another reason. Engineering as a discipline usually involves a degree of responsibility. Architects can be held liable for design flaws in buildings, for example. Similarly, image engineering implies some responsibility for information content. Designing a presentation is not a matter of merely rendering data accurately, but of visualizing your understanding of the data. If you are afraid that this means interpreting the data, with a risk of distortion, your fears are well founded. But you cannot avoid the need to interpret. Any translation from ideas to images will involve many subjective, judgmental—even intuitive—factors. This chapter describes some of them.

Put another way, this chapter is a kind of crash course in graphic design for people who don't necessarily have to be artists, but who cannot avoid being image engineers.

VISUAL STYLE IN BUSINESS PRESENTATIONS

Effective business presentations are designed around the expectations of the audience. One set of expectations concerns *visual style,* which relates to the manner of presentation rather than to information content. Elements of style can reinforce or can detract from information content. The key to good communication is to recognize these hidden elements and to use them to support your objectives.

The Visual Vocabulary

Visual style addresses aspects of human perception that are, to a large extent, subconscious. Human communication depends on a wealth of common experience and unwritten rules that are shared by presenter and audience. We hardly think about these biases. For the most part, they are so deeply rooted that it would be useless or even counterproductive to try to change them. The image engineer, then, must recognize visual biases and use them in such a way that they amplify rather than detract from the intended message.

Elements of visual style encompass a kind of graphic vocabulary used to build pictures. These elements include:

- Form
- Proportion
- Balance
- Symmetry

- Perspective
- Color
- Texture
- Symbolism
- Composition

In this context, visual elements are characteristics, or properties, of graphic objects or groups of objects.

Form

Form   is the shape of an object. Form also can refer to properties of shape: roundness, flatness, hollowness, irregularity, intricacy, and so forth.

Proportion

Proportion   is the relative size of objects or portions of objects.

Balance

Balance   refers to the physical positioning of objects in space, or within a frame, in a pleasing manner.

Symmetry

Symmetry   is the correspondence of size, shape, and position of objects or groups of objects on either side of an axis, or imaginary line of division. Symmetry can be thought of as a special type of visual balance.

Perspective

Perspective   is the representation of three-dimensional objects in a two-dimensional frame of reference to give the illusion of depth. An example would be a drawing of a three-dimensional block on a flat piece of paper.

Color

Color   is both an attribute of objects and an element of composition. The relationships among colors of objects in a grouping is called *color composition*.

Texture

Texture   as used in the graphic arts, usually means the surface quality of an object. Thus, the texture of an object might be described as rough or smooth. Texture also refers to *patterns* with which object outlines can be filled, as an alternative to filling them with solid color. In this sense, plaid, houndstooth check, and gingham are textures. In computer graphics, filling outlined objects with colors and textures is called *rendering*.

Symbolism

Symbolism is graphic form infused with information content. That is, some objects are so closely associated with specific meanings that they can be used as a kind of visual shorthand. International signs are examples of symbolism. Symbolism also may be used in relatively narrow contexts, as in schematic diagrams. For example, within the context of computer networks, a lightning-bolt symbol always stands for a data-communication link.

Composition

Composition is the conscious grouping and coordination of visual elements to achieve a finished design or picture. The following discussion deals with two aspects of composition: orientation and framing.

Orientation

The term *orientation* has a special meaning in computer applications, referring to whether the long dimension of printed pages is horizontal (landscape orientation) or vertical (portrait orientation). Further, in Freelance Graphics, the term can also be used to describe the positioning of axes, or chart frames. In vertical orientation, the *y* axis runs up and down; in horizontal orientation, it runs left to right.

In this discussion, however, let's consider orientation in a wider sense—as a description of screen direction.

As a designer of business graphics, you should be aware of shared assumptions among presenters and viewers about the meaning and importance of orientation, or screen direction.

Left, Right, Up, and Down

People in Western cultures read from left to right. For these read-ers, a transition from left to right is associated with positive motion and progress. Motion from left to right also is associated with the progress of time. Conversely, movement from right to left is consid-ered backward and negative.

Movement along the vertical axis is associated with magnitude. Motion upward connotes increasing magnitude or gain, and down-ward movement means decrease or loss. Also, text-oriented viewers usually will begin at the top of a frame and read, or scan, downward.

Much effort in the graphic-design field recently has been devoted to finding more universal means of expression to minimize the effects of cultural bias. The development of international signs from simple, generic symbols is an example. However, when the audience shares a set of biases, a presentation will be more effective if its design deliberately plays to those assumptions. After all, the use of a language such as English depends on such conventions.

Different sets of assumptions and visual biases may apply to native speakers of Hebrew, Chinese, and Farsi, for example. You should not necessarily assume that if a presentation made a big hit in the New York office, it will be interpreted exactly the same way at an international conference in Geneva.

As discussed in Chapter 2, a classic example of spatial conven-tions is the XY chart. This basic format for many types of charts used in business presentations is presented in Figure 3-1.

Bar, line, area, and scatter charts all are based on XY plotting conventions. The quantity-versus-time relationship is most com-monly used: Time progresses from left to right along the horizontal axis and magnitude varies in the vertical direction. People who share these assumptions can determine much about a trend line even if the graph has no scales or labels.

Freelance Graphics for Windows offers a number of other plot-ting formats that do not adhere to the time-magnitude relationship.

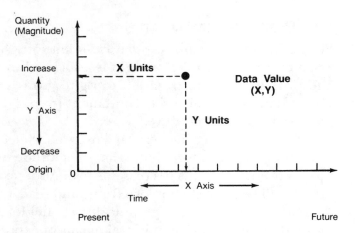

FIGURE 3-1.   Quantity versus time, displayed in an XY data chart

However, as a presenter, you depart from this convention at some risk. It generally would not be appropriate, for example, to use a horizontal bar chart to represent sales volumes. Your intention might be to introduce variety to the presentation, but the result instead will be to add confusion.

Horizontal bars, though, are an excellent way to show time spans and durations. A chart of staff-hours by task might use this format (Figure 3-2).

Gantt charts, or schedule charts, are a specific format used in project management for showing task durations and timing relationships as horizontal bars (Figure 3-3). Specialized software products have been developed for project management (PM), which typically can generate Gantt charts as output from a scheduling process called *time analysis.* Although Gantt charts are not specifically supported in Freelance Graphics for Windows, its horizontal stacked bar chart can be adapted for this purpose.

Another guideline for using left-right, up-down relationships effectively is to remember that there are always two determinants of screen position for a given object. That is, there is a horizontal component and a vertical component. Note the differences among the three designs in Figure 3-4.

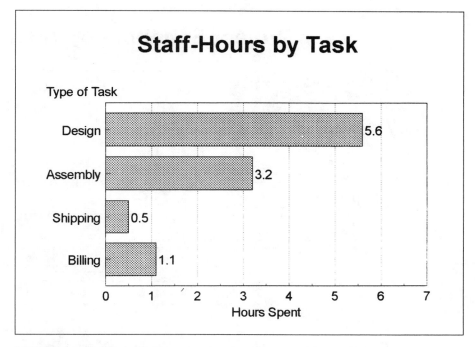

FIGURE 3-2. Horizontal bar chart, a format that departs from the quantity-versus-time relationship

An arrow pointing to the right connotes progress in time only. An arrow pointing upward shows an increase in magnitude but implies a static situation. The third design uses an arrow pointing upward and to the right to convey a sense of both forward motion and growth or gain. The combination of *both* positive biases in this graphic makes it by far the strongest visual statement of the three examples.

North, South, East, and West

Linguistic and graphic conventions about left-right and up-down carry over to concepts about geography. From early childhood, North Americans have been taught to visualize the earth in terms of a Mercator projection map with the continental United States at its center (Figure 3-5).

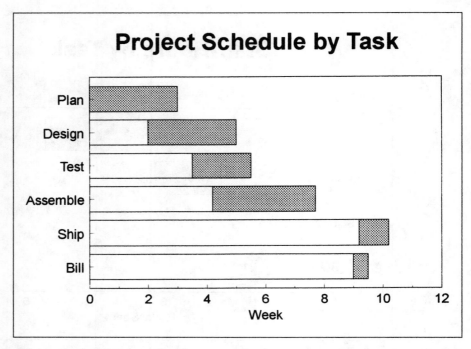

FIGURE 3-3. A Gantt chart may be simulated in Freelance Graphics for Windows by using a horizontal stacked bar chart.

Consider the following item from *Omni* magazine:

We are all taught that the earth rotates counterclockwise on its axis and that it also orbits the sun taking a counterclockwise path. That *seems* to be the case, however, only when viewed from the North Pole, at "the top of the world."

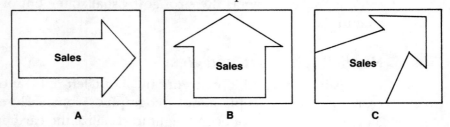

FIGURE 3-4. You can use screen orientation to produce desired psychological effects.

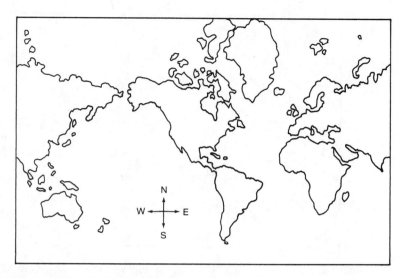

FIGURE 3-5.   The world according to Mercator

The earth, you see, is just a sphere spinning in space and has no objective "top" side. We think of the North Pole as being at the top of the world, because the first mapmakers drew it that way. You could just as easily observe the movement from the South Pole and argue that the planet is traveling in a *clockwise* direction.

The piece goes on to describe McArthur's Universal Corrective Map of the World, as shown in Figure 3-6, an upside down (or "down under") version drafted in Australia. Try thinking about how your assumptions might be different had you been taught this map in elementary school!

With the conventional biases of Mercator, travelers planning a trip from the United States to Europe often have a mental model of flying in an easterly, even rightward, direction. Some people are surprised to learn that the flight plan from most U.S. cities would follow a Great Circle route that goes "up," over the North Pole, as shown in Figure 3-7.

This cultural convention also can be seen in television advertising for air travel. (See the example in Figure 3-8.) In California, an

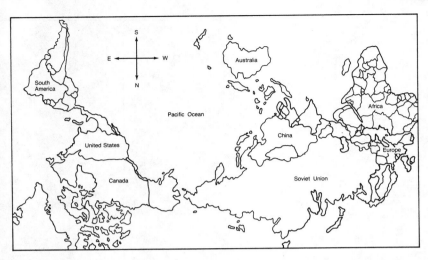

FIGURE 3-6. McArthur's Universal Corrective Map (a view from "down under").
Reproduced with permission of Omni Publications International Ltd.

airline that advertises flights between Los Angeles and Chicago
shows an aircraft flying from left to right, with its nose pointed
toward the upper right of the screen. Viewers in Los Angeles, who
are thinking primarily about their departure rather than their

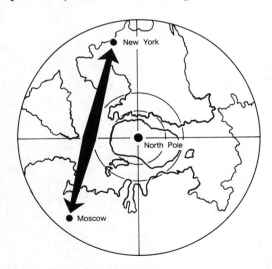

FIGURE 3-7. Polar projection of the North Pole with a Great Circle route from
New York to Moscow

FIGURE 3-8.   Influence of "Mercator bias" in television advertising

return, perceive this screen direction as meaning "northeast." It's fascinating to view similar spots that are prepared for Chicago audiences: as you might expect, the plane is pointed in exactly the opposite direction ("southwest"). In such cases, the art director is designing the scene to meet viewers' expectations.

As a visual technique, playing to this bias can be a kind of narrative shortcut. For example, film director John Huston used it very effectively in *Prizzi's Honor*. The plot involves a bicoastal romance. Each shift of location in the story is signaled by a shot of an airliner pointed in the appropriate direction. Without further explanation, the movie audience knows immediately that, when the plane is flying to screen right, the next scene will find the lovers in New York.

Map conventions are so internalized that they influence almost involuntary eye and body movements. When you read a map, you have been taught to turn it so that north is at the top. Some of us will also go to the extreme of turning our bodies to face north while reading the map.

Photographs or drawings of seacoasts also can play to this prejudice. Again, because of our dependence on Mercator, people in North America think of the Atlantic Ocean as being on the right and the Pacific on the left. If this seems silly to you, look at the sketches in Figure 3-9. Many people would feel somehow uncom-

FIGURE 3-9.   *Q.* Which is a picture of sunny California? *A.* Either might be, but most North American viewers would be more comfortable with the image on the right.

fortable seeing the picture on the left, although they might not be able to tell you why.

These distinctions are purely arbitrary. The real information content of the airline commercials or of the beach scene is not affected by screen orientation. However, to the extent that people have deep-seated expectations, a design that ignores these conventions will be needlessly distracting and, thus, its information content may be not be grasped as readily.

SPATIAL COMPOSITION AND FRAMING

In designing business presentations, considering the left-right, up-down expectations of the audience can affect how you divide a visual frame into areas of interest. This is one aspect of spatial composition. *Framing* can be thought of as the relationship of objects within a picture to the edges of the picture or screen. (In Freelance Graphics for Windows, the term *frame* has three narrower meanings: *(a)* the *plot frame* bordering the plotting area of an XY data chart, *(b)* a *text frame* bordering a block of text, and *(c)* a *table frame* bordering the data table for a chart.)

Composition is a complex subject and is the topic of entire courses in art direction and graphic design. The basic, practical approach to spatial composition described here can be applied to the design of business presentations and to your application of Freelance Graphics for Windows.

For perhaps the majority of charts that you can create with Freelance Graphics, the program takes care of the basic elements of composition automatically. However, sometimes the result that the program produces will not be correct for your case. You need to exercise some judgment about composition so that you know, for example, when to use the drawing utilities to move or resize objects to produce a more pleasing and effective image.

Using Major and Minor Elements

For purposes of composition, the objects in a given picture can be subdivided into major elements and minor elements, as shown in Figure 3-10. This is not a feature of Freelance Graphics for Windows but a conceptual tool to help you think about composition.

The title of a page or slide would be considered a minor element because it is generally smaller than the body (text or chart), which would be the major element. In general, you want your design to guide the viewer's eye from the minor element to the

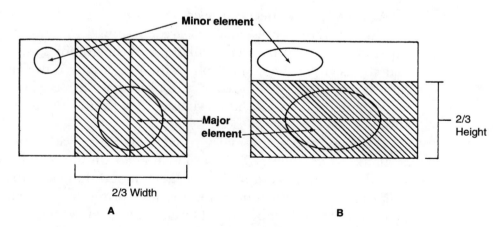

FIGURE 3-10. A practical approach to the design of business graphics: A. left-right composition, B. top-down composition

major element. That is, you want the final, lasting emphasis to be on the major element.

Note that this emphasis is somewhat different from a print-oriented approach. When you write, the major idea, or topic sentence, is expected at the beginning of a paragraph. But in a visual presentation, you want the eye drawn to the elements that support your conclusion.

Artists will tell you that viewers grasp a painting at a glance. Vision specialists will tell you that the eye makes thousands of movements around an image, literally in a wink. For the purposes of this discussion, these factors aren't relevant. Most informational graphics in business involve text or charts; either type of graphic is designed, in some sense, to be "read." Like a sentence, each graphic has a subject and a predicate, or, if you prefer, a lead-in and a pay-off.

Staying within the realm of informational graphics, think about the effect if the eye were to be attracted to the *major* element first. An effective presentation aims at guiding the viewer from premise to conclusion, from subject to predicate, from minor to major elements. It's much like ordering a series of nouns when you list them in a sentence. The greatest emphasis will always be given to the last item in the list.

Again, you can't necessarily use the rules of thumb taught in the fine arts. Business presentations are not purely visual, nonverbal experiences. The presenter is talking, and the graphics must follow that syntax. If, at the conclusion of the presentation, the audience cannot articulate your message, the presentation has failed. Since text-oriented biases will be inevitable, they should be used to best advantage.

Don't confuse minor-major visual composition with *visual cuing*, as discussed in Chapter 2. As a slide appears on the screen, you do want the first words out of the speaker's mouth to match the initial visual impression. To cue a photograph properly, you will sometimes find yourself explaining literally what it shows before moving on to explore the ideas it supports.

Positioning Elements for Best Results

In business presentations, you are seldom dealing with a simple photograph. Slides may contain multiple elements, such as symbols and connectors in a flow diagram. The way to lead the viewer is to place the minor elements in the screen position that the eye naturally is drawn to—either on the left or at the top of the screen. Starting on the left calls for a viewing sequence that proceeds from left to right (example A in Figure 3-10). Starting at the top requires a top-down sequence (example B in Figure 3-10).

Note also in Figure 3-10 that each composition has been divided into thirds. As a rule of thumb, the major element of the composition should occupy two-thirds of the space. Now, this guideline isn't mandatory, and you won't find that Freelance Graphics for Windows always arranges pages this way. However, I've found that this simple rule usually produces an effective composition.

Though individual designs will vary, these basic working rules can be an excellent way to approach initial designs for business graphics. By composing according to minor-major, and left-right or top-down biases, you are anticipating the expectations of the viewer and using them to support your message.

The next six chapters cover the specific functions and capabilities of the Freelance Graphics program for charting and drawing.

COLOR

Color is such an important element of graphic design that I give it a chapter all by itself—Chapter 12.

Learning Freelance Graphics for Windows

C hapters 4 through 10 amount to a quick course in hands-on use of Freelance Graphics for Windows. Chapter 4 includes a discussion of some of the operational aspects of the Windows environment itself. In the other chapters, through step-by-step examples, you will learn to generate all the predefined types of charts and graphs. Drawing and editing tools are also covered, along with advanced techniques that can extend the usefulness of the program.

CHAPTER 4

WORKING IN WINDOWS

This chapter covers those features of Microsoft Windows that affect your use of Freelance Graphics in that environment. You will want to familiarize yourself with this material particularly if you are upgrading from a previous version of Freelance Graphics that runs under the MS-DOS operating system—or if you are just becoming acquainted with Windows.

If you are already comfortable with Windows, you might skim this chapter, then work through the tutorial at its conclusion. If you have difficulty with any part of the tutorial, go back and review that topic before you read Chapter 5.

Windows is a *graphical user interface* (GUI) that replaces much of the keyboarding required to enter commands in DOS with actions that are similar to pointing at pictures. The appearance of its computer screens and its control techniques are similar to GUIs that have been developed for other operating systems, so perhaps quite soon it will be possible to access most computer systems—large and small alike—through this visual vocabulary, with a minimum of prior knowledge.

In Windows, program commands and selections are performed in two-step actions that involve pointing to an item on the screen

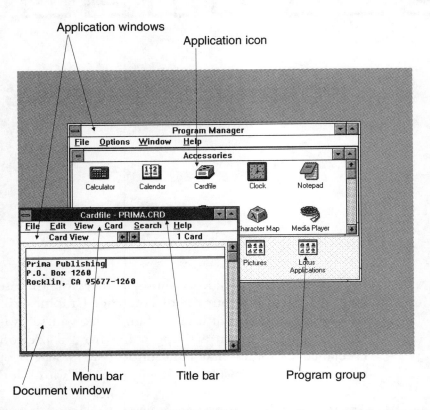

FIGURE 4-1. This view of the Windows desktop shows the open application windows Program Manager and Accessories, as well as a document window in the Cardfile application. Note the arrow-shaped pointer near the menu bar in Cardfile, as well as program groups and icons.

and selecting or activating it. Pointing is done by moving the mouse. The position of the mouse is shown by an arrow-shaped indicator, called the *pointer*, on the screen. After you have moved the pointer to an item you want, you select the item by pressing the mouse button. Pressing the mouse button is called *clicking*. (If the mouse on your system has more than one button, the left button is used for most selections.)

As shown in Figure 4-1, a *window* is a rectangular work space. Windows are of two types: *application* (task or program) and *docu-*

ment. Multiple windows can be open on the screen, or *desktop*, at a given time. The window in which you are currently working is called the *active window.*

In Freelance Graphics for Windows, the display in the Current Page view is a document window for the current presentation file. Shown within the window is one page from the sequence of pages in the presentation document. Displays in the Outliner and Page Sorter, two other program modules of Freelance Graphics for Windows, are also document windows—simply alternate views of the data in the same presentation file.

RUNNING APPLICATIONS

The Windows environment can be started by typing **WIN** at the DOS command prompt and then pressing the Enter key.

 For convenience, the WIN command can be added as the last statement in the DOS file AUTOEXEC.BAT, causing Windows to be started automatically whenever you turn on or restart your computer.

Whenever Windows is started, its Program Manager application is also started automatically. (Refer again to Figure 4-1.) Applications are stored in Windows in collections called *program groups.* Each program group is shown within the Program Manager window as a labeled symbol, or *icon.* The Freelance installation typically places the program icon in the group Lotus Applications.

To open a program group, move the pointer to its icon and *double-click* on it, or press the (left) mouse button twice in very rapid succession.

A window for the program group will open, displaying a labeled icon for each application program it contains. To start an application, such as Freelance Graphics, move the pointer to its icon and double-click.

WINDOWS, PULL-DOWN MENUS, AND DIALOG BOXES

An application window, including Freelance Graphics, has a *title bar* across its top that is labeled with the name of the program.

The title bar of a document window may display its filename, if a name has already been assigned. Otherwise, a blank document window may be presented with the label UNTITLED in the title bar.

Program selections in Windows and within the Freelance Graphics application appear in a *menu bar* beneath the application window's title bar. The menu bar is the main menu, or primary list of program commands, for the application:

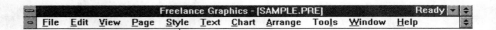

When you select an item from a menu bar, the submenu for that item appears (Figure 4-2). This submenu is called a *pull-down menu* because it appears below the item, much as if a window shade had been pulled down.

A pull-down menu contains a list of commands. There are several ways of making selections from pull-down menus, all of which have the same effect. You can choose the one that is most comfortable for you:

- Click on the item you want in the menu bar. Then, in a separate action, click on the submenu item in the pull-down menu.

- Drag the pull-down menu from the item in the menu bar, and release when you've highlighted the submenu item you want. To *drag*, first move the pointer to the desired item on the menu bar. Then hold the mouse button down, and keep holding it down as the pull-down menu appears. Continue to hold the button down as you move the pointer downward. A *highlight* (colored bar) moves with it. When the submenu item you want is highlighted, release the mouse button. In

Menu-bar selection

Highlighted command

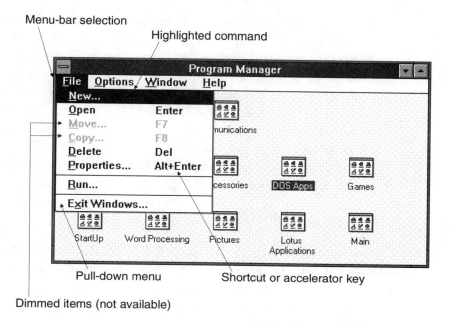

Pull-down menu

Shortcut or accelerator key

Dimmed items (not available)

FIGURE 4-2.   This pull-down menu appears when you select File from the menu
bar of Program Manager.

other words, dragging is a continuous action composed of
the following steps: point, click and hold, move the pointer,
and release. Dragging a pull-down menu selection most
nearly resembles the action of pulling on a window shade.
With this technique, you can execute a compound command
(two selections) in a single motion.

• Press the Alt key, then the key for the underscored letter of
the menu-bar item you want. The pull-down menu will
appear. Then press the key corresponding to the underscored letter of the item in the pull-down menu.

• Press the Alt key, then move the menu highlight in the status
bar with the Right Arrow key. Press Enter to activate the pull-
down menu of the item you want. Then use the Down Arrow
key to move the highlight to the desired command, and press
Enter to select it.

- Press a key combination that is equivalent to the command you want, bypassing the menu system. In Windows and in Freelance Graphics for Windows, certain frequently used selections have been implemented as one- or two-key operations. In Lotus applications such as Freelance Graphics, these are called *accelerator keys*. (In Windows, they are called *shortcut keys*. In other applications, they might be called *hot keys* or *speed keys*.) For example, the accelerator key for printing a presentation from within Freelance Graphics is Ctrl-P. That is, while holding down the Ctrl key, you press the P key. Accelerator keys are listed to the right of their equivalent commands in pull-down menus.

Any menu item or option that appears with its label *dimmed,* or subdued, is not operable at that point in the program. To activate it, you usually must make some other selection first.

When you make a selection from a pull-down menu, one of three things will happen:

- If the menu item is followed by a right arrowhead (▶), a submenu containing a further set of selections will appear to the right of the pull-down menu, as shown in Figure 4-3. You must then make a selection from this list.

- If a menu item is followed by an ellipsis (. . .), a *dialog box* appears. Refer to Figure 4-4. A dialog box is a special window that shows current option settings. You can change settings by selecting various types of switches, or graphical controls, as well as by keying in text or data where required.

- If a menu item is not followed by a right arrowhead or an ellipsis, there are no further selections to make, and the command will simply be executed.

A sequence of menu selections has the same effect as entering a command sequence through the keyboard in a conventional DOS application. For example, in Freelance Graphics for Windows, you can change the format for display of calendar dates by making the following menu selections on page 88.

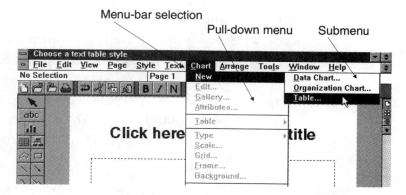

FIGURE 4-3. This submenu appears when you select Chart➤New➤from the menu bar of the Current Page view of Freelance Graphics.

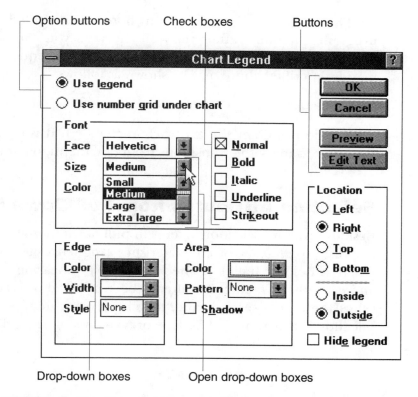

FIGURE 4-4. This dialog box appears in Freelance Graphics when you select Chart➤Legend.

1. Select Tools from the menu bar of the Current Page view.

2. Select User Setup from the Tools pull-down menu.

3. The Tools User Setup dialog box will open. Select the International button.

4. The Tools User Setup International dialog box will open. Click on one of the options in the Date Format box.

5. Select OK twice, once to close each of the open dialog boxes.

 Changes that you make in Tools➤ User Setup or its submenus will apply to future work sessions and other presentations, as well.

The procedures covered in this book are intended to describe program functions rather than all the ways you can select those functions. So, for both clarity and brevity, the sequence of commands described above may be shown as follows:

Tools➤User Setup➤International

You do not enter the arrow character (➤). It is used here as a separator to mark the transitions from one menu to another.

Selecting Attributes from Pull-Down Menus

Besides program selections, items in pull-down menus can also correspond to *attributes,* or characteristics assigned to text or graphics (such as Bold or Italic). A check mark (✓) appearing to the left of an item indicates that it has already been selected or is active. If you select the item a second time, the check mark disappears and the selection is deactivated. This type of two-way switch is called a *toggle.*

Making Option Settings in Dialog Boxes

Again, if an item in a pull-down menu is followed by an ellipsis (...), selecting it will bring up a special window, or dialog box, that contains a set of options. Various types of controls are used to set options, most of which have an initial, or default, setting. Change whatever options you wish, then click on the OK button to accept them (same as pressing Enter) or the Cancel button to ignore them and return to the previous menu (same as pressing Esc).

Different types of controls are used in dialog boxes, depending on the number of selections available in each and whether data entries are needed. With the mouse, click on an item to select or reset it. Or, using the keyboard, press the Tab key to move among the options and use the arrow keys to change the settings. (Pressing Tab repeatedly will move the cursor to the right and downward through the options, and Shift-Tab will move it to the left and upward.) To activate any labeled button, press Alt-*letter*, where the letter key corresponds to the character that is underlined in the button label. Finally, to complete your work in a dialog box, press Enter or select the OK button to accept the changes; press Esc or select the Cancel button if you want to ignore them and close the window.

Dialog-Box Controls

In Windows, there can be as many as six types of controls in a dialog box. (Refer again to Figure 4-4, in which all control types except text box are shown.) These controls are:

- Check box
- Option button
- List box
- Drop-down box
- Text box
- Button

Check Box

A selection that can be only on/off or yes/no is indicated by a hollow square, or *check box*. A check box is a type of toggle. If the square contains an *X*, the setting is on; if the square is empty, it is off. A check box can be set individually, separate from other options. Check boxes that are dimmed represent options that are not available. In some applications, you may also see a check box that is filled with a shaded area. Such shaded check boxes may indicate that related options have not been set. The check box will become active if the related selection is made. The shaded area inside indicates that the current setting is null (neither on nor off) in which case the option is ignored.

Option Button

A small, hollow circle next to an option name is an *option button,* which is another kind of toggle. It can be either on or off. If on, the circle contains a solid dot. Option buttons appear in sets and, like the controls on an old car's push-button radio, only one option in the set can be on at any given time. In effect, a set of option buttons can be regarded as a multiple-choice question for which there can be only one response.

List Box

A *list box* contains a list of text items—usually options or names for things such as fonts, devices, or files (Figure 4-5). Entries inside the box can *scroll,* or roll vertically so that lists can extend beyond the borders of the box. You select an item in the list by clicking on it. You can scroll the list by clicking on the arrows at the side of the box or dragging the slider (the square button located between the arrows).

Drop-Down Box

Another type of list has been collapsed to form a single line that can expand, or drop down, to show the full list. Such a *drop-down box*

Selected item

List box

Up-arrow button

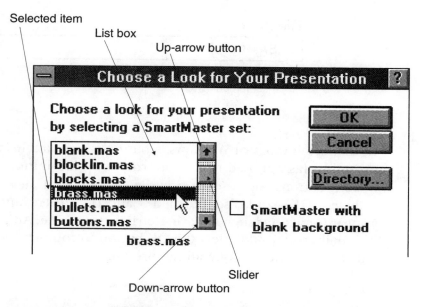

Slider

Down-arrow button

FIGURE 4-5. A list box can scroll, permitting the list to be longer than the size of the box. Scrolling can be controlled by the slider or arrow buttons in the right side of the box.

expands when you click on the down-arrow button at its right end. Once you have made a selection from the list, the box collapses to show the current selection as the single line of text:

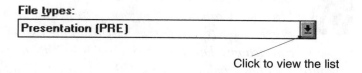

Click to view the list

Text Box

Fields in which you can enter data are *text boxes*. Click on the box to make it active; a blinking vertical-bar cursor appears. This vertical bar is the *insertion point* at which characters will appear in a text string. Type in the data as shown on the next page.

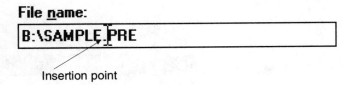

File name:

`B:\SAMPLE.PRE`

Insertion point

Button

In the terminology of Windows, a button is a rectangle labeled with an action (as opposed to a small, round option button). In dialog boxes, buttons are used primarily as the equivalents of Enter (labeled OK) and Esc (labeled Cancel). Other buttons might appear for actions such as Save, Retrieve, Continue, Add, and so on. Normally, you would select the OK button to complete your work in a dialog box after making all required settings.

Don't confuse this type of control with the Button attribute in Freelance Graphics, a program feature that permits you to create graphic objects that can be selected by the user of a screen show to trigger specific actions. This feature in Freelance Graphics permits you to create controls that are similar in effect to the buttons in Windows.

MULTITASKING

One of the much-touted advantages of Windows is the ability to work on more than one application, or task, at a time. In computer terminology, this is called *multitasking*. Advocates of multitasking on personal computers claim that it mirrors the way people actually think and work—juggling several tasks at a time, including the need to respond to interruptions while other ongoing work pauses temporarily. For example, when you are in the midst of building a new spreadsheet, your manager might call and ask you to look up an entry in your database. You need to be able to respond immediately, but with a minimum of disruption to your original task.

In Windows, multiple applications can be running at the same time. Open application windows are always on the screen, even if obscured by the one that is currently active. The window in which you are working (the current, or active, window) is shown with its title bar highlighted. In effect, the task windows are layered, with the active window highlighted and on top.

To activate a different application, simply click anywhere within its window. If the desired window is not visible, as when it is obscured by the active window, other procedures must be used. These procedures are covered in the following discussion.

A quick and convenient way to switch among currently running applications is to press Alt-Tab, which will activate the previous application you used. Or, hold down Alt and press Tab repeatedly. With each press of the Tab key, Program Manager displays the title of another open application. To select a title, press the Alt key again. Another technique is to press Alt-Esc repeatedly, which causes active control to cycle among all the open applications.

Multitasking of non-Windows (DOS) applications is possible only in *386 enhanced mode,* which requires an 80386 processor or higher and at least 2MB (megabytes) of memory.

The other multitasking mode of Windows is *standard mode,* which requires an 80286 processor or higher and at least 1MB of memory. You can run DOS applications in this mode, but not concurrently.

You can make DOS applications available to Windows by adding them as program items, or use the File➤Run command in Program Manager to start them.

TIP

*In 386 enhanced mode, when the DOS application appears, press Alt-Enter to place it in the active window. To end the program, you cannot necessarily use File➤Close or Exit commands; you must exit the application by using the menu selection that is required in DOS. (Your system will run in 386 mode automatically if it is configured properly. To force this mode, type **WIN /3** when you start Windows.) To quit a DOS application window that is not responding to the system, select its Control box, then Settings➤Terminate. Or, press Ctrl-Alt-Del and then Enter.*

CONTROLLING APPLICATION WINDOWS

In Windows and in Freelance Graphics, application or document windows can be *minimized*—shrunk to an icon—or *maximized*—enlarged to fill the screen. You might minimize a window to keep it out of the way (but still ready for use) while making room on the desktop for other windows. Minimizing an application also reduces its processing priority and possibly its memory allocation, freeing computer resources for other tasks. You might maximize a window to allow yourself more room to work within it. This also gives it higher processing priority and more memory.

To minimize or maximize a window, click on either the Minimize (down triangle symbol) or Maximize (up triangle symbol) buttons in the top-right corner of the window's title bar:

Minimize ⟶ ◀ Maximize

Or, from the keyboard, press Alt-Hyphen to activate the window's Control menu. (If the window is the Freelance Graphics application window itself or any dialog box, press Alt-Spacebar instead.) Then, from the Control pull-down menu, select Minimize or Maximize. (There's more about the Control menu in the following section of this chapter.)

The procedure for *restoring* a window to its previous size depends on the current state of the window. If it has been shrunk to

an icon, simply double-click on the icon. If the window has been
maximized, double-click on the Restore (up/down triangle symbol)
button in the top right corner of its menu bar:

To restore a window through the keyboard, press Alt-Hyphen
(or Alt-Spacebar) to activate the window's Control menu box. Then
select Restore from the Control pull-down menu.

THE CONTROL MENU

The small bar in the box in the top-left corner of an application or
document window is the access point to the Control menu for that
window:

The Control menu has selections for manipulating the window,
including Minimize, Maximize, and Restore, as shown in Figure 4-6.
Other selections in the Control menu for an application or document window can include

- Move
- Size
- Close
- Next *or* Next Window
- Paste
- Edit *and* Settings
- Switch To

Control box   Control menu

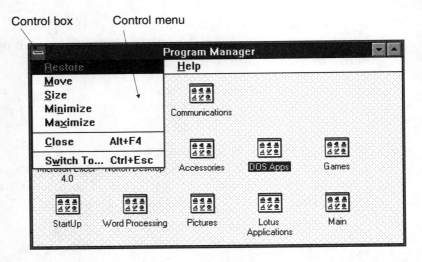

FIGURE 4-6. The Control menu for the Program Manager application window allows you to control the program itself, rather than the contents of its window.

Move

This selection lets you move the window to another location on the desktop (screen) by pressing the arrow keys. However, you can move a window without going through the Control menu simply by dragging its title bar to a new location with the mouse.

Size

This command lets you change the size of a window by pressing the arrow keys. Or, you can bypass the Control menu and perform the same action by dragging a border or corner of the window to a new location with the mouse. Dialog boxes cannot be resized.

Close

This command terminates the running of the window's task or closes the file it represents. Or, the same thing can be achieved by double-clicking on the Control box. If the window is a document and it has not been saved in its current version, the program will prompt you to do so before closing the window. In any presentation document window of Freelance Graphics and in Windows itself, the keystroke equivalent for this command is Ctrl-F4. To close the main program, Chart Data & Titles windows, or dialog boxes of Freelance Graphics, press Alt-F4.

Next or Next Window

When multiple document windows are displayed, this command switches to the next open document. (Examples of document windows include Freelance Graphics presentations, Chart Data & Titles windows, and Help displays.) In either Windows or Freelance Graphics, you can press Ctrl-F6 to execute this command.

Paste

This command, sometimes encountered in Control menus, lets you copy data (such as text, graphics, sound, or pictures) from the Clipboard, or scratch-pad memory area of Windows, into a document window. In Freelance Graphics and in most other Windows applications, the Paste command is usually found instead in the Edit pull-down menu. (There is more about the Clipboard later in this chapter.)

Edit and Settings

These commands appear only on Windows Control menus. They apply to non-Windows applications in 386 enhanced mode and are not available with Freelance Graphics. The Edit command displays a submenu of Clipboard operations, and the Settings command controls multitasking. Use these commands when running DOS applications, such as spreadsheet programs, concurrently with Freelance Graphics for Windows.

Switch To

Select this command to change the active application by making a further selection from the Windows Task List (a listing of currently running programs). In Windows and in the Freelance Graphics main program, you can press Ctrl-Esc to execute this command.

USING FILES

Windows applications use a system of directories and filenames to organize and store disk files that contain programs and data. In 16-bit versions of Windows (as opposed to Windows NT), the underlying file-management system is actually provided by DOS.

All Windows applications use the same system of file access. The File pull-down menu is always the leftmost item in the menu bar of any application.

In addition, Windows includes the utility program File Manager, which can be used independently of applications to create directories, inspect the contents of directories and files, copy or delete files, and generally manage all aspects of data storage. The icon for File Manager is a file cabinet, and it is usually installed in the program group Main (Figure 4-7).

A full discussion of file management in Windows is beyond the scope of this book. Covered here are some of the topics that should be the most helpful in your work in Freelance Graphics:

- File types and associations
- Managing file storage in directories
- Using the Windows file system
- Navigating the file system

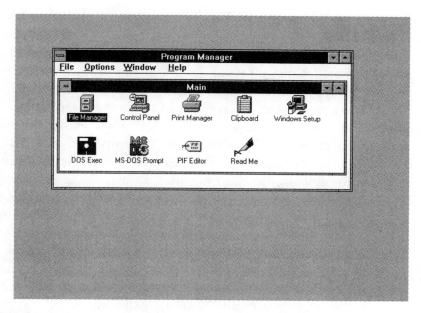

FIGURE 4-7. The icon for File Manager is a file cabinet, found in the program group Main.

File Types and Associations

A *file type* classifies the contents of a computer file stored on disk. File types include text and alphanumeric (character) data, executable (ready-to-run) programs, descriptions of graphic objects, pictures (bitmaps), and even digital sound and movie files. In DOS and in Windows, the file type is indicated by a three-character file extension that is appended to the filename, separated from it by a period.

Some types of data files are proprietary, or unique to specific programs. Typically, when you save a data file to disk, you supply the filename, which can contain as many as eight characters, and the program adds the extension. For example, graphics are stored by Freelance Graphics for Windows as presentation files, which always have the .PRE file extension. So if you save a presentation called REPORT, the name of the file as it appears in the disk directory will be:

report.pre

The file type is important because it gives you, and any program using that file, information about the program that created it. The file type also indicates how the file is to be used. For example, a chart generated by Freelance Graphics for DOS has a .CH1 extension. You would know immediately upon seeing this extension in a file listing that this chart must be translated to .PRE format to be used by Freelance Graphics for Windows. The program can do this automatically, but knowing the file type gives you the information that some attributes, such as colors or fonts, might not be exactly the same after the file is translated.

In Windows, file extensions serve another important purpose. A type of data file, as referenced by its extension, can be *associated*, or linked, with the name of the program file that typically uses it. When you are running File Manager, the association makes it possible to start a program automatically any time you select (double-click on) the name of one of its data files from a listing. File Manager not only starts the program but also loads the selected data file so that you can begin working with it immediately.

The association also tells the file system the appropriate extension for any new data file so that it can be appended automatically any time you are prompted for a filename. That is, the application program adds the extension it requires, and you seldom have to type it in.

File associations are stored in the Windows data file WIN.INI, which is a text file that contains *parameters,* or options, for applications. All associations that have been created within your Windows installation will appear in a section of the file headed [Extensions]. The association for Freelance Graphics presentation files appears as:

    pre=flw.exe   ^.pre

This statement associates files having .PRE extensions with the main Freelance Graphics program file, FLW.EXE. (The .EXE extension means that the file is an executable program.)

Managing File Storage in Directories

Again, Windows applications, including File Manager, use DOS as the method of organizing and storing computer files on disk. If you are familiar with DOS, you already know that files are stored within a hierarchy of categories called a *directory structure,* or *directory tree,* as shown in Figure 4-8. Each directory can be thought of as a file drawer that contains a set of named files.

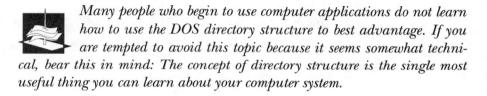

Many people who begin to use computer applications do not learn how to use the DOS directory structure to best advantage. If you are tempted to avoid this topic because it seems somewhat technical, bear this in mind: The concept of directory structure is the single most useful thing you can learn about your computer system.

What is at stake here is the very power of being organized, which is one of the main things that a computer can do for you. And learning to create and manage file directories can pay direct benefits as you begin to build presentations with Freelance Graphics.

To ignore this topic is analogous to throwing paper files haphazardly into a closet. You might not be able to find information quickly when you need it. Also, you will probably waste storage space—perhaps eventually fill up the capacity of a large hard disk—because you have no idea what is contained in all that clutter.

A directory provides a way of grouping and accessing files by topic, job, client, or other convenient category. Whether in DOS or in Windows File Manager, you are the creator of any new directories—so *you* control the directory structure of disk storage on your computer.

Refer again to Figure 4-8. This structure resembles an inverted tree, which can have multiple branches. The base of the tree, or the basic starting point for any search of its directories, is called the *root.* The tree grows downward from the root as directories are created. Each new directory forms a new branch. In turn, a directory can have multiple branches, or *subdirectories,* beneath it. A directory that contains subdirectories is called the *parent directory.*

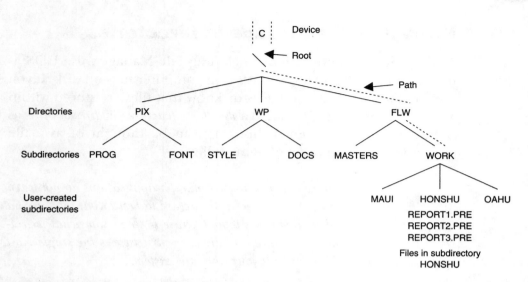

FIGURE 4-8. A directory structure, or tree, shows the organization of all the files, by directory, on your disk. (The tree is usually shown inverted, with the root at the top.)

The location of a file within the directory structure can be specified by tracing the *path* to it through the tree, starting at the root:

c:\flw\work\report.pre

This path description begins with the *device name* of the disk drive that holds the file. The device name is a letter followed by a colon. On most personal computers, the removable-disk (floppy-disk) drives are named A and B. Hard-disk drives (or subdivisions of the same hard disk, called *partitions*) might be designated C, D, and E. On most single-user systems, C is the primary hard-disk drive, on which application programs such as Freelance Graphics normally reside. (On a local area network, many users typically share a common disk device, called a *file server*. It might have a device name like S:.)

Immediately following the device name in the path is the back-slash character (\). When the backslash follows a device name, it means, "starting at the root," or beginning at the base of the tree. As shown in the example of the path description, this character also separates directory names and filenames. The example therefore shows that the Freelance Graphics presentation file REPORT.PRE can be found on drive C by starting at the root and *traversing* directories FLW and WORK.

Specifically, how can you use the directory tree to manage data files in Freelance Graphics? The default directory for data files, such as presentations, is FLW\WORK. That is, unless you specify otherwise, the program will save all presentations in that directory. Now, saving all your presentations here is about as effective as throwing all your paper files on the same shelf of that closet. The situation is improved, but not much.

 When saving Freelance Graphics presentations, I suggest that you create different subdirectories for each major category of work. For example, you might maintain a separate subdirectory for each client, account, or project. So, if you had projects named Maui, Honshu, and Oahu, you would need to create the following subdirectories:

    c:\flw\work\maui
    c:\flw\work\honshu
    c:\flw\work\oahu

The following discussion tells you how to create directories and how to save files in them.

Using the Windows File System

Remember that the File menu is always the leftmost item on the menu bar of any Windows application. The pull-down menu for this item on the startup menu bar of Freelance Graphics for Windows is shown in Figure 4-9.

Regardless of the application, the command to access an existing file is File➤Open. When you select this command, you are requesting the Windows file system to access an existing data file and read its contents into the computer's memory so that you can use the application to work with the data.

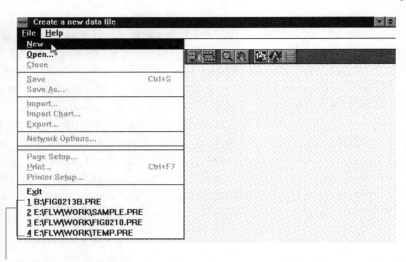

Last files you worked on

FIGURE 4-9.   Startup menu of Freelance Graphics, showing the File pull-down menu. A similar menu is available on all applications that run under Windows.

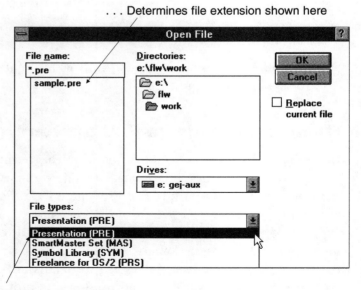

. . . Determines file extension shown here

File type selected here. . .

FIGURE 4-10.   This dialog box appears when you select File➤Open.

Whenever you select File≻Open or File≻Save As, a dialog box will appear, as shown in Figure 4-10. Note that the default data-file type is already displayed in the File Name text box. Any files with this extension in the default data directory are shown in the Files list box. In some cases, you can select a different File Type from the drop-down box. When you do, the extension changes in the File Name box, along with the listing of available files.

Navigating the File System

Whenever you are working in a file-access dialog box such as the one in Figure 4-10, you can *log on,* or change, to another directory by typing its DOS path in the File Name text box and then pressing Enter.

Another effective way of changing directories or finding a file involves *navigating* the file system, or selecting different devices and directories through the dialog box. A convenient way to do this involves pointing and clicking with the mouse.

To navigate the file system, you traverse the directory tree in the same order that you would if you were to type in the DOS path. If the desired directory or file is on a different device (disk drive), first select the drive letter in the Drives list box. When you select a different drive, a listing of its directories will appear in Directories box. To move "down" the inverted tree, simply select the name of the directory on the next lower branch. Then, a listing of its subdirectories will appear. Keep selecting subdirectories until the correct path appears in the File Name text box.

You can also move up—toward the rest of the inverted tree. The parent directory, if there is one, is shown in the listing as two dots enclosed in braces: [..]. Select this symbol to move to the next higher branch in the tree and to display its subdirectories. When you arrive at the root, the [..] symbol will not appear, and assuming you are logged on to the C drive, the following will appear in the File Name text box:

c:\

To see the entire contents of a directory or subdirectory, regardless of file type, use the *wildcard* character (*) in the File Name box instead of the name and extension:

c:\flw\work*.*

You can also use the question mark (?) as a wildcard character to stand for individual characters in a filename; for example:

c:\123w\data*.wk?

In this example, 1-2-3 worksheets with both .WK1 and .WK3 extensions will appear in the listings.

To open an existing file, you can simply double-click on its filename in the Files list box (Figure 4-11). Or, highlight the filename and select OK (or press Enter).

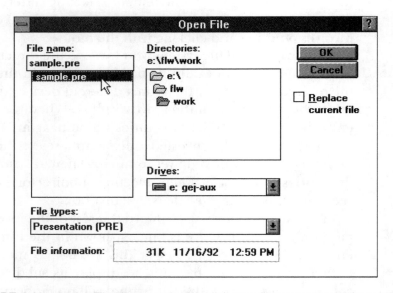

FIGURE 4-11. In the Files list box, double-click on a filename to open it, or highlight the item and select OK.

Within Freelance Graphics for Windows, you can change the currently logged disk and working directory with the File➤Directory command. You can reset default data directories by executing Tools➤User Setup➤Directories.

USING FILE MANAGER

Primary uses of File Manager are to create new directories and to copy files.

To start File Manager, open its program group (usually Main) and select its icon. When you do this, a *device window* will open, which is split into two parts, as shown in Figure 4-12. On the left is a listing of directories for the current storage device, or disk drive. On the right is a listing of files in the current directory. If you select a different directory from the listing on the left, the listing of files on the right will change accordingly.

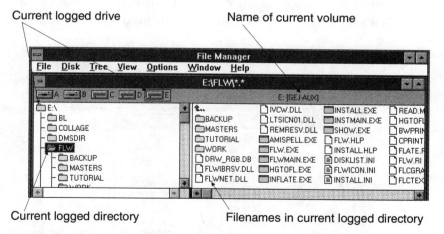

FIGURE 4-12. A device window in File Manager displays the files and subdirectories in the current directory.

Creating a New Directory

To create a new directory, first log on to the directory that will serve as its parent, or the location on the tree from which the new branch will grow. You can do this with the mouse by double-clicking on the directory name in the left portion of the device window.

If the directory will be on a different device, log on to it by clicking *once* on the device icon from the group of pictures of drives in the top left of the device window. (Or, perform Disk➤Select Drive.) Then, navigate its directories to select the branch from which the new directory will grow.

Once you are logged on to the parent directory (as confirmed by the path shown in the window's title bar), select File➤Create Directory. The Create Directory dialog box will appear (Figure 4-13). Type the name of the new directory in the Name text box, then select OK (or press Enter).

The new directory will appear under its parent in the directory listings.

Be aware that you cannot delete a directory that contains files. To remove a directory, first delete the files or move them to another storage location, then delete the directory. Select it and then execute File➤Delete. You will be prompted to confirm the deletion.

Enter name of new directory

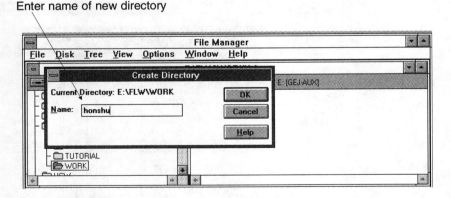

FIGURE 4-13. The Create Directory dialog box appears when you select File➤Create Directory in File Manager.

Copying Files

There is no facility *within* Freelance Graphics for Windows itself for creating directories or for copying files. You must use the Windows File Manager, the DOS Shell, DOS commands, or a file-management utility program.

Using File➤Copy

You can use DOS commands for copying files by first selecting the DOS Prompt icon in the Main program group and then typing in the appropriate command. However, the recommended method is to use File Manager. You can select the filename in the device window, execute File➤Copy, and then type the path to the new location in the Copy dialog box (Figure 4-14).

Drag and Drop

As of the release of Windows 3.1, there is a much more convenient way to use File Manager to copy files—*drag and drop.*

As the term implies, you can drag the file from one window to the other, releasing the mouse button (dropping the file) when you are pointing to the destination file listing.

Enter drive, path, and optional filename for the new file

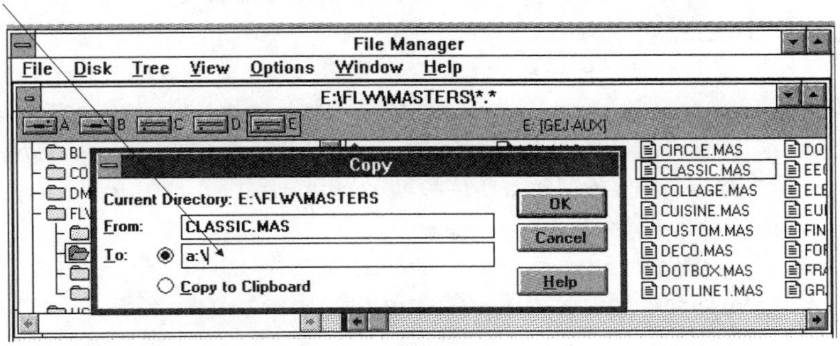

FIGURE 4-14. The Copy dialog box appears when you select File➤Copy in File Manager. This is a quick way to copy a file from one location to another.

In File Manager of Windows 3.0, you can copy by drag and drop if you hold down the Ctrl key while dragging. If you do not use the Ctrl key, the file or files will be moved—that is, copied to the new location and also deleted from the original location. This is an important difference between versions 3.0 and 3.1 of Windows.

To copy a file by the drag-and-drop method, first open File Manager and select the desired file in the device window, navigating the directory tree if necessary until the filename is listed.

Recalling that multiple windows can be open on the desktop at the same time, open a second window in File Manager by double-clicking on the icon of the device that will hold the file copy.

A second device window will open, as shown in Figure 4-15. Navigate its directory tree to log on to the directory that will receive the file copy.

Next, position the two windows so that both their listings are visible. Either drag their title bars to different locations on the desktop, or perform Window➤Tile.

Point to the desired file in the first window. Press the mouse button down to select the file, and *keep holding the button down* as you move the pointer (which has changed to a document symbol) to the desired location in the second window. When the pointer is in the right-hand window that shows the file listing of the receiving directory, release the mouse button. (You need not specify the exact position in the listing; the program will do this for you, according to the current View option. The default setting is to list files alphabetically by name.)

If you are copying the file to a different directory on the same drive (if both windows show the same device), you must hold down the Ctrl key while performing drag and drop.

When you release the mouse button (drop the file), a Confirm Mouse Operation warning will appear:

Are you sure you want to copy the selected files or directories to
<path>?

Drag filename from here. . .

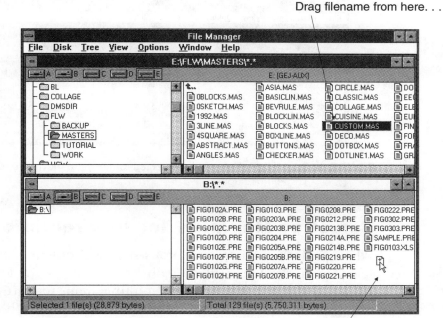

. . .to here

FIGURE 4-15.   Use the drag-and-drop method to copy files by dragging them from one device window to another in File Manager (Windows 3.1 and later versions).

To confirm the copy operation, select Yes (or No to cancel). The filename and its contents now appear in *both* locations. (To copy the file and also delete its first instance, perform File>Move instead. You can also do this with the mouse if you hold down the Shift key while performing drag and drop.)

Copying Directories

When you are performing drag and drop, if you select a directory instead of a file, the directory and all the files it contains—*including its subdirectories and their files*—will be copied to the destination.

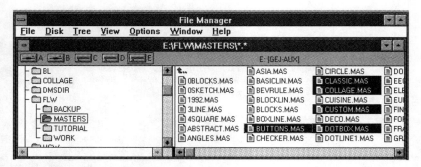

FIGURE 4-16.   Multiple files can be selected for copying, moving, or deletion in File Manager.

Selecting Multiple Files or Directories

When performing File operations such as Copy or Move, you can select multiple items (files or directories) for a single operation. (Refer to Figure 4-16.) To select multiple items that are adjacent to one another in the listing, click on the first item with the mouse. Then, while pressing the Shift key, select the last item. To use the keyboard, hold down the Shift key while pressing an arrow key to move from first item to last.

To select items that are not adjacent, hold down the Ctrl key while clicking on each item. To do this using the keyboard, press Shift-F8, move the pointer with the arrow keys through the listing, and select items with the Spacebar. To complete the selection, press Shift-F8 again.

To select files with similar names or extensions, use the File➤Select Files command and specify the filenames using wild-card characters.

COPYING DATA AND PICTURES THROUGH THE CLIPBOARD

One of the real conveniences of the Windows environment is the ability to easily exchange data—including text, alphanumeric data, graphics, pictures, animation, video, and audio—among applications. This is made possible by two key features of Windows:

Standardization   Certain file types have been standardized for purposes of data exchange. These include ASCII or ANSI text (.TXT or .PRN files), graphics (.CGM and .WMF metafiles), and pictures (.BMP, .PCX, and .TIF bitmaps).

Clipboard   Data exchange is performed through a common memory area called the Clipboard. That is, all applications that support data exchange can access this area. Data are passed from one application to the Clipboard, then moved from the Clipboard into another application.

Within an application, data are passed to the Clipboard by selecting (highlighting) the data and then performing Edit➤Copy or Edit➤Cut. Copying leaves the original item intact; cutting removes it from the application, leaving the only copy on the Clipboard. Once data have been placed on the Clipboard, they can be retrieved by performing Edit➤Paste in the receiving application.

Note that the Clipboard can hold the results of only *one* Edit➤Copy or Edit➤Cut operation, although that item can be quite large, perhaps several megabytes. When you perform Edit➤Copy or Cut again, the prior contents of the Clipboard are lost.

Edit➤Paste can be performed repeatedly to retrieve multiple copies of a data item into one or more active application windows. The contents of the Clipboard will not change until you perform Edit➤Copy or Cut again, or until you end the Windows work session.

Linking Applications through DDE

Further, it is possible to link applications that share data so that if an update is performed in one of them, it will be triggered automatically in the other. This process is called *dynamic data exchange* (DDE). For example, a spreadsheet application can be linked to

Freelance Graphics so that any change in the spreadsheet triggers replotting of a graph that uses its data.

 There is more about multitasking, DDE, and OLE in relation to Freelance Graphics in Chapter 14.

In Windows, the ability to use DDE can depend on the direction of data transfer. The application that is the source of the data is called the *server,* and the receiving application is called its *client.* (Equivalent terms used with OLE are *source* and *destination.*)

DDE is initially set up simply by performing Edit➤Paste Link instead of Paste when retrieving data from the Clipboard. This not only copies the data but also establishes an ongoing link between the applications and the data files, a link that persists even after the applications and files have been closed.

Note that the Edit➤Paste Link command will work only if both applications support DDE for the type of data being exchanged. If this is not the case, the Paste Link option will be unavailable, appearing dimmed in the Edit pull-down menu.

Some programs can act as either server or client. In most cases, you will be using Freelance Graphics for Windows to act as the client DDE application, moving data into its Chart Data & Titles window from other applications. For example, Freelance Graphics can receive spreadsheet data from an application that supports DDE. (Such a data table is called a *linked array.*) In this case, the spreadsheet application is the server, and Freelance Graphics is the client. While both applications remain open, any change of the data in the source spreadsheet will cause the Freelance Graphics chart data to be updated also.

You can sever the link within the client application by using the Edit➤Links command to delete the reference. You can then edit the data or paste other data that are not linked. However, DDE will no longer operate on the data, which will have no relation to the data in the source file.

If you do not sever the links, they will persist even after the applications are closed. In the case of the linked spreadsheet, consider what would happen if you were to open the spreadsheet and change the data while Freelance Graphics remains closed. The next time you open the corresponding Freelance Graphics presentation file, the program will reopen the source file so that the update can be completed.

Object Linking and Embedding (OLE)

Freelance Graphics for Windows also supports the *object linking and embedding* (OLE) feature of Windows, which is an enhancement of DDE. If the server application also supports OLE, double-clicking on the linked object in Freelance Graphics will open the server application so that the data can be edited there. For more information, see Chapter 14.

JUGGLING TASKS

Operations like DDE involve multitasking, or running multiple applications concurrently. There are several ways to switch among open Windows applications:

- As discussed previously, one method is simply to click on the title bar of the application window you wish to activate. This presumes that the desired window is visible on the desktop and not obscured by other windows.

- Select the Control menu of the active application window and then select Switch To. (The shortcut key equivalent for this command is Ctrl-Esc.) The Task List dialog box will appear, listing applications that are already open. You then select another application from this list, completing the command by selecting the Switch To button.

- Press Alt-Esc repeatedly (or hold down Alt while pressing Tab repeatedly) to cycle the open windows through active status until the title bar of the window you want is highlighted.

- Among Windows applications that support OLE, double-click on a linked object to start the source application.

- Minimize the active application, then select (or start) another by selecting its program group and icon. If DDE is being performed, the required document window should remain open as the application is minimized. In some applications, the filename of the open document will appear in the label of the minimized application icon at the bottom of the screen.

This last method is often preferable because it reduces the processing priority and memory allocation of the first application, permitting the second task to run faster. Minimizing the first application has no effect on its ability to participate in DDE, as long as the required data files remain open.

WINDOWS TUTORIAL

As a recap of some of the procedures covered in this chapter, here is a brief tutorial in which you start Freelance Graphics, retrieve a presentation file, manipulate task and document windows, and perform data exchange through the Clipboard.

This tutorial assumes that you have worked through the exercise in the Introduction, which created the presentation file SAMPLE.PRE. To complete the following steps, you need the title page saved as Page 1 in this file. Instructions are included here for creating this page if you have not done so already.

1. Start Program Manager.

   If Windows is not already running, type **win** at the DOS prompt, then press Enter. Program Manager should start automatically. If it appears as an icon, double-click on it to restore it.

2. Select the program group (usually Lotus Applications) that contains Freelance Graphics.

The Program Manager window contains labeled icons representing groups of application programs. Double-click on the group icon.

3. Select the Freelance Graphics application icon.

The program group will open, showing a collection of application icons, including Freelance Graphics. Double-click on this icon to start the program.

4. The Welcome to Freelance Graphics window will open. Select the option button Work on an Existing Presentation. (If you did not work through the tutorial in the Introduction, simply select OK here to create a new presentation, then select OK again.)

5. A file listing of presentations in the directory FLW\WORK will appear. In the Files box, double-click on the filename SAMPLE.PRE.

If you are creating a new presentation, omit steps 5 and 6.

6. Page 2, the chart "Quarterly Results," appears in the Current Page view. Click on the Previous Page icon at the lower left of the screen to switch the display to Page 1.

Previous page

Next page

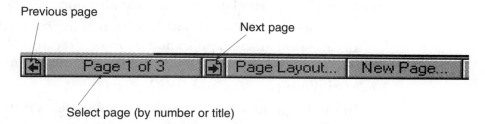

Page 1 of 3   Page Layout...   New Page...

Select page (by number or title)

7. The title page of the sample presentation will appear in the Current Page view. Click on the text "Sales Report" in the Freelance Graphics page (Figure 4-17).

If you are creating a new presentation, click the text "Click here to type presentation title," type **Sales Report**, and click on OK.

Selected text

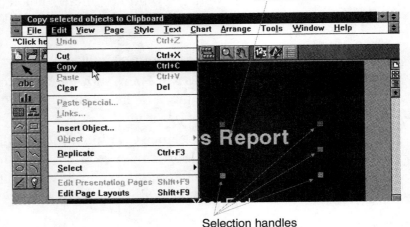

Selection handles

FIGURE 4-17. Freelance Graphics Current Page view with text-block selection

8. Copy the selected text to the Windows Clipboard.

   Execute the command Edit➤Copy from the Freelance Graphics pull-down menu.

9. Minimize the Freelance Graphics application.

   Click on the Minimize button (down triangle) at the top-right corner of the application window. Freelance Graphics will be shrunk to an icon at the bottom of the screen.

10. Start the application Windows Notepad.

    In the Program Manager window, double-click on the Accessories program group and then on the Notepad application icon (Figure 4-18). (If the Accessories program group is not visible, execute Window➤Accessories.) The Notepad application (a text editor) will open, displaying a blank document window.

11. Paste the selected text from the Clipboard into the Notepad document window.

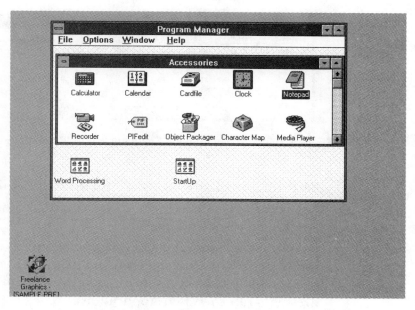

FIGURE 4-18. Accessories program group, containing the Notepad application.
(The Freelance Graphics icon at the bottom of the screen indicates
that this application is still running.)

From the Notepad menu bar, execute Edit≻Paste. The text
you selected in the Freelance Graphics slide will now appear
in the Notepad document, as shown in Figure 4-19. You have
successfully exchanged data between two Windows applications that are running concurrently.

12. Save the text to a Notepad document file.

Select File≻Save As. The Save As dialog box will appear. To
practice navigating the file system, change the directory to
save the new file in C:\WINDOWS\TEMP. Do this by double-
clicking on the TEMP directory in the list box. Type in **SAM-
PLE.TXT** in the File Name text box, then select OK. The text
will be saved to disk according to the path:

c:\windows\temp\sample.txt

13. Close the Notepad application.

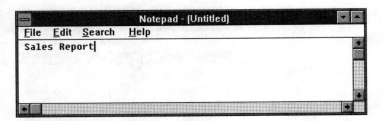

FIGURE 4-19. Text pasted from the Clipboard into Notepad

Perform File➤Exit or select Close from the Control menu of Notepad.

14. Restore Freelance Graphics.

Double-click on the Freelance Graphics icon at the bottom of the screen. (Or, click once on the icon, then select Restore from the pop-up menu that appears. If the icon is not visible, press Alt-Tab to switch applications.) The sample slide will reappear in the Current Page view. Note that this document has remained open while you worked in Notepad and remains unchanged. The program is ready for you to resume work where you left off.

15. Conclude the tutorial by closing Freelance Graphics.

Perform File➤Exit. The Freelance Graphics application window will close, returning you to the Program Manager window. Because you made no modifications to the presentation file SAMPLE.PRE, you are not prompted to save your changes, and the file remains unaltered on disk. If you created a new presentation during this exercise, respond OK to the prompt, "Do you want to save modified windows before closing?" Enter the filename **sample**, then select OK.

The following chapters move on to explore the charting and drawing capabilities of Freelance Graphics for Windows.

COMPOSING PAGES

Freelance Graphics for Windows comprises three modules: the Current Page view, the Page Sorter, and the Outliner. Each module provides a different way of viewing and working with the data in a presentation. This chapter deals with the Current Page view, which is the primary window for creating and editing charts and drawings that will be reproduced as printed pages, slides, or handouts.

As discussed previously, the basic unit of data storage in Freelance Graphics for Windows is a presentation file (.PRE extension). Such a data file contains a sequence of individual graphics, or pages. In turn, one or more charts or drawings can be shown on a page. The *drawing area* of the Current Page view is a document window in which one page can be displayed and manipulated at a time. The Current Page view incorporates tools for editing chart data, as well as for drawing and modifying graphic objects.

A QUICK OVERVIEW

The essential steps for creating pages in Freelance Graphics for Windows are covered in the Introduction. To recap, the basic steps are as shown on the next page.

1. Start the program.

2. Select OK in the first dialog box to create a new presentation.

3. Choose a look (SmartMaster set) in the next dialog box, and select OK.

4. In the next dialog box, choose a page layout (chart type) for the first page you will create, then select OK.

5. The page layout you select will appear in the drawing area of the Current Page view. Click once on any of the "Click here . . ." areas, type the data required, and select OK.

And that's all that is required to create a page! To continue with your presentation:

6. Click on the New Page button in the status bar at the bottom of the screen.

7. Repeat the page-creation steps above, starting with step 4.

8. When you have finished creating your presentation, select Save from the File menu, type a filename, and select OK.

9. To print your presentation, select File➤Print➤Print.

From this short sequence of steps, you might assume that there really isn't very much to learn about Freelance Graphics for Windows. And that is the absolute truth: The program was designed to be easy to learn and use. It is also intended to be easy to relearn— important when you consider that many people won't need to use the program every day.

Beyond the elegant simplicity of this "overview layer" of the program, Freelance Graphics for Windows offers all the power and richness of competing PC-based business graphics software. This chapter begins to explore these underlying layers.

STARTING THE PROGRAM

If you want to work on an existing presentation, there is a very fast way to start the program. In File Manager, log on to the FLW\WORK directory and simply double-click on the presentation filename.

Otherwise, you normally take two steps to start Freelance Graphics for Windows:

1. In Program Manager, select (double-click on) the program group that contains the application, typically Lotus Applications.

2. In the Lotus Applications window, select (double-click on) the Freelance Graphics application icon.

 For instructions on starting Windows applications from the keyboard, see Chapter 4.

When you do this, the program asks you to:

1. Choose whether you want to create a new presentation or work on an existing presentation.

2. If you select OK to accept the default Create a New Presentation, you must then choose a look for your presentation by selecting a SmartMaster set.

3. Choose a layout for the current page. Usually, the first page of a new presentation will be a Title chart.

To get a quick start, you can simply accept the default settings in each step by selecting OK for each of the three dialog boxes presented to you.

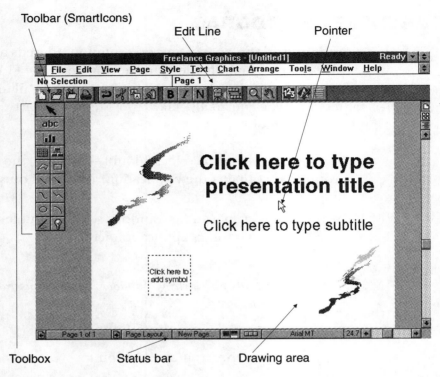

Toolbar (SmartIcons)

Edit Line

Pointer

Toolbox

Status bar

Drawing area

FIGURE 5-1. When you are creating a new presentation, the program window in the Current Page view looks like this.

When you have responded to each of the three dialog boxes, the Current Page view will open, showing the SmartMaster layout you selected. (See Figure 5-1.)

WORKING WITH SMARTMASTERS

SmartMaster layouts are predesigned pages that have placeholders for data that you will provide. These placeholders are identified as "Click here ..." areas. Simply click once with the left mouse button on the element you want to add, key in the data or respond as prompted by the program, and finish by clicking on OK. That's the basic procedure for creating any of the predefined types of pages in Freelance Graphics for Windows.

In effect, a SmartMaster layout is a form, and you create a finished page by filling in its blanks.

If you enter data into any of the "Click here . . ." areas, the prompt is replaced in the display by the text or chart generated from the data. You need not enter data into every one of the "Click here . . ." areas. An area that is empty of data will always display the prompt in the Current Page view, but the prompt will never appear on printouts or in screen shows.

Options such as text color and size, as well as more extensive choices for charts, have been preselected for each of the "Click here . . ." areas. If you don't need to change these default options, you can create entire presentations simply by entering the data for each page.

Giving your presentation a customized look and tailoring the layouts to your own preferences mainly involve resetting these chart options, of which there are many for each of the page layouts in a SmartMaster set. Chapters 6–9 cover each of the available chart types and their options.

SETTING UP YOUR DESKTOP

Program options allow you to control displays and printed output to suit your preferences. Certain program options set for one work session will be applied to other work sessions, potentially affecting the appearance of other presentations.

You may want to get in the habit of reviewing these options at the beginning of your work session, before you start to work on a presentation.

Among the system settings that affect presentations are the sizes, margins, and other specifications for printers and output media. You should set these initially in Freelance Graphics for Windows, especially if the settings for that application differ from those you need for other Windows applications. For example, you normally would use portrait page orientation for word processing, but you might prefer landscape for chart output.

In Freelance Graphics for Windows, there are separate groups of settings for printers and for pages. In general, it is good practice to select a printer or output device first, then the page specifications. The proportions, orientation, and margins of the Current Page view of Freelance Graphics will then be adjusted automatically to match these output settings.

Selecting a Printer

Output devices, including printers, must be installed through Windows Program Manager. The command is Main➤Control Panel➤ Printers, by which you also specify the default system printer. (See Figure 5-2.) Freelance Graphics will use this printer unless you change the selection through the Control Panel or within the application. So, if you will be using the system printer in Freelance Graphics, you need not select it from within the program. However, you probably will need to adjust page settings, as described in the following section "Setting Up Page Orientation and Margins."

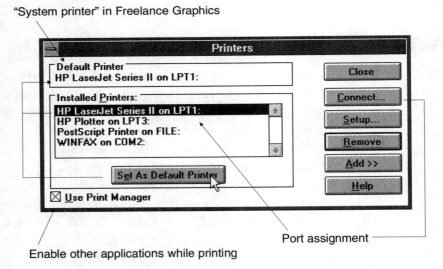

"System printer" in Freelance Graphics

Port assignment

Enable other applications while printing

FIGURE 5-2. System printer selection in Windows Control Panel➤Printers

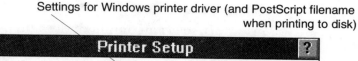

Settings for Windows printer driver (and PostScript filename when printing to disk)

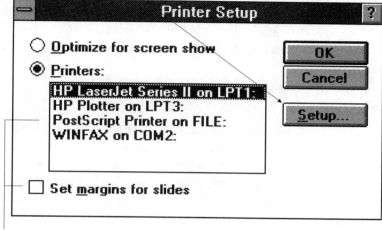

Mark only for film recording

FIGURE 5-3.   Choose from previously installed Windows printer drivers and ports in the Printer Setup dialog box.

When you set up a printer from within Freelance Graphics, you are selecting from the list of previously installed Windows printer drivers, which are shared among Windows applications. If you select something other than the system printer, your selection will apply to the current work session only. Also, your printer selection and page settings will be saved with any presentation files that you create or update during the session.

To select a printer within Freelance Graphics, perform File▸ Printer Setup. The Printer Setup dialog box will appear, as shown in Figure 5-3.

Optimizing Output for Screen Shows

If you will be making your presentation primarily as a screen show or SmartShow, select the option button Optimize for Screen Show, then select OK to close the dialog box.

Specifying the Printer Driver and Port

For printouts, select an output device and port from the Printers list box. (You will see only output devices that have been installed previously through the Windows Control Panel, through which port connections, such as LPT1, can be made to each printer.)

Printer Setup Options

Before exiting the Printer Setup dialog box, you may need to select the Setup button to change printer options such as Resolution, Paper Size, Paper Source, Memory, Orientation, and printer-resident Fonts. A dialog box containing options for the specific printer driver will appear. An example for the Hewlett-Packard LaserJet II is shown in Figure 5-4. (This same dialog box and its settings can be accessed through Windows➤Control Panel➤Printers.) Change the

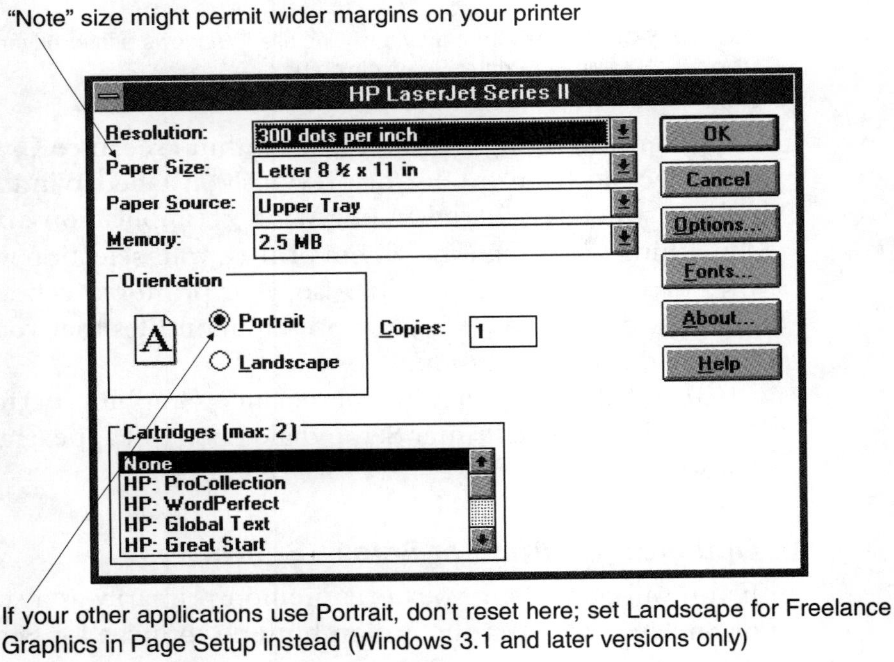

"Note" size might permit wider margins on your printer

If your other applications use Portrait, don't reset here; set Landscape for Freelance Graphics in Page Setup instead (Windows 3.1 and later versions only)

FIGURE 5-4.   Shown here are setup options for the Hewlett-Packard LaserJet II. The options available will vary considerably among printers.

settings, select OK, then select OK again to close the Printer Setup dialog box.

 If the printer driver is current with Windows 3.1, it will permit Freelance Graphics to override the system page settings, such as Size and Orientation, regardless of the setup options you select here. If you are using the system printer and if its normal page settings differ from those you need with Freelance Graphics, do not reset them here. Instead, control the appearance of presentation output with the File➤Page Setup command. If you are using an older printer driver, the page settings in File➤Printer Setup and File➤Page Setup must be the same.

Printing to Disk for Film Recording

To output your presentation on a film recorder for color slides or transparencies, you generally must use a printer driver that can send its output to a disk file. This file must then be processed in a separate step by the film recorder's software. For example, to create the color PostScript (.CPS) files used by Autographix, the printer selection is

Autographix on FILE:

If you select such a device for slide output, you should also mark the check box Set Margins for Slides, which will adjust the display and output to match the aspect ratio of a standard 35mm double-frame slide aperture.

Procedures for color-film recording are covered in Chapter 13.

Setting Up Page Orientation and Margins

To control the appearance of pages, select File➤Page Setup in any view of Freelance Graphics. The File Page Setup dialog box will appear, as shown in Figure 5-5.

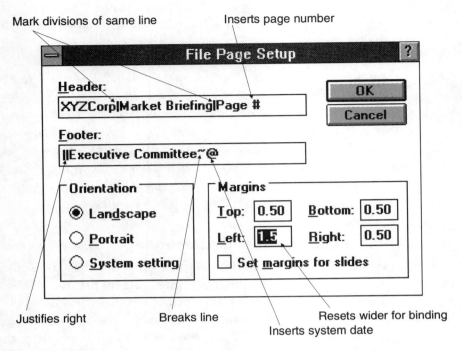

FIGURE 5-5. The File Page Setup dialog box: Text and print codes have been entered for a header and a footer to be printed at the top and bottom of each presentation page.

Remember that settings you make in this dialog box will:

- Apply only to the current work session

- Override any page setup options in File≻Printer Setup, provided that the printer driver supports software control of these settings

- Not affect existing presentation files or other Windows applications

- Control the proportions of the drawing area in the Current Page view

- Be saved with any presentation files that you create or update during the session

Orientation

Select one of the following option buttons: Landscape (long dimension of page is horizontal), Portrait (long dimension of page vertical), or System Setting.

 A presentation file can have only one orientation setting. If you need to intermix portrait and landscape pages, create separate presentation files for each.

If you select System Setting, Freelance Graphics will follow any changes you make for the default printer in Windows➤Control Panel➤Printers.

It can be convenient to select System Setting for pages if you will be using several Windows applications to work on different pages of a report or long document. Network users also might want to set this option if it is difficult to predict in advance which of several dissimilar printers eventually will produce the presentation.

Margins

In each of four text boxes, you can enter numeric values for the distance from the top, bottom, left, and right edges of the printed page. The units of measurement shown are determined by the Units setting in View➤Units & Grids: Millimeters, Centimeters, Inches, Points, or Picas.

The minimum allowable margins define the *printable area* of the selected output device. After you select OK, the program will warn you if the margins you set are outside the ranges permitted by the printer driver. You can cause the margins or the printable area to be displayed as dotted lines in the drawing area of the Current Page view by selecting View➤View Preferences➤Margins or View➤View Preferences➤Printable Area, as shown in Figure 5-6.

To specify margins for color slides, mark the check box Set Margins for Slides. If you do, the other Margins settings will be dimmed, and the program will set them automatically. This is the same

Letter 8.5 × 11" page size
(landscape orientation)

Margins: Top 0.5"   Bottom 0.5"
Left 0.5"   Right 0.5"

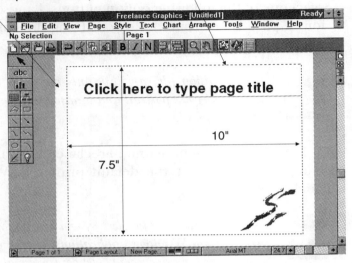

Printable area

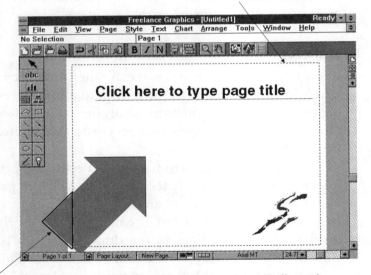

This part will not be printed (Note: objects can "bleed" off page)

FIGURE 5-6.   By setting View➤View Preferences, you can select a dotted-line border in the drawing area that shows either (top) current Margins settings in File➤Page Setup, or (bottom) the printable area on the page as defined by the Windows printer driver.

option available in File➤Printer Setup. However, for most printer drivers, the Page Setup options will apply.

Specifying Page Headers and Footers

Also in the File Page Setup dialog box, you can enter text for a header and a footer to be printed on each page. The text will appear only on printed outputs, not in the Current Page view or in Screen Shows.

Text will be printed in the Arial (True Type)or Arial MT (Post-Script) font, 10-point size, just within the printable area of the page (not in the margins).

The header and footer each can have as many as 512 characters on as many as three segments and on multiple lines. Mark the beginning of the second and third segments with the vertical bar (|) character:

Alpha Project|Product Launch Meeting|Preliminary

These three elements will be justified left, center, and right, respectively, on the same line:

Alpha Project   Product Launch Meeting   Preliminary

To create multiple lines, precede the beginning of each line with the tilde (~) character within its segment. For example,

Alpha Project~Introduction~Ms. Rawlings|

will be printed as:

Alpha Project
Introduction
Ms. Rawlings

Single-line headers or footers can be justified left, center, or right. If no leading character precedes a line, it will be justified left. One leading vertical bar (|) character will cause it to be justified center, and two (||) will justify it right. For example,

Alpha Project
|Beta Project
||Gamma Project

will be printed as:

Alpha Project

Beta Project

Gamma Project

A number sign (#) appearing anywhere in a string will be replaced with the page number, for example, the string

||Page #

will appear as

Page 1

To begin with a specific page number, precede it with two number signs, such as:

##5

This code will cause the first page in the presentation to be numbered 5, the second page 6, and so on.

To insert the system date, place the at sign (@) anywhere within a string.

To produce any one of the special characters (~ | # @) as itself (as a literal character), precede it with a backslash (\). For example, \@ will be printed as @.

Setting Display Preferences

To control the appearance of the drawing area, select View➤View Preferences. (You can perform this command in any view, but it will affect only the Current Page view.) The View➤View Preferences dialog box will appear, as shown in Figure 5-7.

Press when drawing to toggle this option

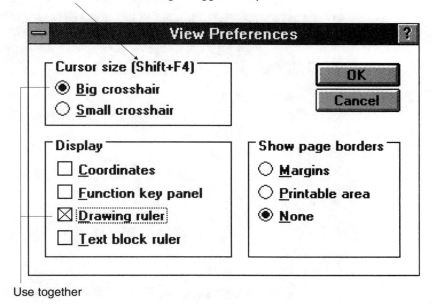

FIGURE 5-7. Make settings in the View Preferences dialog box to control the appearance and behavior of the Current Page view.

Cursor Size

Two option buttons here determine the pointer shape when you are using the drawing tools. The default, Small Crosshair, produces a pair of crossed lines that are about the size of the arrow-tipped pointer. If you select Big Crosshair, the lines extend in each direction to the edges of the drawing area. Use this option particularly to measure vertical and horizontal distances on the optional Drawing Rulers, as shown in Figure 5-8.

When you are drawing, you can toggle between Small Crosshair and Big Crosshair by pressing Shift-F4.

Display

Four check boxes here help you further customize the Current Page view.

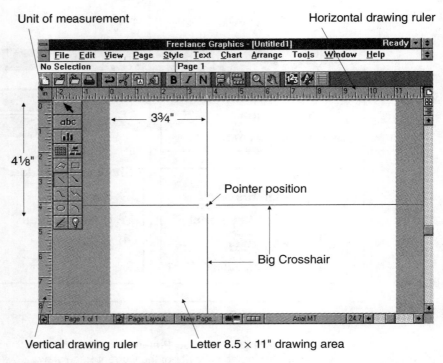

FIGURE 5-8.   Use the Big Crosshair option in conjunction with the Drawing Ruler to position the pointer precisely within the dimensions of the printed page.

Coordinates   Marking this check box will display the cursor position within the drawing area as a pair of numeric coordinates. The readout will appear at the top right of the program window, in the edit line just beneath the menu bar, as shown in Figure 5-9. The first number is the horizontal position (*x* coordinate), and the second is the vertical position (*y* coordinate). The unit of measurement corresponds to your selection in View➤Units & Grids.

In Freelance Graphics for Windows Release 2, the origin is at the top left of the page, not at the bottom left, as it is in Release 1 and in the conventional Cartesian coordinate system.

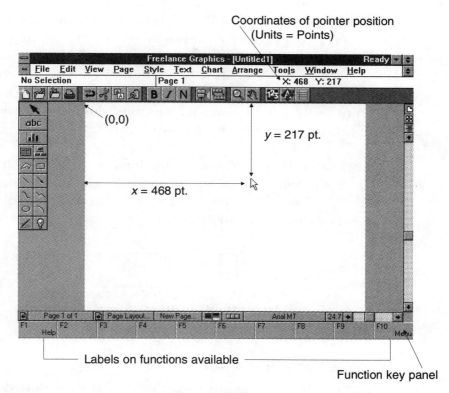

Coordinates of pointer position
(Units = Points)

FIGURE 5-9. Readout of coordinates appears on the right end of the edit line. Numeric values are given in the units set in View≻Units & Grids. Shown at the bottom of the screen is the optional Function Key Panel.

Function Key Panel   Selecting this option turns on the display of a set of on-screen buttons that correspond to the numbered F keys on the keyboard. (Refer to Figure 5-9.) Labels will appear on the function-key display to indicate which commands are available at that point in the program. That is, labels will appear only on those function keys that apply to your current task. When this feature is selected, you can activate function-key commands by clicking on your selection in the key panel with the left mouse button. (See Table 10-1.)

Drawing Ruler   Turning on this option will show a pair of on-screen rulers at the left and top edges of the drawing area. (Refer again to Figure 5-8.) Markings are in the units of measurement selected in View➤Units & Grids, as indicated at the intersection of the rulers. Use this option in conjunction with Big Crosshair to pinpoint vertical and horizontal positions within the drawing area and in precise relation to the measurements of the output page.

Text Block Ruler   This option turns on the display of a ruler along the top edge of an open text block. Use it to measure the lengths of text lines, particularly when you are designing for print media with Units set to Picas.

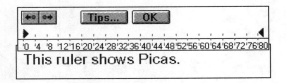

Show Page Borders

Optionally, you can turn on the display of a dotted-line border around the drawing area, showing either the margins chosen in File➤Page Setup or the maximum printable area allowed by the printer device driver for the selected page size. (Refer to Figure 5-6.) The default is None, or no border shown.

Even though the program will accurately display the printable area or margins on the page, it will not constrain you to keep objects within them. In fact, you can place objects anywhere on the screen, thus permitting them to bleed *off the edges of the printable area.*

Specifying Units of Measurement and Grids

To select the units of measurement for page margins, drawing rulers, and grids, perform View➤Units & Grids. Then, select one of

Affects rulers, grids, coordinates, margins

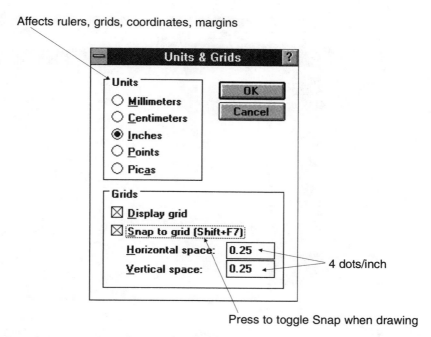

4 dots/inch

Press to toggle Snap when drawing

FIGURE 5-10.   Set units of measurement, as well as grid spacing and Snap
options, in the Units & Grids dialog box.

the option buttons: Millimeters, Centimeters, Inches, Points (72 per
inch), or Picas (about 6 per inch). The Units & Grids dialog box is
shown in Figure 5-10. In general, pick units that are compatible with
the dimensions of the output medium, such as Paper Size in
File➤Printer Setup➤Setup.

In Freelance Graphics, a *grid* is an array of points that can fill the
drawing area as a positioning aid. The check box Display Grid turns
on its display, and the Horizontal and Vertical Space settings control
the spacing between grid points according to the current Units setting. The option Snap To Grid will force points selected for drawn
objects to coincide with, or *snap* to, points on the grid. A grid set for
4 dots to the inch (0.25-inch spacing) is shown in Figure 5-11. When
you are using a drawing tool, you can turn Snap on and off by pressing Shift-F7. For tips on using a grid, see Chapter 10.

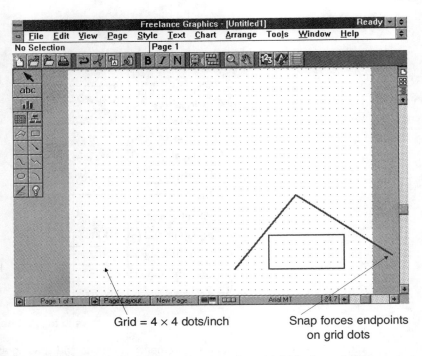

Grid = 4 × 4 dots/inch

Snap forces endpoints
on grid dots

FIGURE 5-11.　The grid shown here has spacing of 0.25 inch, or 4 dots per inch.

User Setup Selections

Other options that affect the overall behavior of the program can be set when you select Tools≻User Setup. Unlike printer or page settings, the settings you make for the options shown in Figure 5-12 will apply to all future work sessions until you reset them.

Startup Options

If you mark the check box Skip the Standard Startup Dialogs and Bring Up a Blank Page, the program will begin as though you selected File≻New with the last SmartMaster set you used. You might turn this option on if you usually make single-page drawings.

Option buttons here also control the default view, which will appear immediately after you open the application. You can select Current Page (the default), Page Sorter, or Outliner. Select Page

Use for special effects (replicate with rotation)
when duplicating objects

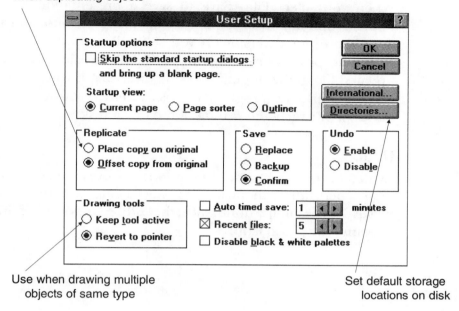

Use when drawing multiple
objects of same type

Set default storage
locations on disk

FIGURE 5-12. The User Setup dialog box has options that will apply to current
and future work sessions.

Sorter if you are preparing existing presentations for production, or
choose Outliner if you prefer to compose your speeches initially as
text pages generated from outlined topics.

Replicate

This setting controls the duplication of graphic objects when you
perform Edit➤Copy and then Edit➤Paste, or when you select
Edit➤Replicate. The options are Place Copy on the Original (which
superimposes on center) or Offset Copy from Original (which only
partially obscures the first object). Normally, you will want to leave
this setting at Offset, the default, so that you can more easily select
among the duplicates. The other option might be preferred for
some types of special effects. (See "Copying Objects" in this chapter.)

Save

When you select File➤Save to save a presentation to disk, the Replace option will cause the updated file to automatically over-write the original version. If you select Backup, the program will place the prior version in the BACKUP directory and write the updated file in the original working directory. If you select Confirm (the default), the program will ask whether you wish to replace, back up, or cancel the writing of the file to disk.

Undo

By default (set to Enable), the program stores the last 10 edits you made, permitting them to be restored one at a time, in reverse order. This can be done with the Edit➤Undo command or by selecting the Undo icon:

When set to Disable, Edit➤Undo does not operate, increasing the amount of computer memory available.

Drawing Tools

Normally, the program is set to Revert to Pointer, so that the pointer appears immediately after you draw an object. This allows you to select a menu command, pick another tool, select an object for edit-ing, or activate any other program operation. Change the setting to Keep Tool Active if you usually want to be able to draw a series of the same type of object, as when making a line drawing that has many line segments.

Other Options

Three check boxes enable other user-controllable actions of the program:

Auto Timed Save   Marking this check box will cause the program to save the current presentation file automatically to disk at a specified interval of time. Choose the interval by selecting from a range of 1 to 99 minutes. (You can change the setting by clicking the arrow buttons.) If you are working on an untitled presentation, you will be prompted for a filename during the first save operation; thereafter, the file will be saved without prompting.

Recent Files   To speed access, the File pull-down menu can list the filenames of up to five of the last presentations you worked on. You can then select File➤<Filename> to open one of these presentations, instead of having to specify the path or navigate the file system.

Disable Black & White Palettes   If this check box is not marked (the default), the program will use its own special palettes to translate color outputs for monochrome printers. (You can preview the monochrome output by clicking on the Color/BW button in the status bar at the bottom of the Current Page view.) If marked, the translation will be handled instead by the color-texture mapping tables of the Windows printer driver for the selected output device. Use the setting that produces the most consistently good results on your printer.

International Settings

Selecting this button brings up the International User Setup dialog box, as shown in Figure 5-13. Settings can be changed here for the same time, currency, date, and number formats found in Windows➤Control Panel➤International. However, settings here will apply only to Freelance Graphics and need not match those in Windows unless you want consistency with other applications.

The drop-down box File Translation (Code Page) determines the internal table by which ASCII data files are translated when

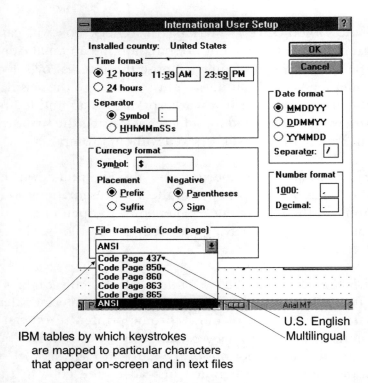

IBM tables by which keystrokes
are mapped to particular characters
that appear on-screen and in text files

U.S. English
Multilingual

FIGURE 5-13. The International User Setup dialog box has options much the same as Windows➤Control Panel➤International, but the settings apply only within Freelance Graphics.

imported to or exported from the program. For more on code-page translation, see Chapter 14.

Default Directories

Selecting this button permits you to enter the paths of disk directories that will be used to store the various kinds of program files. The default settings are FLW\WORK, FLW\MASTERS, and FLW\BACK-UP. You might want to change the Working directory setting if you segregate projects for different clients by directory, and you might want to specify a floppy-disk drive for the Backup setting.

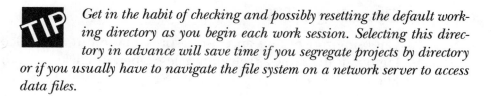

Get in the habit of checking and possibly resetting the default working directory as you begin each work session. Selecting this directory in advance will save time if you segregate projects by directory or if you usually have to navigate the file system on a network server to access data files.

CREATING AND OPENING PRESENTATION FILES

Besides selecting various user setup options, you cannot do anything in Freelance Graphics for Windows until you open a presentation file. The program will create a new presentation automatically when you choose that option in the Welcome to Freelance Graphics startup dialog box.

Creating a File

The equivalent menu-bar command for creating a new file is File➤New. Or, click the New File icon:

When you make this selection, the program opens a new document window for the presentation. The name of this window initially is UNTITLED1. At this point, the document is simply a work area in memory. No disk file is created until you save your work with the File➤Save or File➤Save As commands, or with the Save File icon in the toolbar:

The program will prompt you for a filename the first time you save the file or if you select File➤Close.

Opening a File

Choosing to work on an existing presentation in the Welcome dialog box is the same as selecting File➤Open or clicking on the Open File icon:

The Choose Presentation dialog box will appear, listing all the presentation (.PRE) files in the default working directory (Figure 5-14). Double-click on a filename, or select it and then select OK.

 By first making a selection from the File Type drop-down box, you can open any SmartMaster set (.MAS), symbol library (.SYM), or presentation created by Freelance Graphics for OS/2 (.PRS). Opening a SmartMaster Set for editing has the same effect as selecting Edit➤Edit Page Layouts when you are working on a presentation. Opening a symbol file permits you to modify symbol drawings directly rather than importing them to and exporting them from a presentation. For more information on using symbols, see Chapter 10.

When you select OK to close the Choose Presentation dialog box, the file you specified is read into memory and a document window is opened in the Current Page view. (The program will display the last page you worked on, which may be something other than Page 1.)

Opening Multiple Presentations

Several presentations can be open at the same time in Freelance Graphics. Simply perform separate File➤New or File➤Open commands to open each document window.

When multiple presentations are open, they appear initially as maximized windows, or full screens that overlay one another. The file most recently opened will be on top. To access another open

presentation, select the Window pull-down menu and then the
number or title of its document window:

If there is already a presentation open when you select
File➢Open, you can mark the check box Replace Current File to
retrieve the file into the active window, closing the presentation it
replaces. (Refer to Figure 5-14.) If the option is unmarked, the
existing file is placed in an inactive window, and the selected file is
retrieved into a new, active window.

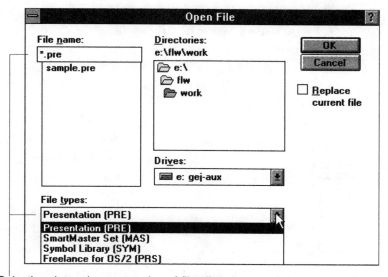

Selection determines extension of files listed

FIGURE 5-14. This dialog box appears when you select File➢Open.

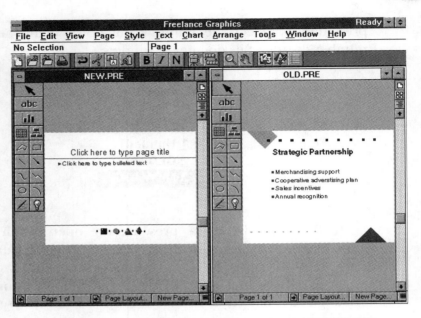

FIGURE 5-15. Two presentations are shown here after the Window➤Tile command has been performed.

To view presentation windows side-by-side on the same screen, select Window➤Tile. The result is shown in Figure 5-15. To view them in an overlapping stack, select Window➤Cascade. To select from among windows shown in either mode, simply click on the title bar of the window you want to activate.

 A common reason to open multiple presentations is to copy pages between them. This is done most easily if all presentations are in the Page Sorter view. You can then select a page or pages and pass them to other windows through the Clipboard.

CONTROLLING THE PAGE DISPLAY

The Current Page view has a variety of controls for navigating among the pages in a presentation and controlling the display of the current page in the drawing area.

Creating a New Page

There are several ways to add a new page to the current presentation:

- Select File➤New.
- Click on the New Page icon:

- Click on the New Page button in the status bar at the bottom of the screen:

The New Page dialog box will appear, as shown in Figure 5-16. Select a chart type, or page layout, from the list. Then select OK. Optionally, you can type an entry in the Page Name text box. The default is Page *n*, where *n* is the next number in presentation sequence. This page name will appear in the edit line just above the toolbar in the Current Page view, as well as just beneath each miniature page view in the Page Sorter.

 You can also create a new page by pressing the F7 accelerator key. However, the New Page dialog box will not appear. Instead, the new page will conform to the layout of the current page.

Moving Around in the Page Sequence

To navigate the page sequence in the Current Page view, you can click on the Previous Page or Next Page icons in the status bar:

Previous page ⟶  ⟵ Next page

Enter your own label or accept Page # (default)

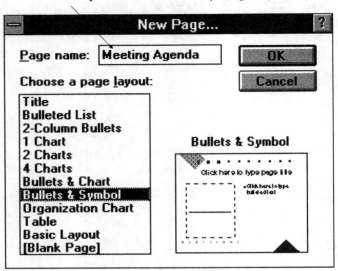

FIGURE 5-16. Selecting Page➤New brings up this dialog box, in which you can enter an identifying name for the page (not its title) and the SmartMaster layout it will follow.

At the keyboard, you can press PgUp or PgDn. (If you use the numeric keypad, the Num Lock must be off.)

Or, you can click on the Page icon and select the page number or title from a pop-up menu:

Current page

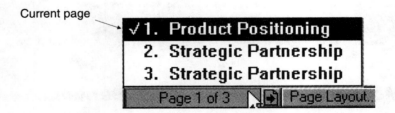

When you are working in the Page Sorter, double-click on a page, or move the highlight to it with the arrow keys and press Enter. The selected page will appear in the Current Page view.

Changing the Page Layout

Assume that you have entered the text for a Bulleted List layout and you decide you would prefer the Bullets & Symbol layout instead. In the Current Page view, select Page➤Choose Page Layout, or click on the Page Layout button in the status bar:

> Page Layout...

The Choose Page Layout dialog box will appear, which is a listing of the chart types available in the current SmartMaster set. Double-click on the layout you want, or highlight it and then select OK. The data you entered will now be shown in the Current Page view, arranged according to the new layout.

Using the Basic Page Layout

If you select Basic Layout and Edit➤Edit Page Layouts, any charts or drawings that you add to that layout will appear on all pages in the presentation, with the exception of the first Title chart or any pages you create with the Blank Page layout. Use this feature particularly when you want to add drawings or logos to the background, or to create a consistent page title.

Viewing a Page in Monochrome

Freelance Graphics for Windows uses a set of its own mono-chrome palettes when producing pages created from full-color SmartMasters on monochrome printers. Each full-color palette has a counterpart in black and white. The default display in the Current Page view is the full-color version, unless you have selected a SmartMaster that has a black-and-white palette as its default selection.

152

LEARNING FREELANCE GRAPHICS FOR WINDOWS
· ·
Part II

Problems can arise when adjacent areas or objects with different colors have the same gray-scale value, or look the same in monochrome.

The program has a feature that lets you preview any page in its monochrome version in the Current Page view. To switch between full-color and monochrome display, select Style➤Use Black & White Palette or Style➤Use Color Palette. Or, toggle the display by clicking on the Color/BW button in the status bar:

Hiding the Toolbar

You can choose to hide or to display the toolbar of SmartIcons, which normally appears across the top of the Current Page view between the top of the drawing area and the edit line. Hiding the toolbar makes the drawing area slightly larger, which you might prefer if you mainly use the menu commands.

The Default toolbar normally is shown. To hide it or to select another named toolbar, click on the Display➤Hide SmartIcons button in the status bar. A pop-up menu will appear:

Current toolbar —————— 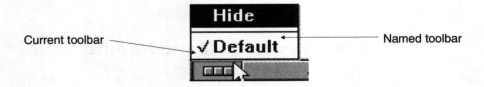 —————— Named toolbar

To suppress the toolbar display, select Hide. To turn the display back on, click on the button again and select Show. To pick a different toolbar (such as Charting or Drawing), select its name. Tips on building your own custom toolbars are presented in Chapter 10.

To select a different custom toolbar, you can also click on the Next Toolbar icon:

Magnifying the View

To magnify the view of the page in the drawing area, select View➤Zoom In. The page will be magnified by a predetermined increment. You can repeat the command as many as nine times in all to magnify the view further.

Another technique for magnifying the view is to click on the Zoom Page icon in the toolbar:

The pointer in the drawing area will change to a magnifying-glass symbol. Move the magnifying-glass pointer and click on the area you want to enlarge, or drag a rectangle that contains it.

To undo the most recent Zoom operation, select View➤Last. To restore the whole page, select Zoom➤Full Page.

To move back from a magnified view by increments, select View➤Zoom Out. You can also perform this command as many as three times to move back from the Full Page view. You might need to do this when creating objects that will bleed, or extend off the edges of the printable area.

Moving Around in a Magnified View

To move around the page in a magnified (Zoom In) view, adjust the horizontal and vertical scroll bars at the bottom and right edges of the window:

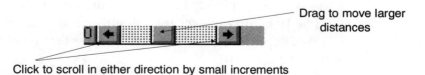

Drag to move larger distances

Click to scroll in either direction by small increments

Click either of the arrow buttons to move in that direction by increments, or drag the slider in the direction you want to move.

As an alternative, click on the Move Page icon in the toolbar:

The pointer in the drawing area will change to a hand symbol. You can then drag the page around on the screen.

Controlling Screen Regeneration

Normally, the program will redraw, or regenerate, the Current Page view automatically after each edit or drawing operation. However, redrawing can be time consuming (depending on the speed of your computer), particularly when objects become complex.

To suspend screen regeneration, press Esc in the Current Page view. Redrawing will resume when you do one of the following:

- Press F9
- Select View➤Redraw
- Click on the Redraw icon

WORKING WITH GRAPHIC OBJECTS

The bottom 10 tools in the toolbox on the left side of the Current Page view can be used to create graphic objects in the drawing area. If you have worked with drawing tools in other Windows applications, you will probably find these quite familiar.

The basic procedures for using these drawing tools are outlined in this chapter. More extensive drawing features and tips are covered in Chapter 10.

As an aid to positioning points on objects, select View▶Units & Grids and turn on Display Grid and Snap to Grid before you begin drawing.

Controlling the Appearance of Objects

Each object type in Freelance Graphics has a set of default attributes, such as color and width, that affect its appearance. To control the appearance of objects that you draw, you have three options:

- Draw the object with default attributes.
- Just prior to selecting a drawing tool, reset attributes to affect all objects of that type that you create thereafter.
- Edit attributes for particular objects after those objects have been drawn.

Resetting Attributes for New Objects

To inspect or to reset the default attributes for any of the drawing objects, first select its tool from the toolbox, then select Style▶ Default Attributes. The current settings for that object type will appear in a dialog box. If you change them here, the new settings will apply to all objects you draw thereafter during the work session. (However, color assignments may vary with the palette selection.)

Resetting Attributes for Existing Objects

To change the appearance of an existing object, click on it to select it, then select Style▶Attributes. (See "Selecting Objects" in this chapter.) Current attribute settings for that object will appear in a dialog box. If you alter the settings, only the selected object will be changed; objects you draw thereafter will take on the default attributes.

Appearance options for each type of object are covered under "Editing Object Attributes" below. Sample objects of each type are shown in Figure 5-17.

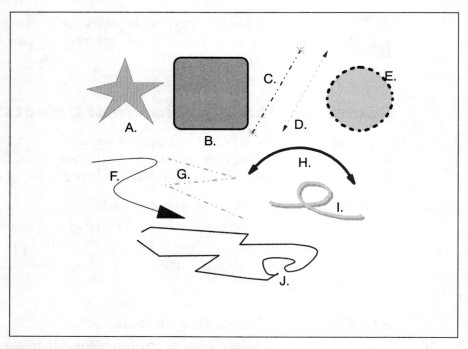

FIGURE 5-17. These objects were created with each of the drawing tools: A. Polygon, B. Rectangle (rounded), C. Line, D. Arrow, E. Circle, F. Open Curve, G. Polyline, H. Arc, I. Freehand, and J. A compound object (having both polyline and open-curve segments).

In general, you probably will want to draw with a mouse, pen, or other pointing device. For greater precision, you can draw by selecting points with the Spacebar and moving the pointer by small increments with the arrow keys. The procedures below first describe the drawing procedure with the mouse, then with the keyboard.

Polygons

A polygon is an irregular, closed area. To create a polygon, select the Polygon tool:

To Use the Mouse: The pointer in the drawing area will change to cross hairs. Move the cross hairs to the first point, or *vertex,* on the object and select it by clicking once. Move the cross hairs and click again to select the second point, and repeat the procedure for each point on the polygon except the last one. Double-click on the last point (or click the *right* mouse button once), and the program will connect it automatically to the first, closing the object and filling it.

An alternative to clicking on each point is to drag each line segment of the polygon: Press and hold down the left mouse button at the first point, move the cross hairs to the second point, and release the button; repeat the dragging procedure for each line segment that defines the edge of the polygon; and double-click on the last point.

To Use the Keyboard: After you have selected the Polygon tool, move the cross hairs to the first point and with the arrow keys and select it by pressing the Spacebar. Select each of the other points by pressing the Spacebar *twice,* once to end the current line segment and once to start the next one. When you reach the last point, press Enter to close the polygon and fill it.

 Whether you are using the mouse or the keyboard, you can create right and 45-degree angles by holding down the Shift key while you create a line segment. (The program constrains the segment to the nearest angle of 0, 45, 90, 135, 180, 225, 270, or 315 degrees. Refer to Figure 5-18.)

Rectangles and Squares

To draw a rectangle, select the Rectangle tool:

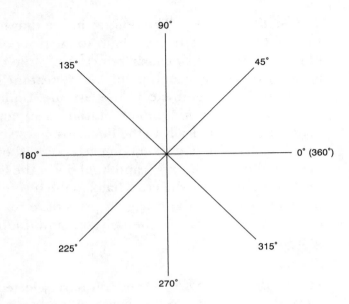

FIGURE 5-18. Holding down the Shift key while drawing a line segment or object side will constrain it to the nearest 45-degree angle.

To Use the Mouse: In the drawing area, drag the cross hairs from one corner to the opposite corner of the rectangle. (You cannot select the corners by clicking.)

To Use the Keyboard: Move the cross hairs with the arrow keys to the first corner and select it by pressing the Spacebar. Move to the opposite corner, and press Enter.

To create a square, hold down the Shift key while you are drawing, and release it only after you have selected the opposite corner.

Lines and Arrows

To create a straight line segment, select the Line tool:

To Use the Mouse: Click on each of the endpoints of the segment or drag the crosshairs from one to the other.

To create a straight line segment that is tipped with an arrowhead, select the Arrow tool instead and use the same procedure.

To Use the Keyboard: Move the cross hairs with the arrow keys, and press the Spacebar to select each of the segment's endpoints.

 You can select the second point by pressing Enter instead, but it will be faster just to keep your thumb or finger on the Spacebar.

To constrain a line or arrow to the nearest 45-degree angle, hold down the Shift key as you draw with either the mouse or the arrow keys.

To connect multiple objects that have been created as separate lines or arrows, select all of them (click on each while holding down the Shift key), and then select Arrange>Connect Lines. The lines will be joined at their closest points.

 To create series of concatenated lines (such as a chain of arrows that would be difficult to do as a polyline), select Tools>User Setup>Keep Tool Active, then use the Line or Arrow tools. Drag each line segment, releasing and clicking again on each vertex.

Open Curves

An open curve is also called a *polycurve, compound curve,* or *Bézier curve.* To draw an open curve, select the Curve tool:

To Use the Mouse: Drag a series of line segments that define the curve. The first segment will appear straight until you start to drag the second one. After that, the dotted-line preview of the curve will "bend" as you drag the segments. Double-click (or click the right mouse button) once on the last point to finish the curve.

As an alternative, you can simply click on a series of vertices, double-clicking on the last one. However, dragging is recommended because you have more control over the curvature as you create it.

To Use the Keyboard: Move the cross hairs with the arrow keys, and press the Spacebar to select the first point. Select each of the other points by pressing the Spacebar *twice,* once to end the current segment and once to start the next one. When you reach the last point, press Enter to finish the curve.

 To create a cusp, *or sharp break in the curve, click twice (not a rapid double-click) at that point, or press the Spacebar twice. Then resume drawing the curve. (See Figure 5-19.)*

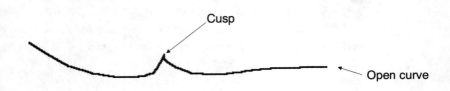

FIGURE 5-19.   To create an open curve with a cusp, or sharp bend, click twice or press the Spacebar twice at the point of the cusp as you are drawing the curve.

Polylines

A polyline is a series of connected, or *concatenated,* line segments. To draw a polyline, select the Polyline tool:

To Use the Mouse: The pointer in the drawing area will change to cross hairs. Move the cross hairs to the first point and select it by clicking once. Move the cross hairs and click again to select the second point, and repeat the procedure for each point on the polyline except the last one. Double-click on the last point to finish the polyline.

An alternative to clicking on each point is to drag each line segment of the polyline: Press and hold down the left mouse button at the first point, move the cross hairs to the second point, and release the button; repeat the dragging procedure for each line segment; and double-click on the last point.

To Use the Keyboard: After you have selected the Polygon tool, move the cross hairs to the first point with the arrow keys and select the point by pressing the Spacebar. Select each of the other points by pressing the Spacebar *twice,* once to end the current line segment and once to start the next one. When you reach the last point, press Enter to finish the polyline.

 As when drawing polygons, you can constrain line segments to the nearest 45-degree angle by holding down the Shift key as you draw the segment.

Ellipses and Circles

To draw an ellipse, or oval, select the Circle tool:

162 ·

LEARNING FREELANCE GRAPHICS FOR WINDOWS

Part II

To Use the Mouse: Move the cross hairs in the drawing area to a point that would lie on the edge of the ellipse. Drag the dotted-line preview of the ellipse until it is the shape and size you want.

To Use the Keyboard: Move the cross hairs with the arrow keys to a point that would lie on the edge of the ellipse. Select that point by pressing the Spacebar. Move the arrow keys to adjust the size and shape of the dotted-line preview, then press Enter to finish the ellipse.

To create a circle when drawing with either the mouse or the keyboard, hold down the Shift key while you are defining the shape.

Arcs

An arc is a segment of the circumference, or edge, of a circle. In Freelance Graphics, arcs can have any of the attributes of lines or arrows; however, an arc requires three, not two, points to define it (or two endpoints and the amount of curvature).

To create an arc, select the Arc tool:

To Use the Mouse: Move the cross hairs to one endpoint of the arc. Then, drag to the other endpoint. A straight, dotted line will appear. Drag this line until it assumes the amount of curvature you want.

As an alternative, you can click on three points: Click on each of the endpoints, and then on a third point that would lie on the arc.

To Use the Keyboard: Move the cross hairs to the first endpoint and select it by pressing the Spacebar. Use the arrow keys to move the cross hairs to the second endpoint, and press the Spacebar *twice*. Press the arrow keys to adjust the curvature. Finish by pressing Enter.

Freehand Drawing

In Freelance Graphics, a freehand drawing (or freehand object) is any unconstrained line that you trace in the drawing area.

To create a freehand drawing, select the Freehand tool:

With the mouse, move the cross hairs to the point in the drawing area at which the freehand line will begin. Hold down the left mouse button while you trace the object. When you reach the endpoint, release the button.

Additional Drawing Tips

Here are some further tips for using the drawing tools:

Undo Segment (Backspace)

When selecting points to create an object, you can press Backspace to undo the last selection. For example, if you were defining a polygon, pressing Backspace would erase the last line segment you had drawn. Then, you could resume the drawing operation.

Mixed Objects

You can intermix line segments created with the Polygon, Curve, and Polyline tools within the same object by selecting the tool that will control the next segment as you draw the object. For example, assume you want to include a curved edge on a polygon. Start drawing with the Polygon tool. Before you select the starting point of the curved edge, select the Curve tool and draw the edge. Then select the Polygon tool to complete the object.

Regular Polygons

Regular polygons have sides that are all of equal length. The program has no automatic feature for generating these objects. However, when you draw with the Polygon or Polyline tools, you can use Grid and Snap to constrain the positions of vertices to create some kinds of regular polygons.

Smoother Curves

To create smoother curves and freehand lines, increase the mouse tracking speed by resetting it through Windows Control Panel➤ Mouse. This causes more vertices to be generated as you draw.

Converting between Lines and Areas

Normally, even if the endpoints of a curve or freehand line are joined, the object cannot be filled. To fill a polyline, curve, or freehand line, select it and perform Arrange➤Convert➤To Polygons. The program will join the endpoints to close the object and fill it with the default area color for polygons. With the object selected, perform Style➤Attributes to change its Area and Edge colors settings.

You can also do the reverse: Select any solid object, such as a polygon or an ellipse, and then perform Arrange➤Convert➤To Lines. This will have the effect of making the fill transparent, permitting the background or objects beneath to show through.

Symbols

Select the Symbol tool to import ready-made drawings into the current page:

For procedures for selecting and manipulating symbols with the drawing tools, see Chapter 10.

MANIPULATING OBJECTS

Once an object has been drawn, it can be moved, resized, or manipulated with other objects in a group.

Selecting Objects

Before you can make any change to an individual object, you must select it. Usually, the easiest way to select an object for manipulation is to click on it once. Your selection is confirmed by a set of handles (small, solid squares) surrounding the object, as shown in Figure 5-20.

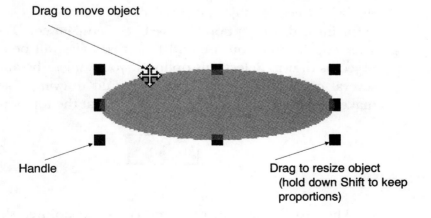

Drag to move object

Handle

Drag to resize object
(hold down Shift to keep
proportions)

FIGURE 5-20. Handles will surround an object that has been selected successfully. Drag the four-way pointer to move the object, or drag the two-way pointer at one of the handles to resize the object.

Another way to select one or more objects is to drag a box around them. Remember that only the objects that lie entirely *within* the box you draw will be selected.

Selecting Multiple Objects

To select multiple objects, hold down the Shift key while clicking on each of them.

In the terminology of Freelance Graphics, a multiple-object selection is called a *collection*. A collection that has been consolidated to form a single object with the Group command is a *group*. In contrast to a collection, a selected group will display only a single set of handles.

Reasons to select a collection might be to move or resize the gathered objects as a unit, to group them, or to change the same attribute—such as area color—for all of them.

Using the Selector Tool

If Tools➤User Setup➤Revert to Pointer is activated (the default), handles will appear around an object immediately after you draw it, and it will be ready for manipulation. The drawing cross hairs will revert to the pointer shape—allowing you to make menu selections that will affect the object, if you like.

If instead, the option Tools➤User Setup➤Keep Tool Active is selected, the tool you use and the cross hairs will persist after an object is drawn. Select this option if you want to be able to create several objects of the same type. To quit drawing objects and to make selections, click on the Selector tool at the top of the toolbar:

The cross hairs will then revert to the pointer shape in the drawing area, permitting you to select objects for editing and manipulation.

Making Selections through the Edit Menu

The Edit menu has a variety of commands for selecting objects that are difficult to isolate from other objects that surround or overlap them.

Selecting All Objects on the Page To select all objects in the drawing area (excepting any in the background, or drawn on the Basic Layout), perform Edit➤Select➤All, press F4, or click on the Select All icon:

Handles will appear around each of the objects.

 See Chapter 10 for procedures for adding Select All and other SmartIcons to the Default or custom toolbars.

Cycle through the Objects To select an object from many objects on a page, you can perform Edit➤Select➤Cycle. The Cycle Selection dialog box will appear, along with a dashed box surrounding one of the objects on the page (Figure 5-21).

The object type of the first selection will be displayed in the dialog box. Select the Next or Previous button to move the dashed-box selection among the available objects. When the object you want is highlighted, choose the Select button. Handles should appear around the object you want. If not, choose Deselect and repeat the procedure. To confirm a selection and close the dialog box, select OK.

 If the object you want is obscured by the dialog box, drag the box's title bar to reposition it.

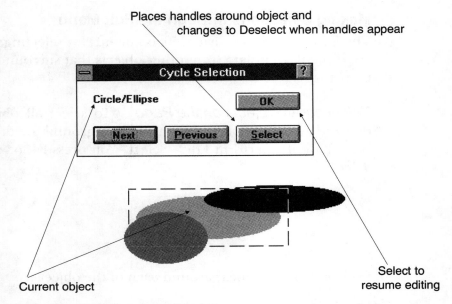

FIGURE 5-21. The Cycle Selection dialog box permits you to identify and select objects one by one within a complex drawing.

Selecting Objects That Share Specific Attributes   A handy feature of the program permits you to select all objects on the page that share characteristics that you specify. First, select an object you want to match. Then, perform Edit➢Select➢Like. The Select Like Objects dialog box will appear, as shown in Figure 5-22.

    Mark check boxes for the characteristics you want to match: Color, Width, Style, 1st Color Area, 2nd Color Area, or Pattern. (Other options are available only when matching text objects.) When you select OK, handles will surround all objects that meet these criteria.

Dragging a Collection of Objects   You can control how the program will select objects when you drag a box around them. First perform Edit➢Select➢Inside. Then drag a box that surrounds the objects you want to select. The program will select only objects that lie entirely within the box you drew.

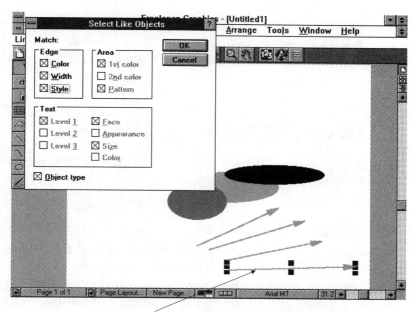

Program will match this object for attributes
you select, creating a collection

FIGURE 5-22. In the Select Like Objects dialog box, you can specify attributes by
which a collection of objects will be selected.

Then, perform Edit≻Select≻Touching and drag a new selection box. (This is an exception to the rule requiring you to make a selection before executing the command.) The program will select all objects that touch the box you drew, even if they extend beyond the box.

Releasing Objects

To release, or deselect, an object or collection of objects, click anywhere outside its handles (but not on another object).

To release an object from a multiple selection, hold down the Shift key while you click on the object.

To release all currently selected objects, perform Edit≻Select≻None or click on an area of the page that has no objects.

To select a few objects from a complex collection, you might first perform Edit⊳ Select⊳ All to include them all, then select Edit⊳ Select⊳ Cycle and use the Deselect button on each object you want to release.

Moving Objects

There is no explicit command for moving an object. Instead, you simply select it and drag it to a new location. (Refer back to Figure 5-20.)

To Use the Mouse: When handles surround a selected object, move the pointer to any location inside the handles. The pointer shape will change to a four-way arrow, indicating that movement is possible. Drag the four-way pointer and a dotted-line preview of the object will move along with it. Release the mouse button at the new location.

To Use the Keyboard: Select the object or objects to be moved. Press the arrow key corresponding to the direction of movement. Press the key once to move one pixel (or one grid position if Snap is on) in that direction. Hold down the key to move continuously.

Resizing Objects

There is also no explicit command for sizing objects. Rather, you simply drag one of its handles.

To Use the Mouse: When you move the pointer to a handle, the pointer shape changes to a two-way arrow. The directions of the arrow tips indicate the possible directions of growth or shrinkage. Select a handle on the side to resize horizontally, on the top to resize vertically, or at one of the corners to resize in both dimensions. As you drag the handle, a dotted-line preview of the object

changes size. Release the mouse button when the preview is the size
you want. (Refer again to Figure 5-20.)

To Use the Keyboard: Select the object or objects, then press the
period (.) key. A small cross will appear on one of the object handles. You can press the period key repeatedly to cycle through the
handles. When the cross is on the handle you want, press the arrow
keys to resize the object. Finish by pressing Enter.

 *Resizing an object can distort it. To constrain the shape of the
object, or to resize it proportionally, hold down the Shift key while
you drag one of the handles.*

Copying Objects

You can copy any object in Freelance Graphics by passing it through
the Clipboard, either to the same or to a different page. Select the
object and perform Edit➤Copy, then Edit➤Paste.

For any selected object or objects, an alternative that bypasses
the Clipboard—leaving its existing content intact—is Edit➤Repli-
cate. In the Current Page view, this command applies only to duplicating objects on the same page.

The command can also be done by pressing Ctrl-F3 or by selecting the Replicate icon:

 *The position of the copy on the page will depend on the current set-
ting of Tools➤User Setup➤Replicate: either offset from the original or superimposed on it.*

The Replicate command can also be used to create special
effects. See Chapter 10.

Grouping Objects

Especially when you are working with complex drawings such as symbols and logos, it can be inconvenient to make changes to component objects individually. The solution can be to combine the objects to form a group, which the program manipulates as though it were a single object.

To combine objects into a group, first perform a multiple selection so that handles surround all the desired objects. Then perform Arrange➤Group or click on the Group icon:

Ungrouping Objects

To disassociate the objects in a group so that they can be manipulated separately, select the grouped object, then perform Arrange➤ Ungroup or click on the Ungroup icon:

As an alternative, after you have selected a group, hold down the right mouse button. A pop-up menu will appear. Keep holding the button down as you drag the pointer to select Ungroup from this menu.

EDITING OBJECT ATTRIBUTES

As discussed previously in this chapter, you can reset the attributes, or appearance options, of drawn objects either before or after you draw them.

To set attributes for all objects of that type that you will draw in a session, select Style>Default Attributes and select from among the options described in this section. You need not repeat the command to reset other types of objects; just click on the corresponding Object Type button before closing the dialog box and its options will appear.

There are several ways of resetting attributes for individual objects or collections of objects:

- Select the object or objects and perform Style>Attributes.

- Double-click on the object.

- Select the object and then hold down the right mouse button. A pop-up menu will appear. Keep holding the button down as you drag the pointer to select Attributes from this menu.

When you take any of these actions, the Style Attributes dialog box will appear for the selected object type and you can reset the options.

If your selection in the drawing area includes dissimilar objects, the Style Attributes Mixed dialog box will appear. Groups, collections of dissimilar objects, or compound objects are treated as the Mixed object type.

Be cautious about resetting options for an entire group. All objects that share a given attribute will be reset. To have greater control, perform Ungroup, change the objects individually, then group them again.

Attributes of Lines

Lines and objects that are composed of lines—such as arrows, polylines, curves, and freehand drawings—share the following set of attributes:

- Color
- Width
- Style
- Marker
- Arrowheads
- Position
- Size

Edges of filled objects are also treated as lines, but selections are limited to the Color, Width, and Style options. The Style Attributes Line & Curve dialog box is shown in Figure 5-23.

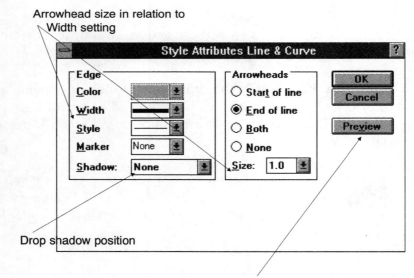

FIGURE 5-23.   The Style Attribute Line & Curve dialog box shows the options for lines, arrows, open curves, polylines, and arcs. Edges of solid objects also share some of these attributes.

Color

When you activate a Color drop-down box, the current palette will appear for your selection. An object assigned a palette color (one of the top 32) will change color if you change palettes. The color of an object assigned a library color will always be the same.

Width

The Width drop-down box has eight selections for line width, ranging from thin to thick. (Even thick lines are one solid color; they cannot be hollow or filled with a different color.)

Style

The Style setting for a line can be solid, dotted, or any of three variations of dashed-and-dotted. The option None hides the line (or edge).

Marker

A variety of dots, squares, or other symbols can be spaced evenly along the line. Each line can have one type of marker. The default is None (no marker).

Arrowheads

Only lines created with the Arrow tool can have arrowheads as default attributes. However, any line object or curve (with the exception of an edge) can have an arrowhead. Simply select the object and reset its Arrowhead attribute.

Position   Option buttons control the position of the arrowhead on a line segment: Start of Line, End of Line, Both, or None (no arrowheads). The arrowheads always point away from the line.

Size   The size of the arrowhead can be controlled by numeric settings in this box. Settings range from 0.5 to 10, in relation to the current Width setting. The default size is 1.0.

Attributes of Shapes

Solid objects, or shapes, can have the edge attributes described above, as well as the area (fill) attributes shown in the dialog box in Figure 5-24. Rectangles (but no other type of object) can have rounded corners, as well.

1st Color

Your selection from this drop-down box controls the fill color within the object, unless a pattern other than solid is also chosen. (Remember that palette colors are subject to change, but library colors remain the same.)

2nd Color

If a pattern has also been selected in this dialog box, this color is intermixed with the first color. If the pattern is solid, this setting is ignored.

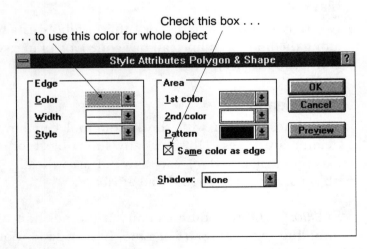

FIGURE 5-24. The Style Attribute Polygon & Shape dialog box shows the options for polygons, circles, and ellipses. The Style Attribute Rectangle dialog box (not shown) has the same options, with the addition of the Rounded Rectangle setting, which controls rounding of corners.

Pattern

In this drop-down box, you can choose from a variety of hatched or gradient blends of the two selected colors.

Same Color As Edge

If this check box is marked, all the Area options will be ignored, and the fill color will be set to the color selected in the Edge box. The effect will be to produce a filled object without an outline.

Shadow

A shadow effect can be added behind any object (except a bitmap). Options for the direction of offset are None (no shadow), Bottom Right, Bottom Left, Top Right, or Top Left.

Rectangle Rounding

For rectangles only, select from the options in the drop-down box: None (sharp corners) or Low, Medium, or High for the degree of rounding at the corners.

Charting Tools

Between the Selector tool and the drawing tools in the toolbox, are four tools for creating text and chart objects.

The Text Tool

For details about using the Text tool, see Chapter 6.

The Data Chart Tool

This tool has the same effect as the command Chart➤New➤Data Chart. Data charts are covered in Chapters 7 and 8.

The Table Tool

This tool has the same effect as the command Chart➤New➤Table. Tables, along with various kinds of lists and text charts, are covered in Chapter 6.

The Organization Chart Tool

This tool has the same effect as the command Chart➤New➤ Organization Chart. For procedures, see Chapter 9.

TRYING YOUR HAND AT DRAWING

As a way of becoming acquainted with the drawing tools, you might try making each of the objects shown in Figure 5-17. Create a new presentation using the SKETCH.MAS SmartMaster set. Choose the Blank Page layout. On one page, use the drawing tools to create each of the objects shown, using default attributes. Then, select any of the objects that don't match the illustration and reset options in Style➤Attributes.

Complete the exercise by printing the page and saving your work. If you are using a monochrome printer, note how colors have been converted to textures on the printout.

CREATING TEXT AND TABLES

TYPES OF TEXT AND TABLE CHARTS

Freelance Graphics for Windows offers several different ways to use text to compose presentation pages and annotations to charts. A SmartMaster set typically contains layouts for the following types of text and table charts:

- Titles
- Bulleted lists
- Tables

Title Charts

The Title page layout can be used for main topic, or *signpost,* pages in a presentation, as well as for various kinds of printed output such as report covers and flyers.

In Freelance Graphics for Windows, Title charts typically have two "Click here..." fields—one for a main title and the other for a subtitle. Each field is a text block that can be rendered in a different set of styles, changing options such as paragraph indentation, typeface, point size, and color. Optionally, attributes of text strings within blocks can be made different from the rest of the block.

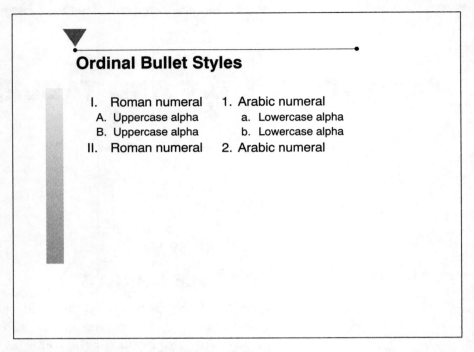

FIGURE 6-1. For a given level of indentation, the program will generate bullets as lowercase or uppercase alphabet letters, Roman numerals, or Arabic numerals.

Bulleted Lists

Bulleted List charts contain lines of text organized as lists, or topic items. Items can be preceded by bullets in various styles, or by *ordinal* characters such as letters or numbers, as shown in Figure 6-1.

In Freelance Graphics for Windows, SmartMaster sets typically include a Bulleted List page layout, as well as the following variations:

- 2-Column Bullets
- Bullets & Chart
- Bullets & Symbol

Examples of these layouts are shown in Figures 6-2a through 6-2d.

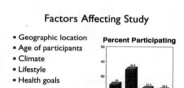

A.   B.

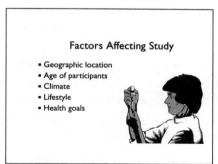

C.

D.

FIGURE 6-2.   SmartMaster page layouts: A. Bulleted List, B. 2-Column Bullets,
                  C. Bullets & Chart, and D. Bullets & Symbol

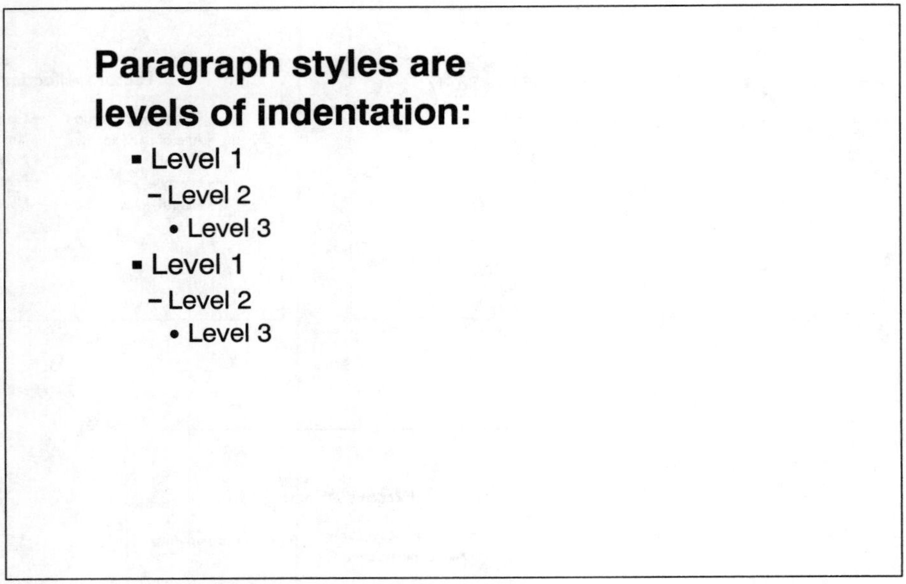

Paragraph styles are levels of indentation:

- Level 1
  - Level 2
    - Level 3
- Level 1
  - Level 2
    - Level 3

FIGURE 6-3. In a block, three possible levels of indentation correspond with three paragraph styles.

Bulleted charts are particularly useful for giving an audience a preview of a presentation topic by listing its subtopics. Each subtopic, in turn, becomes the title of one or more subsequent pages that form a segment of the presentation.

Bulleted lists can contain multiple levels of indentation, as shown in Figure 6-3. This kind of text organization—a hierarchic list of topics—is related closely to traditional outline style. Freelance Graphics for Windows takes advantage of this similarity by permitting you to compose and view the text of a presentation in outline form in the Outliner view. Using the Outliner to create Bulleted List charts is covered in this chapter.

Table Charts

Table charts are *text arrays* arranged by columns and rows. Another commonly used term is *column chart.*

In Freelance Graphics for Windows, a table can have as many as 50 columns and 50 rows. Just as in a spreadsheet, the intersection of a column and a row is called a *cell*. The entire table is a single "Click here..." data-entry area. When you click on this area, you are prompted for the number of rows and columns. The program then displays the table as an empty grid with the specified number of rows and columns. To make an entry into a cell, you click on the cell to move the insertion point there and then type the text.

By default, the program justifies alphabetic labels left and numeric data right within each cell. However, justification (and other attributes) of text in a table can be reset selectively for individual cells or for groups of adjacent cells.

CREATING A TITLE CHART

As covered in the Introduction, the procedures for creating a Title chart in Freelance Graphics for Windows are:

1. Create or open a presentation.
2. Create a new page (by the Page➤New command or its equivalent command).
3. Select Title in the New Page dialog box. The SmartMaster page layout will appear in the Current Page view.
4. Click on "Click here to type presentation title." A text block will open.
5. Type the main title, then select OK to close the block.
6. Click on "Click here to type subtitle," type your entry, then select OK.
7. Optionally, click on "Click here to add a symbol," select a predrawn graphic from one of the symbol libraries, then select OK to close the Add Symbol to Page dialog box.

The appearance of the chart will follow the SmartMaster layout named Title. Elements contained in the Basic Layout will appear on all pages of the current presentation, with the exception of the first

Title chart, which is assumed to be the main title of the presentation.

TITLE CHART OPTIONS

There are no Option selections in the Chart menu for Title charts. That is, when you are working with a Title chart in the Current Page view, if you try to select Chart➤Options, you will find that the command is dimmed, indicating that it is unavailable.

In fact, there are many options available, but changing them does not involve commands in the Chart menu. Rather, changing the appearance of a Title chart is a matter of manipulating its component text blocks for:

- Layout
- Attributes

Changing the Layout of Titles

To change the composition, or layout, of a Title chart, simply drag either of its text blocks to a different position in the drawing area.

If you do this while editing presentation pages, the change will affect only the current page. If instead you first select Edit➤Edit Page Layouts, you will be changing the underlying master layout, which will affect all Title charts in your presentation.

You can select a text block (or any graphic object) for manipulation in the Current Page view by clicking on it or by drawing a box around it (Figure 6-4). When the object has been selected, or captured, handles will surround it. When you press the left mouse button and hold it down to drag the object, a dotted outline of the block moves with the pointer. Release the mouse button at the new object location to complete the operation.

 When you are editing a presentation page (as opposed to its layout), you cannot move or change the attributes of a "Click here..." block that is empty of text.

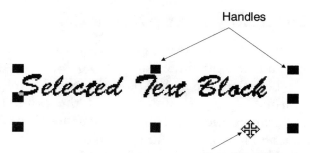

FIGURE 6-4.   When you select a text block for editing or manipulation, handles appear around it.

You can also control the size of a text block by dragging its handles individually. When you select just one handle for dragging, the pointer will change to a two-way arrow. You can resize the block in the directions indicated by the arrow tips, as shown in Figure 6-5.

Resizing a text block alters the area within which text will be composed, or the size of block boundaries. The size of the text characters remains the same, and the program will adjust line breaks, if possible, to fit the text to the new block size. To change text size, you must adjust its Size setting, as described later in this chapter. It is also possible to distort, or stretch, text. The procedure is described in Chapter 10.

FIGURE 6-5.   Drag a handle to resize a text block. Resizing affects block boundaries and line breaks, not text size.

Changing Text Attributes

Other aspects of the appearance of a Title chart can be changed by resetting the attributes of text blocks. Text attribute settings that affect appearance include font Face and Size, Color, and Attributes (Normal or any combination of the Bold, Italic, Strikeout, and Underline options). Other settings include Bullet, Paragraph Styles (determines spacing and indentations within the block), and Frame (places a border around the block).

For any text block, attributes can be reset by selecting (clicking on) the block, then selecting the desired command or attribute from the Text menu. Or, press the *right* mouse button and make an equivalent selection from the pop-up menu. Text attributes are covered in depth in this chapter, immediately following the discussion of the Text tool.

Special effects can also be added to text blocks in the Current Page view. These include rotation, multiple instances (replication), and curvature. However, such effects cannot be added to "Click here..." blocks unless you are editing the master layout (Edit➤Edit Page Layouts). The topic of enhancing text, which includes use of these special effects, is covered in Chapter 10.

CREATING AND EDITING TEXT BLOCKS

In Freelance Graphics for Windows, all text blocks can be manipulated directly in the Current Page view, whether they have been entered into a "Click here..." area or created as free-form graphic objects. Creating free-form text, as in annotating a chart, is done with the Text tool (icon labeled *abc*).

The Text tool can also be used to open a block, allowing you to edit its characters and change indentation (margins and tab stops)

within the block. As background for discussions of text attributes and the page layouts Bulleted List and Table, a detailed explanation of text blocks and the usage of the Text tool follows.

Text Block Definitions

Attribute options such as Bold and Italic affect the appearance of text characters. Other attributes control the layout and positioning of the text block as a whole. These attributes are

- Block size
- Alignment and justification
- Paragraph styles

Block Size

As mentioned previously, the size of a text block refers to its boundaries in the drawing area, not to the size of the text characters it contains. You can resize a block by selecting it and dragging the handle that corresponds to the direction of growth or shrinkage. (Refer again to Figure 6-5.)

A text block can be composed of multiple lines of text in multiple paragraphs. Optionally, a paragraph can begin with a bullet or a number. When you are typing the characters, breaks between lines can be inserted by pressing Ctrl-Enter; to insert a break between paragraphs, press Enter. These typed breaks are marked by *hard carriage returns* in the data. A hard carriage return is a mandatory break. However, the program will also automatically insert *soft carriage returns,* or movable line breaks, so that the text *wraps,* or flows, within the boundaries of a block. The program may adjust these "soft" line breaks if you resize a block.

The program will cause a block to grow downward, *maintaining its right boundary, if you enter more text into it than can be displayed in the current text point size.*

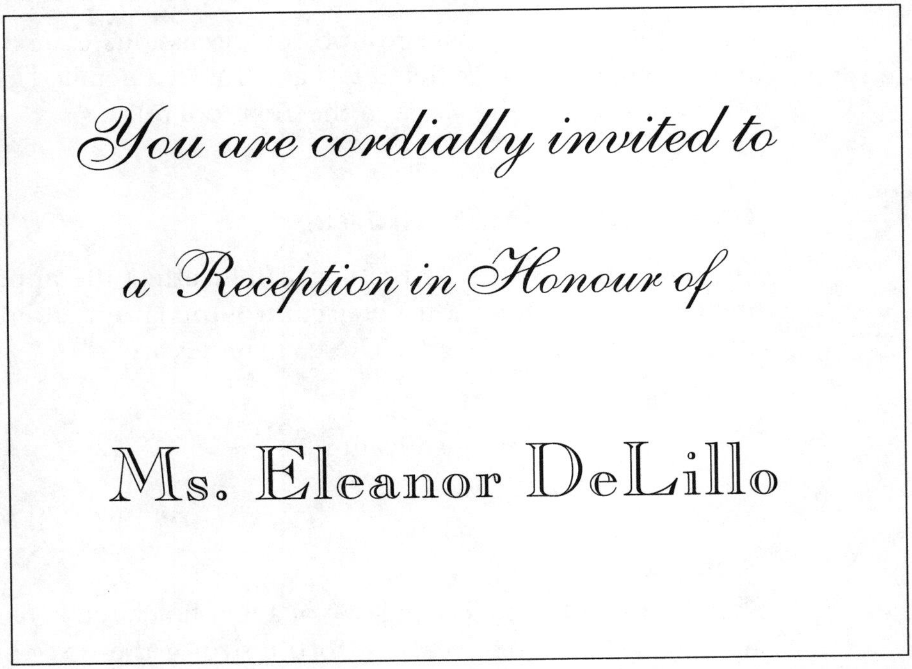

You are cordially invited to

a Reception in Honour of

Ms. Eleanor DeLillo

FIGURE 6-6. Three text blocks are shown here aligned vertically on their centers.

Alignment and Justification

With respect to text blocks, note the differences between the terms *alignment* and *justification*. Alignment refers to the relative positioning of two or more graphic objects, including text blocks. For example, the centers of three blocks might be aligned vertically, as shown in Figure 6-6.

Justification refers to positioning text relative to the margins or boundaries of a page, text block, or cell. These options include Left, Center, Right, and Both Left and Right. *Vertical justification* is another way to position text in relation to the top and bottom boundaries of a block; the applicable settings are Top, Center, and Bottom. Examples are shown in Figure 6-7.

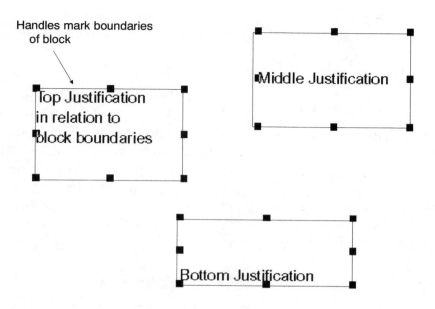

FIGURE 6-7.   Vertical justification options: Top, Middle, and Bottom

Paragraph Styles

In Freelance Graphics for Windows, a text block can contain three different sets of attributes, margins, and indentations that apply to entire paragraphs, or indentation levels. Accordingly, a block can be thought of as a miniature text document that can be opened within a page.

A paragraph style is a set of text attributes that applies to multiple lines of text within a block until a hard carriage return is entered. Each block can have as many as three different paragraph styles. In a bulleted list, paragraph styles correspond to three possible levels of indentation: Level 1, Level 2, and Level 3.

Attributes that can be set for each paragraph style are described in "Using the Text Tool." When you change the attribute settings of a paragraph style, your changes will affect all paragraphs in the block that use the style. (For more information, see "Switching among Default Paragraph Styles" and "Resetting Paragraph Styles" later in this chapter.)

Using the Text Tool

Before using the Text tool, you may want to select View≻View Preferences and mark the check box Text Block Ruler. This option causes a ruler to be displayed along the top margin of any open text block, with units marked according to the current Units setting in View≻Units & Grids. The ruler is handy for measuring the lengths of text lines in relation to the dimensions of the output page.

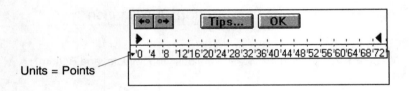

Units = Points

To create a text block, or text object, select the Text tool (the toolbox icon labeled *abc*) in the Current Page view. In the drawing area, place the cursor on one corner of the new text block (usually the top left). Then, drag to create a dotted rectangle that defines the boundaries of the block. When you release the mouse button, a text block will open. The pointer will change to an I-beam cursor:

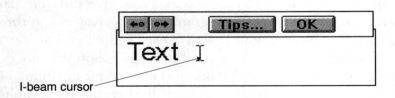

I-beam cursor

Dragging the boundaries of a text block permits you to control the area within which text will appear, turning word wrap on automatically. To create a block that will grow as you type—one without word wrap and requiring hard returns—click the top left corner of the block in the drawing area instead of dragging the block boundaries.

The open text block is the area to be filled with text. As you type, the insertion point within the block will be indicated by a flashing vertical bar. The normal keyboard mode is Insert, but you can toggle Typeover mode by pressing the Ins key. You can also use the Del key to delete the character to the right of the insertion point, or press Backspace to delete the character to the left.

Avoid starting a new text block on top of an existing one: The existing block will open for editing instead. Create the new block in a blank area of the page and then drag it to the desired position.

Press Enter to insert hard carriage returns, dropping down one line and starting a new paragraph. Or, as you reach the right margin, keep typing and the program will wrap the text to the next line. Such a soft carriage return will permit word wrap to adjust automatically if you later resize the block or adjust its margins.

When you have entered all the text in the block, click on OK. The block will close, and handles will surround the new text so that it can be manipulated. Alternative methods of closing a text block are clicking on the Selector tool or pressing Esc.

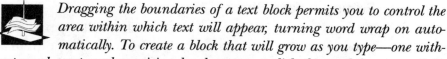

To close the block and release (deselect) the text in a single operation, click a blank area outside the block instead of selecting OK.

Editing a Text Block

To edit your text entry while the block is still open, move the I-beam cursor with the mouse and click to indicate the point of an insertion between characters. Or, move the insertion point (vertical-bar cursor) with the arrow keys. Then, type the inserted characters.

 Other key commands for editing text are Home or End (beginning or end of line), and Ctrl-Left Arrow (left one word). Ctrl-Backspace or Ctrl-Del erase the word to the left or to the right of the insertion point.

To replace a string of characters, drag the I-beam cursor to highlight the string, which will appear in reverse color. To use the keyboard, press Shift at the beginning of the string and keep holding it down as you press the Right Arrow key to move the insertion point through the string. Then, type the replacement string. Pressing the Delete key will erase the highlighted string.

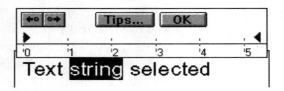

To edit the text data in any previously entered block, first click on the block to select it, then click on the Text tool. As alternatives, you can select Text➤Edit or press F2 (Edit). The block will open, allowing you to perform insertions, replacements, and deletions as just described.

 To edit a "Click here..." entry, click just once on it to open the block. You do not need to select the Text tool.

If there are multiple blocks on a page, you can open the next block by positioning the insertion point at the end of the last text line and then pressing the Down Arrow. To move to the previous block, position the insertion point at the beginning of the first line and press the Up Arrow.

When you are finished making edits, select OK or click outside the block. (Or, click on the Selector tool or press Esc.)

Changing Attributes as You Type

As an alternative, you can change text attributes as you are entering text into the block. With the text block open, and just prior to typing the characters that will share the attribute, select the attribute you want. For example, select Text➤Bold or click on the Bold icon, then type a word that you want in boldface. Then select Text➤Normal or the Normal icon to resume typing in normal style. At any point, you can select Text➤Revert to Style to type new characters in the default style of the current paragraph level.

Dragging Text into or out of "Click Here..." Areas

Having entered a text block, you might decide to use it as a page title or subtitle. If you drag a text block into a "Click here..." area, the program will recompose it automatically, applying the styles in the SmartMaster layout.

If you press the Ctrl key as you drag text *out* of a "Click here..." area, the text block will retain its composition and styles but will lose its ability to change automatically to reflect edits to the SmartMaster.

Using the Text Block Ruler

Margins and paragraph indentations can be set when you are using the Text tool by adjusting icons within the Text Block Ruler. (See Figure 6-8. Be sure that View➤View Preferences➤Text Block Ruler is marked.) The white space *inside* the ruler (not in the text box) is an area in which margins and indentations can be set.

Margin indicators

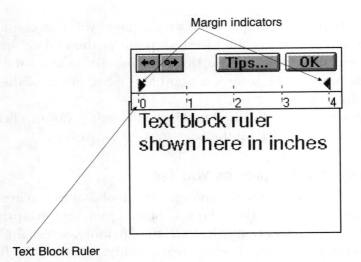

Text Block Ruler

FIGURE 6-8.   A Text Block Ruler will appear in open blocks if you select
View➤View Preferences➤Text Block Ruler.

*The unit-of-measure markings on the Text Block Ruler are deter-
mined by the Units setting in View➤Units & Grids. This setting
should be consistent with the Paper Size units specified in
File➤Printer Setup and Windows➤Control Panel➤Printers. The unit of
measure also affects Margins settings in File➤Page Setup.*

At the left edge of the white space in the Text Block Ruler is a
right triangle:

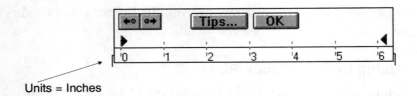

Units = Inches

Although not apparent at first, this triangle actually has separately movable top and bottom parts. For the current paragraph,
the top part represents the first-line indent and the bottom part is
the left margin.

Setting Block and Paragraph Margins   To set the left margin of
a block that contains a single line or paragraph, drag the bottom
part of the left-margin indicator in the white space of the Text Block
Ruler. This will reposition the left edge of the text-entry field:

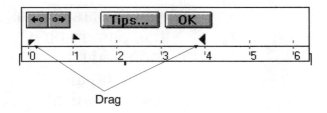

Drag

Blocks can contain multiple paragraphs in any of three styles, or
levels. Each paragraph style can have different margin settings. See
the following section "Resetting Text Attributes" and "Resetting
Paragraph Style Options."

Setting Paragraph Indentations   To set the first-line indentation
for the current paragraph, drag only the *top portion* of the left-margin indicator in the white space above the Text Block Ruler. When
you type the text, only the first line will be indented by this distance.
(You do not need to press Tab first.) Subsequent lines will wrap
within the block to follow the left margin (marked by the bottom
part of the indicator), until you type a paragraph break (Enter). An
example is shown in Figure 6-9. After the break, the next line will be
indented to the first-line indent, beginning another paragraph.

   To indent only the first line of a paragraph, drag the top portion
(first-line indent) of the indicator further to the right than the bottom portion (left-margin indicator):

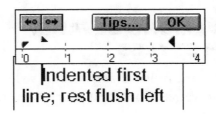

First-line indent indicator

Left-margin indicator

Right-margin indicator

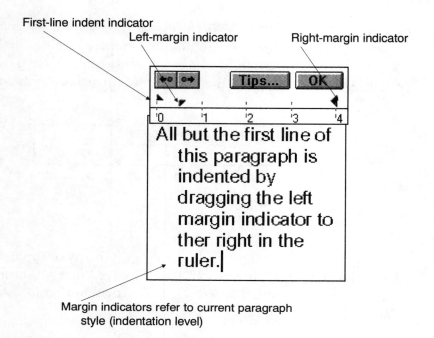

Margin indicators refer to current paragraph
style (indentation level)

FIGURE 6-9.   You can adjust left and right margins, as well as first-line indentation, within the Text Block Ruler.

To indent all lines except the first one, drag the bottom portion
(left margin) to the right of the first-line indent indicator:

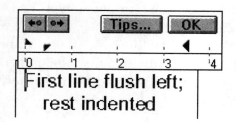

SWITCHING AMONG DEFAULT
PARAGRAPH STYLES

The program holds three default styles for paragraph indentation
and appearance. Each text block can contain multiple paragraphs,

and each paragraph can be displayed in any one of those three styles. (A paragraph cannot be displayed in more than one style.) Paragraph styles are treated as levels of indentation, although you can adjust the margins of each style so that they are not necessarily indented.

Changing paragraph styles is easiest if the Text Block Ruler is turned on (View➢View Preferences➢Text Block Ruler). To use this feature to edit paragraphs in an existing block, first select the block to open it. Then, click anywhere within the paragraph to be changed. Click on the Demote icon in the top-left corner of the ruler to change to the next-lower level of indentation:

Remember that each level of indentation corresponds to a paragraph style. So, changing the level of indentation can change the appearance of the text, as well.

For example, by default paragraphs are displayed in Level 1 style. If you move the insertion point into a paragraph and click on the Demote icon, the paragraph will be redisplayed in Level 2 style, as shown in Figure 6-10.

If a paragraph has been demoted to a lower level, it can be changed to the style of a higher level by placing the insertion point within it and clicking on the Promote icon:

You can also demote or promote paragraphs by using the keyboard, whether or not the Text Block Ruler is on. To demote a paragraph, use the arrow keys to move the insertion point to the beginning of the first line, then press the Tab key. To promote a paragraph, do the same but press Shift-Tab.

Demote icon shifts margin
rightward to next level

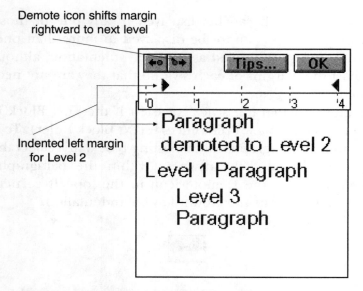

Indented left margin
for Level 2

FIGURE 6-10. The first paragraph in this block has been demoted from Level 1 to Level 2 indentation.

RESETTING TEXT ATTRIBUTES

Freelance Graphics for Windows provides some quick ways to change the appearance of text blocks, or of characters, words, or lines of text within blocks.

Selecting Text Strings

To change the attributes of a string within a text block, select the text to open the block, then highlight the string by dragging the I-beam pointer over it. The highlighted string appears in reverse color:

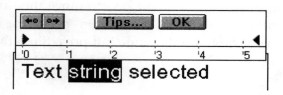

Changing Text Appearance Quickly

To reset attributes for just the selected string, select commands from the Text menu or from the pop-up menu that appears when you click the *right* mouse button. Or, click on a SmartIcon, such as Bold, Italic, or Normal:

After you have selected a string or block, a convenient way to change the typeface is to click on the Face box in the status bar at the bottom of the screen:

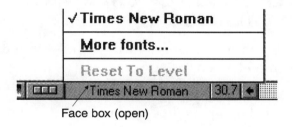

Face box (open)

A pop-up menu will appear, listing the available typefaces. Simply click on your selection and the selected text will change accordingly.

To change the point size of a selected string or block, click on the Point Size box in the status bar:

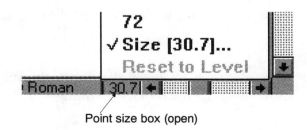

Point size box (open)

A pop-up menu will appear, listing point-size increments ranging from 8 to 72. To enter a nonstandard size, click on the Size command in this menu, type a numeric point size in the dialog box that appears, and select OK. (Numeric point sizes can include four digits with one decimal place, with values ranging from 1 to 200.)

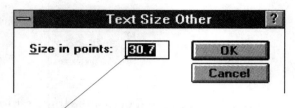

Type value (decimals permitted)

OTHER METHODS OF CHANGING TEXT ATTRIBUTES

You can also change attributes of selected text blocks or strings within blocks by using

- Text menu commands
- Pop-up menu commands
- Accelerator keys
- SmartIcons

These different methods are equivalent, so use the one you find most convenient or easiest to remember.

Text Menu Commands

The Text pull-down menu has the following commands:

Edit

For text surrounded by handles in the drawing area, the Text➤Edit command opens the block for editing.

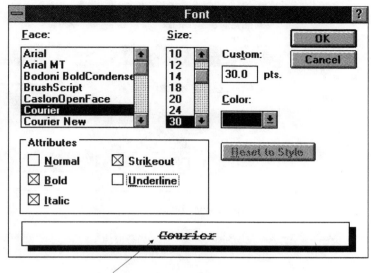

Sample in current settings

FIGURE 6-11. Change attributes for the current text selection in the Font dialog
box.

Font

After you have selected an item in an open text block, selecting
Text➤Font will open the Font dialog box shown in Figure 6-11.
Here you can select a typeface from a list of installed fonts; choose a
point size from a list of specific increments or type in your own
value under Custom; select a color from the current palette; and set
other attributes such as Normal or any combination of Bold, Italic,
Strikeout, and Underline.

If you reset font attributes, the Reset to Style button becomes
available so that you can restore all the default settings with a single
selection.

When you have finished changing font attributes, select OK to
close this dialog box.   ∘

Choose numbered or lettered styles,
shapes, or symbols

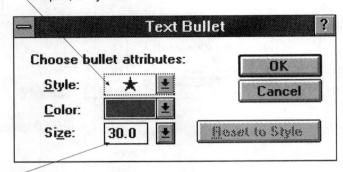

Text point size for bullet

FIGURE 6-12. Choose bullet attributes in the Text Bullet dialog box.

Bullet

For a selected block or string, performing Text≻Bullet will open
the Text Bullet dialog box (Figure 6-12), which contains the following options. For any selection but Style=None, the options specify a
bullet that will precede the text selection.

Style   Select from any of the bullet shapes in the drop-down
menu. Or, select ordinal letters (lowercase *a* or uppercase *A*) or
numbers (Roman *I* or Arabic *1*), which will be incremented automatically by the program for subsequent paragraphs of the same
style in the block.

   If you select Symbol here, the Choose Symbol for Bullet dialog
box will appear, in which you can select a predrawn graphic from
the symbol library. (This is the same dialog box that appears when
you select the Symbol tool; here, however, your selection will be
used as a bullet.)

Color   Select a color for the bullet from the current palette.
Remember that palette colors will change with SmartMaster selections but library colors will remain the same.

Size   Specify a numeric point size from 8 to 72 for the bullet, or type a custom size in this box. The default is the same point size as the selected text item.

Reset to Style   This button will become available if you have reset the default bullet attributes. Select it to restore all the defaults in a single operation.

Style Attributes

The Text menu makes style attributes available as commands, which can be set to Normal or any combination of Bold, Italic, Underline, and Strikeout. The current selection will be preceded by a check mark (✓) in the pull-down menu. If the setting is other than the default for the current style, the command Reset to Style will become available.

Paragraph Styles

The Text➤Paragraph Styles command will open the Paragraph Styles dialog box. This controls sets of text attributes, as well as spacing and indentation, for the three available paragraph styles, or levels. See "Resetting Paragraph Style Options" below.

 When a text block is selected, choosing Style➤Attributes will open the Paragraph Styles dialog box for the current block. Selecting Style➤Default Attributes permits you to reset the appearance of styles in all new blocks.

Frame

This option draws a frame, or border, around an entire selected *block* (but not around individual paragraphs, lines, or strings within blocks). You can set the edge, area, and drop-shadow styles just as you can for objects you create with the Rectangle tool. For the frame to be visible, Edge Style must be set to something other than None.

Curved Text

This command is available only for an entire block, and only when that block is selected (surrounded by handles) but not open for editing. Techniques for creating text that follows a curve, or arc, are covered in Chapter 10.

Pop-Up Menu Commands

For a selected block or string within an open block, pressing the *right* mouse button will cause a pop-up menu to appear (Figure 6-13). Commands on this menu are equivalent to commands in the Text pull-down menu just described. In addition, Cut, Copy, and Paste commands are available for performing the Clipboard operations Edit➤Cut, Edit➤Copy, and Edit➤Paste. (Paste will be available only if there is already a text item on the Clipboard.)

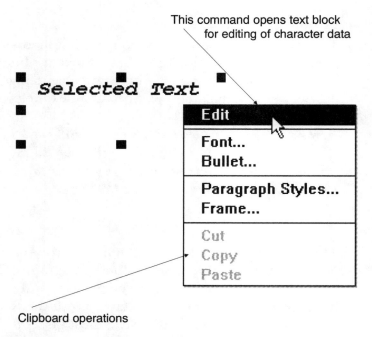

This command opens text block for editing of character data

Clipboard operations

FIGURE 6-13.   When you select a text item and press the right mouse button, this pop-up menu will appear.

TABLE 6-1. Accelerator Keys for Editing Text and Text Attributes

Accelerator Key	Command Equivalent
F2	Text➤Edit
Ctrl-N	Text➤Normal
Ctrl-B	Text➤Bold
Ctrl-I	Text➤Italic
Ctrl-U	Text➤Underline

Accelerator Keys

Keyboard selections are available as alternatives to some of the Text or pop-up menu commands that affect the appearance of selected blocks or strings. These accelerator keys are listed in Table 6-1.

SmartIcons

SmartIcons for changing text appearance (including some that are not shown in the default toolbar) are listed in Table 6-2.

RESETTING PARAGRAPH STYLE OPTIONS

To reset paragraph styles, simply double-click on the block you want to change. Or, select the block, then do any of the following:

- Select Text➤Paragraph Styles.
- Select Style➤Attributes.
- Click the right mouse button and select Paragraph Styles from the pop-up menu.
- Click on the Paragraph Styles SmartIcon.

Any of these actions will cause the Paragraph Styles dialog box to open, as shown in Figure 6-14.

TABLE 6-2. SmartIcons That Affect Text Appearance

SmartIcon	Name	Command Equivalent	Default Toolbar
B	Bold Text	Text≻Bold	X
N	Normal Text	Text≻Normal	X
I	Italic Text	Text≻Italic	X
(scissors)	Cut to Clipboard	Edit≻Cut	X
(copy)	Copy to Clipboard	Edit≻Copy	X
(paste)	Paste Clipboard Contents	Edit≻Paste	X
S	Paragraph Style	Text≻Paragraph Style	
U	Underline Text	Text≻Underline	
abc	Curved Text	Text≻Curved Text	
az	Change Font	Text≻Font	
abc	Show Text Block Ruler	View≻View Preferences≻ Text Block Ruler	

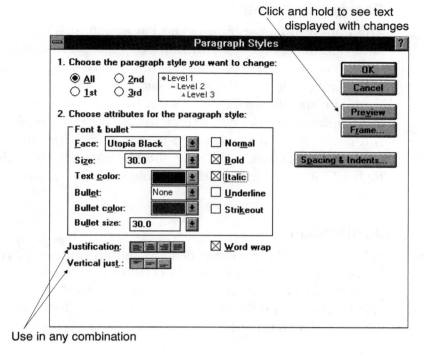

FIGURE 6-14. You can control sets of text attributes by paragraph in the Paragraph Styles dialog box.

A similar dialog box with the same options will appear if you select Style➤Default Attributes or if you double-click on the Text tool. Settings made here will apply to all subsequent text blocks that you create in a work session.

Specifying Styles by Level

The top portion of the Paragraph Styles dialog box has four option buttons for choosing the style to which the settings will apply: All (same changes for the three styles that can be defined for a block), 1st (first-level indent, or title), 2nd (second-level indent, or topic), and 3rd (third-level indent, or subtopic).

Font and Bullet Attributes

The Font & Bullet section of the Paragraph Styles dialog box contains options for the text attributes covered previously in this chapter. Remember that changes you make here will apply to all complete paragraphs that share the same level.

If you specify a paragraph style, you are still free to add effects for emphasis to selective strings within paragraphs. For example, you could make a word bold within a paragraph of normal text. (With the text block open, drag the I-beam cursor over the word to highlight it, then perform Text➤Bold or make an equivalent selection.)

Justification

Select one of the four Justification setting buttons to control the horizontal positioning of text in relation to the side margins of the paragraph that contains it. These buttons are Left, Center, Right, and Both Left and Right (also called *spread* justification). Examples are shown in Figure 6-15.

Vertical Justification

Select one of the four Vertical Justification setting buttons to control the vertical positioning of text in relation to the top and bottom

```
This text is            This text is
justified left            justified
in relation to               right
the block
boundaries
```

```
 This text is           This    text   is
  justified             justified  both
   center               left and right
```

FIGURE 6-15. Examples of justification settings: Left, Center, Right, and Both Left and Right

boundaries of the block. These buttons are Top, Middle, and Bottom. Refer again to Figure 6-7.

Word Wrap

By default, this check box is marked to permit the program to realign soft line breaks when you resize a text block. Turning the option off will cause each paragraph to be displayed as a single line, requiring you to insert hard carriage returns (Ctrl-Enter) for line breaks within paragraphs. However, if you resize a block in which Word Wrap has been turned off, the option will be turned back on automatically and the lines will wrap, conforming to the new boundaries.

Frame

Selecting this button will open the Text Frame dialog box, which contains the options described previously for a frame (border), surrounding the block. Remember that this option will apply to the entire block, regardless of the paragraph style level currently selected.

Preview

To see how new attribute settings will affect the selected text, click and hold on this button to see the results displayed in the drawing area. Releasing the mouse button will cause the Paragraph Styles dialog box to reappear. Select OK to close the dialog box when you are satisfied with the previewed text.

Controlling Spacing and Indentation

While working in the Paragraph Styles dialog box, you can select the Spacing & Indents button to control these aspects of paragraph appearance. When you select the button, the Spacing & Indents dialog box will open, as shown in Figure 6-16.

Mixed appears when all styles
are being changed

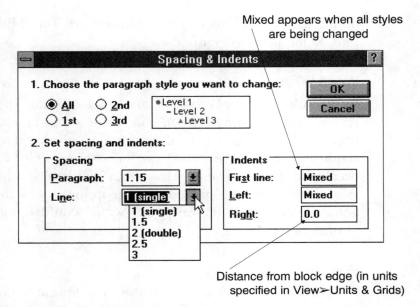

Distance from block edge (in units
specified in View≻Units & Grids)

FIGURE 6-16. Control line and paragraph spacing, as well as numeric values for indentation in this dialog box.

As in the Paragraph Styles dialog box, four option buttons at the top permit you to select the style to which the spacing and indentation options will apply. Each of the three style levels can have a different set of options, or you can select All to create uniform spacing and indentation throughout the block.

Spacing

Numeric settings in two drop-down boxes control the vertical distance between each paragraph and between each line. Select increments ranging from 1 to 3 for single to triple spacing, or type a value. Decimal values are permitted. If single spacing is set for Line (1), the default spacing between paragraphs is 1.15.

Indents

Numeric values for first-line indent, left margin, and right margin can be entered in the corresponding text boxes. Decimal values are permitted, and values are expressed in the units selected in View➤ Units & Grids as distances from the block boundaries.

If you dragged the margin indicators in the Text Block Ruler to adjust the margins or first-line indent for a paragraph, the equivalent numeric values will be shown here. In most cases, it will be easier to make adjustments by dragging the indicators than by entering numeric values. Remember that if you change the margins of a paragraph, all paragraphs at that style level within the same block will change accordingly.

TUTORIAL: WORK WITH TITLES AND TEXT BLOCKS

To review text blocks and their attributes, open the presentation SAMPLE.PRE that you created in the Introduction and work through the following steps with Page 1 in the Current Page view, as shown in Figure 6-17:

1. Change the attributes of the subtitle.

   Click on the subtitle block YEAR END to select it. Handles will surround the text. Then, click the *right* mouse button. Select Font from the pop-up menu that appears. Change the Face option to Times New Roman. Select attributes Bold and Italic. Change the Size setting to 42. Click on the Color drop-down box and click on another color from the top row of the palette colors. Then, click on OK to close the Font dialog box. Handles still surround the selected text. Click on a blank area of the page to release the text.

2. Add a line of text as a footnote.

   Click on the Text tool. Drag to create a long, thin box at the bottom left corner of the page, as shown in Figure 6-18. A text block will open. Type the words: **Unaudited results** and select OK to close the text box. The footnote text appears on the page. Adjust the font and size, if necessary. The footnote shown is in Arial MT, about 30 points.

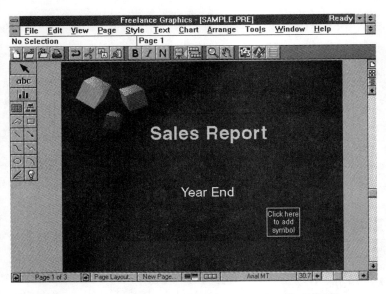

FIGURE 6-17. Begin the tutorial with this page of the SAMPLE.PRE presentation that you created in the Introduction.

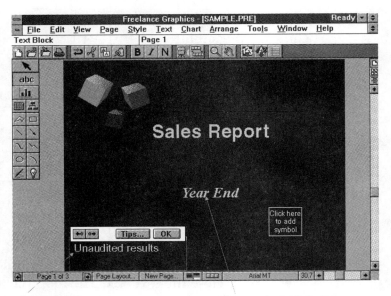

Add footnote   Change text attributes

FIGURE 6-18. Drag a text block to hold a footnote.

3. Save your work!

   Select File≻Save or press Ctrl-S. You have been working on an existing file, so the program will ask whether you wish to update it. Select Replace to confirm the update.

TUTORIAL: CREATE A BULLETED LIST CHART

Still working with SAMPLE.PRE in the Current Page view, continue with the tutorial to add a bulleted-list chart to the presentation:

1. Add a new page.

   Click on the New Page button in the status bar or press F7. The New Page dialog box will appear. Select the Bulleted List page layout, then click on OK.

2. Enter the title.

   Click on the area labeled "Click here to type page title." A text block will open. Type **Meeting Agenda** and click on OK.

3. Enter the text for the bulleted list.

   Click on the area labeled "Click here to type bulleted text." A text block will open. If you have not done so already, select View≻View Preferences≻Text Block Ruler to display the Text Block Ruler across the top of the block. Note how the margin indicators just above the ruler change position as you move from topics to subtopics. Type **Market briefing** and press Enter. Press Tab to indent one level, then type **Competitive share** and press Enter. Then, type the rest of the list shown in Figure 6-19. Remember to press Shift-Tab to unindent (promote) or Tab to indent (demote) topics and subtopics.

   Before you close the block, click on the beginning of the first line to move the insertion point there. Then, click on the Demote icon and watch the indentation level change. Click on the Promote icon to restore the original text position. Finally, click on OK to close the block.

4. Save your work!

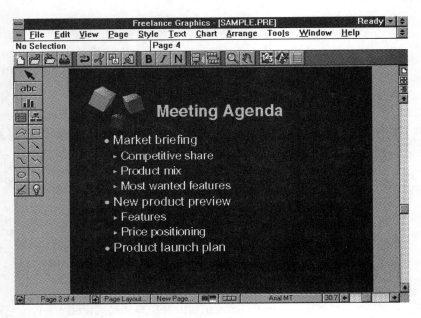

FIGURE 6-19.   Create this bulleted list.

VARIATIONS ON BULLETED LISTS

Each SmartMaster set also has 2-Column Bullets, Bullets & Chart,
and Bullets & Symbol layouts. From the standpoint of entering text,
you use each of these layouts as just described. In the case of a two-
column layout, however, each column is treated as a separate block.

EDITING BULLETED LISTS

As with Title charts, there are no special Chart options for the text
lists in any of the bulleted layouts. However, the appearance can be
changed by moving and resetting the attributes of text blocks, or by
resetting the attributes of paragraph styles within the list block.

Each paragraph style within the list block corresponds to one of
three levels of indentation. A different set of styles can be specified
for each; see "Resetting Paragraph Style Options" above.

Again, bullets specified as numerals or letters will be incremented automatically by the program, in ordinal (counting) sequence for each paragraph at the same level. For example, Level 1 topics might proceed 1, 2, 3, and so on; Level 2 subtopics underneath these headings might be labeled a, b, and c.

To specify numbers or letters for bullets, select the list block, move the insertion point to a paragraph (line) on that level, and perform Text➤Bullets (or its equivalent). Select the Style drop-down box, and select one of the lettered or numbered styles: a (lowercase alphabet), A (uppercase alphabet), I (Roman), or 1 (Arabic).

ENTERING BULLETED TEXT THROUGH THE OUTLINER

Text for charts, including bulleted lists, can also be entered through the Outliner. To open the Outliner, select View➤Outliner, or click on the Outliner icon (the third one from the top in the top right corner of the current window). The data from the preceding tutorial is shown in the Outliner view in Figure 6-20.

You enter text data for a bulleted list in the Outliner just as you would in a text block. Press Enter at the end of each text line, and press Tab or Shift-Tab to demote or promote text to the next bullet level.

To add a second column to a list in the Outliner, select Page➤Choose Page Layout➤2-Column Bullets. A *second-column indicator* will appear in the outline at the beginning of the second list:

For procedures for using the Outliner to create text charts, see Chapter 13.

Page 2 text

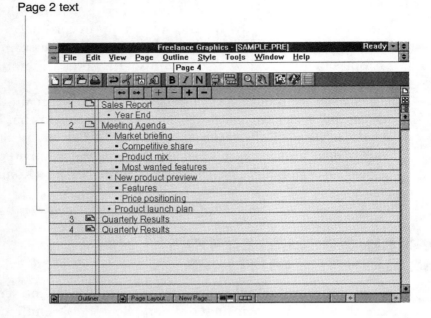

FIGURE 6-20.   The bulleted list from Figure 6-19 is shown here in the Outliner view.

CREATING TABLE CHARTS

In Freelance Graphics for Windows, a table is a special kind of text block that is subdivided into rows and columns of cells. Text in each cell can be selected separately; you are not required to make changes to the table as a whole. Attributes can be set for any column, row, group of adjacent cells, or individual cell.

To create a table chart, select Page➤New (or its equivalent). The New Page dialog box will appear. Select the Table page layout, then OK.

The Table page layout will appear in the drawing area of the Current Page view. Click on the area labeled "Click here to create a text table."

The Table Gallery dialog box will open, as shown in Figure 6-21. Choose a table style from one of the gallery buttons shown. The

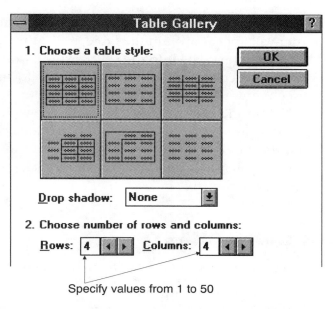

Specify values from 1 to 50

FIGURE 6-21.   Change grid styles in the Table Gallery dialog box.

selections include variations on grid lines separating rows and columns.

Optionally, make a selection from the Drop Shadow drop-down box for the position of a shadow that will surround the entire table. Your options are Bottom Right, Bottom Left, Top Right, and Top Left. The default selection None omits the shadow.

Change the settings in the Rows and Columns text boxes to indicate the number of rows and columns you require. A text table can have up to 50 rows and as many columns.

If you are not sure of the number of rows and columns you need, make an approximate selection. You can always add or delete rows or columns in subsequent steps as you work on the chart.

An empty block of cells will appear in the drawing area. To enter text in a cell, click on it. The text insertion point will appear as a flashing vertical bar in the top left corner of the cell. Also, a thick border will appear around the table, indicating text-entry mode.

Type the text data into the cell. Text will wrap within the boundaries of the cell, or you can press Enter to insert a hard break between multiple lines.

Click inside the next cell that will receive text, and repeat the text-entry procedure. The text in the previous cell will not be justified until you have moved the insertion point to a different cell.

When you are finished entering text, click on a blank area of the page outside the table.

EDITING TABLE CHARTS

Editing operations you can perform on a table include

- Changing text attributes
- Resizing columns or rows
- Moving columns or rows
- Adding or deleting columns or rows
- Clearing cell contents

CHANGING TEXT ATTRIBUTES

Attributes of table-cell text can be changed by individual cell, by groups of adjacent cells—including columns and rows—or for the table as a whole. In all cases, the editing commands are the same; which part of the table will be affected depends on the text selection you make before you perform an editing command.

Selecting Items within a Table

Here are the procedures for selecting different items in a table for editing:

Selecting the Whole Table

To select the table as a whole so that you can make changes to all the text it contains, click on the table once. Handles will appear at its edges.

Selecting and Editing Cell Data

To edit the character data in a cell, first select the whole table by clicking on it once. Then, click on the cell you want to edit. A thick, colored border will surround the table, indicating that you are in text-editing mode. The pointer will change to an I-beam cursor. To move the insertion point (vertical-bar cursor), place the I-beam cursor on the point of insertion and click. Or, move the insertion point with the arrow keys. When you type, your changes will be inserted to the right of the vertical-bar cursor. You can also press the Ins key to toggle Typeover mode. Just as in other types of text blocks, you can drag the I-beam cursor over a string to highlight it before you type a replacement string.

Selecting a Cell or a Group of Cells

To edit an individual cell, first select the entire table in text-entry mode. That is, click once on the table, then click again inside the cell you want to edit. Text-entry mode is indicated by a thick, colored border and handles surrounding the table.

To select a single cell, drag the I-beam cursor over it and just past one of its edges. The entire cell should become highlighted in reverse color.

To select a group of adjacent cells, continue dragging until all the cells are highlighted.

To select a row or column, drag from the first to the last cell until all are highlighted.

Controlling Text Attributes in a Table

To reset attributes for part of a table, first make a selection as just described. The extent of the selection will determine the cells to be affected. Then, do one of the following:

- Select Style➤Attributes (Table).
- Click the right mouse button and select Attributes from the pop-up menu.

To reset attributes for the entire table, you can:

- Without making a selection first, double-click on the table.
- With the table selected, click on the Table tool in the toolbox. The Table Choices dialog box will appear. Select Change Attributes, then OK.

When you take any of these actions for part or all of a table, the Table Attributes dialog box will open, as shown in Figure 6-22.

Note that the dialog box has two main sections, labeled 1 and 2. This is actually three dialog boxes in one. The choice you make in

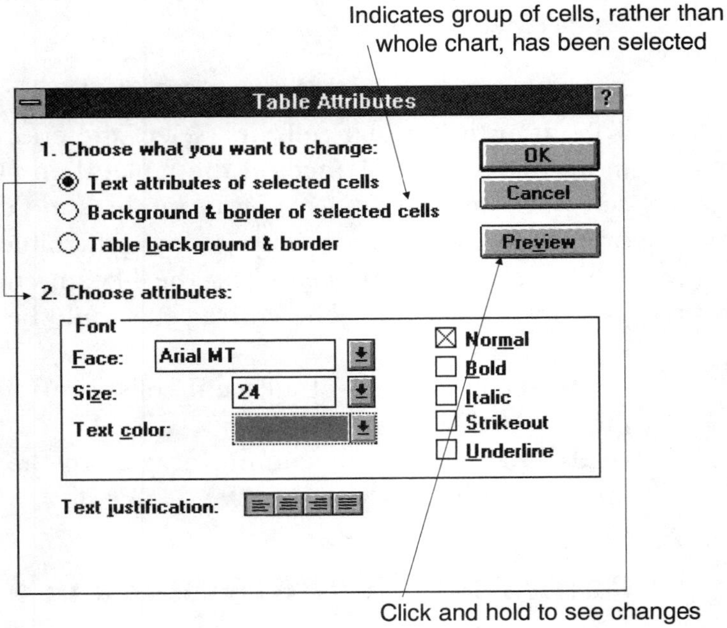

Indicates group of cells, rather than whole chart, has been selected

Click and hold to see changes

FIGURE 6-22. Section 2 of this dialog box will change, depending on your choice in section 1. Shown here are text attributes, which can apply to the whole table or to selected cells, depending on the current selection.

section 1 will cause the set of options displayed in section 2 to change. The default display allows you to change text attributes. If you have selected the whole chart, the option button will be labeled Text Attributes. If you have selected one or more cells, the option will be Text Attributes of Selected Cells.

With the Text Attributes option button selected, section 2 of this dialog box has the usual settings for text: Face, Size (increments from 8 to 72, or type in a value), Text Color (make a selection from the current palette), and Normal style or any combination of Bold, Italic, Strikeout, and Underline.

Just beneath these choices are four buttons that control text justification: Left, Center, Right, and Both Left and Right. *This setting is very important to the correct composition of your table.* By default, the program justifies alphabetic data left and numeric data right with respect to cell boundaries. However, the default justification might not be appropriate in some cases. If you have selected a cell or group of cells, this is the only place where you can change the justification for those cells.

TIP *Freelance Graphics for Windows Release 2 has no facility for aligning numeric table data vertically on the decimal point. Therefore, to align numeric data properly, make sure that each value in a column has the same number of decimal places. For best results, you might use a monospace (nonproportional) font, such as LetterGothic or Courier.*

Changing Borders and Backgrounds

In the Table Attributes dialog box, you also can reset the color and pattern of the background. In addition, you can set the color and line style of the border of selected cells, the border of the whole table, or the borders of both.

The second option button in section 1 of the dialog box controls the appearance of cells. If you have selected the whole chart, the option is labeled Cell Background & Borders. This setting will

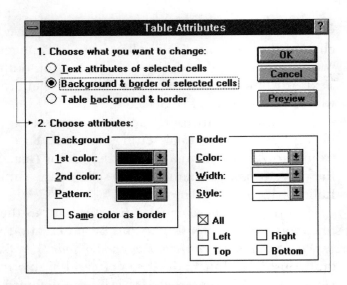

FIGURE 6-23.　These options control cell appearance.

override all selections made from among the Table Background & Border options, except Shadow. If you have selected a cell or group of cells, the option is Background & Borders of Selected Cells. The rest of the table will conform to your selections for cell or table background and borders.

When you select this second option button, the display in section 2 of the dialog box changes as shown in Figure 6-23. These attributes are the same as the Area and Edge selections for rectangles and other filled objects. If the pattern chosen for the background is solid, only the 1st Color selection will be used to fill the selected cells. For any other pattern, the 2nd Color selection is alternated with the first to produce the patterned effect. If the check box Same Color as Border is marked, all the Background settings are ignored, and the border color will fill the cell.

Cell-border options are Color, Width, and Style, and refer to the grid lines within the table. Additionally, you can specify which edges of the cell will be bordered by selecting All, Left, Right, Top, or Bottom. (Some boxes may be marked in solid gray here, indicating

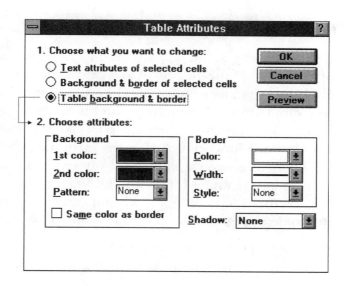

FIGURE 6-24.   These options apply to the appearance of the whole table even if group of cells has been selected.

options that do not match the grid style you selected in the Table Gallery. You can, however, reset them if you wish.)

The third option in section 1 of the dialog box refers to the background and border of the whole table, regardless of the current selection. When you select this option button, the display in section 2 changes as shown in Figure 6-24. The Background and Border options are the same as those for cells, with the addition of Shadow position. This lets you specify a drop shadow that will be offset from the table boundaries at the bottom right, bottom left, top right, or top left. If you select None, no shadow will be shown.

To preview any of your changes in the drawing area, click and hold on the Preview button in this dialog box. When you release the button, the dialog box will reappear.

When you are satisfied with your changes, select OK to close the dialog box.

RESIZING COLUMNS OR ROWS

If you are using a mouse, perhaps the easiest way to adjust the width of columns or the height of rows involves dragging cell borders. Click on the table to select it. Place the pointer on the cell border you want to move. When the pointer is correctly positioned over the border, its shape should change to a two-way arrow. Drag the border in either direction indicated by the arrow tips.

There are several command alternatives that permit you to enter numeric values for width and height. With the table selected in text-entry mode, drag the I-beam cursor to select the column or row to be changed. Then, do one of the following:

- Select Chart≻Table≻Size Column-Row
- Click the right mouse button and select Size Column-Row

In either case, the Size Column/Row dialog box will appear, as shown in Figure 6-25. You can enter numeric values here for the Row Height, Column Width, Row Spacing, and Column Spacing settings. Values are expressed in the units selected in View≻Units & Grids. You can change the unit by clicking on the button that is

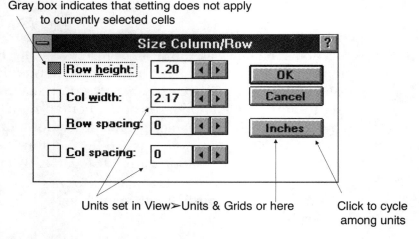

Gray box indicates that setting does not apply
to currently selected cells

Units set in View≻Units & Grids or here   Click to cycle
among units

FIGURE 6-25.   The Size Column/Row dialog box permits you to adjust width and
height by specifying new numeric values.

labeled with the current unit; each time you select this button, its
label will show a new unit. These include points, picas, millimeters,
centimeters, and inches. The numeric settings will be converted to
whichever unit appears as the button label.

If the selection includes rows or columns of different dimensions, the corresponding check box will be gray and the size of the
first column or row (starting at the top left of the table) will be
shown.

MOVING COLUMNS OR ROWS

To move a column or row, as well as its text entries, select it and do
one of the following:

- Select Chart➤Table➤Move Column-Row.
- Click the right mouse button and select Move Column-Row
  from the pop-up menu.
- Click on the Table tool in the toolbar. Then, select Move a
  Column or Row in the Table Choices dialog box and select
  OK.

The Move Column/Row dialog box will appear. Choose whether you will move a column or a row. For its new position, select
either Move the Selected Columns One Column Left or Move the
Selected Columns One Column Right. Then select OK to close the
dialog box.

ADDING OR DELETING COLUMNS OR ROWS

To add, or insert, a column or row to a table, select the table and a
cell in an adjacent column or row. Then, do one of the following:

- Select Chart➤Table➤Insert Column-Row.
- Click the right mouse button and select Insert Column-Row
  from the pop-up menu.

- Click on the Table tool in the toolbar. Then, select Insert a Column or Row in the Table Choices dialog box and select OK.

- Click on either the Insert a Column or Insert a Row icon:

The Insert Column/Row dialog box will appear, as shown in Figure 6-26. Choose whether you want to insert a column or a row. Select whether the new position will be before (left or above) or after (right or below) the currently selected cell. Enter the number of columns or rows to be added, and select OK.

Deletion of a column or row works much the same way. The menu command is Chart>Table>Delete Column-Row, and you have the same alternative ways of selecting it, including the Delete Column and Delete Row icons:

The Delete Column/Row dialog box will appear, and you must choose whether the current column or row will be removed. Then, select OK.

To delete an entire table, select it and press the Delete key. Or, select it, click on the Table tool, select Delete Entire Table, then select OK. The entire table chart and its contents will be removed.

CLEARING CELL CONTENTS

To delete the character data within a cell, select it and perform Edit>Clear or press the Delete key.

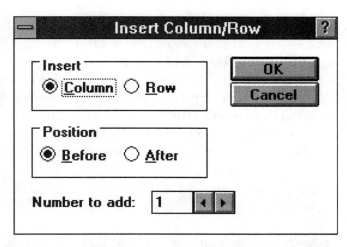

FIGURE 6-26. The Insert Column/Row dialog box is used to make additions to the number of columns or rows in a table.

CHANGING THE GRID STYLE

You can change the grid style of an existing table. Select the table and do one of the following:

- Select Chart➤Gallery.
- Click the right mouse button and select Gallery from the pop-up menu.
- Click on the Table tool in the toolbar. Then, select Change Table Style in the Table Choices dialog box and select OK.

The Table Gallery dialog box will open. Click on the button that shows the grid style you want, then select OK.

CREATING A TABLE AS A NUMBER GRID

If the body of your table contains only numbers (possibly with labels as column and row headings), you can use a different technique to create it. In the New Page dialog box, select 1 Chart (or any of the multiple-chart layouts). When the page layout appears in the drawing area, click on the area "Click here to create a chart." The New

Chart Gallery will open. Select the Number Grid button, choose one of the grid styles shown, and select OK.

The Chart Data & Titles window will open. This is the same input form used for other types of data charts. The form is laid out like a spreadsheet, and the arrangement of table data will match the columns and rows of the finished chart. Enter the labels for column headings in the row labeled Columns, and enter the labels for row headings in the column labeled Rows. Each of the numeric cells is designated by the letter of its column and the number of its row, such as A1. Remember that the program will not accept alphabetic data in these cells.

TIP   *Create a table as a number grid if you might want to convert it to a graph later. In Freelance Graphics for Windows, this can be done simply by choosing Chart➤ Gallery and selecting a different chart type in the Chart Gallery dialog box.*

There's more information on the use of the Chart Data & Titles window in Chapter 7.

PASTING TEXT AS A TABLE FROM ANOTHER APPLICATION

In some cases, you may want to create a presentation page from an existing table that you have built in a spreadsheet or word-processing application. If the application supports the Table data type of the Windows Clipboard, you should be able to pass the table directly into Freelance Graphics.

Select the table in the source application and perform Edit➤ Copy. Switch to Freelance Graphics, create or open a page in the Current Page view, and select Edit➤Paste Special. If the data have been copied as a table, Table Options will appear in the Paste Special dialog box. Choose the Table (Formatted) data type, then select Paste. The table should appear on your presentation page.

Select and center text in cells

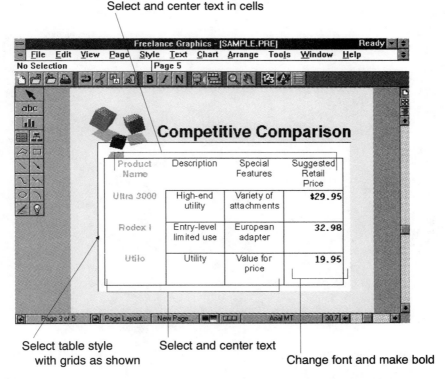

Select table style
with grids as shown

Select and center text

Change font and make bold

FIGURE 6-27. As an exercise, create this table. Then, select the third column and change its justification to Center. Select the fourth column and change the font to LetterGothic, Bold style.

EXERCISE: CREATE A TABLE CHART

Follow the procedures under "Creating a Table Chart" to make the table shown in Black-and-White mode in Figure 6-27. First, add a page to the SAMPLE.PRE presentation used in the tutorial in this chapter. Then, see "Controlling Text Attributes in a Table" to change the appearance of the table. Make sure to reset the Justification to Center for those cells that contain alphabetic labels. Select the bottom three cells in the fourth column and change the face to LetterGothic, in Bold style. (Be sure to save your work.)

BUILDING X-Y DATA CHARTS
AND NUMBER GRIDS

F reelance Graphics for Windows provides a wide variety of formats for plotting data in graphs. Most of these formats, or chart types, are X-Y data charts. These are plotted against perpendicular *x* and *y* axes, in either vertical or horizontal chart orientation. Data sets, or data series, can be plotted as any combination of bars, lines, regression curves, areas, or points. They can be plotted in a variety of styles, including three-dimensional.

Creating X-Y data charts and exploring their many options is the subject of this chapter. Data charts that do not have perpendicular axes—pie and radar charts—are covered in Chapter 8.

Although most of the X-Y plotting styles can be intermixed on the same chart, the SmartMaster sets of Freelance Graphics have separate page layouts for:

- Bar
- Stacked Bar
- Horizontal Bar
- Horizontal Stacked Bar
- Line
- Bar-Line
- High-Low-Close-Open (HLCO)

- Area
- XY (Scatter)
- Number Grid
- 3D Bar
- 3D Stacked Bar
- 3D Bar (XYZ)
- 3D Area-Line

Applications of these chart types include the following:

- Bars might be used to separate the results of different time periods or to show performance by different entities.
- Line plots can show continuous change, particularly over time.
- Use an area chart to emphasize continuous change with emphasis on volume.
- Point charts, or scatter charts, can show the clustering of discrete data points that have been gathered through experiments or statistical surveys.
- Use high-low-close-open (HLCO) charts to show the results of financial trading or to present empirical results that include error bars.
- Number grids are tables of data values arranged in columns and rows. Typically, the top row and the first column contain labels and the rest of the chart is numeric. Number grids can be used as tables of values to accompany graphs or as standalone table charts in which spreadsheet-style number formats can be displayed.

X-Y GRAPHING CONCEPTS

As background for working with various types of X-Y charts, you should be familiar with the following concepts:

- Orientation of axes
- Data sets
- Data typing
- Cumulative data
- Dual *y* axes

Some of these Freelance Graphics features work differently from what you might expect or from what you've learned elsewhere about graphs.

Orientation of Axes

As discussed in Chapter 2, perhaps the most common and readily understood X-Y graph format shows the progress of time along a horizontal *x* axis and changes in magnitude along a vertical *y* axis, although Freelance Graphics offers a much wider range of options.

When getting acquainted with the X-Y charting format, visualize the plotting area in *vertical chart orientation,* or with the *x* axis running horizontally and the *y* axis vertically (Figure 7-1). The origin of the chart is assumed to be in the lower-left corner. This will usually be the point $x=0, y=0$ unless you specify different starting points for the axes.

Although you won't find this terminology in Freelance Graphics, it is sometimes convenient to refer to boundaries of the plotting area this way: The origin is the point of minimum *x* and minimum *y*, or x_{min}, y_{min}. The greatest values on each axis are x_{max} and y_{max}.

In horizontal chart orientation, which is an option built in to some chart types, the *x* and *y* axes are transposed so that the *x* axis runs vertically on the left side of the plotting area (Figure 7-2). Only special types of charts use horizontal plotting, however, and you should avoid it unless you need one of these special types, as when plotting time spans (durations) in a schedule chart.

Whether the chart orientation is vertical or horizontal, the *y* axis is always numeric, with values that are *continuously variable.* By contrast, the *x* axis can include discrete as well as variable data.

VERTICAL PLOTTING
Y Axis Runs Vertically

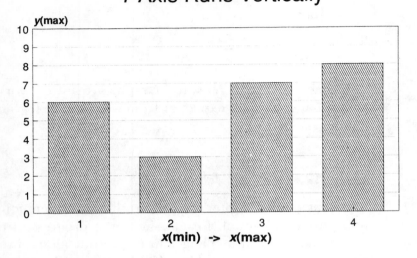

FIGURE 7-1. Vertical chart orientation

When you're starting out with Freelance Graphics, there can be a tendency to confuse vertical and horizontal chart orientation with portrait (vertical) and landscape (horizontal) orientation for output. The two types of orientation are independent of one another. To keep the charting formats straight, think about whether the bars in a bar chart would be vertical or horizontal. For output orientation, think of a piece of letter paper: With a long vertical dimension, it is in portrait format; turned on its side with a long horizontal dimension, it is in landscape format.

Data Sets

Each data set on an X-Y graph is a sequence of *pairs* of data points, an *x*-axis value and a *y* value. For any X-Y chart type (except scatter)—whether in vertical or horizontal orientation—all data sets share the same set of labeled *x*-axis scale divisions, which are set off in equal increments. When you enter a series of numbers to be plotted, you are entering only the *y* values. But remember that each data

HORIZONTAL PLOTTING
Y Axis Runs Horizontally

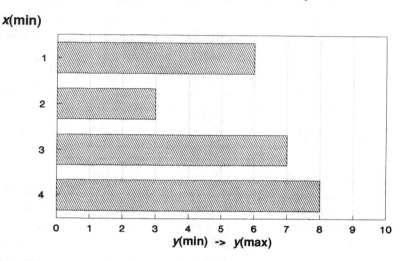

FIGURE 7-2. Horizontal chart orientation

point on the graph has two coordinates: its labeled division on the *x* axis, which it shares with other data sets, and its *y* value. If no *x* labels are entered, the graph is plotted with one unlabeled *x*-axis division for each *y* value entered.

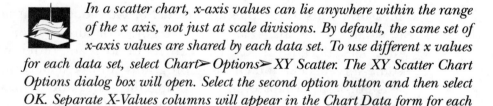 *In a scatter chart, x-axis values can lie anywhere within the range of the x axis, not just at scale divisions. By default, the same set of x-axis values are shared by each data set. To use different x values for each data set, select Chart➤ Options➤ XY Scatter. The XY Scatter Chart Options dialog box will open. Select the second option button and then select OK. Separate X-Values columns will appear in the Chart Data form for each data set.*

In a bar chart, each data set is plotted as one bar for each *division,* or major increment, on the *x* axis. For clarity, all bars in a set are given the same color or pattern. In a line chart, the data points in a set are connected by a continuous line. If the chart shows multiple data sets, each line will have a different color, width, line style, or marker for data points, or any combination of these features.

In Freelance Graphics, plotting styles can be intermixed. For example, bars and lines might be used on the same chart. One use for such a chart would be to show a primary data set as a series of bars and a line to show a related trend.

On plots with multiple data sets, the color/pattern coding is shown in a key, or legend. Freelance Graphics can do this automatically for X-Y charts, and you can specify the labels and position of the legend on the chart.

Data Typing

In computer terminology, particularly in spreadsheet and database applications, *data type* refers to particular formats of data entries. Data types can include labels (text, or alphabetic data), numbers (as integers, decimals, or scientific notation), currency amounts, calendar dates, clock time, and so on.

Some computer programs *enforce* data typing. That is, for fields that have been designated for specific data types, the program will reject entries of other types. For example, a program might reject entry of text into a field that is supposed to hold numeric data.

In conventional charting, the *x data type* usually corresponds to the units in which *x* data are expressed or to the intervals at which measurements or samples are taken. So, *x*-axis data might be calendar dates, time spans, labels of categories or different entities, or numbers. Because *x*-axis data can be of so many different types, some spreadsheet and charting programs enforce data typing for *x*-axis entries, perhaps even generating the series automatically. For example, a spreadsheet program might be able to generate a series of calendar dates based on the first and last date and an increment, or based on the first two dates and the number of items in the series.

Data Typing in Freelance Graphics

Freelance Graphics for Windows Release 2 does enforce data typing, but in a limited way. For all chart types except XY (scatter), the program follows a simple rule:

x-axis data are labels; *y* data must be numeric values

In a scatter chart, both *x* and *y* values must be numeric.

The program therefore places no restrictions on *x*-axis labels: Any characters you enter will be shown as a label. The program will reject nonnumeric entries for any of the data sets; however, if any *y* entry includes an alphabetic character, it will not be accepted.

This means that if you enter numeric values for the *x* axis, they will be treated as text labels on evenly spaced divisions of the axis—not as numeric point coordinates. The difference is shown in Figure 7-3. Freelance Graphics does not place any other requirements on *x*-axis data that you enter.

However, the program can generate calendar data automatically for the *x* axis. See "Generating Calendar Data" later in this chapter.

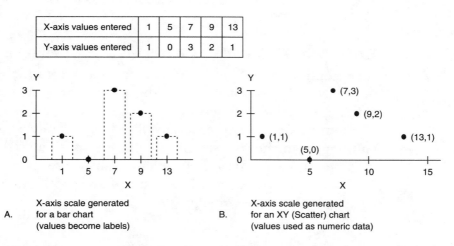

X-axis values entered	1	5	7	9	13
Y-axis values entered	1	0	3	2	1

A. X-axis scale generated
    for a bar chart
    (values become labels)

B. X-axis scale generated
    for an XY (Scatter) chart
    (values used as numeric data)

FIGURE 7-3. Differences between *x*-axis plotting of A. Bar charts and B. XY (Scatter) charts

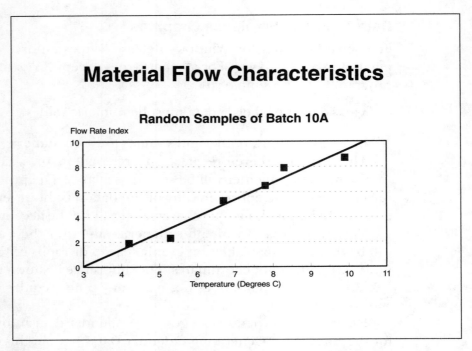

FIGURE 7-4.   This example shows the plotting of data values on an XY (Scatter) chart.

Exception: XY (Scatter) Charts

An exception to the rule is XY (Scatter) charts, for which x and y values must *both* be numeric. Also, the x axis is generated differently: You can enter any numeric values for x, which need not be incremented uniformly. The program will then generate an x-axis scale, running from the lowest to the highest values entered, with even divisions. Data points can be plotted anywhere along the either axis—not just at x-axis divisions—depending on the values entered. An example is shown in Figure 7-4.

Cumulative Data

In Freelance Graphics, data can be plotted only as *absolute,* not as *cumulative,* values. That is, actual data values are plotted independently of one another. The program will not generate cumulative totals *within* a given data set (as in Figure 7-5). But data that are cumulative *among* series can be plotted in one of the stacked styles, as shown in the figure's bottom chart. (This topic is covered in greater depth in Chapter 2.)

If you need to plot cumulative data, you might generate the values in a Windows spreadsheet program, then paste them through the Clipboard into Freelance Graphics.

Dual Y Axes

Another topic covered in Chapter 2 is dual y axes. Data sets that differ widely in range or that are measured in incompatible units can be plotted against separate y axes. In vertical orientation, the y_1 axis is on the left side and the y_2 axis is on the right side of the plotting area, as shown in Figure 7-6. In horizontal orientation, the y_1 axis runs along the bottom and the y_2 axis is on top.

In Freelance Graphics, the y_1 axis is designated Y, and the y_2 axis is designated 2Y.

Chart legends and color coding of plots with axis labels can help the audience read a graph that has dual y axes. I recommend dual-y plotting in vertical format for comparing and contrasting two trends that are expressed in dissimilar units. However, many viewers will be confused by this technique if there are too many series or if the plot is in horizontal format.

I mention the dual-axis capability here because you won't find any reference to the 2Y axis when you begin to enter data into an X-Y chart in Freelance Graphics. At this point, some users become discouraged and incorrectly assume that dual-axis plotting isn't possible. Rest assured that, if you want to have two y axes, you can go ahead and enter all the data sets even though the units might not be consistent. You select which series will be plotted against the 2Y axis in a later step, as will be explained in this section.

A. # STACKED CUMULATIVE BARS

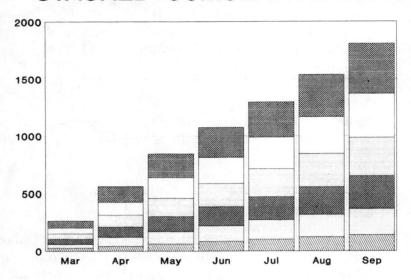

B. # STACKED BARS
Same Data, Not Cumulative

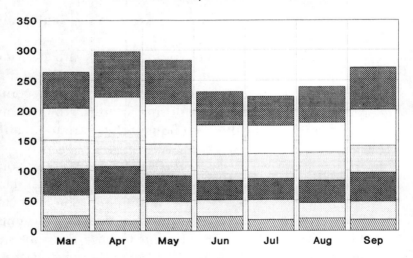

FIGURE 7-5. A. Stacked cumulative bars; B. Stacked noncumulative bars. Note the differences in the *y* scales. (Freelance Graphics will not generate cumulative plots automatically.)

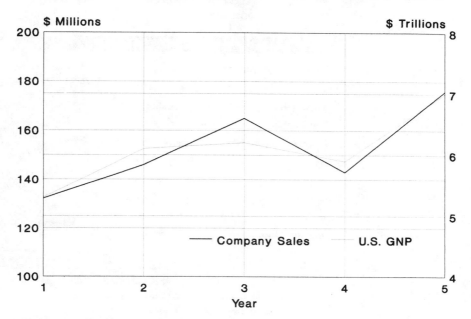

FIGURE 7-6. Dual *y* axes in vertical chart orientation

ENTERING CHART DATA

To create an X-Y chart to a presentation in the Current Page view, select Page➤New (or an equivalent command).

The New Page dialog box will appear. From the list box, select the 1 Chart page layout. (To create a page with multiple charts, select 2 Charts or 4 Charts instead. To create a chart accompanied by a bulleted list, select Bullets & Chart. From the standpoint of data entry, all these layouts work the same.)

The SmartMaster page layout will appear in the drawing area. Click on the area labeled "Click here to create chart."

The New Chart Gallery dialog box will appear, as shown in Figure 7-7. Select the option button that corresponds to the type of X-Y chart you want to create.

Styles shown here
depend on your
chart type selection
in section 1

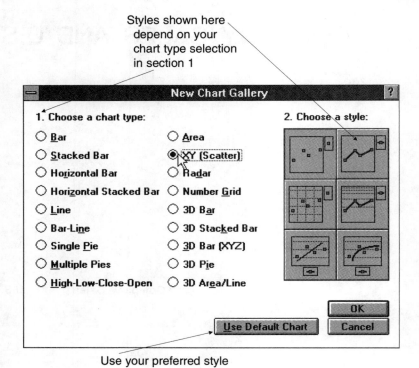

Use your preferred style

FIGURE 7-7.   Select a chart type and a style in the New Chart Gallery dialog box.

*The distinctions among chart types here is largely a matter of con-
venience. Among the X-Y charts (all charts but pie and radar),
you can select any of these chart types and change the plotting style
to make it become one of the other types. You can make the change later by
selecting the chart, choosing Chart➤Gallery, and then making a different
selection from the dialog box.*

Before closing the New Chart Gallery dialog box, select one of
the plotting styles shown as buttons in section 2. Each button shows
a different set of preselected options for styles of legends and grids.

Select OK to close the dialog box. Or, select the Use Default
Chart button to bypass the style selection and close the dialog box.

Select to add or edit headings, notes, or axis titles

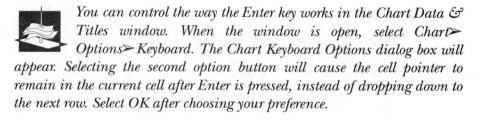

Click and hold to view chart in drawing area

FIGURE 7-8. The Chart Data window is arranged as a spreadsheet-style data-input form.

The Chart Data & Titles window will appear, as shown in Figure 7-8. This is a spreadsheet-style form: Each data-entry cell in the form is identified by the number of its row and the letter of its column.

You can control the way the Enter key works in the Chart Data & Titles window. When the window is open, select Chart▷ Options▷Keyboard. The Chart Keyboard Options dialog box will appear. Selecting the second option button will cause the cell pointer to remain in the current cell after Enter is pressed, instead of dropping down to the next row. Select OK after choosing your preference.

In the data form, each data set corresponds to one of the lettered columns. The first column, Axis Titles, is reserved for x-axis labels. The first two unnumbered rows are reserved for one- or two-line column headings for each data set. If the chart includes a legend, these headings will be shown as its labels.

The current cell, which will receive any entries you type, is highlighted by a box. Click on a cell to move the highlight to it, or use the arrow keys.

As you type chart data into the cells, the entry appears both in the cell and on the Edit line, just above the toolbar. You can edit the entry on the Edit line as you would a text block: Move the insertion point and drag any portion of a string to type its replacement. To accept the entry, click on the Confirm button to the left of the Edit line:

Cancel   Confirm

If you prefer, you can simply click on any other cell or, at the keyboard, press Enter to accept the entry and drop down to the next-lower cell in the column.

To reject an entry, click on the Cancel button to the left of the Edit line, or press Esc.

As an alternative to typing the chart data, select the Import button in this window and specify an external data file. Procedures are covered in Chapter 14.

Generating Calendar Data

When you are working in the Chart Data form, the program can generate a series of calendar dates automatically. Such a date series can be used for either *x*-axis data (first column of the form) or legend labels (first or second rows of the form).

To generate a series of dates, first select the cell in which the series will begin. To generate *x*-axis data, select cell 1 in the Axis Labels column. To generate legend labels, select one of the two cells just beneath the A column heading. After selecting the cell, choose Chart➤Options➤Date Fill. The Chart Options Date Fill dialog box will open. Select a date style from the list box, then enter a start date and an end date in the text boxes. Choose an interval of weekdays, days, weeks, or months. Optionally, mark the Use Fiscal Years check box and specify the first month of the fiscal year. (A fiscal year can be any 12-month accounting period. For example, many corporations keep accounts according to fiscal years beginning each July and ending the next June.)

When you select OK to close the dialog box, the Chart Data window will reappear, with the calendar data filled in.

Entering Chart Titles

When you have entered the chart data, select the Edit Titles button. The display in the Chart Data & Titles window will change to a set of text boxes for chart titles: Headings, Notes, and Axis Titles, as shown in Figure 7-9.

The positions of these headings, notes, and titles are shown in relation to the chart frame in Figure 7-10.

Remember that, unlike the page title, chart titles can be moved and resized with the chart itself. If you do not reposition the chart, headings will appear as subtitles beneath the page title.

To see the chart data in the currently selected style, click and hold on the Preview button in either Chart Data & Titles window. Keep holding the button down as you inspect the change. When you release the mouse button, this window will reappear.

To change the chart type or style, click on the Chart Sample button in the top-left corner of the window:

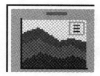

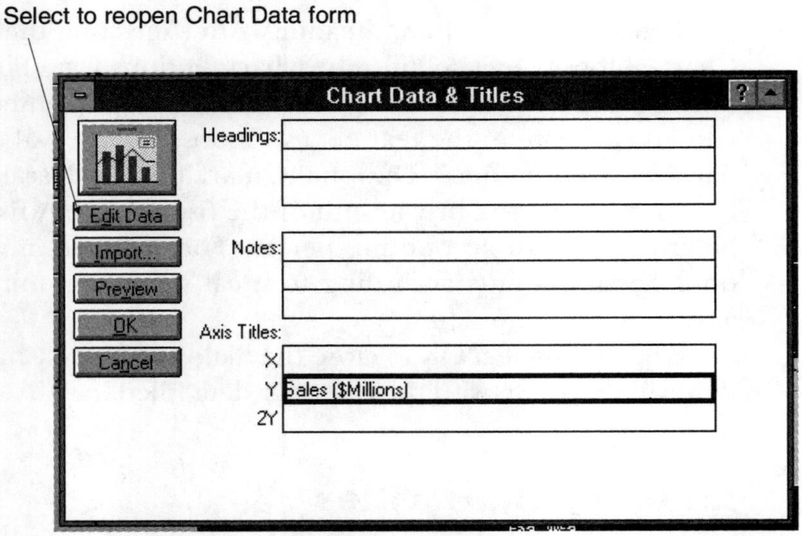

Select to reopen Chart Data form

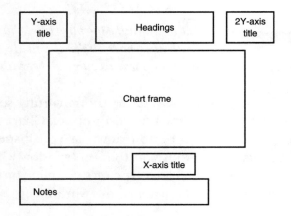

FIGURE 7-9.   Selecting the Edit Titles button in the Chart Data window changes
the display to Chart Titles. (Note that the label on the button
changes to Edit Data.)

FIGURE 7-10.   Location of headings, notes, and titles in relation to the chart frame.

The Chart Gallery dialog box will reopen, and you can make another selection. (The Chart Sample button shows the currently selected chart type, but not necessarily its style.)

When you have entered all the data and titles in the Chart Data & Titles window, select the OK button.

The X-Y chart will appear in the drawing area of the Current Page view. Use menu commands or the drawing tools to annotate or edit the chart.

As a general rule, you can double-click on any chart element, such as a heading or a data plot, to change its attributes. A dialog box will open, showing the options available for the selected element. The options are covered in depth in this chapter.

Number of Data Points

For most types of X-Y charts, the number of columns on the data form is limited to 26, labeled *A* through *Z*. The number of rows is limited to 4,000. (Radar charts can have as many as 36 rows. Pie charts can have up to 16 rows (slices) and 4 columns (pies).) Adjust the scroll bars in the data-entry window to move around the form, as shown in Figure 7-11. You can drag the borders of the window to make it larger. For a still larger view of the form, click its Maximize button (top-right corner).

You will probably not require a large number of rows unless you are importing data from a spreadsheet program or other application that has generated a long number series, as in describing a curve or other continuously variable plot. Remember that x-axis labels will overlap if you enter too many of them. You can improve this situation somewhat by selecting the chart and performing Chart➤Axis Titles & Labels➤Labels➤Adjustments and using Slant, Stagger, or Shrink for the labels. (For this feature to work, labels have to be long enough to require adjustment.) If there are a great many divisions, you can also specify a numeric skip factor, placing a label at every nth division.

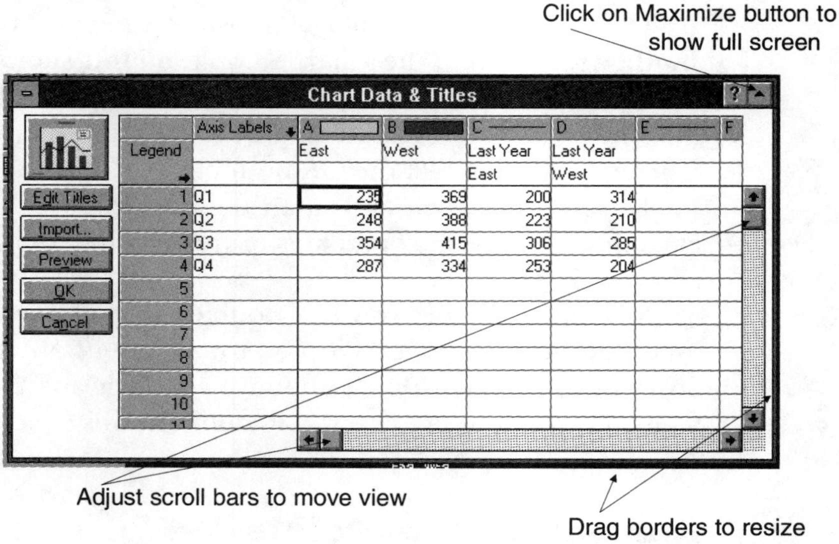

Click on Maximize button to
show full screen

Adjust scroll bars to move view

Drag borders to resize

FIGURE 7-11. Use the controls shown here to adjust the display in the Chart Data
& Titles window.

REOPENING THE CHART DATA & TITLES WINDOW

When you are working on a chart in the Current Page view, the data
and titles input forms can be reopened several different ways for
editing. First click on the chart to select it, then do any of the following:

- Click on the Chart tool in the toolbar.
- Select Chart➤Edit.
- Place the pointer within the chart area, click the right mouse
  button, and select Edit Data and Titles from the pop-up
  menu.
- Select the Edit Data button whenever it appears in a dialog
  box:

Edit Data

Within the Chart Data & Titles window, the Edit Data or Edit Titles button will toggle between the input forms for data and chart titles.

Correcting Editing Mistakes

When you are working in the Chart Data & Titles window, the Edit➤Undo command will be available for canceling as many as 10 previous edits, in reverse order of entry.

Using the Clipboard

Also in this window, the following commands are available for moving data to or from the Windows Clipboard and other applications: Edit➤Cut, Edit➤Copy, and Edit➤Paste. To select a set of items for copying or a portion of the form into which data will be pasted, highlight the range by dragging the pointer from one corner to the opposite corner of the range. (The highlighted range will be shown in reverse color.) Or, to select an entire row or column, click on its lettered or numbered heading. The selected portion of the data form will be shown in reverse color:

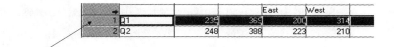

Click here to select whole row

To select all the data in the form, click on the unlabeled box in the top-left corner:

Click here to select all data in form

For more information on exchanging data with other applications, see Chapter 14.

EDITING CHART APPEARANCE

The appearance of an X-Y chart can be changed in the Current Page view by double-clicking the specific element of a chart to be changed. This feature, called *subselection,* permits the selection of bars, grid lines, labels, and other elements of a chart as graphic objects for which attributes can be reset. When you click on the chart to select it, handles surround it. If you click again on a specific element, small hollow handles will surround the element as well. If the element is a text block, such as a heading or axis label, clicking on it one more time will open the block for editing.

Double-clicking on an element will open the dialog box that contains its attributes, such as color or font.

CHART ATTRIBUTES

To change an attribute, such as color, of chart data sets, do any of the following:

- Select the chart and perform Chart➤Attributes.
- Select the chart, click the right mouse button, and select Attributes from the pop-up menu.
- When the chart is displayed in the drawing area, double-click on one of the data-set plots, such as a bar, line, or area.
- When you are working in the Chart Data window, double-click on a lettered column heading.

When you take any of these actions, the Chart Attributes dialog box will open for the corresponding chart type. Options for each type are described below.

Choose data set to which other options will apply
Select for dual *y* plotting

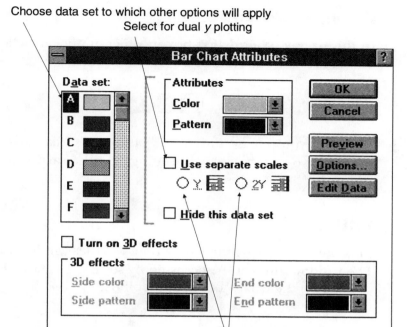

Select scale against which selected
data set will be plotted

FIGURE 7-12.   Change attributes of data sets selectively in the Bar Chart Attributes dialog box.

Options that work much the same for all chart types are as follows. Figure 7-12 shows options for bar charts.

Data Set

Settings in the rest of the dialog box refer only to the currently selected data set (A–Z for most chart types). Adjust the slider to scroll from the list and make a selection. When you have changed the settings for one data set, pick another, then change its settings. When you have made adjustments to all the data sets you want to change, select OK to close the dialog box.

Preview Button

In this or any other dialog box in which it appears, click and hold
on the Preview button to see the revised chart:

> **Preview**

When you release the mouse button, the dialog box will reappear, and you can revise your settings, if necessary, before selecting
OK.

Edit Data

This button reopens the Chart Data & Titles window for the table.
The window also can be accessed by selecting Chart➤Edit Data or
clicking on the Chart tool in the toolbox.

Use Separate Scales

Mark this check box to turn on dual-*y* axes. When you do this, the
option buttons Y and 2Y become available. Select the *y* axis against
which the currently selected data set will be plotted.

*Dual-y plotting is not available for some chart types, including
HLCO.*

Hide This Data Set

Marking this box will suppress the display of the currently selected
data set, but its data will be retained in the Chart Data window.

*Do not use this feature to create buildup sequences (multiple-page
sequences that add chart elements in stages); the chart might be
recomposed each time an element is deleted or added. Instead, set
the color of the data set you want to hide to match the chart background.*

Other dialog boxes use these relative terms
  rather than numeric settings

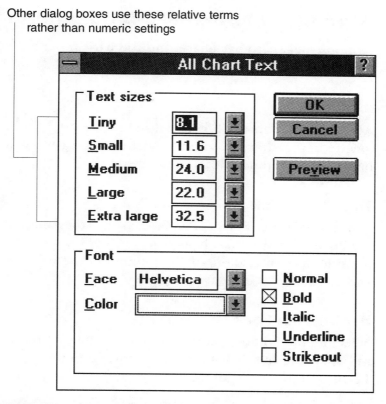

FIGURE 7-13.   Relative text-size options (such as Small) reset numerically here
will be used in other dialog boxes that control chart text.

Global Settings for Chart Text

In various chart-attribute dialog boxes, relative rather than numeric text sizes are used for chart headings and notes, axis titles, and labels of scales and data values. The choices are Tiny, Small, Medium, Large, and Extra Large. You can control the numeric point-size equivalents of these settings by performing Chart➤All Chart Text. The All Chart Text dialog box will open, as shown in Figure 7-13. You can reset each size here, as well as the overall font attributes of chart titles and labels.

Attributes of Bar and 3-D Bar Charts

Options specific to bar charts and the bars in bar-line charts are as follows:

Attributes

Attributes for bars are fill color (make a selection from the current palette) and pattern. A setting of Pattern=None will cause the bar to be shown in outline, with a transparent fill.

Turn On 3-D Effects

Marking this check box for a bar chart has the same result as selecting 3D Bar for the chart type. Select colors from the current palette for side and end colors of three-dimensional bars, as well as side and end patterns, if desired.

Bar Chart Options

Selecting the Options button in the Bar Chart Attributes dialog box will open another dialog box, Bar Chart Options, shown in Figure 7-14. Its options are as follows:

Bar Width   A value from 1 to 100 here specifies bar width as a percentage of its axis division. A setting of 100 will cause the bars to touch one another.

Bar 3-D Effect   A value from 1 to 100 determines the depth of the three-dimensional effect (if selected) as a percentage of bar width.

Bar Angle   A value from 0 to 360 determines the angle of any three-dimensional effect. Zero is at 3 o'clock (or east on a compass), and the setting increases counterclockwise.

Bar Edges   As with rectangles and other filled objects, line color, width, and style can be selected for the bar edges. If the Contrasting Color check box is unmarked, the edge will be the same color as the

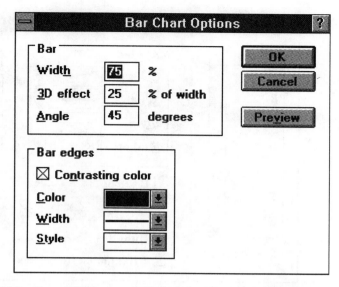

FIGURE 7-14. Reset dimensions of bars in the Bar Chart Options dialog box.

fill (data-set color attribute), and the Color option here will be dimmed.

Comparison Lines For stacked types only, marking the Display check box turns on lines that link data-set segments from one bar to another. You can specify the width and the style of the lines.

Line Chart Attributes

The Line Chart Attributes dialog box is shown in Figure 7-15. Attributes for the line plotted for each data set can be varied by color, width, and style, with an optional marker at each data point.

If the Offset Lines from Frame check box is marked, a gap will appear between the Y- and 2Y-axis lines and the endpoints of the line. If the option is unmarked, the line will begin and end on the *y* axes.

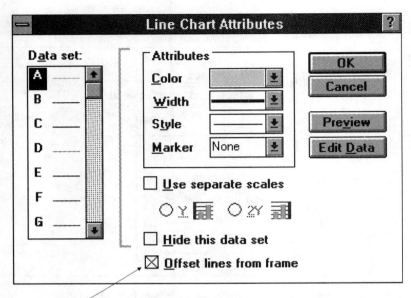

Mark so that line plots do not intersect Y or 2Y axes

FIGURE 7-15. Change the attributes of data sets selectively in the Line Chart Attributes dialog box.

Bar-Line Chart Attributes

If the chart type is bar-line, an additional option appears in the Bar-Line Attributes dialog box:

Option buttons specify whether the selected data set will be displayed as a bar or as a line. Attributes that do not apply to your selection will become dimmed.

Selecting the Options button here opens the Bar-Line Chart Options dialog box, which displays a further choice for bars:

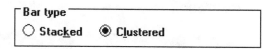

Option buttons here determine whether data sets plotted as bars will be stacked to form a single bar or clustered at each axis division as a set of individual bars.

HLCO Chart Attributes

The high-low-close-open chart type is designed specifically for reporting price fluctuations in financial trading of stocks, bonds, commodities, and so forth. The HLCO Attributes dialog box is shown in Figure 7-16.

HLCO-chart elements are shown in Figure 7-17. Data sets are assigned as follows: High (data set A), Low (data set B), Close (data set C), and Open (data set D). You must enter high and low points for each *x*-axis item (typically a day of the week). Close and open series are optional. The Vert data set specifies the attributes of the line that connects high and low values. Data set E is reserved for volume bars, which will be displayed below the chart. Data sets F–Z can be used for conventional line plots that might show averages, cumulative totals, or other data.

Markers cannot be specified for data sets Vert or A–D. Also, an HLCO chart cannot have a 2Y axis. The separate y axis used for data set E (volume) bars is called the Bottom Y axis.

Appropriate *x*-axis labels for high-low-close-open charts should be calendar data, such as days of the week, dates, or month and day.

HLCO charts can also be used to show empirical data gathered in scientific and statistical studies. The span between high and low data sets is called an error bar *and represents a range of experimental error or reliability. If you use an HLCO chart for this purpose, you might plot the average or net result in data set F as a line plot.*

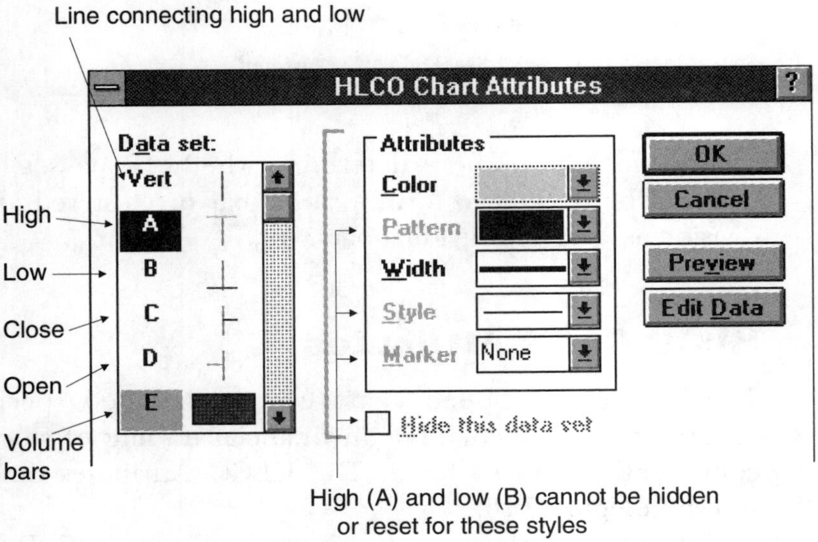

Line connecting high and low

High (A) and low (B) cannot be hidden
or reset for these styles

FIGURE 7-16.   Attributes of high, low, open, close, volume bars, and other data
sets can be changed in this dialog box.

Area Chart Attributes

The Area Chart Attributes dialog box is shown in Figure 7-18. For
data sets A–Z, you can specify the same attributes that apply to filled
polygons: color (of area fill), pattern (if any, of area fill), edge color
(outline), width (of outline), and style (of outline).

   If the Stack Data check box is marked, each data-set area will use
the previous set as its base line, causing the areas to be stacked upon
one another (Figure 7-19a). (See "Cumulative Plotting" in Chapter
2.) If the option is unmarked, all areas will use y_{min} as their base line,
causing the areas to be layered over one another (from back to
front, as shown in Figure 7-19b).

XY (Scatter) Chart Attributes

The XY Scatter Chart Attributes dialog box is shown in Figure 7-20.
Recall that in this chart style, data items are plotted as discrete

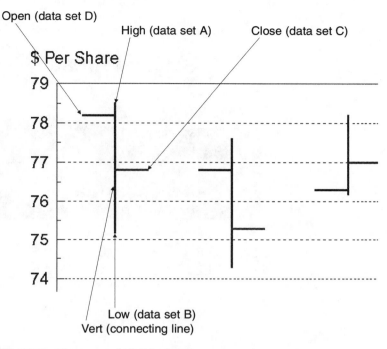

FIGURE 7-17. Elements of HLCO charts

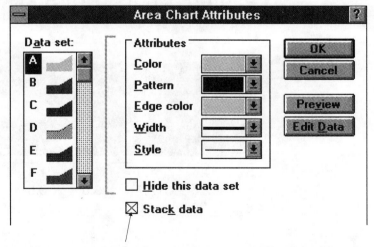

If marked, y_{max} values of prior data set will be used as y_{min} values of next

FIGURE 7-18. Change the attributes of data sets selectively in the Area Chart Attributes dialog box.

A.

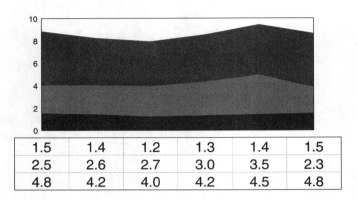

1.5	1.4	1.2	1.3	1.4	1.5
2.5	2.6	2.7	3.0	3.5	2.3
4.8	4.2	4.0	4.2	4.5	4.8

B.

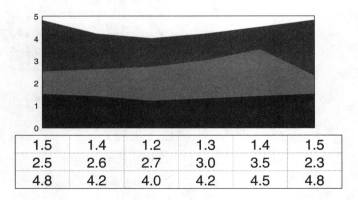

1.5	1.4	1.2	1.3	1.4	1.5
2.5	2.6	2.7	3.0	3.5	2.3
4.8	4.2	4.0	4.2	4.5	4.8

FIGURE 7-19. Plotting options for Area charts: A. Stacked areas and B. Layered (not stacked) areas. Notice the different *y*-axis scales.

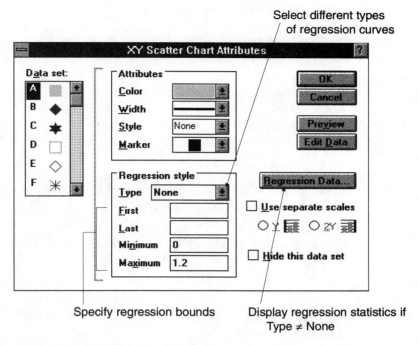

Select different types
of regression curves

Specify regression bounds

Display regression statistics if
Type ≠ None

FIGURE 7-20. Change the attributes of data sets selectively in the XY Scatter
Attributes dialog box.

points, not necessarily at *x*-axis divisions. For each data set, points can be displayed with a different marker symbol. Style and Width settings refer to an optional line that will link the points. No line will be generated if Style=None.

Another option for each data set will cause the program to generate various types of regression curves based on the data points. A regression shows a pattern in the data. Mathematical formulas used for each type of regression are shown in Table 7-1. The program generates values for *a* and *b* and substitutes them in the formulas along with the *x,y* values in the chart data.

In the Regression Style box, you can specify the regression type as Linear, Exponential, Logarithmic, or Power. You can also enter the first and last numeric values to be used in the regression calculation, as well as its bounds: Data points outside of minimum and

TABLE 7-1. Regression Formulas

Regression Type	*Formula*
Linear	$y = a + bx$
Exponential	$y = ae^{bx}$
Logarithmic	$y = a + b\,(\ln x)$
Power	$y = ax^b \quad a > 0$

maximum values will be excluded from the calculation. If Type=None, no curves will be generated.

If you have specified one of the regression styles, you can select the Regression Data button to display statistics that the program has calculated. These include R Square (the result of multiplying the *correlation coefficient,* by itself)—the selected mathematical relationship between the x and y values—a and b (the component values of the regression), and Number of Points (the number of nonblank data items used in the regression calculation).

3-D Chart Attributes

If the chart type is 3-D Area/Line, the 3-D Area/Line Chart Attributes box has the additional option Type, by which each data set can be made either a dimensional area or line:

Selecting the Options button opens another dialog box that contains settings for edges (Color, Width, and Style) as well as for objects. Depending on the chart type, Object settings are as follows (Figure 7-21).

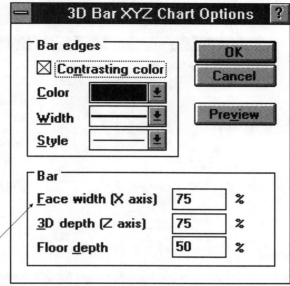

This option will not appear for 3D Area/Line

FIGURE 7-21. These additional choices will appear in the Options dialog boxes for 3-D chart types.

Face Width (X Axis)

For 3-D Bar (XYZ) charts only, you can specify the width of bars as a percentage (1–100) of x-axis divisions.

3-D Depth (Z Axis)

For 3-D Bar (XYZ) or 3-D Area/Line charts, this setting controls the apparent depth of the 3-D effect (sides of the object) as a percentage (1–100) of z-axis divisions.

Floor Depth

For 3-D Bar (XYZ) or 3-D Area/Line charts, this setting controls the apparent depth of the plotting area (z-axis dimension) as a percentage (1–100) of the available space. Varying this setting also adjusts the height of the wall (usually the y axis), so that the total of the

These options will appear for 3D Bar (XYZ) only

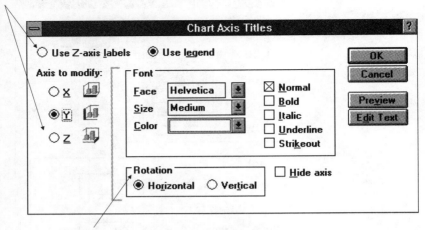

Applies to *y*- and 2Y-axis titles only

FIGURE 7-22.   Control positioning and attributes of axis titles in the Chart Axis Titles dialog box.

floor depth and the wall height is always 100 percent. That is, increasing the floor depth decreases the wall height, and vice versa.

AXIS TITLES

For any X-Y chart type, selecting the chart and then performing Chart➤Axis Titles & Labels➤Titles will open the Chart Axis Titles dialog box, shown in Figure 7-22. Axis titles are entered in the Chart Titles window (open the Chart Data window and select the Edit Titles button.)

The dialog box will also open if you double-click on an axis title in the drawing area.

For each axis—*x*, *y*, or 2Y (if used)—you can specify font options for its title. (Font sizes are relative; set numeric point sizes in Chart➤All Chart Text.)

For *y* or 2Y axes only, you can specify rotation as horizontal or vertical:

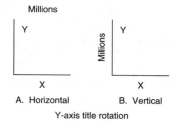

Y-axis title rotation

You can mark the check box Hide Title to suppress the display of the axis title, while retaining the entry in the Chart Titles window.

AXIS LABELS

For any X-Y chart type, selecting the chart and then performing Chart➤Axis Titles & Labels➤Labels will open the Chart Axis Labels dialog box, shown in Figure 7-23. (*X*-axis labels are entered in the first column of the Chart Data window and identify divisions of the *x* axis. *Y*-axis labels identify numeric scale divisions.)

These options will appear for 3D Bar (XYZ) only

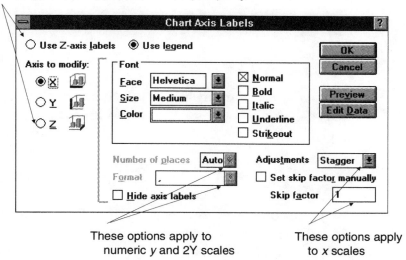

These options apply to numeric *y* and 2Y scales

These options apply to *x* scales

FIGURE 7-23. Control positioning and attributes of scale labels in the Chart Axis Labels dialog box.

The dialog box will also open if you double-click on axis labels in the drawing area.

For each axis—*x, y,* or 2Y (if used)—you can specify font options for its labels. (For this purpose, font sizes are relative; set numeric point sizes in Chart➢All Chart Text.)

Adjustments

If the *x* axis is crowded with too many labels, you can set the Adjustments option to Slant, Stagger, or Shrink:

$$S_{L_{A_{N_T}}} \qquad \text{STAGGER} \qquad \text{STAGGER} \qquad \text{SHRINK}$$
$$\text{STAGGER}$$

Skip Factor

By default, the program will determine the number of *x*-axis increments at which labels will appear. To set this manually, mark the Set Skip Factor Manually check box, and enter a whole number *n* as a skip factor, which will generate a label at every *n*th increment of the *x* axis.

Number of Places

For *y* axes only, you can specify the Number of Places (1–5) for decimal-valued labels (or select Auto to accept the program's default labels).

Format

For *y* axes only, you can specify various spreadsheet-style numeric display formats: Fixed, Scientific, Currency, Comma, General, Percent, or X Suffix. (For more information, see the "Format" subsection in the discussion of number grids later in this chapter.)

Format options determine how values entered in the Chart Data window are interpreted and displayed on the chart. But the values shown in the data form will remain the same.

Hide Axis Labels

For any axis, you can mark this check box to suppress the display of its labels, while retaining the entries in the Chart Data window.

SCALING THE Y AXES

Normally, the program will generate the starting and ending values of the *y* axes (Y or 2Y) based on the lowest and highest data values you enter. To change this default scaling, select the chart and perform Chart➤Scale. The Chart Scale dialog box will open, as shown in Figure 7-24.

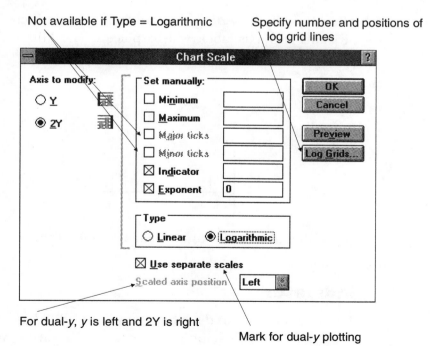

FIGURE 7-24. Control scaling of axes, including starting and ending values, in the Chart Scale dialog box.

If you have not already specified dual-*y* axes and wish to do so, mark the check box Use Separate Scales. The 2Y option button will become available, and you can make changes to either axis depending on the button you select.

The Set Manually box holds numeric entries for various scale parameters. Parameters that have been generated by the program are shown as defaults. Mark the boxes of options for which you will enter new values.

Minimum and Maximum Scale Values

You can reset the minimum (starting) and maximum (ending) values to adjust the range of values spanned by the scale.

Major and Minor Ticks

The Major Ticks setting determines the scale increment at which divisions and axis labels will be placed. The Minor Ticks setting is for fractional increment markings within divisions:

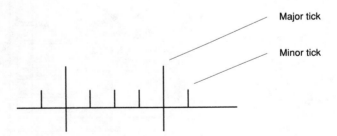

By default, the minor increment is half of the major.

Indicator

This text box can hold a label that will be added as a second line to the axis title. For example, the axis title might be SALES and the indicator might be MILLIONS OF UNITS. The axis label would appear as:

SALES
MILLIONS OF UNITS

Exponent

This parameter is also called a *scaling factor.* Enter a whole-number power of 10 by which scale labels must be multiplied to yield the actual data values. For example, if you enter 2 and the scale label is 5, a data point with a *y* value of 5 will be interpreted as 500 (5×10^2). Note that the default value is 0, not 1, because $10^0 = 1$.

Type

You can specify that the scale will be linear (the default) or logarithmic (division by powers of 10). See "Notes on Logarithmic Plotting" in this chapter for more information.

If you choose the Logarithmic option, the Log Grids button becomes available for specifying grid attributes.

Log Grids

When you specify logarithmic scaling and select the Log Grids button, the Log Grids dialog box will open, as shown in Figure 7-25.

You can specify the Number of Grid Lines (1–20) that will be generated for scale divisions (at major ticks). If the Set Grid Manually check box is marked, you can enter a numeric value at which each of the grid lines will appear. Values can range from –1.0E+99 to 1.0E+99 (-1.0×10^{99} to 1.0×10^{99}).

If you set a logarithmic scale manually, the automatic Major Ticks and Minor Ticks options will be unavailable. For tips on using semi-log and log-log scales, see "Notes on Logarithmic Plotting" in this chapter.

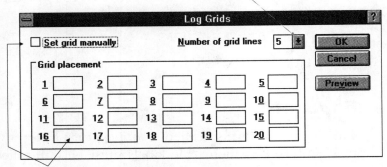

Select 1–20 lines

Enter values in scientific notation (1.5E+05) here
only if check box is marked

FIGURE 7-25. Control the number and position of logarithmic grid lines here.

Scaled Axis Position

If only one y axis is used, the Scaled Axis Position option can be set to Left, Right, or Both (for vertical orientation); or Bottom, Top, or Both (for horizontal orientation).

If separate scales (Y and 2Y) are used, Y is on the left (or bottom) and 2Y is on the right (or top).

GRIDS

Selecting a chart in the drawing area and performing Chart➤Grid will open the Chart Grid dialog box, shown in Figure 7-26. Separate settings can be made for each axis: X, Y, or 2Y (if used).

Marking check boxes here turns on display of grids, ticks, or both at major and minor increments of the scale. Grid lines can be shown in selected color, width, and line style.

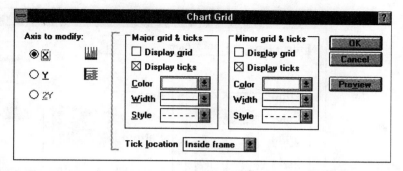

FIGURE 7-26.   Adjust the attributes of major and minor grids and ticks in the Chart Grid dialog box.

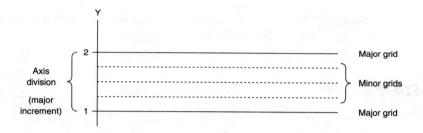

Tick location can be inside the frame, outside the frame, or across the frame:

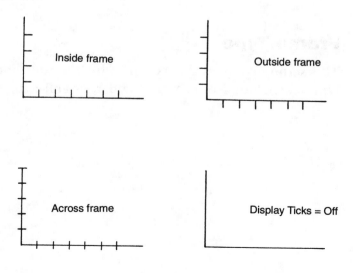

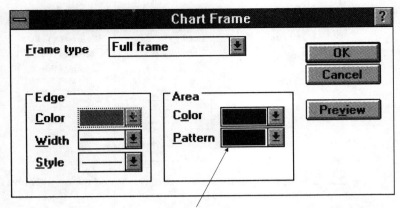

Frame will not be filled if Pattern = None

FIGURE 7-27. In this dialog box, you can control the attributes of the rectangle bounded by the chart axes.

FRAME

Selecting a chart in the drawing area and performing Chart⊳ Frame will open the Chart Frame dialog box, shown in Figure 7-27. (It will also open if you double-click on the chart frame.)

Frame Type

This setting controls the axes on which border lines will be drawn. Options include None, X, Y, X and Y, or Full Frame:

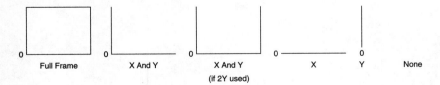

Edge and Area

As you can for any rectangle, you can specify a color, width, and line style for the edge (frame outline), and a color, pattern, or both for the area (fill).

 To see the Edge or Area attributes in the chart, the Style or Pattern settings must be something other than None.

CHART BACKGROUND

Selecting a chart in the drawing area and performing Chart➤Background will open the Chart Background dialog box, shown in Figure 7-28.

A rectangle will be drawn around the outside of the chart (with axis labels as well as the chart frame inside), if the Display check box

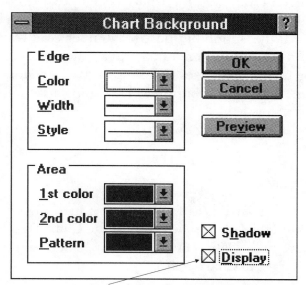

No background or shadow will appear if unmarked

FIGURE 7-28. Settings in this dialog box will generate a rectangle around the entire chart.

is marked. Optionally, the Shadow check box can be marked to generate a drop-shadow behind the chart background.

If the Display check box is marked, you can select a color, width, and line style for the edge (chart background outline) and two colors and a pattern for its area (fill). (The second color is used only if a two-color pattern is also selected.)

 To see the Edge or Area attributes in the chart, the Style or Pattern settings must be something other than None.

LEGEND

A legend is a key that correlates colors, patterns, styles, and markers to data sets in a graph. The chart style you select in the Chart Gallery dialog box usually will determine the placement of the chart legend.

Selecting a chart in the drawing area and performing Chart➤Legend will open the Chart Legend dialog box, shown in Figure 7-29. (It will also appear if you double-click on a legend.)

If the option button Use Number Grid Under Chart is on, a legend will not be generated and all the options in this dialog box will be unavailable. See "Creating a Data Table for a Chart" in this chapter. (This option button will not appear if the chart type is XY (Scatter).)

The following options apply if Use Legend is on.

Font

Set text attributes for the labels in the legend. The label text is entered in the top two rows of the Chart Data window. (Sizes shown here are relative but can be specified as numeric point sizes in Chart➤All Chart Text.)

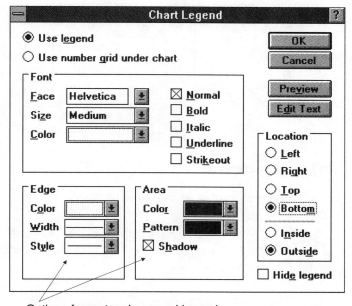

Options for rectangle around legend

FIGURE 7-29.   This dialog box controls the location of a chart legend, if any.

Edge and Area

Rectangle attributes can be set for the legend: a color, width, and line style for its edge (outline), and a color, pattern, or both for its area (fill). Optionally, mark the Shadow check box to add a drop-shadow behind the legend rectangle.

Location

The position of the legend can be specified here in relation to the chart frame, or plotting area. The options are Left, Right, Top, and Bottom; for any of these you can also choose Inside or Outside (of the plotting area). For example, if you choose Bottom and Inside, the legend will be located as shown here:

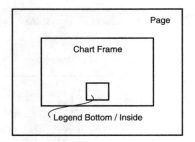

Hide Legend

Mark this check box to omit the legend.

You might omit the legend to permit more space on the page for the chart. If you do, it might be necessary to add free-form text blocks as labels for the plots.

HEADINGS AND NOTES

Selecting a chart in the drawing area and performing Chart➤Headings & Notes will open the Chart Headings & Notes dialog box, shown in Figure 7-30.

Attributes set here affect the headings and notes you enter in the Chart Titles window (open the Chart Data window and select the Edit Titles button).

Different sets of attributes can be specified for each line of heading and note, which you select from the option buttons on the left: Heading 1–3 and Note 1–3.

Font

Text attributes can be set for each line of headings or notes. Remember that size is relative but can be specified numerically in Chart➤All Chart Text.

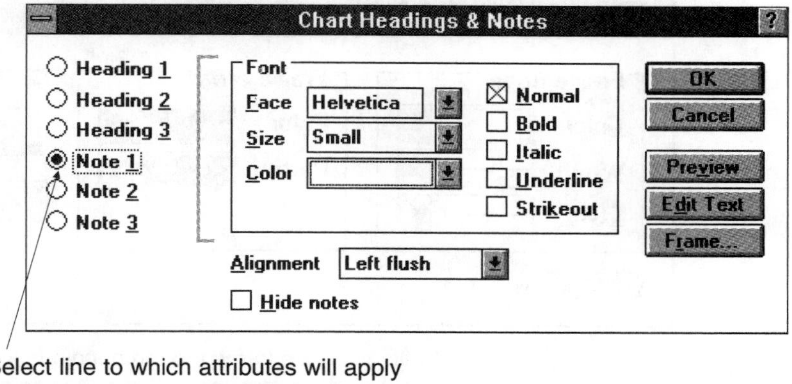

Select line to which attributes will apply

FIGURE 7-30.   For each line of headings or notes, attributes can be set separately here.

Alignment

Justification of each line can be controlled here in relation to the chart frame. The options are Left Flush, Centered, or Right Flush.

Hide Headings or Hide Notes

Mark this check box to suppress the display of *all* headings or notes (depending on the option-button setting at the left).

Frame

Selecting this button permits you to specify a frame (filled rectangle) behind either the headings or the notes (or both, depending on your selection in the Chart Headings & Notes dialog box). Selections for the Frame Edge and Frame Area settings will appear in the Chart Headings & Notes Frame dialog box (Figure 7-31). Optionally, mark the Shadow check box to place a drop-shadow behind the frame.

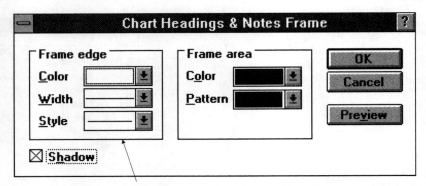

Settings create frame around headings and/or around
notes, depending on option button selected in Chart
Headings & Notes dialog box

FIGURE 7-31.   Settings in this dialog box will draw a rectangle around headings,
notes, or both.

VALUE LABELS

Selecting a chart in the drawing area and performing Chart➤Value
Labels will open the Chart Value Labels dialog box, shown in Figure
7-32. (It will also appear if you double-click on a data-value label in a
chart.)

To show labels for the data values at each point on a graph,
mark the Display check box.

Font

Select font attributes for the text, remembering that size here is relative. (Specify point sizes in Chart➤All Chart Text.)

Number Display

You can specify 1–5 for Number of Places (for decimal values) or
Auto (to accept program-generated labels), as well as an option for
spreadsheet-style numeric display format: Fixed, Scientific, Cur-

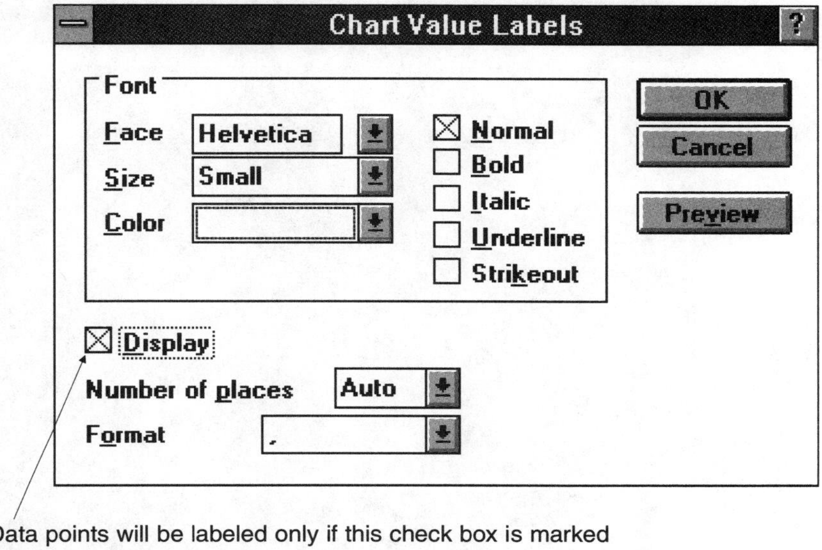

Data points will be labeled only if this check box is marked

FIGURE 7-32. Make settings here to generate value labels at each data point in the chart.

rency, Comma, General, Percent, or X Suffix. (For more information, see the "Format" subsection in the discussion of number grids later in this chapter.)

If you use 3-D chart effects, display data values as labels or in a number grid so that the audience need not estimate the values visually.

TUTORIAL: EDIT A BAR CHART

The variety of options available for X-Y charts is extensive, but the following tutorial should help you become acquainted with techniques for changing a chart's appearance and options.

In this series of steps, you will work with the 3-D bar chart you created in the Introduction as Page 4 of SAMPLE.PRE. Recall that the discussion at the conclusion of Chapter 2 points out several

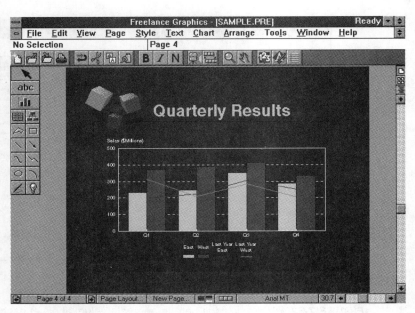

FIGURE 7-33. Following the instructions in the tutorial, edit the bar chart you created in the Introduction to produce this chart.

problems with this chart. To address some of these problems, you
will edit the page to produce the graph shown in Figure 7-33.

Open the presentation SAMPLE.PRE and display Page 4 in the
Current Page view:

1. Add a *y*-axis title.

   Click on the chart area so that handles surround it. Click on
   the Chart tool in the toolbar, or select Chart➤Edit. The
   Chart Data & Titles window will open. Click on the Edit Titles
   button on the left side of the window. The display will change
   to a Chart Titles entry form. Click on the left edge of the Y
   text box of the Axis Titles area, and type **Sales ($Millions)**.
   (Proceed to the next step; do not close this window yet.)

2. Change the chart type to Bar-Line with a style that has horizontal grids and a legend.

In the Chart Data & Titles window, click on the Sample Chart button in the top-left corner. (If you have closed this window, you can select Chart≻Gallery instead.) The Chart Gallery dialog box will open. Select the Bar-Line option button in section 1. The data form will open. In section 2 of the dialog box, click on the second button in the second row (middle right). This chart style includes horizontal grid lines and a legend at the bottom of the chart frame.

Select OK to close the Chart Gallery dialog box. You will be returned to the Chart Data & Titles window. In this window, select the Edit Data button.

3. Add the prior year's sales data to the chart as line plots.

In the data form, click on the cell just beneath the column C heading (in the row labeled Legend). Type **Last Year**. Press Enter to drop down one cell, and type **East**. Press Enter to drop down another cell in the same column, and type the following data items: **200, 223, 306, 253**. (Press Enter after typing an item to drop down to the next line, or click in the next cell.)

Click the right arrow button in the scroll bar at the bottom of the display to move column D into the data form. As you did for column C, enter the following items for data set D: **Last Year, West, 314, 210, 285, 204**.

4. Change the color of data set D.

Still working in the Chart Data & Titles window, double-click on the D column heading. (If the window is closed, you can double-click on the line in the graph or select Chart≻Attributes.) The Bar-Line Chart Attributes dialog box will open. Make sure that data set D is highlighted in the list on the left, then click on the Color option. Click on a different color in the current palette. (To be consistent with other palettes, pick one of the colors in the Chart section of the palette.)

Select OK to close the dialog box.

5. Make the titles and labels bigger, in boldface.

   With the chart still selected in the drawing area (surrounded by handles), select Chart➤All Chart Text. The All Chart Text dialog box will appear. Click on the Medium drop-down box, then click on the setting 24. In the Font area, mark the Bold check box. Select OK to close the dialog box.

6. Save your work! Select File➤Save or press Ctrl-S.

GENERATING NUMBER GRIDS AND DATA TABLES

There are two main uses of the Number Grid feature:

- As an alternative to a legend as a key to data sets, you can create a *data table,* or listing of values, beneath a graph.
- As an alternative to the Table chart layout, you can create a stand-alone table that is composed entirely of numeric data, except for labeled column and row headings.

Creating a Data Table for a Chart

If you create a chart on the current page and select it, the command Number Grid Under Chart will appear in the Chart pull-down menu. When you select this command, the Number Grid Under Chart dialog box will appear, as shown in Figure 7-34.

With the option button Use Legend selected (the default), a legend will be generated according to the options in Chart➤Legend. If instead Use Number Grid Under Chart is selected, the rest of the options in this dialog box will become available for defining a data table.

Percent of Total Chart Area for Number Grid

Enter a number from 10 to 80 in this text box to control the size of the grid as a percentage of the chart area. The default is 30 percent.

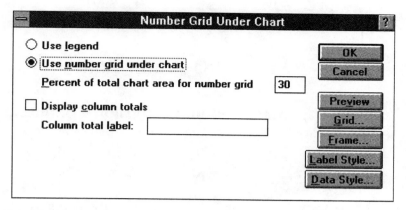

FIGURE 7-34. In this dialog box, you can specify a data table that will appear beneath a chart.

 Click and hold on the Preview button to see the grid in different sizes. You can also drag the size of a selected grid in the drawing area.

Display Column Totals

If this check box is marked, the program will add the values for each column (data set) and display a total in the bottom row of the table.

Column Total Label

If you marked the check box, your entry in this text box will be shown as the bottom-row label for the data-set totals. A data table with labeled column totals is shown in Figure 7-35.

Creating a Stand-alone Numeric Table

When you create a new chart, you can create a stand-alone table by selecting the Number Grid chart type in the Chart Gallery dialog box. Or, you can convert any selected chart to tabular format by performing Chart➤Gallery and selecting this option.

The number-grid chart type is well suited to conversion among other chart types because:

Opinion Polls

Respondents with High Confidence
Number of 'Yes' Answers to Survey Questions

	#1	#2	#3
January	45	34	32
February	34	23	56
March	23	67	34
April	56	89	76
Totals	158	213	198

Eastern Region

FIGURE 7-35. The number grid is shown here as the labeled column totals that were generated by the program.

- It uses the same spreadsheet-style data-input form (the Chart Data window).

- It enforces data typing the same way: Unlike the Table chart page layout, the table body of a numeric grid must be all-numeric, but row and column headings can be labels. The program will reject the entry of labels into numeric cells.

 You can override numeric data typing for specific data sets in a number grid by selecting the grid and performing Chart➤Attributes➤Object Type, selecting a data set, and choosing Text instead of Number.

Number Grid Chart

☒ Customize number grid width and height

Set the height to `100` %

Set the width to `100` %

☐ Equal column widths

☐ Display column totals

Column total label: [   ]

OK
Cancel
Preview
Frame...
Grid...
Label Style...
Data Style...

FIGURE 7-36.   Specify the dimensions of a number grid in this dialog box.

When you select the Numeric Grid option button in the Chart Gallery dialog box, the Number Grid Chart dialog box will open, as shown in Figure 7-36.

Customize Number Grid Width and Height

If this check box is unmarked, the program will size the table automatically based on the number of entries and the text size. If marked, numeric settings from 1 to 100 can be entered for height and width as percentages of the "Click here..." chart area.

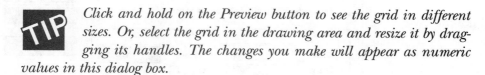

Click and hold on the Preview button to see the grid in different sizes. Or, select the grid in the drawing area and resize it by dragging its handles. The changes you make will appear as numeric values in this dialog box.

Equal Column Widths

If this check box is marked, the grid will have a uniform column width. Otherwise, the program will size the columns to fit the longest entries in each.

Display Column Totals

If this check box is marked, the program will add the values for each column (data set) and display a total in the bottom row of the table.

Column Total Label

If you marked the check box, your entry in this text box will be shown as the bottom-row label for the data-set totals.

Frame

This button opens the Number Grid Frame dialog box, shown in Figure 7-37. (It also appears if you select the table and perform Chart➤Frame.)

For a numeric grid, the frame is an area surrounding the table, excluding its body, or numeric cells. Optionally, the frame can have a contrasting edge color and can include the row labels, column labels, or both.

Remember that a frame is different from a chart background, which surrounds the entire chart. An example of a number grid with a chart background is shown in Figure 7-38.

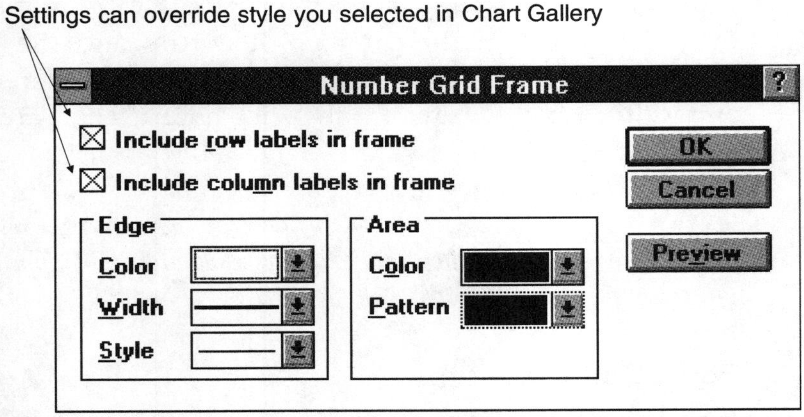

Settings can override style you selected in Chart Gallery

FIGURE 7-37. Settings in this dialog box control the rectangle attributes of a number grid.

	Last Year	This Year	% Change
	Units Sold (000s)		
Cars	12,543	11,324	(9.7)
Trucks	9,876	10,145	2.7
RVs	4,328	3,218	(25.6)

FIGURE 7-38. This number grid has a chart background. By contrast, a frame would surround only the grid.

Grid

This button opens the Number Grid Style dialog box, shown in Figure 7-39. (It also appears if you select the table and perform Chart➤Grid.)

Option buttons on the left control the grid lines within the table to which the color, width, and style settings to the right will apply: First Horizontal, Other Horizontal (all but the first), First Vertical, or Other Vertical (all but the first).

For vertical lines only, you can also specify one of the following types: Data & Column Headings (grid surrounds the labels), Data Area (numeric cells, or table body), or Column Heading Area (top-row labels only).

Not available for horizontal grids

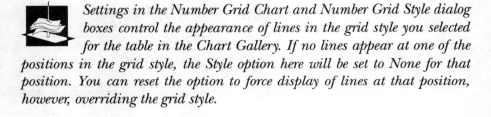

FIGURE 7-39.   Settings in this dialog box control the line attributes of grids at different positions in a table.

 Settings in the Number Grid Chart and Number Grid Style dialog boxes control the appearance of lines in the grid style you selected for the table in the Chart Gallery. If no lines appear at one of the positions in the grid style, the Style option here will be set to None for that position. You can reset the option to force display of lines at that position, however, overriding the grid style.

Label Style

This button opens the Number Grid Label Style dialog box, shown in Figure 7-40. You can specify whether font attributes you select here will apply to the top row (as column headings) or first column (as row labels) of the table.

 Greatly increasing the size of labels can have the effect of reducing the size of text (numeric entries) in the data area.

Data Style

This button opens the Number Grid Chart Attributes dialog box (described in the next section), in which text attributes and formatting can be specified for each data set.

Column labels are in first *row* of table

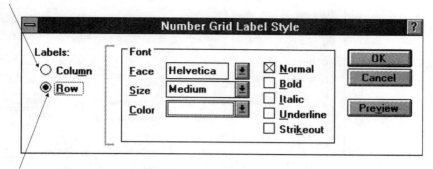

Row labels are in first *column* of table

FIGURE 7-40.   Settings in this dialog box control the attributes of text in the top
row (Column) or first column (Row) of a table.

Numeric Grid Chart Attributes

When you select a number grid and perform Chart>Attributes, or
if you double-click on a data set in the table, the Number Grid
Chart Attributes dialog box will open, as shown in Figure 7-41. Here
you can reset options for each data set in the chart. (Adjust the
slider in the list box at the left to see more data-set choices.)

Font

Text attributes can be specified by data set: Face, Size (Tiny, Small,
Medium, Large, or Extra Large), Color (from the current palette),
and Normal style or any combination of Bold, Italic, Underline, and
Strikeout. (To reset point sizes for chart text, select Chart>All
Chart Text.)

Object Type

For the selected data set, you can specify whether its entries will be
shown in text or number formats. Selecting Text has the effect of
overriding numeric data typing of table entries and dims numeric-
formatting options in this dialog box.

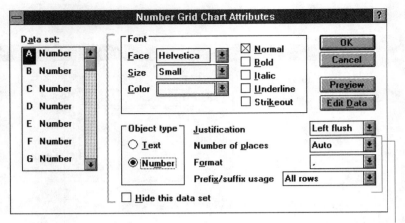

Apply if Object Type =
Number

FIGURE 7-41. These settings control the text attributes of each data set in a table.

Justification

By default, text is justified left and numbers are justified right with respect to the cell boundaries in a table. Regardless of the object type selected, you can specify Left Flush, Centered, or Right Flush for each data set to override the default justification.

Number Of Places

For number entries only, you can specify the number of places (0–5) displayed for decimal values. If the setting is Auto (the default), the number of places will vary: If the value is less than 10,000, as many as five decimal places will be displayed; no decimal places will be displayed for numbers greater than 10,000.

Format

For number entries only, this setting controls spreadsheet-style numeric display formats in the table. (Formats will not appear in the Chart Data window.) Choices are Fixed (using Number of Places setting), Scientific notation, Currency (according to Tools➤ User Setup➤International), Comma (thousands separator speci-

TABLE 7-2. Number Format Options

Format Setting	*Thousands Separator?*	*Minus Sign?*
Fixed	No	Yes
Scientific*	No	Yes
Currency	Yes	†
Comma	Yes	No (Parentheses)
General	No	Yes
Percent	No	Yes
X Suffix	Yes	Yes

*Base-10 exponent (−99 to 99); very large and very small numbers default
  to Scientific format

†Minus sign or parentheses, as set in Tools➤User Setup➤International

fied in Tools➤User Setup➤International), General (overrides
Number of Places setting), Percent (multiplies entry by 100 and fol-
lows it with a percent sign), and X Suffix (follows the entry with the
X factor symbol). These options differ in their use of thousands sep-
arators and leading minus signs for negative values, as shown in
Table 7-2.

 *Format options determine how values entered in the Chart Data
window are interpreted and displayed on the chart. But the values
shown in the data form will remain the same.*

Prefix/Suffix Usage

For Currency, Percent, or X Suffix formats, you can specify that the
prefix or suffix will be used for the top row, top and bottom rows, or
all rows of the selected data set.

Hide This Data Set

Marking this box will suppress the display of the currently selected
data set in the table, but its data will be retained in the Chart Data
window. Empty cells will not be shown; the entire column will be

omitted, and the table will be recomposed, showing one column for each of the unhidden sets.

 Do not use this feature to create buildup sequences (multiple-page sequences in which chart elements are added in stages) because the table might be recomposed each time an element is added or deleted. Instead, set the text color of the data set you want to hide to match the cell background.

EXERCISE: MAKE AN AREA CHART WITH A NUMBER GRID

The entries in the Chart Data & Titles window in Figure 7-42 cause the area chart in Figure 7-43 to be generated. Add an area chart to SAMPLE.PRE and see if you can reset the options to match the example. (In the Chart Gallery dialog box, choose the style button at the bottom right, which generates a data table, or number grid, of chart values.)

	Axis Labels	A	B	C	D
Legend					
→		#1	#2	#3	
1	J	5	21	55	
2	F	3	23	34	
3	M	4	25	43	
4	A	3	28	37	
5	M	4	26	42	
6	J	2	23	21	
7	J	1	21	10	
8	A	0	18	5	
9	S	0	16	0	
10	O	5	17	5	
11	N	4	27	4	
12	D	3	26	3	
13					

Chart Data & Titles

[Edit Titles] [Import...] [Preview] [OK] [Cancel]

FIGURE 7-42.   Sample area-chart data

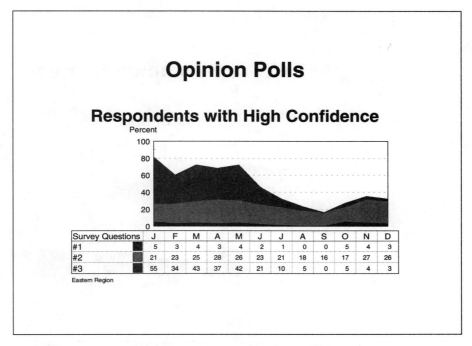

FIGURE 7-43. Area chart with number grid generated from data in Figure 7-42.

EXERCISE: MAKE A HIGH-LOW-CLOSE-OPEN CHART

The entries in the data form shown in Figure 7-44 cause the HLCO chart in Figure 7-45 to be generated. Add a new chart page to SAMPLE.PRE, enter the data for this chart type, and see if you can reset the options to match the example.

Axis Labels	A High	B Low	C Close	D Open	E Daily Volume	F
Legend						
1 MON	78.5	75.2	76.8	78.2	3045	
2 TUE	77.6	74.3	75.3	76.8	3128	
3 WED	78.2	76.2	77	76.3	3076	
4 THU	77.1	74.1	74.5	75.1	3102	
5 FRI	75	73	74.8	74.5	3115	
6						

Chart Data & Titles

Edit Titles / Import... / Preview / OK

FIGURE 7-44. Sample HLCO-chart data

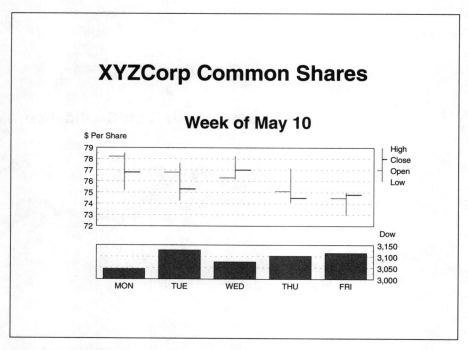

FIGURE 7-45.   HLCO chart generated from data in Figure 7-44

NOTES ON LOGARITHMIC PLOTTING

The use of logarithmic scales is another specialized application of X-Y charts that deserves some further explanation. The option settings, already covered, can be accessed by executing Chart➤Scale➤ Type and selecting Logarithmic for an axis.

If the Log option is set for any axis, its scale is marked off in logarithmic divisions, or by powers of 10. In a typical style called *semi-log,* the *y* axis is logarithmic and the *x* axis is linear. In *log-log* plotting, both axes are logarithmic.

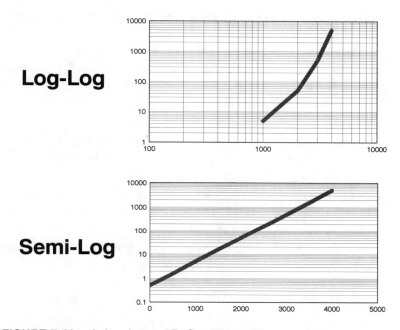

FIGURE 7-46. A. Log-log and B. Semi-log plotting examples

In Freelance Graphics for Windows, the only chart type that will support log-log plotting is XY (Scatter). Logarithmic scaling is not usually appropriate for calendar- and time-based *x*-axis data.

The primary use of logarithmic plotting is in scientific and engineering applications to show data items of widely different magnitudes on the same chart. Examples of log-log and semi-log plotting are shown in Figure 7-46.

To make the graph easier to interpret, if you make the *y* axis logarithmic, make the 2Y axis logarithmic also or omit it entirely.

If a great many data points are to be plotted, consider importing the data from spreadsheets or other external data files (see Chapter 14).

Avoid logarithmic scales if your audience is not familiar with this type of charting.

CONVERTING AMONG CHART TYPES

In Freelance Graphics for Windows, you can convert a data chart to another type just by selecting the chart, performing Chart➤Gallery, and making a different selection in the Chart Gallery dialog box. However, depending on the organization of the data, the new chart type might not necessarily be appropriate.

For example, data sets of X-Y charts can be converted to pie charts. The *x*-axis data become the pie labels. If you choose the Multiple Pies option, as many as the first four sets of *y*-axis data will be used for pie values. (By default, all pies share the same set of slice labels.) Only the first 16 data values in each set can be used, because a pie in Freelance Graphics for Windows has a maximum of 16 slices, or wedges. Furthermore, only four pies can be displayed in each chart, even though as many as 26 data sets can be entered in an X-Y chart.

In similar manner, a pie chart can be converted to any X-Y chart type. But it will usually not be appropriate to show pie data in a format such as High-Low-Close-Open, for example.

For more on creating various types of pie charts, see Chapter 8.

REPLACING CHART DEFAULTS

If you find yourself resetting chart options the same way repeatedly, you can save work by creating a typical chart and then performing Chart➤Replace Defaults. This command will reset the default options for new charts. You can retrieve the settings by selecting the Use Default Chart button in the Chart Gallery dialog box.

BUILDING PIE
AND RADAR CHARTS

[T] his chapter covers the capabilities of Freelance Graphics for Windows for generating graphs that do not use *x-y* perpendicular axes. (Such X-Y data charts are covered in Chapter 7.)

The discussion here assumes that you have read Chapter 7 and learned the techniques for editing charts and changing attributes and options in the Current Page view. You will need these skills in working through the examples here. In particular, you may want to review the data-entry procedures for the Chart Data & Titles window.

For a discussion of design principles that apply to all sorts of graphs, see Chapter 2.

CREATING PIE CHARTS

A pie chart shows data as slices, or wedges, of circular areas. Pies are ideal for showing percentages. In Freelance Graphics for Windows, from one to four pies can be shown on the same chart. For clarity, a pie is limited to 16 slices.

Use one of the Single Pie chart styles to show contributions of a few items to a whole entity, as shown on the following page.

Use one of the Multiple Pie chart styles to illustrate shifts in ratios among time periods, such as prior years and the current year, or to compare results from competing entities, as shown here:

TIP *It is rarely necessary to show more than two pies in the same chart. Even the comparison between two pies might not be clear to your audience unless there are marked differences in the values of corresponding slices. Perhaps the most useful comparison is of a pie linked to a second pie, where the second pie is a breakdown of the pie slice to which it is linked. An example is shown in Figure 8-1. (Freelance Graphics for Windows will not link the pies automatically, but you can draw the linking lines with the Line tool.)*

ENTERING PIE DATA

To create a pie chart, first open or create a presentation, then create a new page (select the New Page button in the status bar at the bottom of the Current Page view window or select Page➤New). The New Page dialog box will appear.

Select one of the following page layouts, depending on the number of charts that will appear on the page. (Remember that a Multiple Pie can be plotted in a single chart area, such as that in the 1 Chart layout). Page layouts available for data charting are:

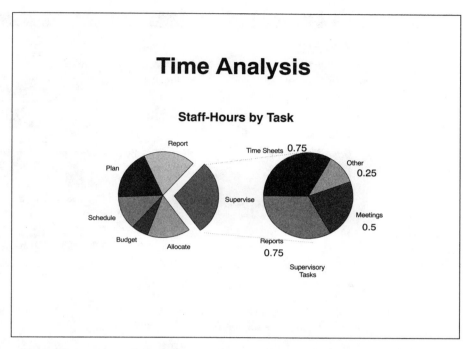

FIGURE 8-1. The linked second pie is an itemization of the slice on the left. You can create the connecting lines with the Line tool.

- 1 Chart
- 2 Charts
- 4 Charts
- Bullets & Chart

After choosing a chart type, select OK to close the dialog box.

The selected SmartMaster layout will appear in the drawing area of the Current Page view. Click once on the area labeled "Click here to create chart."

The New Chart Gallery dialog box will appear, as shown in Figure 8-2. Select one of the following option buttons:

- Single Pie
- Multiple Pies
- 3D Pie

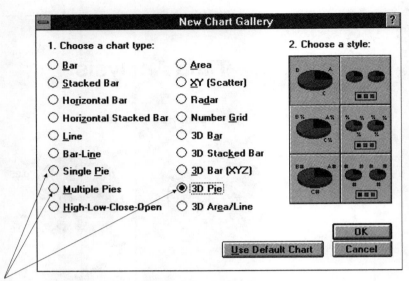

3-D effects can be selected for any of these types

FIGURE 8-2. The New Chart Gallery dialog box has three option buttons for pie charts, each with a variety of styles.

 You can reset chart options to turn three-dimensional effects on or off for any of these chart types.

Select one of the chart styles shown as buttons in section 2 of the dialog box. These styles vary as to position of the legend, display of data labels as values or as percentages, and display of pie slices as normal or exploded (cut). Select OK.

The Chart Data & Titles window will open. Like the data form for X-Y data charts, its layout resembles a spreadsheet composed of numbered rows and lettered columns.

Chart Data Form Layout

The arrangement of the data form will vary, depending on the chart type you have selected:

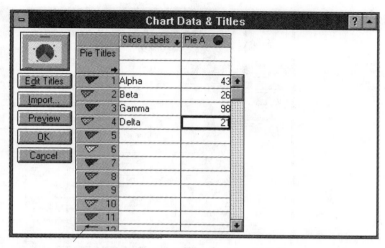

1 to 16 slices (rows)

FIGURE 8-3. This Chart Data & Titles window appears if the chart type is Single Pie.

- If you chose Single Pie or a single-pie style of 3D Pie, the form will have only two columns: Slice Labels and Pie A (for slice values). The window is shown in Figure 8-3.

- If you chose Multiple Pies or a multiple-pie style of 3D Pie, the form will have five columns: Slice Labels and Pies A–D, as shown in Figure 8-4.

By default, multiple pies are assumed to share a single set of slice labels (the first column of entries in the data form). You can change this, however, so that the pies are labeled differently from one another. From the menu bars that appear above either the Chart Data & Titles window or the drawing area, select Chart> Options>Pie. The Multiple Pie Chart Options dialog box will appear, as shown in Figure 8-5. Select the option button Separate Attributes (No Legend), and then OK.

After you reset this option, the number of columns in the data form will change, as shown in Figure 8-6. Now, the first column is headed Labels, and a new Labels column is inserted just to the left

Chart Data & Titles					
	Slice Labels	Pie A ●	Pie B ●	Pie C ●	Pie D ●
Pie Titles					
1	Alpha	43	78		
2	Beta	26	45		
3	Gamma	98	67		
4	Delta	21	29		
5					
6					
7					
8					
9					
10					
11					
12					
13					
14					
15					
16					

Edit Titles
Import..
Preview
OK
Cancel

FIGURE 8-4. This is the data-form arrangement for multiple pies that share labels.

of each Pie (values) column. Each Labels column holds slice labels
for the Pie column to its right. Therefore, each label-value pair in a
given row holds the data for one pie slice.

*Data values longer than nine digits will be converted to scientific
notation in the data form, but not necessarily on the graph itself.*

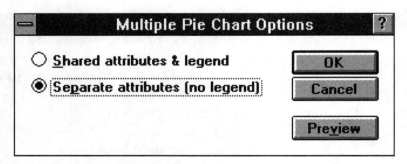

FIGURE 8-5. To label pies differently, use the Multiple Pie Chart Options dialog
box.

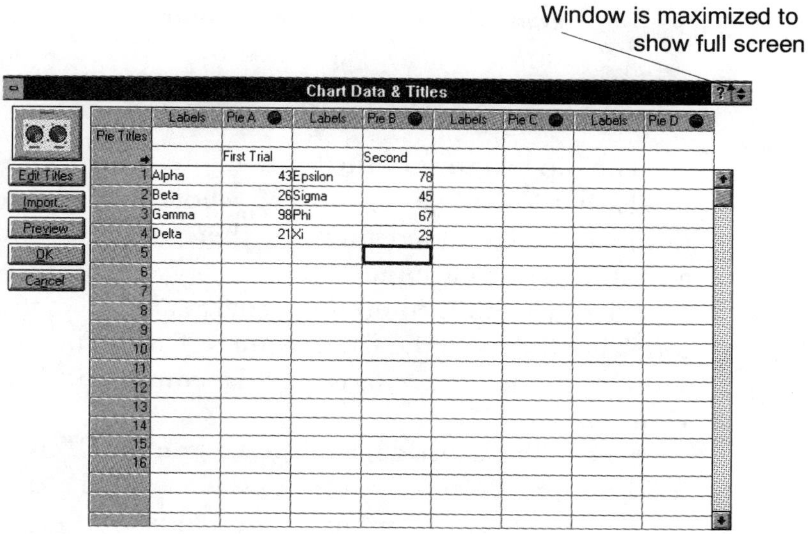

FIGURE 8-6. If multiple pies have different labels, the data form will be arranged as shown here.

Entering Data

You make entries into the Chart Data & Titles forms just as you do for X-Y data charts. The current cell, which will receive any entry you type, is highlighted by a box. Click on a cell to move the highlight to it, or use the arrow keys.

As you type chart data into a cell, the entry appears both in the cell and on the Edit line, just above the toolbar. You can edit the entry on the Edit line as you would a text block; move the insertion point and drag any portion of a string to type its replacement. To accept the entry, click on the Confirm button to the left of the Edit line, click on any other cell, or press Enter to accept the entry and drop down to the next-lower cell in the column.

To reject an entry, click on the Cancel button to the left of the Edit line or press Esc.

As an alternative to typing the chart data, select the Import button in this window and specify an external data file. Procedures are covered in Chapter 14.

The top two rows of the form are for one- or two-line pie titles—labels that identify each pie as a whole. If a legend is used, these titles will be displayed there. If there is no legend, the titles will appear beneath each pie.

When you have entered the chart data, select the Edit Titles button. The display in the Chart Data & Titles window will change to a set of text boxes for chart titles: Headings and Notes, as shown in Figure 8-7.

To see the chart data in the currently selected style, click and hold on the Preview button in either Chart Data & Titles window. When you release the mouse button, this window will reappear.

To change the chart type or style, click on the Chart Sample button in the top-left corner of the window. The Chart Gallery dialog box will reopen, and you can make another selection. (The Chart Sample button shows the currently selected chart type, but not necessarily its style.)

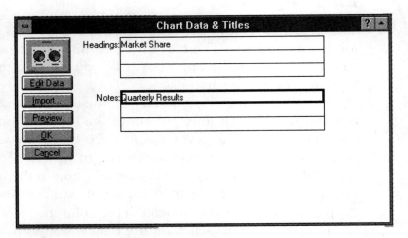

FIGURE 8-7. The Chart Data & Titles window for pie charts has data-entry fields for headings and notes.

When you have entered all the data and titles in the Chart Data & Titles window, select the OK button.

The pie or pies will appear in the drawing area of the Current Page view. Use menu commands or the drawing tools to annotate or edit the chart.

 As a general rule, you can double-click on any chart element, such as a heading or a pie slice, to change its attributes. A dialog box will open, showing the options available for the selected element. The options are covered in depth in this chapter.

Number of Pies and Slices

To restate the rule, pie charts in Freelance Graphics for Windows can have as many as four pies (Pie A–Pie D), each with as many as 16 slices. The data form will not permit more entries.

 If you need to show more than four pies on a page, use the 2 Charts or 4 Charts layouts and create a different set of Multiple Pies in each chart area.

TUTORIAL: CREATE A PIE CHART

Follow the data-entry procedures just described to add a pie chart to the presentation SAMPLE.PRE. Perform the following steps:

1. Open the presentation in the Current Page view.
2. Create a New Page.

   Click on the New Page button in the status bar, or select Page➤New. The New Page dialog box will appear.
3. Select a page layout.

   Select 1 Chart from the list, then OK.
4. Enter the chart title.

The SmartMaster layout will appear in the drawing area. Click on the area labeled "Click here to type page title." A text block will open. Type **Time Analysis** and select OK.

5. Select the chart type and style.

   In the drawing area, click once on "Click here to create chart." The New Chart Gallery dialog box will open. Select the 3D Pie option button in section 1 and the middle-left style button in section 2 (data labels as percentages):

   Select OK.

6. Enter the chart data.

   The Chart Data & Titles window will open. Refer to the sample data form in Figure 8-8. Type the pie-slice labels in the first column and the data values in the Pie A column.

	Slice Labels	Pie A
Pie Titles		
1	Plan	1.5
2	Schedule	1
3	Budget	0.5
4	Allocate	1.25
5	Supervise	2.25
6	Report	1.5
7		
8		
9		
10		
11		

Chart Data & Titles

Edit Titles
Import...
Preview
OK
Cancel

FIGURE 8-8. The data shown here generate the Single Pie chart in Figure 8-9.

7. Enter a heading and a note.

   Select the Edit Titles button. The Chart Titles window will open. Enter the heading shown below:

   Then, select OK to close the Chart Data & Titles window.

   The pie chart will appear in the drawing area of the Current Page view, as shown in Figure 8-9. Note that the data values are converted to percentages automatically.

8. Save your work!

   Select File➤Save or press Ctrl-S.

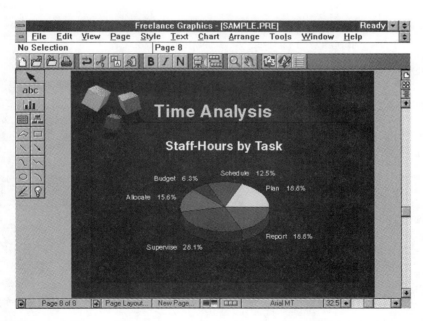

FIGURE 8-9. The tutorial creates this Single Pie chart, which shows how managers spend their time.

CHANGING THE APPEARANCE OF A PIE CHART

To change an attribute, such as color, of pie slices, do any of the following:

- Select the chart and perform Chart➤Attributes.
- Select the chart, click the right mouse button, and select Attributes from the pop-up menu.
- When the chart is displayed in the drawing area, double-click on one of its slices.
- When you are working in the Chart Data window, double-click on a lettered column heading.

When you take any of these actions, the Pie Chart Attributes dialog box will open, as shown in Figure 8-10. The same dialog box appears for Single, Multiple, and 3D Pie chart types. Options are as follows:

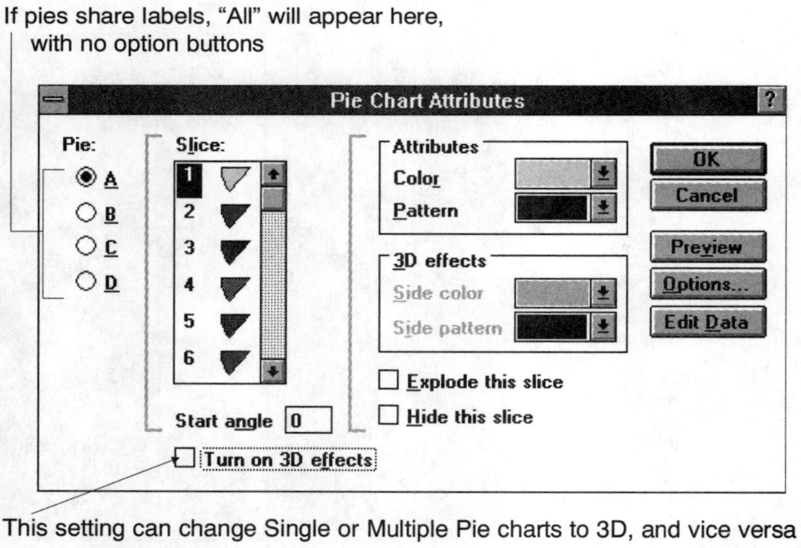

If pies share labels, "All" will appear here, with no option buttons

This setting can change Single or Multiple Pie charts to 3D, and vice versa

FIGURE 8-10.   The same Pie Chart Attributes dialog box will appear for Single, Multiple, and 3D Pie chart types.

Pie

If you have specified Single Pie or Multiple Pies that share a single set of labels, this option will be set to All. If pies will have different labels (as selected in Chart➤Options➤Pie), separate option buttons appear for Pies A–D. (Refer again to Figure 8-10.) When separate option buttons are displayed, you can adjust attributes of the pies separately.

Slice Number

Pie slices are numbered 1–16 in counterclockwise order, starting at the 3 o'clock position (0 degrees). Settings in the rest of the dialog box refer only to the currently selected slice number. Adjust the slider to select from the list. When you have changed the settings for one slice, you can pick another and change its settings. When you have made adjustments to all the slices you want to change, select OK to close the dialog box.

Preview and Edit Data Buttons

In this or any other dialog box in which it appears, click and hold on the Preview button to see the revised chart. When you release the mouse button, the dialog box will reappear, and you can revise your settings, if necessary, before selecting OK.

The Edit Data button reopens the Chart Data & Titles window for the pie. The window can also be accessed by selecting Chart➤ Edit Data or clicking on the Chart tool in the toolbox.

Explode This Slice

To *explode* a slice, or remove it from the rest of the pie, mark this check box for the selected slice number. This setting can override the chart style option you selected in the Chart Gallery.

Slices of 3-D pies can be neither exploded nor hidden.

Hide This Slice

Marking this box will suppress the display of the currently selected slice, but its data will be retained in the Chart Data window.

Do not use this feature to create buildup sequences (multiple-page sequences in which elements are added in stages), because the chart might be recomposed as elements are added or deleted. Instead, set the color of the slice you want to hide to match the chart background.

Start Angle

Enter a value from 0 to 359 degrees to rotate the entire pie counter-clockwise in relation to a 0-degree (3 o'clock) default starting position.

You cannot use the command Arrange➤Rotate to rotate a pie. You must change the Start Angle setting here instead.

Turn On 3D Effects

Marking this check box for Single Pie or Multiple Pies has the same result as selecting 3D Pie for the chart type. Select colors from the current palette for side color of three-dimensional pies, as well as side pattern, if desired. The dimensional side will appear as the bottom edge of a pie that appears to be tilted backward from the viewer.

Pie Chart Options

Selecting the Options button in the Pie Chart Attributes dialog box will open another dialog box, Pie Chart Options, shown in Figure 8-11. Its options are as follows.

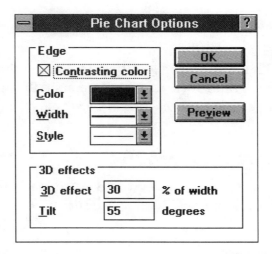

FIGURE 8-11. Control 3-D effects by using the Pie Chart Options dialog box.

Edge

As with other types of filled objects, line color, width, and style can be selected for the slice edges, or outlines. If the Contrasting Color check box is unmarked, the edge will be the same color as the fill (slice-color attribute), and the Color option here will be dimmed.

3D Effect and Tilt

These settings affect the currently selected pie as a whole if three-dimensional effects are turned on. The thickness of the dimensional edge can be entered here as a percentage (1–100) of pie width. The Tilt setting is the number of degrees (0–89) by which a 3-D pie will appear to be rotated backward. A Tilt setting of 0 degrees results in a two-dimensional pie, and 89 degrees would produce a pie viewed edge-on.

OTHER CHART COMMANDS

Chart menu commands work the same for pie charts as explained in Chapter 7 for X-Y data charts. You must select a chart in the drawing area before performing any of these commands.

Chart Type

Select Chart➤Type to reopen the Chart Gallery dialog box. Select a different chart type and style to convert the current chart to a different graph format. But remember that pies can have far fewer data sets (1–16 slices for 1–4 pies) than X-Y charts.

Chart Background

Perform Chart➤Background to set the attributes of a rectangle, with optional shadow, that will surround the entire chart.

Legend

Select Chart➤Legend to set the text attributes, location, and style of a legend, or data key. For pie charts, if the Use Slice Labels option is selected, all the settings in this dialog box will be ignored:

Headings and Notes Options

Select Chart➤Headings & Notes to control the alignment and text attributes of headings and notes entered in the Chart Titles window. Optionally, headings, notes, or both, can be surrounded by frames.

Pie Titles and Labels

Select Chart➤Pie Titles & Labels to control the text attributes of pie titles (first two rows of data form) and slice labels (text-entry columns to the left of Pie columns). If a legend is used, the Slice Labels option will be dimmed.

The option Use Legend or Use Slice Labels also appears in this dialog box (as well as in the Chart Legend dialog box, if the legend has been turned off):

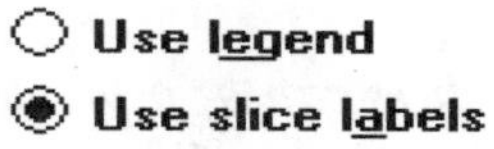

○ Use le̲gend

◉ Use slice la̲bels

Resetting the option in one dialog box will reset it in the other also.

Value Labels

Select Chart≻Value Labels to generate text showing the data values of each pie slice. In the Pie Chart Value Labels dialog box (Figure 8-12), mark the Values check box to display the data in the units entered on the data form. Mark the Percents check box to translate the values into percentages of the total pie. You can mark Values or Percents—or both.

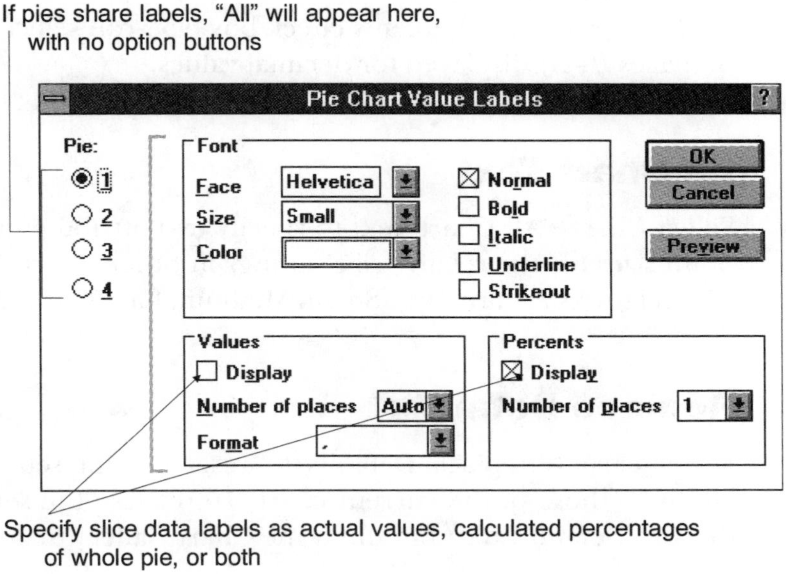

If pies share labels, "All" will appear here,
  with no option buttons

Specify slice data labels as actual values, calculated percentages
  of whole pie, or both

FIGURE 8-12. In the Pie Chart Value Labels dialog box, you can specify whether slice data will appear on the chart as value labels, percent labels, or both.

Normally, pie data would be labeled by choosing either the Values or the Percents check box. However, you can mark both check boxes to display two sets of data labels for each slice.

Small slices can be a problem in pie charts, because they are hard to read and it is difficult to visually estimate proportion in relation to the other slices. One solution can be to combine two or more small slices to form a single slice labeled Other or All Others. If a data value is very small in relation to the other slices, it may be necessary to "fudge" that slice—enter a higher-than-actual value on the data form—to produce a slice that is visible on the chart. If you do this, be sure to add a slice label showing the actual value. You must add this label as a free-form text block, since value or percent labels would be calculated from an incorrect data item.

If you select the Values check box, you can specify spreadsheet-style formatting of the numbers. (For more information, see the "Format" subsection in the discussion of number grids in Chapter 7.)

If you select the Percents check box, you can select the number of places (0–5) displayed for decimal values.

All Chart Text

Select Chart➤All Chart Text to specify text attributes and numeric point sizes for the relative size settings in other Chart dialog boxes. The relative sizes are Tiny, Small, Medium, Large, and Extra Large.

Replace Defaults

Select Chart➤Replace Defaults to reset default settings for new charts to those of the current chart. To retrieve the settings, select the Use Default Chart button in the Chart Gallery dialog box.

NOTES ON CREATING PROPORTIONAL PIES

As discussed in Chapter 2, proportional sizing of pies can be a misleading presentation technique, because audiences usually have difficulty estimating the relative sizes of areas.

In fact, Freelance Graphics for Windows has no feature for sizing pies differently based on the ratios of their total data values.

However, if you must use proportional pies, you can produce them. An example is shown in Figure 8-13. Use the 2 Chart format, and create separate Single Pie charts. Select each chart separately in the drawing area, resize it by dragging one of its corner handles, then drag the charts to recompose the page correctly. To prevent distortion of pie shape when resizing, hold down the Shift key when you are dragging a handle.

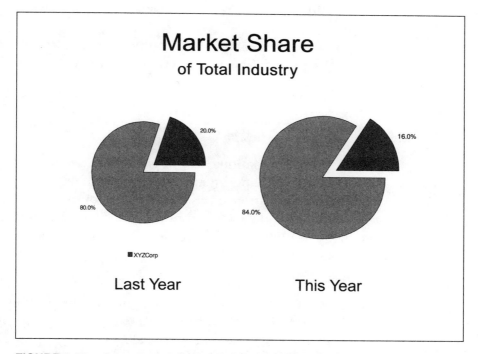

FIGURE 8-13. An example of proportional pies: The pie on the right indicates that the overall size of the market has increased.

NOTES ON LINKING PIES

In a linked-pie chart, two pies are shown. (Refer back to Figure 8-1.) Pie B is shown on the right and is an expanded view of one slice of pie A. Freelance Graphics for Windows does not generate linked pies automatically, so here are some guidelines for creating them.

Use the 1 Chart and Multiple Pies type and style unless the pies must be different sizes.

The slice to be expanded as pie B should be designated slice 1 in pie A, or pie A should be rotated so that the slice is in the 3 o'clock position. In the Pie Chart Attributes dialog box, mark the option Explode This Slice to remove slice 1 from the rest of the pie.

Use the Line tool to add connecting lines between slice 1 of the first pie and the edges of the second pie.

Use a different set of slice colors for pie B than you did for pie A. Or, build pie B entirely from shades of the color of slice 1 in pie A.

Optionally, the second chart can be a single stacked bar instead of a pie: Use the 2 Chart page layout to create separate charts on the same page.

TUTORIAL: EDIT A PIE CHART

There are many variations on the pie chart format. In this tutorial, you will be able to experiment with some of them.

Continue with the exercise begun previously ("Tutorial: Create a Pie Chart") to add a second pie to the chart and edit its appearance. Start in the Current Page view with the pie chart you created in the presentation SAMPLE.PRE.

1. Change to Multiple Pies format.

    In the Current Page view, click once on the pie chart to select it. Handles will surround the chart. Then, perform Chart‣ Gallery. The Chart Gallery dialog box will open. Select the option button Multiple Pies in section 1. Select the middle-left style button in section 2 (legend with percent labels).

Note these new labels

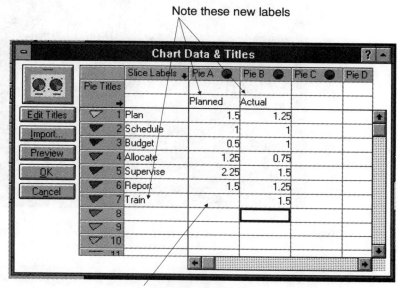

Leave this cell blank

FIGURE 8-14. For this tutorial, enter the data shown here.

Then select OK. The revised chart will appear in the drawing area, surrounded by handles.

2. Enter the data for pie B.

With the pie still selected, perform Chart➤Edit. The Chart Data & Titles window will reopen. Enter the data shown in Figure 8-14. Note that the pie-B data include a slice ("Train") not found in pie A. It will not be necessary to enter a data value in cell A7, since a blank is treated as a zero, and the slice and its labels will be omitted from pie A. Be sure to enter the pie titles **Planned** and **Actual** in their respective column headings.

Close the window by selecting OK.

3. Change the location of the legend.

With the chart still selected in the drawing area, select Chart➤Legend. The Chart Legend dialog box will appear. From among the Location option buttons in the lower-left corner, select Left. Select OK to close the dialog box.

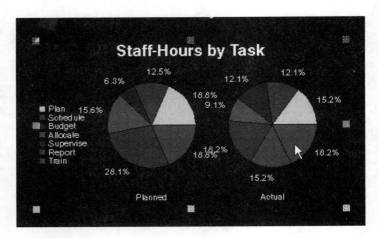

FIGURE 8-15. Double-click on the "Train" slice to change its attributes.

4. Explode one of the pie slices for emphasis and change its color.

In the drawing area, double click on the "Train" slice in pie B, as shown in Figure 8-15.

The Pie Chart Attributes dialog box will open, with slice 7 preselected. Mark the check box Explode This Slice. Then, click on the Color drop-down box in the Attributes section. The current color palette will appear. Click on another color in the Chart section of the palette.

The Pie Chart Attributes dialog box will reappear. Select OK to close it.

The completed chart is shown in Figure 8-16.

5. Save your work! Select File➣Save or press Ctrl-S.

CREATING RADAR CHARTS

Radar charts are method of plotting pairs of labels and values that departs from conventional *x-y* plotting. A Chart Data window with sample data is shown in Figure 8-17, and the resulting plot is shown in Figure 8-18.

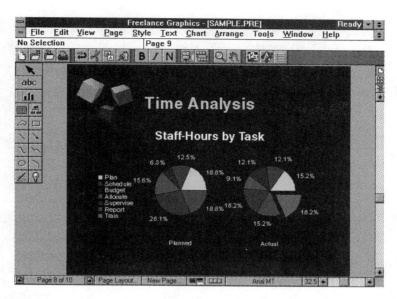

FIGURE 8-16. At the conclusion of the tutorial, the chart should appear as shown.

Interpretation of the Sample Chart

The first column of the data form holds axis labels, and each of the items entered has become a separate numeric axis in the plot. These radiate from a common center like the spokes of a wheel. The numeric values in data sets (A–C, in this case) are plotted as points *on* each axis. Points in the same data set are connected to form line plots.

A radar chart can be used to correlate several data sets according to multiple criteria. The sample chart rates three models of automobile according to five criteria: styling, fuel economy, handling, acceleration, and safety. Each criterion is represented by an axis. Each axis is a set of performance ratings, or possible scores from 1 to 4. Each line plot, then, represents the scores of each model in each of the categories.

The car model with the highest scores in each category will have the outermost line graph. Also, the model with the most consistent scores will have the most symmetrical plot. From a glance at the

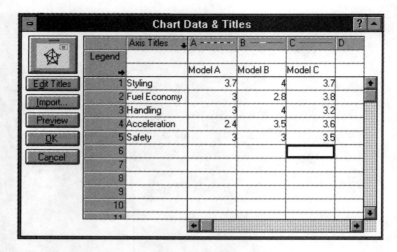

FIGURE 8-17. Sample data for a radar chart: Note differences in the data form.

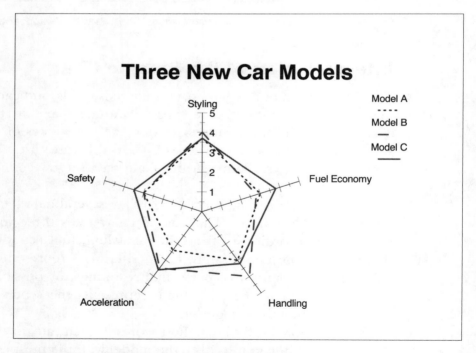

FIGURE 8-18. This radar chart compares three new car models according to five different criteria, one criterion on each axis.

graph, it is apparent that Model B scored higher in some areas, but Model C had a better overall distribution of scores.

Cultural Bias in Radar Charts?

Consider this plotting technique in terms of the left-right and up-down expectations of audiences in Western countries, a subject that was raised in Chapter 2. Perhaps it will come as no surprise that managers in Japan often prefer radar charts to the time-dependent, linear format of x-y plots. Interpreting a radar chart involves looking for the most "well-rounded" alternative. Is there something essentially Eastern in the search for symmetry?

Number of Data Items

In Freelance Graphics for Windows, a radar chart can have 1 to 36 axes (rows in the data form) and data sets from A to Z (columns) displayed as line plots on the chart. Bear these limitations in mind when you are converting larger sets of x-y data to Radar format.

Radar Chart Options

Creating and editing radar charts in Freelance Graphics for Windows is much the same as for other chart types, with the following exceptions.

Attributes

Chart attributes can be specified for each data set (A–Z). For each line plot, you can select a different color, width, line style, and marker symbol. (Options are the same as for line charts.)

Scales

By default, all axes of a radar chart share the same scaling, and only one axis is labeled. To override this feature, select the chart in the drawing area and perform Chart➤Scale. Mark the check box Use Separate Scales. Each axis can then be scaled individually to range from 0 (or a common minimum) to the maximum value in the data. Remember, though, that if the axes have different scales, the chart will be less useful for showing symmetries in the plots, as described previously.

Axes of radar charts cannot have logarithmic scales.

Grids

Grid lines, if used, are shown as concentric circles.

Chart Background

Even though the plotting area is circular, the chart background, if used, is rectangular, as it is for the other types of charts.

Axis Labels

When you select Chart➤Axis Titles & Labels➤Labels, two additional options are available:

☐ <u>H</u>ide axis labels

☒ <u>F</u>irst axis only

If Hide Axis Labels is marked, the scale divisions of *all* axes will be unlabeled, even if you have specified that the axes will be scaled separately. If First Axis Only is marked, numeric scale labels will be generated for only the axis that appears in row 1 of the data form. If the option is unmarked, scale labels will appear on all the axes, even if all the scales are the same.

Other Options

The following commands work the same for radar charts as for other chart types:

- Chart➤Type
- Chart➤Legend
- Chart➤Headings & Notes
- Chart➤Axis Titles & Labels➤Titles
- Chart➤Value Labels
- Chart➤All Chart Text
- Chart➤Replace Defaults

The command Chart➤Number Grid Under Chart is not available for radar charts. You can, however, add a second chart to the page (Chart➤New) as a number grid.

MAKING ORGANIZATION CHARTS AND DIAGRAMS

T his chapter covers one remaining chart type—organization, or hierarchy, charts. Also discussed are the symbol libraries and techniques for building diagrams by using predrawn symbols. The discussion assumes that you are familiar with the pull-down menus in the Current Page view, data-entry procedures, and drawing tools.

CHARACTERISTICS OF ORGANIZATION CHARTS

Organization charts show the hierarchy and reporting relationships among managers and subordinates. Although not specifically designed for this purpose, the Organization Chart type, or template, of Freelance Graphics for Windows can also be used to build programming structure charts, decision trees, computer-system directory trees, genealogical charts (family trees), and many other types of charts based on hierarchies.

Freelance Graphics for Windows automates the drawing of organization charts so that you can get attractive results quickly and easily, without having to be overly concerned with questions of box and text size, layout, alignment, and so on. As a result, charts have a neat, finished appearance. However, because some aspects of chart appearances are predefined, they might be difficult to change.

The layout and composition of the chart will be governed largely by the number of boxes and the length of the text entries within them.

An organization chart in Freelance Graphics for Windows can have as many as 12 levels, or tiers in the hierarchy. As a guideline, try to keep the chart to 20 or fewer boxes, although this is not a rigid constraint. Landscape orientation will usually provide the best layout.

An alternative would be to create the organization chart from scratch as a freehand drawing. If you've ever tried this on a computer graphics system, whether with CAD or with other presentation graphics software, you know it can be tedious. Attempting it with the drawing tools in the Current Page view would also be cumbersome, at best.

So, all things considered, you may be quite comfortable with the organization charts generated by Freelance Graphics for Windows. You might have difficulty if your supervisor or client were to ask you to match existing manually drawn charts, but the Freelance Graphics charts are attractive, and creating them is certainly fast and easy. For most people in business, speed will be the overwhelming advantage. It can mean the difference between getting the job done on time or becoming frustrated and having to work late just to produce an acceptable chart.

CREATING ORGANIZATION CHARTS

To create an organization chart, add a new page to a presentation. (In an existing presentation, select the New Page button at the bottom of the Current Page view window or select Page➤New.) The New Page dialog box will appear, as shown in Figure 9-1. Select the Organization Chart layout from the list, then OK.

The SmartMaster layout will appear in the drawing area of the Current Page view. Click once on the area labeled "Click here to create organization chart."

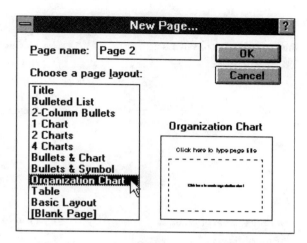

FIGURE 9-1. Select the Organization Chart page layout in the New Page dialog box.

The Organization Chart Gallery dialog box will open, as shown in Figure 9-2. Choose one of the Style buttons: Options include shadowed, rounded, and oval box styles, as well as no boxes. In the bottom portion of the dialog box, select one of the option buttons

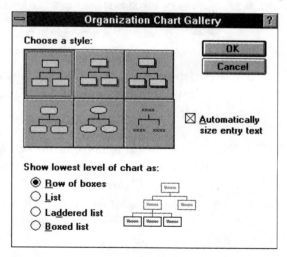

FIGURE 9-2. Select a Style and a Lowest Level option in the Organization Chart Gallery dialog box.

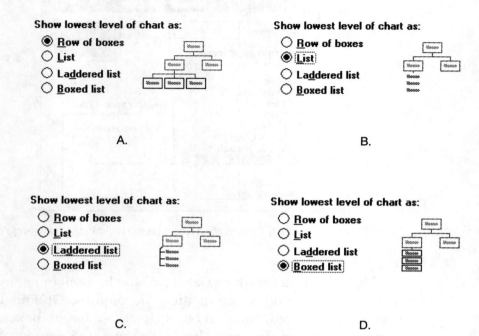

FIGURE 9-3. Options for the lowest level of an organization chart: A. Row Of Boxes, B. List, C. Laddered List, D. Boxed List. Use one of the list types if you want to reduce overall chart width.

to control how the last (bottommost) level of the chart will be drawn. The options are Row of Boxes, List, Laddered List, or Boxed List. (See Figure 9-3.)

Select one of the list options for the last level if you want to reduce its total width; the bottom level will then spread vertically instead of horizontally. Eliminating the width of that last level will also provide more space for the higher levels, possibly increasing the chart-box and text sizes. If there are many boxes in a bottom-level list arrangement, consider using portrait orientation for the page.

The dialog box includes a check box:

☒ <u>A</u>utomatically
size entry text

This option normally should be left marked so that the program will compose text to fit within chart boxes. If this option is off, you can resize box text by double-clicking it and resetting the Organization Chart Attributes dialog box.

When you have selected a Style and a Lowest Level option, select OK to close the dialog box.

The Organization Chart Entry List dialog box will open, as shown in Figure 9-4. The insertion point will appear at the beginning of the first text-entry field.

For each box, or position, in the chart there are three text-entry fields. These are labeled "Enter name here" (usually the name of a

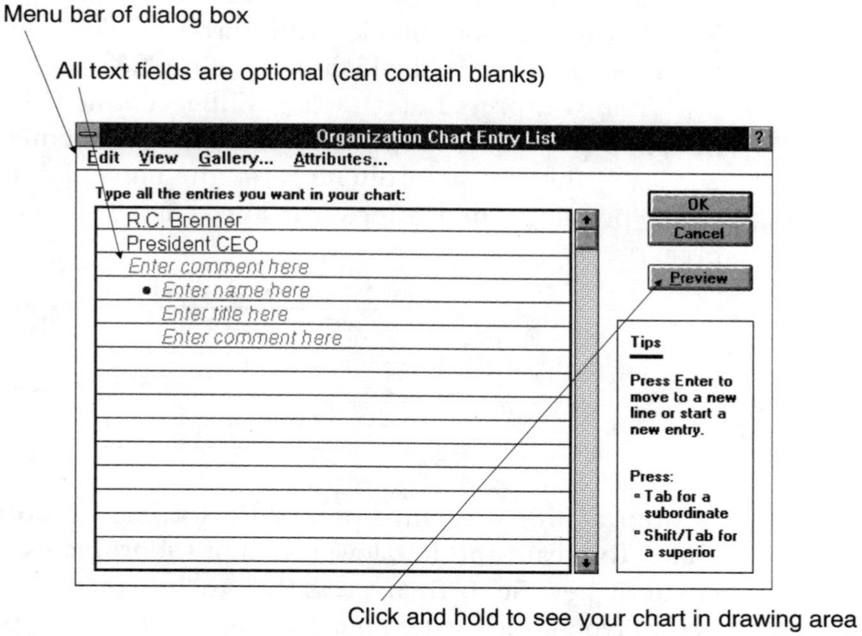

Menu bar of dialog box

All text fields are optional (can contain blanks)

Click and hold to see your chart in drawing area

FIGURE 9-4. Type text data into the Organization Chart Entry List dialog box.

person), "Enter title here" (the person's job title), and "Enter comment here" (an optional third line of text).

The first set of entries are for the top-level box. In Freelance Graphics for Windows, there can be only one box on the top level. Type a name, title, and comment for the top-level box. As you finish typing a line, press Enter to drop down to the next field.

 To break, or split, a line of text, press Ctrl-Enter at the point of the break and continue typing characters:

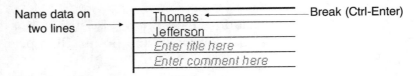

Each of the entry lines is optional: A box will be generated even if all its lines contain blanks. To insert a blank for any field, move the insertion point to the beginning of the field and press Enter.

When you press Enter in the "Enter comment here" field, the insertion point will drop down and will be indented for the text entries of the first subordinate. Type the name, job title, and comment, pressing Enter after each line. (Again, Ctrl-Enter inserts a break.)

R.C. Brenner
President
CEO
• Enter name here
Enter title here
Enter comment here

Repeat this text-entry procedure for each subordinate in the chart. To create another, lower level of subordinates, press Enter to create a new field, then press Tab to indent the insertion point before typing the next name. To move the insertion point back to a higher level, press Shift-Tab.

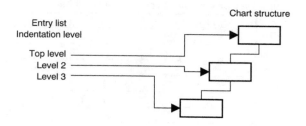

FIGURE 9-5. Relationship of indentation levels to chart levels

 As an alternative to typing your entries, you can use the Edit⊳Paste command in the dialog box to bring in text that you have previously copied to the Clipboard. See Chapter 14 for more information.

Adjust the scroll bar at the right side of the entry list to move up or down on the form.

Each level of indentation in the entry list corresponds to a vertical level on the chart. Subordinates must be entered on the form immediately below the manager to whom they report, as shown in Figure 9-5.

In the entry list, each level of indentation is identified by a different bullet symbol, which precedes a block of text-entry fields. The symbols used for each level are shown in Figure 9-6.

To see the organization structure in the drawing area, click and hold on the Preview button. When you release the mouse button, the entry list will reappear.

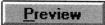

When you have made text entries for all boxes in the chart, select OK to close the entry list. The chart will appear in the draw-

Type all the entries you want in your chart:

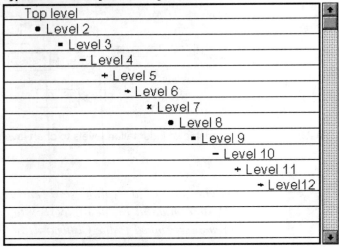

FIGURE 9-6. These bullet symbols identify levels of indentation in the entry list.

ing area of the Current Page view. Use menu commands or the drawing tools to annotate or edit the chart.

A sample organization chart is shown in Figure 9-7.

EDITING ORGANIZATION CHART DATA

Text appearing in boxes on an organization chart can be edited in two ways: You can edit text in the drawing area, or you can reopen the entry list.

Editing Text in the Drawing Area

In the drawing area, click on the chart to select it, then click again on a chart box. It will open as a text block for editing, as shown in Figure 9-8. Drag a text string to highlight it before typing its replacement. When you are finished, click on a blank area of the chart to close the text block.

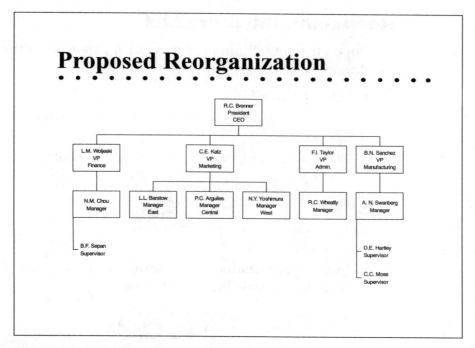

FIGURE 9-7.   Organization chart example

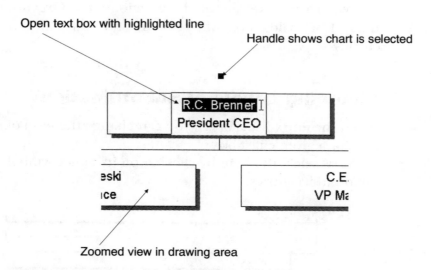

FIGURE 9-8.   To open a box label for editing as a text block, click once to select the whole chart, then click again on the box label.

Reopening the Entry List

To reopen the entry list in the Current Page view, select the chart in the drawing area and do one of the following:

- Select Chart➤Edit.
- Click the right mouse button, and select Edit from the pop-up menu.
- Click on the Organization tool in the toolbar:

- In the Organization Chart Attributes dialog box (discussed below), select the Edit Text button:

When you take any of these actions, the Organization Chart Entry List dialog box will reopen, and you can revise the text entries.

Changing Levels of Subordination

When the entry list is open, you can change the level of subordination for a given chart box.

First, select the item by clicking on its bullet symbol. A box will surround its entries:

CEO
- C.E. Katz
VP
Marketing

From the menu bar of the dialog box, select Edit➤Demote to move the item to the next-lower level (indent one level to the right) or select Edit➤Promote to move it to the next-higher level (unindent one level to the left).

When you demote or promote an item, all its subordinate entries move with it.

 If the Edit➤Demote or Edit➤Promote commands have no effect, the change you are requesting is not appropriate for the selected item. In particular, the top-level manager cannot be demoted or promoted.

Adding a Staff Position (Assistant)

A staff position usually represents an administrative aide who has no subordinates. In Freelance Graphics for Windows, there can be one such staff member in an organization chart, and that position must report to the top-level manager:

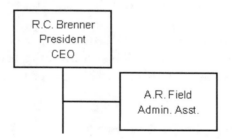

To create a staff position in a chart, you must be working in the Organization Chart Entry List dialog box. From its menu bar, select Edit➤Staff. The Organization Chart Staff dialog box will appear, as shown in Figure 9-9.

The dialog box has three text boxes for staff-member entries: Name, Title, and Comment. Type entries in each, pressing Tab (not Enter) to move the insertion point to the next-lower field or Shift-Tab to move to the next-higher field. You can also click on a charac-

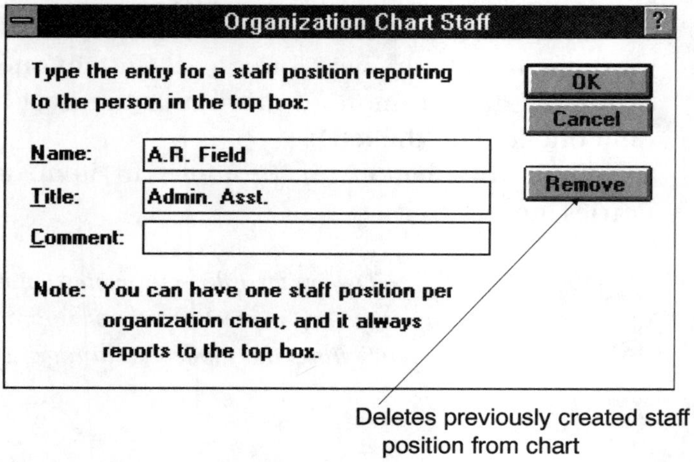

Deletes previously created staff
position from chart

FIGURE 9-9. Enter text data for a staff member here, not in the entry list.

ter position within a field to move the insertion point there. When you have entered as many as three lines of text for the staff-member chart box, select OK.

The staff-member data will not appear on the entry list. To inspect its contents and edit the data, select Edit≻Staff to reopen the dialog box.

To remove the staff-member box from the chart, select Edit≻Staff≻Remove. This command removes the box from the chart display and also clears its text entries.

Hiding Data Entries

To present a less cluttered view of the entry list, you can suppress the display of both the job title and comment fields, or just the comment. From the menu bar of the dialog box, select View≻Names or View≻Names and Titles.

When you do this, the job titles and comments (or just the comments) will disappear from the entry list—collapsing the list and making it possible to see more entries on a single screen. The result

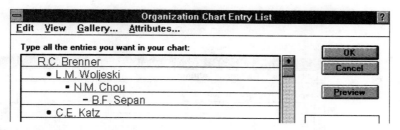

FIGURE 9-10.   Collapsing the entry list with the View➤Names Only command produces this abbreviated listing.

is shown in Figure 9-10. However, the chart display in the drawing
area will be unchanged.

To cause the titles and comments to reappear, perform
View➤All from the menu of the dialog box.

Deleting a Box or a Group

You can remove the data for a box or a group of boxes in a single
operation. In the entry list, select an item to be deleted by clicking
on its bullet symbol. To select a manager and its subordinates, click
on the bullet symbol of the manager item (the topmost box in the
group). Then from the menu bar of the dialog box, select
Edit➤Clear. Remember that all the subordinates, if any, of the
selected item will also be deleted.

If you need to restore the deletion, select the Cancel button to
undo all changes in the dialog box. Or, select OK, then perform
Edit➤Undo from the main menu bar before making any other
changes to the chart.

Moving a Box within the Chart

An item—which represents a box on the chart—can be moved
within the entry list by clicking on the item's bullet symbol to high-

Box surrounds selected item
and all its subordinates

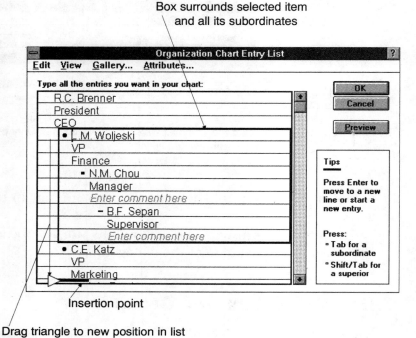

Insertion point

Drag triangle to new position in list

FIGURE 9-11.   When you drag an item within the entry list, the insertion point is
indicated by a horizontal bar.

light the entire entry. Then, hold down the mouse button and a triangle symbol will appear at the cursor location:

When the triangle symbol appears, simply drag the item to
another position in the entry list and release the mouse button. As
you do this, the insertion point will be indicated by a horizontal bar,
as shown in Figure 9-11.

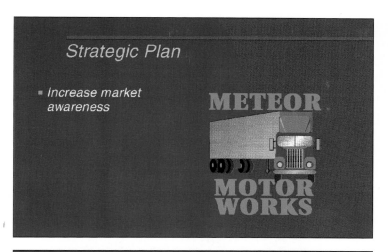

Color Plates 1–3.
This buildup sequence of a bulleted list chart was created in two steps. The last page in the sequence was created first in the Current Page view. The SmartMaster set CORPORAT.MAS was selected with no changes to its default color palette. The page layout is Bullets & Symbol. The truck logo is from the symbol library TRANSPOR.SYM, to which text has been added in 50-point Utopia Black. The two other pages in the sequence were then generated by the command Page ➤ Create Build. The dimming of preceding text items in gray is a feature of the autobuild process, which picks up Color 4 (Autobuild Gray) from the current palette.

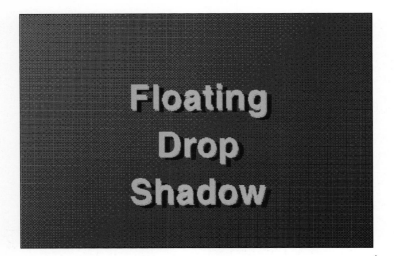

Color Plate 4.
This floating drop-shadow effect includes three instances of a text object, created with the Edit ➤ Replicate command. The first instance of the text block was rendered in the face color (yellow), the second in a darker shade of the same color (yellow orange) in back of it, and the third in black — farther back and offset down and to the right. Procedures for creating this effect are covered in Chapter 10. The background is a diagonal-patterned blend of two colors (red and purple).

Color Plate 5. This multiple drop shadow was produced with a special feature of the Edit ➤ Replicate command. One text block was created first in 69-point Utopia Black (in light blue). The Replicate option in Tools ➤ User Setup was changed to Place Copy on Original. Selecting Edit ➤ Replicate created a second copy of the text. While this object was selected, the Arrange ➤ Rotate command was used to rotate it about 15 degrees. Then Edit ➤ Replicate was performed five more times. Each copy of the text block was not only centered on the first, but was also rotated automatically by 15-degree increments. The last (frontmost) copy of the text was recolored white. All of the objects were selected in a collection, then Arrange ➤ Group performed to combine them into a single object. The Arrange ➤ Rotate command was performed on this object so that the white text was aligned horizontally. The background is a radial-patterned blend of green and blue.

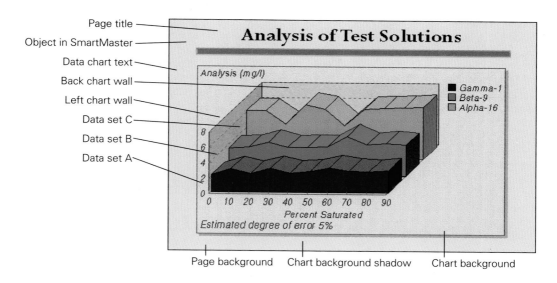

Page title — **Analysis of Test Solutions**

Object in SmartMaster —

Data chart text —

Back chart wall — Analysis (mg/l)

Left chart wall —

Data set C —

Data set B —

Data set A —

Gamma-1
Beta-9
Alpha-16

8
6
4
2
0

0 10 20 30 40 50 60 70 80 90

Percent Saturated
Estimated degree of error 5%

Page background   Chart background shadow   Chart background

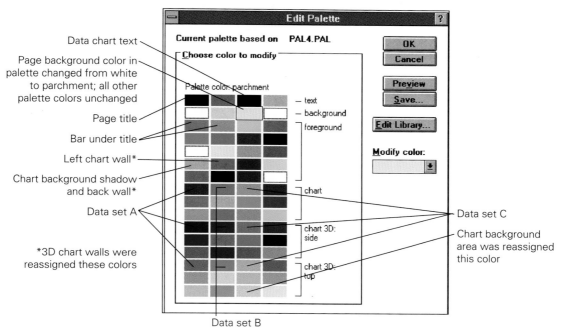

Edit Palette

Data chart text —

Current palette based on PAL4.PAL

Choose color to modify

OK
Cancel

Page background color in palette changed from white to parchment; all other palette colors unchanged —

Palette color parchment

— text
— background
foreground

Preview
Save...

Page title —

Bar under title —

Edit Library...

Left chart wall* —

Modify color:

Chart background shadow and back wall* —

chart

Data set A —

Data set C

chart 3D: side

Chart background area was reassigned this color

*3D chart walls were reassigned these colors

chart 3D: top

Data set B

Color Plates 6–7.

A 3D Area chart is shown here with the color palette used to create it. The SmartMaster set used was BEVRULE.MAS, which normally has a blue background. The Style ➤ Choose Palette command was used to change the palette to PAL4.PAL, which has a white background. Color 7 of this palette was changed to parchment to produce the ivory-colored background shown here. The Chart ➤ Background command was used to create a shadowed chart background, and some colors in the chart were reassigned. For example, the chart wall colors were changed to shades of gray.

Color Plate 8.

Here is a color version of the Radar chart discussed in Chapter 8. Radar charts are particularly useful for making multifactor comparisons among entities. The entity with the most symmetrical plot is the most nearly optimal combination of the factors. This conclusion will be valid, however, only if all factors are scaled the same. (In this case, each of the factors is rated from 0 to 5.) In this example, the SmartMaster set WORLD2.MAS was used, which includes the world map symbol. The command Style ➢ Edit Palette was used to change page and chart background colors. The width of data-set plot lines was increased and line styles were changed by double-clicking on the plot and changing options for each data set in the Radar Chart Attributes dialog box.

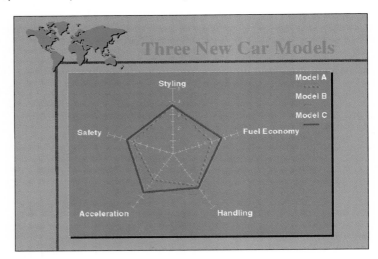

Color Plate 9.

To create this example, the Basic Layout of the SmartMaster set SCRIM.MAS was used, which contains the large shaded rectangle. Selecting Style ➢ Edit Palette changed the background and title colors of SCRIM.PAL. This diagram was created by modifying a symbol from the library file DIAGRAM.SYM. The symbol was broken into its component objects with the Arrange ➢ Ungroup command, then Edit ➢ Replicate was chosen to copy more three-dimensional ellipses. Arrows

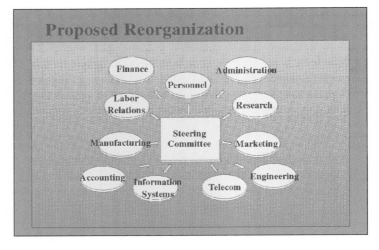

were also copied with this command, and some of these copies were rotated with the Arrange ➢ Rotate command. Finally, Arrange ➢ Group was performed to recombine the ellipses, rectangle, and arrows to form a single object that could be sized and moved as a unit. This example is discussed further in Chapter 10.

Color Plate 10.

This title page for a multimedia Screen Show was created from the SmartMaster set ELEGANCE.MAS. The default color palette and text attributes were used. The logo in the lower-right corner is a cube symbol from the library file _SHAPES.SYM, to which a text block was added in 25-point GillSans UltraBold. The world globe symbol is the multimedia object MMGLOBE.LSM, which is a movie file (with sound) found in the directory LOTUSAPP\MULTIMED. When this page appears in a Screen Show, the globe will rotate once and be accompanied by a musical tone. The object was inserted into the current page with the command Edit ➤ Insert ➤ Lotus Media, specifying Movies for File Type, and then selecting the filename.

Color Plate 11.

This title page for an instructional SmartShow was created from the Title page layout of the SmartMaster set MOUNTAIN.MAS. The Style ➤ Choose Palette command was used to change to the PAL2.PAL palette, which was used unchanged with its white background. A free-form text block was added in the lower right in 29-point Arial MT, and the symbol is a button from the symbol library BUTTONS.SYM. This object can be made into an on-screen control for SmartShows by selecting it in the Current Page view and choosing View ➤ Screen Show ➤ Create-Edit Button. Normally, a Screen Show will advance to the next page if the user clicks anywhere on the screen, but this button could be used to cause the presentation to branch to a master-menu page, which might not necessarily be the next page in numeric sequence.

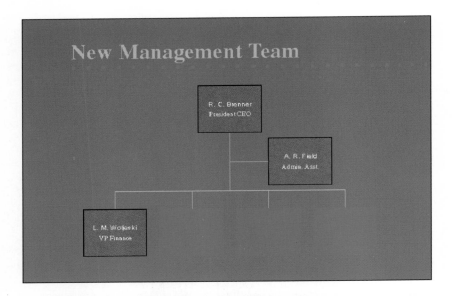

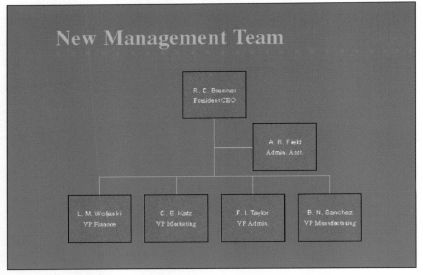

Color Plates 12–13. Here is an example of a buildup sequence created from an organization chart. The full chart (*bottom*) was created first, then duplicated with Page ➤ Duplicate. In the other chart (*top*), the three boxes in the lower right were apparently deleted by changing their area and text colors to match the green background. The color change can be done for each box individually in the Current Page view by double-clicking the box and then resetting options in the Organization Chart Attributes dialog box. Organization charts are covered in Chapter 9.

Color Plate 14.

This table was created from the Table page layout of the SmartMaster set SHADOWBX.MAS. The Style ➤ Edit Palette command was performed to edit the background and chart colors of the default palette. The creation of this chart is covered in Chapter 6, and it is used as an exercise at the conclusion of that chapter. Creating the table involved resetting text justification of selected cells to Center, recoloring the cell backgrounds, and changing the text in three cells of the fourth column to 22-point LetterGothic, a monospace font that provides good vertical justification of numeric entries.

Competitive Comparison

Product Name	Description	Special Features	Suggested Retail Price
Ultra 3000	High-end utility	Variety of attachments	$29.95
Rodex I	Entry-level limited use	European adapter	32.98
Utilo	Utility	Value for price	19.95

Color Plate 15.

This High Low Close Open (HLCO) chart adds the Dow-Jones Industrial Average as a fifth data series, data set E. To make the fluctuations in that data set more apparent, the Chart ➤ Scale command was performed to reset the bottom *y* scale from 2,900 minimum to 3,200 maximum, in increments of 100. The SmartMaster set GRAPHLIN.MAS was used, which includes the pulse symbol at the bottom of the chart area. The default color palette was edited to change the blended background colors to shades of gray, and the chart frame areas were changed to black to make the plot colors stand out. Note that the dashed white horizontal grid lines (a feature of the selected HLCO style) assist the audience in visually estimating the data values.

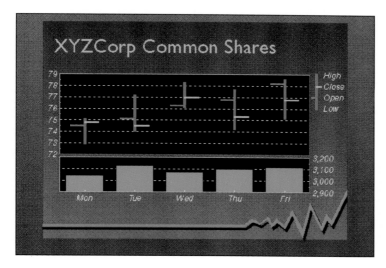

RGB Color Mixing Guide

Red	255	231	207	184	158	134	107	84	59	24	0
Green	0	26	50	74	104	126	150	173	196	225	255
Blue	0	0	0	0	0	0	0	0	0	0	0

Red	255	232	208	186	160	134	109	83	57	24	0
Green	0	0	0	0	0	0	0	0	0	0	0
Blue	0	25	49	74	104	128	151	172	195	226	255

Red	255	231	208	184	158	134	107	84	59	24	255
Green	255	230	207	184	158	134	107	84	59	24	255
Blue	0	24	59	84	107	134	158	184	207	231	255

Color Plate 16. The color patches shown here illustrate just a few of the 16-plus million colors that can be mixed in Freelance Graphics. Library colors in any palette can be adjusted by performing Style ➤ Edit Palette ➤ Edit Library and adjusting the Red, Green, and Blue components from 0 to 255 for any color. In the top row of this chart, proceeding from left to right, Red was decreased and Green was increased in equal increments, while Blue was held at 0. In the second row, Red was increased, Blue was decreased, and Green was held at 0. The third row shows Red and Green decreasing by equal increments, with Blue increasing. In general, add one or two of the component colors to change hues. For example, adding some red and some green will add yellow; adding green and blue will add blue-green; adding blue and red will add violet. To adjust the saturation, or tint, of a color, increase Red, Green, and Blue equally. To adjust the value, or shade, of a color, decrease all components equally. Bear in mind that subtle differences in RGB settings might be apparent even on high-resolution output devices such as color film recorders and true-color video displays.

CHANGING THE APPEARANCE OF ORGANIZATION CHARTS

To change the attributes, such as color, of boxes, text, and lines in the chart, do any of the following:

- Select the chart in the drawing area and perform Chart➤ Attributes.

- Select the chart, click the right mouse button, and select Attributes from the pop-up menu.

- When the chart is displayed in the drawing area, double-click on the element you want to change, such as the solid area within a box or on a connecting line.

- When the Organization Chart Entry List window is open, select Attributes from its menu bar.

To make changes selectively to a box or a group of boxes, click once in the drawing area to select the chart, then again to select the box. Large handles will surround the chart, and small handles will surround the box. With the box or group of boxes selected in the drawing area, perform Chart➤ Attributes or an equivalent command.

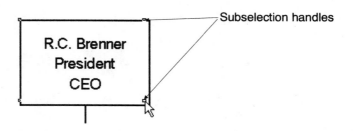

When you take any of these actions, the Organization Chart Attributes dialog box will open, as shown in Figure 9-12. Your selection in the drop-down box (section 1) determines the element you want to change:

Your selection here controls options shown here

If box within chart was selected before this dialog box was opened, its name appears here (name of person)

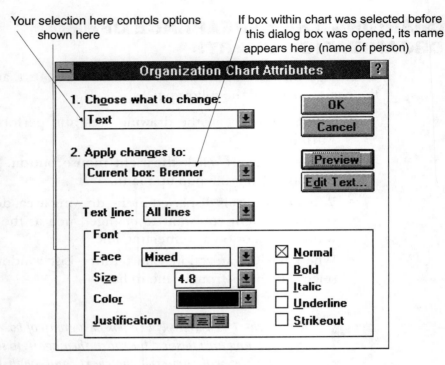

FIGURE 9-12. Change text attributes in this dialog box.

- Text
- Boxes
- Connecting lines
- Frame

The display of options in section 2 will change for each of these selections.

If the selection is either Text or Boxes in section 1, you have the additional option (in section 2), Apply Changes to:

Here you can specify how the settings will apply by selecting All Boxes in Chart, Current Box (which must be selected in the drawing area), Current Box & Subordinates, or Current Box & Peers (all boxes on the same level).

Text Attributes

If you select Text in section 1, the Text Line drop-down box will appear in section 2:

Your selection here determines to which item(s) the changed text attributes will apply. Choose All Lines, Name, Title, or Comment.

Font-attribute options include Face, Size, and Color. Text-style settings can be Normal or any combination of Bold, Italic, Underline, and Strikeout. Justification settings for text within the selected boxes are Left, Center, or Right (shown as buttons).

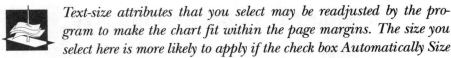

Text-size attributes that you select may be readjusted by the program to make the chart fit within the page margins. The size you select here is more likely to apply if the check box Automatically Size Entry Text is unmarked in the Organization Chart Gallery dialog box.

Box Attributes

If you select Boxes in section 1, you can reset the attributes shown in section 2 of Figure 9-13. For Edge (box outline), make selections for Color, Width, and Style. For Area (box fill), make selections for 1st Color, 2nd Color, and, optionally, Pattern. (The second color will be used only if you select a pattern, as well.) If the check box Same Color as Edge is marked, the Area settings will be ignored, and the Edge Color selection will be used to create solid rectangles.

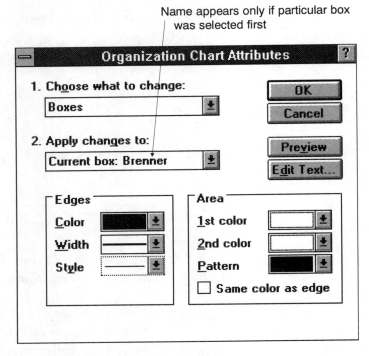

FIGURE 9-13. Change attributes for chart boxes in section 2.

Attributes of Connecting Lines

As shown in Figure 9-14, for Connecting Lines, you can change the Color, Width, and Style settings. If the check box Set Box Edges The Same is marked, the Edge Color attribute in the Boxes options will also be used for the lines that connect the boxes. (This check box will appear only if you opened the dialog box by double-clicking a connecting line in the drawing area.)

Frame Attributes

As shown in Figure 9-15, you can set Edge and Area attributes for a rectangle that will surround the entire chart. No frame will be generated if Edge Style and Area Pattern are set to None.

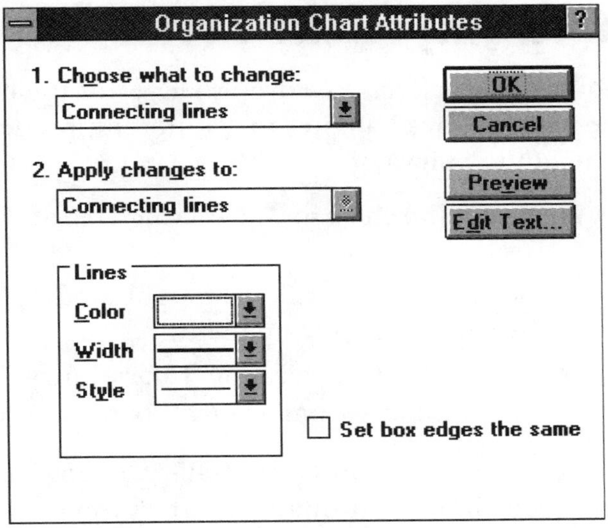

FIGURE 9-14. Section 2 presents these options if you select Connecting Lines in section 1.

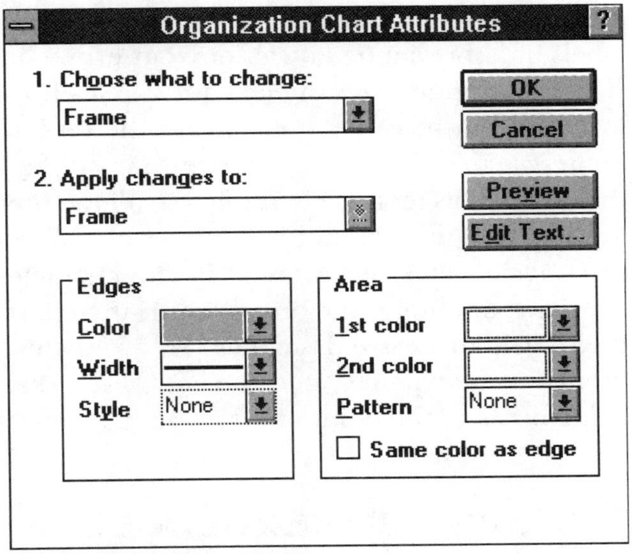

FIGURE 9-15. These options appear for the organization chart frame.

CHANGING THE CHART STYLE

You can add effects like drop-shadow for the boxes or rounded corners simply by changing to a different, predefined chart style. Do one of the following:

- Select the chart in the drawing area and perform Chart≻Gallery.
- Select the chart, click the right mouse button, and select Gallery from the pop-up menu.
- When the Organization Chart Entry List window is open, select Gallery from its menu bar.

The Organization Chart Gallery dialog box will reopen. Select the Style button that shows the effect you want. Then select OK.

CONTROLLING THE SIZE OF TEXT AND BOXES

You can't control the text or box size directly in this type of chart. In general, to increase the size of text and boxes, shorten the box labels by abbreviating entries or by inserting line breaks.

The program sizes the text automatically to compose the best fit in a uniform box size. It calculates the text size required to fit the longest text label into a box size that will be uniform throughout the chart. This text size is applied to all the box labels.

The program will not break lines of text within the boxes unless you specifically enter a break in the character data. Therefore, if you have one long line anywhere in the chart, it can cause all the box labels to be sized smaller. To avoid this, you can insert line breaks as you type text into the entry list. Pressing Ctrl-Enter causes a line break at the point of insertion in a text string.

CREATING BUILDUP SEQUENCES

In some cases, it might be possible to create a buildup sequence for an organization chart by creating the chart, duplicating it in the

Page Sorter, then deleting text entries in selected boxes. However, this approach won't always work. If you happen to enter blanks for the longest line in the chart, the program might recalculate the whole layout, destroying the consistent screen-to-screen matching of objects.

Hiding Text in Buildup Sequences

Another way to achieve a buildup effect is to display the entire chart on each screen—but to selectively color the text labels so that the areas of interest are highlighted and the rest are subdued. Or, hide portions of the chart—including boxes, text, and connecting lines—by selecting them in the Current Page view and setting their Color attributes to match the box fill color or the background color. An example is shown in Figure 9-16.

A variation of this technique is to hide the text but not the boxes. For example, selecting the same color for both a name and its box fill will hide the text, making the box look empty. So, recoloring the name on the next screen or slide in a buildup sequence will make the text appear to pop into the box.

Showing Skip-Level Relationships

In a skip-level reporting relationship, a subordinate has no supervisor on the level above and must report to the manager on the next-higher level. These relationships are relatively common in practice, especially if an organization is understaffed.

Figure 9-17 shows the actual organization structure. The shop technician reports directly to the service manager. Field technicians, however, report to supervisors, who, in turn, report to the manager. The relationship between the shop technician and the service manager involves skip-level reporting because this technician has no middle-level supervisor.

Freelance Graphics for Windows will draw the chart as shown in Figure 9-18. This organization incorrectly implies that the shop

A. Create this slide (the last in the buildup sequence) first.

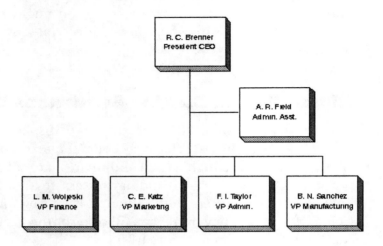

B. Select boxes and set attributes of boxes and text to same as background color.

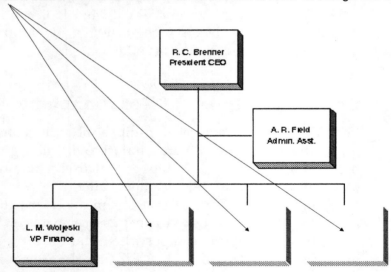

FIGURE 9-16. To hide text during a buildup sequence, recolor it to match the box background. (This method preserves chart composition from one screen to the next.)

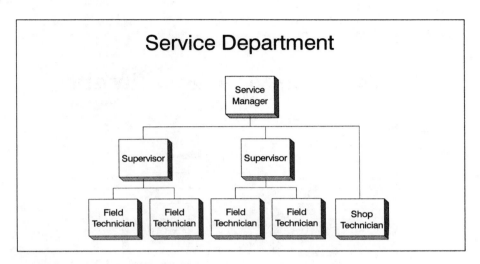

FIGURE 9-17. Skip-level reporting

technician has received a promotion, in effect, and is considered to be on the same level as the supervisors. Levels in an organization chart usually correspond not only to responsibility, but also to compensation. So the mistake is doubly misleading.

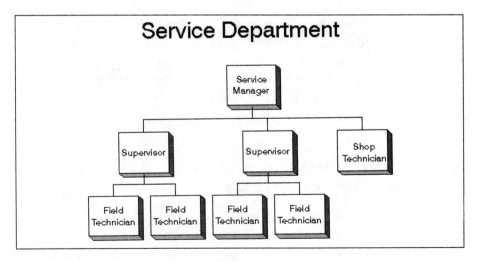

FIGURE 9-18. Chart as drawn by the program

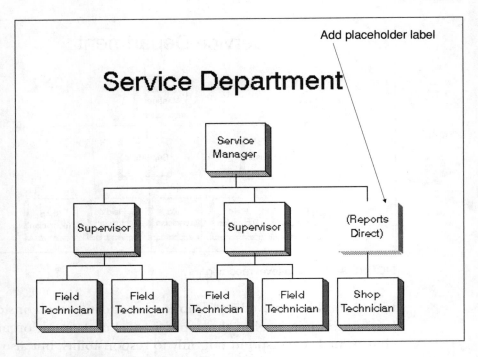

FIGURE 9-19. Workaround solution

One solution might be to enter the placeholder label **Reports To Manager** at the supervisor level for the shop technician, as shown in Figure 9-19.

An alternative solution would be to use the drawing tools to create that portion of the chart so that it shows the actual arrangement in Figure 9-17.

EXERCISE: CREATE AND EDIT AN ORGANIZATION CHART

The data shown in Figure 9-20 cause the chart shown previously in Figure 9-7 to be generated.

Try entering the data as a new page in the presentation SAMPLE.PRE. Then, reset chart attributes to change the appearance to match the chart in Figure 9-21. Specifically, you will need to:

```
R.C. BRENNER
President CEO
        L.M. WOLJESKI
        VP Finance
                N.M. CHOU
                Manager
                        B.F. SEPAN
                        Supervisor
        C.E. KATZ
        VP Marketing
                L.L. BARSTOW
                Manager, East
                P.C. ARGUILES
                Manager, Central
                N.Y. YOSHIMURA
                Manager, West
        F.I. TAYLOR
        VP Admin.
                R.C. WHEATLY
                Manager
        B.N. SANCHEZ
        VP Manufacturing
                A.N. SWANBERG
                Manager
                        D.E. HARLEY
                        Supervisor
                        C.C. MOSS
                        Supervisor
```

FIGURE 9-20.   Data for the chart in Figure 9-7

- Change Lowest Level setting to Row of Boxes
- Change to a rounded box style
- Enter a staff position
- Change the Area Color attribute for all boxes in the chart

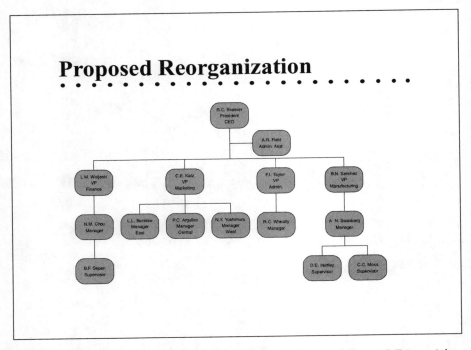

FIGURE 9-21.   In the Exercise, change the chart attributes of Figure 9-7 to match
this example.

CREATING DIAGRAMS FROM SYMBOLS

In Freelance Graphics for Windows, the Organization Chart feature
appears with Release 2. In Release 1, the recommended way of creating these charts was to adapt predrawn charts that were supplied
in the symbol libraries.

Although the newer method of creating organization charts is
much more convenient and certainly more extensive, the original
approach can still be used effectively to create other types of diagrams.

To add a symbol to a page in the drawing area, click on the Symbol tool in the toolbar:

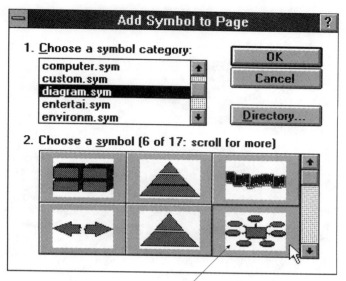

Selected symbol used to create
Figure 9-21

FIGURE 9-22. This dialog box appears when you select the Symbol tool.

The Add Symbol to Page dialog box will appear, as shown in Figure 9-22. In section 1, select a symbol category (library filename) from the list. The drawings it contains will then appear as buttons in section 2. Adjust the scroll bar on the right of the button display to see all the drawings in the file. Click on the drawing you want, then select OK.

As an alternative to clicking on the Symbol tool, you can select File➤Open and specify Symbol Library for the File Type setting. Change to the directory FLW\MASTERS. Select a filename, then OK. Symbols will appear in the Page Sorter. Select Edit➤Copy to move a selected symbol to the Clipboard. Change the active window to your presentation page and perform Edit➤Paste.

The selected symbol will appear surrounded by handles in the drawing area. Drag the handles to resize or move the symbol as you

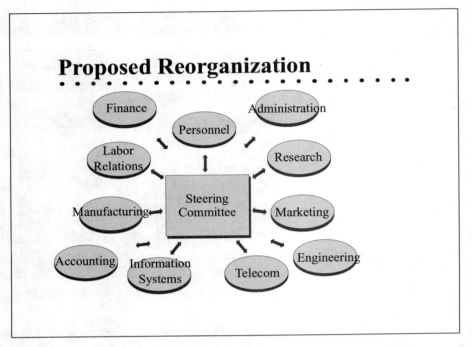

FIGURE 9-23. This diagram was made by modifying the symbol selected in Figure 9-22.

would any graphic object. (Hold down the Shift key as you do so if you want to prevent distorting its shape.)

Two of the supplied symbol libraries may be particularly helpful for creating diagrams: DIAGRAM.SYM contains block diagrams, pyramids, arrows, and three-level organization charts; and FLOW-CHRT.SYM has data-processing flowchart symbols, which can be added to a page individually. Add connecting lines with the Line tool.

A diagram that was created from a drawing in DIAGRAM.SYM is shown in Figure 9-23. (The original symbol is highlighted in Figure 9-22.) After the symbol was brought into the drawing area, the Arrange➤Ungroup command was used to separate it into its component objects. An ellipse in the drawing was duplicated several times, then the duplicates were repositioned within the drawing.

The same procedure was used to duplicate the arrows. Labels were added with the Text tool.

There is more information on drawing techniques in Chapters 5 and 10.

DRAWING AND PRODUCTION SHORTCUTS

Drawing tools and techniques are presented in Chapter 5. This chapter covers other program features that enhance your ability to draw, as well as tips and techniques for creating special kinds of charts and graphic effects.

CREATING MULTIPLE-CHART PAGES

In Freelance Graphics for Windows, a page can contain many charts. Charts can be added to a page in the Current Page view by executing the command Chart≻New.

A submenu will appear, as shown in Figure 10-1. From the submenu, select the type of chart to be added. After you make this selection, the Gallery dialog box for that chart type will open. You then select a style and enter chart data just as you would for a new page. After you have entered the data, the chart will appear surrounded by handles in the drawing area of the current page. You can then manipulate the chart as you would any complex graphic object: You can drag its size, shape, and location, as shown in Figure 10-2.

FIGURE 10-1.   This submenu appears when you select Chart➤New.

Multiple charts will appear in the drawing area overlaid on one another. You will have to drag and possibly resize them to compose the page properly.

An example of a multiple-chart page is shown in Figure 10-3. Don't confuse pages that contain multiple charts with the Handout options for printouts. In Freelance Graphics for Windows, a handout is a printed output that can contain one to six pages. Each of those pages, in turn, could contain multiple charts.

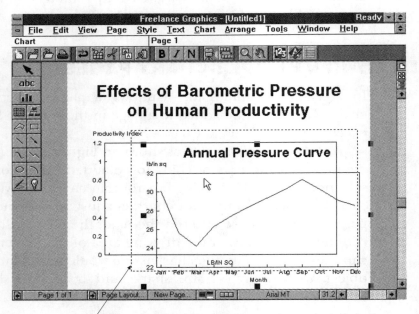

Reference rectangle moves as you drag selected chart

FIGURE 10-2.   Drag multiple charts and resize them to recompose the page.

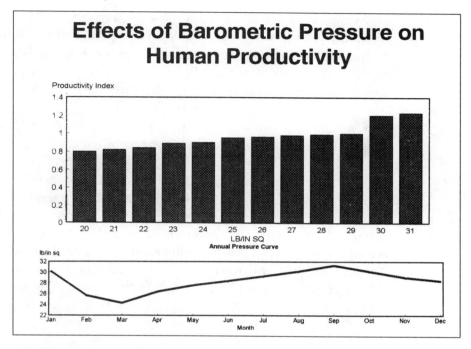

FIGURE 10-3. This page contains multiple charts.

 As an alternative, you can use one of the ready-made multiple-chart page layouts: 2 Charts, 4 Charts, or Bullets & Chart.

USING THE SYMBOL LIBRARY

An important use of drawing capabilities in Freelance Graphics for Windows is to create, recall, and modify symbols, or predrawn electronic art. In practical terms, a symbol is a drawing that you plan to reuse as a design element in other charts. A company logo is an example.

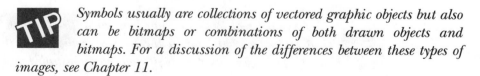 *Symbols usually are collections of vectored graphic objects but also can be bitmaps or combinations of both drawn objects and bitmaps. For a discussion of the differences between these types of images, see Chapter 11.*

Symbols are stored in sets, or *symbol categories,* and these files are given the extension .SYM. Categories typically represent themes, such as people, maps, logos, and so forth. One symbol-category file might hold 50 different symbols or more, which can be retrieved and selected individually through the Current Page view.

 For convenience of access, always store symbols by category and assign filenames that describe those categories.

An assortment of symbols is provided with the program. A library of 2,000 additional symbols is available as a separate product, Lotus SmartPics for Windows. SmartPics category files have the extension .SYl and are compatible with Freelance Graphics for Windows and other Lotus applications for Windows such as Ami Pro and 1-2-3. If you have installed SmartPics, you can access the files by clicking on the Launch SmartPics icon in Freelance Graphics:

Retrieving a Symbol

To add a symbol to the Current Page view, select the Symbol tool:

 The Symbol tool looks almost identical to the Launch SmartPics icon. The tool is found in the toolbox to the left of the drawing area. The icon, used only if you have installed SmartPics, is

among the available icons that can be added to the SmartIcon set, or toolbar that usually runs across the top of the screen.

To add a symbol, you can also click on the following prompt whenever you see it on a page layout:

> Click
> here to
> add
> symbol

The Add Symbol to Page dialog box will open, as shown in Figure 10-4. In section 1, select a symbol category (library filename) from the list. The drawings it contains will then appear as buttons in section 2. Adjust the scroll bar on the right of the button display to see all the drawings in the file. Click on the drawing you want, then select OK.

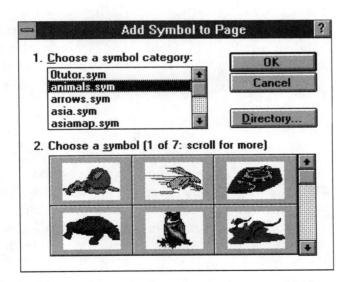

FIGURE 10-4. This dialog box appears when you click on the Symbol tool or on an area labeled "Click here to add a symbol."

As an alternative to clicking on the Symbol tool, you can select File➤Open and specify Symbol Library as the file type. Change to the directory FLW\MASTERS. Select a filename, then OK. Symbols will appear in the Page Sorter. Select Edit➤Copy to move a selected symbol to the Clipboard. Change the active Window to the drawing area of a presentation page and perform Edit➤Paste to add the symbol.

The selected symbol will appear surrounded by handles in the drawing area. Drag the handles to resize or move the symbol as you would any graphic object. (Hold down the Shift key as you do so, if you want to prevent distorting its shape.)

Editing Symbols

You can use the drawing tools and editing commands in the Current Page view to manipulate the symbol as you would any graphic object.

Remember that a symbol typically is a group of objects. To change the shape or size or to edit points within these objects, you must first dissociate them from the group. Select the symbol so that handles surround it. Then select Arrange➤Ungroup, or click on the Ungroup icon:

After you perform Ungroup on a symbol, separate sets of handles will surround each of its component objects, as shown in Figure 10-5. The objects can then be manipulated individually.

Attributes of component objects can be changed without first ungrouping them from the symbol. Simply double-click on the object you want to change, and the Style Attributes dialog box will appear for that object type. Reset the attributes and select OK to close the dialog box.

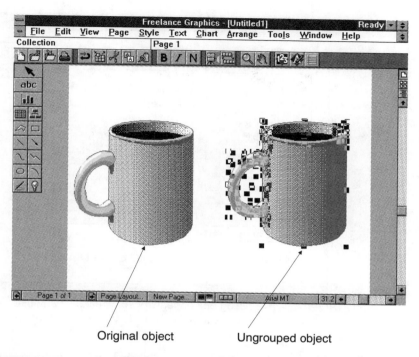

Original object   Ungrouped object

FIGURE 10-5. When you perform Ungroup for a symbol, handles surround each
of the unlinked objects.

Saving a Symbol

To make a new symbol, first create it as a drawing in the Current
Page view. Select all its component objects, then perform Group.
With the group selected, perform Tools➤add to Symbol Library.
The Tools Add to Symbol Library dialog box will appear, as shown
in Figure 10-6. Select a filename from the list of category files or
type a new one, then select OK. The file you select will not be overwritten (replaced) as it would be in a File➤Save operation. Rather,
the selected symbol will be added, or appended, to the existing symbol-category file. (The file CUSTOM.SYM is provided to hold your
custom symbols.)

*If the selection in the drawing area contains multiple objects, they
will be saved as separate symbols, not as a group.*

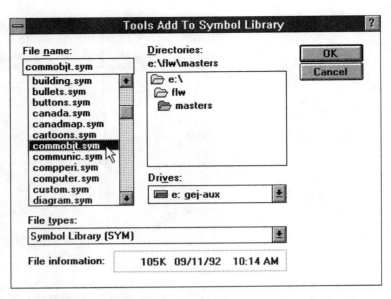

FIGURE 10-6. This dialog box appears when you select an object in the drawing
area and perform Tools➤Add to Symbol Library.

Saving a Chart as a Symbol

Any chart you create in the Current Page view can be saved as a symbol by selecting it in the drawing area and doing the procedure just described. In Freelance Graphics for Windows, the data in a chart that has been saved as a symbol remain accessible and editable. For example, if you retrieve a bar chart that you have saved in a symbol-category file, you can reopen its Chart Data & Titles window by selecting it and performing Chart➤Edit.

This is significantly different from some other graphics software programs, in which saving charts as symbols converts them to images. No charting operations can be performed on charts that have been converted to images.

Using Symbols as Bullets

To add interest to text pages, you can use symbols instead of bullets in any text block that contains a bulleted list.

Click here to select bullet style

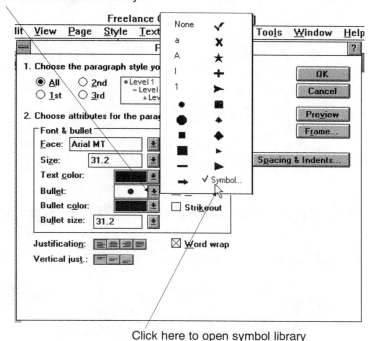

Click here to open symbol library

FIGURE 10-7. To specify a symbol in place of bullets, make this selection in the Bullet drop-down box.

To change a bullet in the drawing area to a symbol, double-click on the text block that contains it. (Remember to double-click on the unselected block, *not* on a block that is open for editing.) The Paragraph Styles dialog box will open. In section 2 of the dialog box, select the Bullet drop-down box. Then, select Symbol from the list, as shown in Figure 10-7.

The Choose Symbol for Bullet dialog box will open. (This is essentially the same dialog box as shown in Figure 10-4.) Retrieve a symbol by first selecting a symbol-category file, choosing one of the symbol buttons, and selecting OK to close the dialog box.

The symbol you have selected will appear as the Bullet selection in the Paragraph Styles dialog box:

Bull<u>e</u>t:

You can adjust the size of the bullet symbol by changing the numeric setting (8–72) in the Bullet Size drop-down box. To see the effect of these changes on the actual size of the symbol, click and hold on the Preview button. When you have made all your changes, select OK to close the Paragraph Styles dialog box.

A sample result, a list that has symbols instead of bullets, is shown in Figure 10-8.

Sharing Symbols with Other Applications

Symbols can be passed through the Clipboard to other Windows applications that support graphics. Select the symbol in the Current

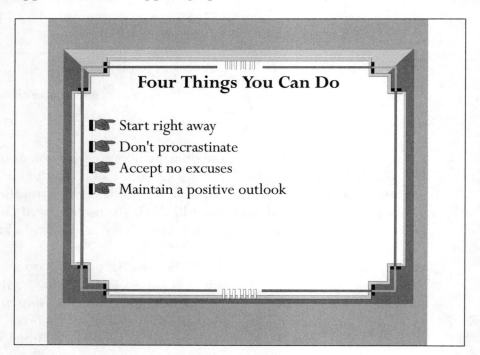

FIGURE 10-8. Symbols have been substituted for bullets in this list.

Page view, and perform Edit≻Copy to place it on the Clipboard. Switch to the other application and perform Edit≻Paste to retrieve the symbol.

A variety of graphic and bitmap formats can be brought in through the Clipboard to Freelance Graphics for Windows.

Graphics and bitmaps can also be exchanged with non-Windows applications by using the Freelance Graphics commands File≻ Import and File≻Export. There's much more information about sharing graphics with other programs in Chapter 14.

DRAWING TIPS AND TECHNIQUES

I offer here some personal preferences for using the drawing tools and editing commands in the Current Page view. Also covered are some tips for creating custom effects.

Tool Locking and Object Selection

In the Current Page view, a feature called *tool locking* controls the manner in which drawing tools are activated. Tool locking can be turned on or off to make object selection more convenient, depending on your current task and your own particular work style.

The tool-locking setting is made by performing Tools≻User Setup. The User Setup dialog box will open. The setting is found in the Drawing Tools box:

```
┌─Drawing tools────────┐
│ ○ Keep tool active    │
│ ◉ Revert to pointer   │
└───────────────────────┘
```

Keeping a Tool Active

Select the option button Keep Tool Active if you want to use the same tool repeatedly. For example, turn it on if you wish to draw a series of circles; the Ellipse tool will remain selected after you have drawn the first circle, and the drawing cross hairs will remain active. The handles around the first object you drew will disappear if you start to draw another ellipse or circle.

Clicking on the Selector tool has the effect of turning tool locking off temporarily and selecting the last object drawn. (The Selector tool is the arrow icon at the top of the toolbox.) When you select another drawing tool, the lock is reinstated.

Reverting from a Tool to the Pointer

By default, tool locking is turned off and the Revert to Pointer option is active. With this option, the Selector tool is activated automatically after you draw an object. Handles appear around the object, ready for editing. You will probably want to leave tool locking off whenever you are making selective changes to a chart or drawing.

Get accustomed to using the tool-locking feature. Verify its setting by selecting Tools➤User Setup, especially before you start any kind of detailed drawing. Your preference will apply from one session to the next, until you reset the option.

Making the Same Change to Several Objects

If you want to change the same attribute *to the same setting* for several objects (such as when filling them all with the same color), simply select them together and perform the edit. If the attribute does not apply to any of the objects selected (if one object is a line, for example), the setting will be ignored for that object. Recall that you can select multiple objects by drawing a box around them or by holding the Shift key while you click on each.

Finding the Center of a Circle

Particularly when used to draw a circle, the Ellipse tool works somewhat differently from what you might expect. Instead of picking the

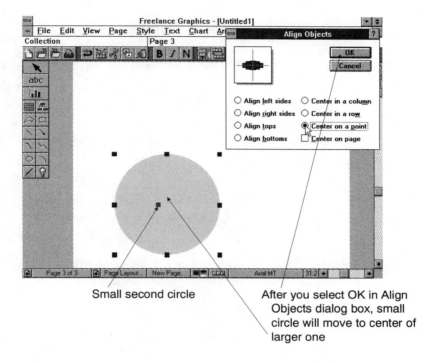

Small second circle

After you select OK in Align
Objects dialog box, small
circle will move to center of
larger one

FIGURE 10-9. You can use this procedure to find the center of a circle.

center point and a point on the circumference, you simply "grow"
the circle from a single point on its edge. For this reason, it can be a
bit more difficult to find the center of a circle or to fit it exactly
among previously drawn objects.

To find the center of a circle, create a small second circle. Select
both this circle and the larger one, then perform Arrange➤
Align➤Center on a Point. The small circle will be aligned in the
center of the larger one. This procedure is shown in Figure 10-9.

Using the Rulers, and Grid and Snap

As covered in Chapter 5, rulers and grids are features that serve as
drawing guides in the Current Page view.

Using Rulers for Visual Measurements

Rulers appear at the edges of the drawing area and track the horizontal and vertical positions of the mouse on a scale marked in inches, centimeters, or other unit of measurement. Use rulers for making measurements visually on the drawing screen.

To show rulers in the drawing area, select View➤View Preferences and mark the Drawing Ruler check box. Or, click on the Show Drawing Ruler icon:

The Big Crosshair option is also recommended for use with rulers. You can activate this option by clicking on the Big Cursor icon:

Rulers are useful for matching your work in the drawing area to the dimensions of specific output devices, such as printers. The dimensions of the vertical and horizontal rulers will correspond to the Paper Size setting in File➤Printer Setup➤Setup.

Using Grid and Snap

A grid in the Current Page view is an array of points spaced evenly throughout the drawing area, as shown in Figure 10-10.

Grid display can be turned on or off, and you can control the spacing between grid points. The position of objects can be made to coincide with (snap to) grid points, simplifying alignment.

The Grid and Snap features can be used to space objects at precise locations with a minimum of effort. This is particularly handy if several objects must be arranged with uniform spacing between them. (As an alternative, use the Arrange➤Space command, described below.) Used by itself, a grid can help you visually esti-

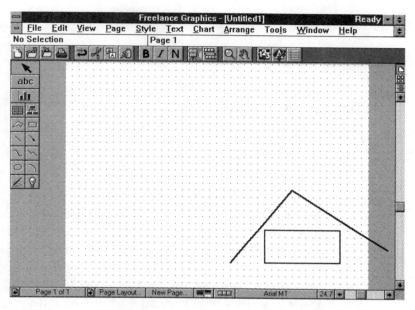

FIGURE 10-10. Turning the Grid option on displays an array of uniformly spaced points in the drawing area.

mate the positions of objects, particularly if the rulers are also displayed.

Turning on Grid and Snap

To display a grid, perform View➤Units & Grids, then mark the check box Display Grid. Or, select the Show Grid icon:

The Horizontal and Vertical Space settings control the spacing between grid points according to the current Units setting. The option Snap to Grid will force points selected for drawn objects to coincide with, or snap to, points on the grid. You can also activate the Snap feature by clicking on the Turn Grid Snapping On icon:

Tips on Using a Grid

Here are some suggestions for using Grid and Snap successfully:

- Particularly when you are using the drawing tools, turn Snap on and off by pressing Shift-F7.

- Unless you want polyline or polygon vertices to be only at points on a grid, turn Snap off when drawing the object. But if Snap is on, you won't need to press the Shift key to constrain line segments to 90- or 45-degree angles: A line segment will follow only the angles that connect grid points. (To produce 45-degree angles, the grid must be square; that is, it must have identical vertical and horizontal settings.)

- As with the Polyline tool, press the Shift key while drawing a line to constrain it to 90- or 45-degree angles. Turn Snap off unless you want the endpoints of the line at points on the grid. Set Snap on if you want to draw straight lines along vertical or horizontal grids without having to press the Shift key.

- Turn Snap on as an aid to creating regular polygons. There is no feature in Freelance Graphics for Windows Release 2 for generating regular polygons based on the number of sides. Once you have created the object, turn Snap off and use the Arrange➤Rotate command to orient the object the way you want it.

Controlling Object Priority

As discussed previously, objects in Freelance Graphics are displayed as though they were created on different overlapping layers, or drawing planes. In general, object priority is the reverse of creation order: Objects created first are said to be in back, and each subsequent object forms the next layer forward. The forward objects appear to be on top, obscuring the overlapping portions of the objects beneath them.

To move an object the farthest back or forward, you need only select that single object and perform Arrange➤Priority➤Bottom or Arrange➤Priority➤Top. Also available for this purpose are the icons:

Send To Back   Bring To Front

You can reposition a selected object with respect to other object layers by performing Arrange➤Priority➤Send Forward One (or press Shift-F8) or Arrange➤Priority➤Fall Back One (or press F8). (See Figure 10-11.) Icon alternatives are:

Forward One   Back One

 Objects in the SmartMaster layout are in the background and are always on the bottommost layer. The priority of objects in "Click here..." areas cannot be changed.

Editing Points

In the Current Page view, selecting Arrange➤Points Mode (or pressing Shift-F6) permits you to select and change individual points, or vertices, within objects. You can also click on the Points Mode icon:

When you are in this mode, the pointer changes to the Points Mode indicator:

In Edit Points mode, when you select an object that contains vertices, the vertices appear with small, hollow selection handles. Then, when you click on a point to edit it, the handle becomes solid:

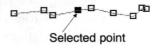

Selected point

To select multiple points, hold down the Shift key while clicking on each of them. Or, drag a box around a collection of adjacent points.

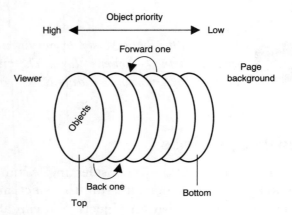

FIGURE 10-11. If an object is higher in priority, it obscures the overlapping portions of objects beneath.

Moving a Point

To move a vertex, select it and drag it to a new location. A reference outline will move with the pointer as you drag it, and the shape of the object will change when you release the mouse button.

Deleting a Point

When you delete points, bends in the shape of an object tend to become sharper. To delete a vertex, select it and perform Arrange➤ Edit Points➤Delete Points or Edit➤Clear (or press Del).

 You cannot delete entire objects in Edit Points mode. Press Shift-F6 to exit this mode before trying the deletion.

Adding a Point

Adding points can make bends smoother. To add a vertex, select it and perform Arrange➤Edit Points➤Add Point (or press Ins). Or, click on the Add Point icon:

The symbol inside the pointer will change to a plus sign:

Click on the location of the new vertex, and it will appear as a solid handle. The new vertex must lie on an edge of the object, but you can drag it to any location.

Breaking Objects

In Edit Points mode, you can *break* an object into its component line segments or polygons. When you perform the break, the object initially will look the same. But you can then drag its line segments or polygonal area apart.

You begin by selecting the point or points at which the object will be broken. Different procedures apply to objects that are open, such as lines or curves, and objects that are closed, such as polygons or rectangles.

Breaking Lines and Curves

To break a line or a curve in Edit Points mode, select the point or points at which connections will be severed. Selected points will change from hollow to solid squares. (Hold down the Shift key while selecting multiple points.) Then, select Arrange➤Edit Points➤Break.

The handles of the selected points will disappear from the object. However, the points are still there and available for manipulation. If you click on the point of a break, it will reappear as a very small, solid handle. You can then drag the point to reposition it. As you do so, the break in the object will become apparent:

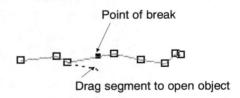

Point of break

Drag segment to open object

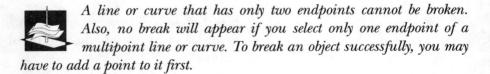

A line or curve that has only two endpoints cannot be broken. Also, no break will appear if you select only one endpoint of a multipoint line or curve. To break an object successfully, you may have to add a point to it first.

Breaking Polygons

To break a polygon or rectangle in Edit Points mode, select two break points by holding down the Shift key as you click on each of them. The points must not be adjacent; that is, the points must mark the boundaries of a polygon, so there must be at least one point between them on the edge or line. (Think of slicing through the object from one selected point to the other.)

After selecting the points, perform Arrange➤Edit Points➤ Break. The solid selection handles will disappear. Press Shift-F6 to exit Edit Points mode. The break will not yet be visible. Click on one portion of the broken object. Solid handles will surround that portion only. Drag it away from the other portion. The break will become visible and the program will reconnect each of the new objects, closing them at the points of the break. An example is shown in Figure 10-12.

 You cannot break rectangles or circles. Convert them first to lines or polygons with the commands Arrange➤Convert to Lines or Arrange➤Convert to Polygons. The vertices of the lines or polygons can then be edited.

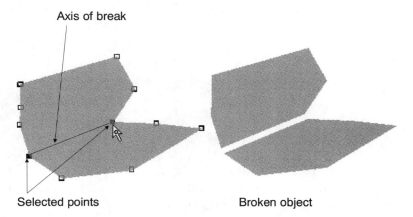

Axis of break

Selected points   Broken object

FIGURE 10-12. The result of breaking a polygon is two closed, filled areas, or polygons.

Editing Curves

Recall that Freelance Graphics generates open curves as Bézier curves. Each vertex on such a curve has two control points:

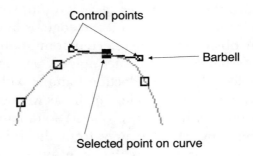

The length of the line segment between the control points and its angle in relation to the vertex on the curve define the shape of the curve at that point.

When you select a vertex on a curve in Edit Points mode, the control points appear as a *barbell*. You can drag the endpoints of the barbell to adjust the shape of the curve:

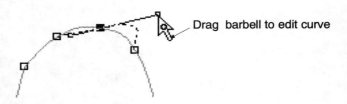

You can adjust the length of either segment of the barbell, or you can rotate it. A dotted reference line shows the revised shape of the curve as you drag the barbell.

In general, if you rotate a barbell to be perpendicular to the original curve, you will create a cusp, or sharp bend in the curve:

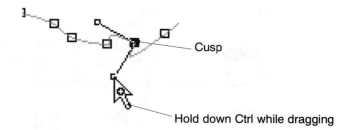

To make a cusp even sharper, hold down the Ctrl key while you drag one end of the barbell. This creates a bend in the barbell itself and a sharp bend in the curve.

Connecting Lines

To connect multiple objects that have been created as separate lines or arrows, select all of them (click on each while holding down the Shift key), and then select Arrange➤Connect Lines. The lines will be joined at their closest points.

When you connect arrows, an arrowhead will appear only at the endpoint of the resulting polyline. That is, there will be only one arrowhead at the end of the series of connected lines. To change the endpoint at which the arrowhead is located, to put arrowheads at both endpoints, or to delete the arrowheads, double-click on the connected line and reset the options in the Paragraph Styles dialog box.

Making Objects Open or Closed

If the endpoints of an object such as a line or arc are not joined, the object is said to be open. An open object cannot be filled with a solid color or pattern. If the endpoints are joined, the object is closed, permitting it to be filled. In Freelance Graphics for Windows, open objects can be converted to closed ones, and vice versa.

The conversion can be done either in the normal drawing mode or in Edit Points mode.

A line that has just two points is open by definition and cannot be converted. In other words, the object must contain at least three points to have the option of being open or closed.

To close an open object, such as a polyline, select it in the drawing area. Then, perform Arrange➤Convert➤To Polygons. The endpoints of the object will be connected, closing it, and it will be filled with the default color and pattern. To change the fill, double-click on the object or select Style➤Attributes and change the settings. To create a closed object that has no fill (the background shows through), set its pattern to None.

To make a closed object open (removing its fill), select the object in the drawing area and perform Arrange➤Convert➤To Lines. Its fill will disappear, but the object will look closed. In fact, the object now contains a break at its starting point. To make the break visible, perform Arrange➤Points Mode, select the starting point, and drag it away from the object:

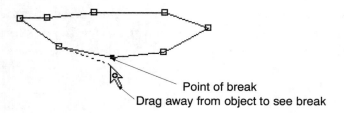

Point of break
Drag away from object to see break

If you select multiple objects for conversion, they will be converted separately rather than combined into a single object.

Replicating Objects

Sometimes you want to replicate, or generate multiple instances of, the same object in the drawing area. This is especially useful for creating special effects such as *sweeps,* or multiple drop shadows (described below).

To replicate an object in the drawing area, select it and perform Edit➤Replicate (or press Ctrl-F3).

The effect of this command depends on the Replicate setting in Tools➤User Setup:

If you select Place Copy on Original, the second instance will be superimposed exactly on the first, so that you will have to drag it away to see the original object beneath.

If instead you select Offset Copy from Original (the default), the second object will appear slightly down and to the right of the original.

Aligning Objects on Each Other

As a drawing aid, the program can align a collection of objects with respect to one another. There is a variety of alignment options.

You cannot change the alignment of objects within a group. Select the object and perform Ungroup first.

Alignment Procedure

To align objects, first select them as a collection. (Hold down the Shift key while clicking on each, or drag a box around all of them.) Handles should surround each of the selected objects. Perform Arrange➤Align. The Align Objects dialog box will appear, as shown in Figure 10-13.

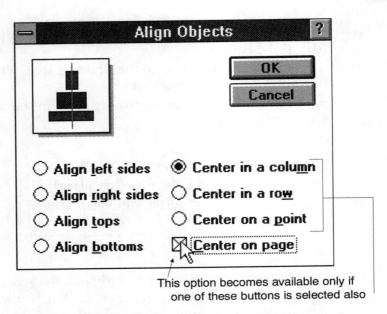

FIGURE 10-13. This dialog box appears when you select a collection of objects and perform Arrange➤Align.

Select the option button for the type of alignment you want. When you make your selection, an illustration of the positioning will be shown in the preview box.

If you select any of the Center option buttons, the Center on Page check box also becomes available. If this box is marked, the objects will be centered both with respect to one another (according to the option button you choose), as well as with respect to the page margins. If the check box is not marked, all the objects will be moved to the point at the center of the collection—which will not necessarily be at the center of the page.

The manner of page centering will depend on the first option. For example, if you choose Center in a Column, the page centering will be done only with respect to the left and right margins—the vertical position of the objects will be unchanged. To center a collection of objects with respect to all margins, select Center on a Point, as well as Center on Page.

When you have made your alignment settings, select OK to close the dialog box.

 If you are not satisfied with the realignment, select Edit➤Undo, then try again, selecting a different option.

Alignment SmartIcons

To align selected objects without making settings in a dialog box, click on the following SmartIcons:

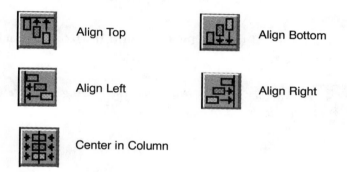

Align Top   Align Bottom

Align Left   Align Right

Center in Column

Creating Uniform Spacing between Objects

The program can create uniform spacing within a collection that contains *at least three* objects.

To space the objects uniformly, first select them in the drawing area. (Hold down the Shift key while clicking on each, or drag a box around all of them.) Handles should surround each of the selected objects. Perform Arrange➤Space. The Space dialog box will appear, as shown in Figure 10-14. Mark the check box Space Vertically or Space Horizontally, or both. Then, select OK. SmartIcon alternatives are

Space Vertically   Space Horizontally

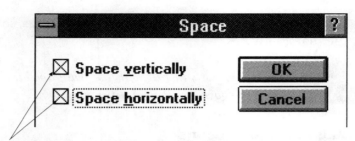

You can space both vertically and horizontally in single operation, if you wish

FIGURE 10-14.   This dialog box appears when you select a collection of objects and perform Arrange➤Space.

Examples of uniform vertical and horizontal spacing are shown in Figure 10-15.

 Another way to create uniform spacing is to use Grid and Snap, as described previously in this chapter.

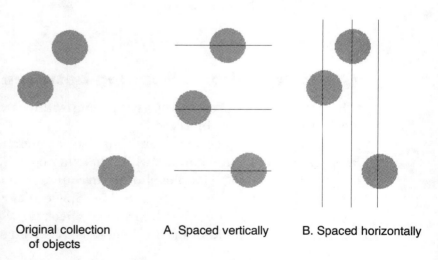

Original collection   A. Spaced vertically   B. Spaced horizontally
   of objects

FIGURE 10-15.   Objects in this drawing have been re-spaced.

Rotating Objects

You can rotate objects—including text blocks—about their centers. Select the object in the drawing area and perform Arrange➤Rotate. Or, click on the Rotate icon:

The pointer will change to an arc with a plus sign:

When this pointer is shown, you can drag the object around its center to any degree of rotation. The operation will end and the pointer will revert to its normal shape when you release the mouse button. You can hold the Shift key down during the rotation to constrain the movement to 45-degree increments.

Text in "Click here..." blocks cannot be rotated. However, you can hold down the Ctrl key, drag the text out of a "Click here..." block, and then perform the rotation. In general, hardware fonts, such as a printer's resident or cartridge fonts, cannot be rotated. If you attempt this, you may see the rotation in the drawing area, but the text will revert to normal horizontal position on printouts.

Objects that cannot be rotated include graphs, tables, and organization charts. Bitmaps can be rotated in increments of 90 degrees.

Skewing Objects

An object that is *skewed* appears to slant. For example a skewed rectangle is a parallelogram:

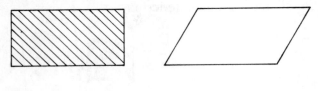

Original object   Skewed to the right

A related effect is *perspective,* which distorts the dimensions of a two-dimensional object in the direction of an imaginary vanishing point to create the impression of the third dimension, as shown in Figure 10-16.

> **TIP** *Methods of achieving perspective and three-dimensional effects vary for different types of objects. For example, you cannot create an ellipse that is initially distorted along a diagonal axis. However, you can create the object and then rotate it, as described above. Remember, however, that you cannot manipulate the pies in pie charts as ellipses. Instead, adjust options for depth, tilt, and starting angle.*

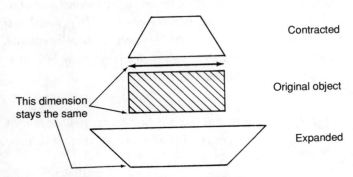

FIGURE 10-16. Distorting an object can help create perspective, or the illusion of depth.

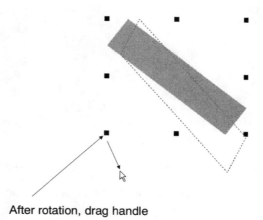

After rotation, drag handle

FIGURE 10-17. Immediately after rotating an object, drag one of its corner handles to skew it.

Perspective in 3D bar, line, and area charts can also be created by setting chart options, such as the floor depth of the plotting area for the 3D Bar (XYZ) chart type. To change these settings, select the chart and then perform Chart≻Attributes≻Options.

Skewing can be done in the Current Page view by using the Rotate tool in a way that causes the object to slant. The skewing operation can involve both rotation and distortion, which can also be useful in adding perspective.

To skew an object in the Current Page view, first select it and rotate it, as described above. When you release the mouse button to complete the rotation, the changed object will be surrounded by handles. Drag one of the object's corner handles, as shown in Figure 10-17. The distorted shape will be shown as a dotted outline as you drag the handle. Release the mouse button when the outline is the desired shape.

It will usually be necessary to reposition an object after performing this skew operation. If the object is a text block or a group that contains text, the skewing operation will not distort the characters.

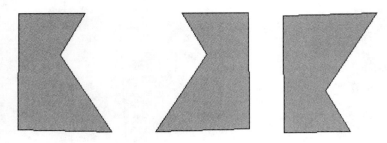

Original object   A. Flipped left to right   B. Flipped top to bottom

FIGURE 10-18. The object in this drawing has been flipped two ways.

Flipping Objects

You can flip an object, creating its mirror image. Select the object in the drawing area and perform Align➤Flip. A submenu will appear. Select either Left to Right (flipping the image on its vertical axis, as you would turn the pages of a book), or Top to Bottom (flipping the object on its horizontal axis, as you would flip the pages of a sketchpad.) SmartIcon alternatives are:

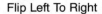

Flip Left To Right   Flip Top To Bottom

Examples of flipped objects are shown in Figure 10-18.

Adding Text Frames

A text frame is a border around a text block:

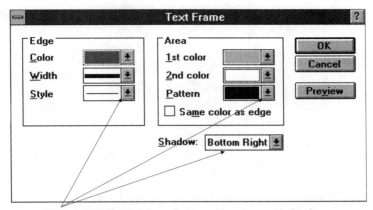

These settings produce frame with edge and shadow

FIGURE 10-19. This dialog box appears when you select a text block and perform Text➤Frame.

To add a text frame to an existing block, click on the block *once* to select it. (Do not open the block for editing.) With the block selected, perform Text➤Frame. The Text Frame dialog box will appear, as shown in Figure 10-19. Select options for the Edge and Area settings of a solid rectangle that will surround the text. Optionally, also select the position of a drop shadow from the drop-down box.

 By default, text blocks have no frames. To remove the frame from a block, set its edge style to None.

Curved Text

In Freelance Graphics for Windows Release 2, a line of text can be curved or bent in several predefined ways, or the text can be made to follow the edge of any other selected object.

Using Predefined Curves or Bends

To create curved text, select a text block (but not a "Click here..." block) in the drawing area. Then, perform Text➤Curved Text, or click on the Curved Text icon:

The Curved Text dialog box will open, as shown in Figure 10-20. Choose one of the buttons to define the shape of the curve. (Use the scroll bar to see more shapes).

For any of the predefined circular or oval shapes, you can enter a starting point as an angle 0 to 359 degrees clockwise from the top (*not* counterclockwise from 3 o'clock, as you specify rotation of pie charts). Select OK to close the dialog box.

Examples of text blocks to which some of the predefined curves and bends have been applied are shown in Figure 10-21.

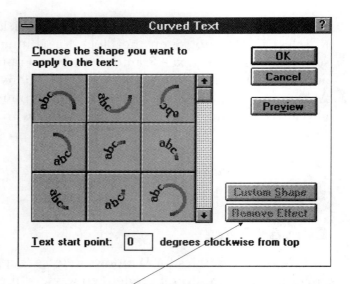

This button becomes available when the selected
text block already has curved effect

FIGURE 10-20.   This dialog box appears when you select a text block and perform Text➤Curved Text.

FIGURE 10-21.   Predefined curves and bends have been applied to these text
blocks.

Creating Custom Shapes

To bend text around an object, select the text, hold down the Shift
key, and select the object. Then, perform Text➤Curved Text. In
this case, the dialog box will not appear, and the text will be moved
to follow the closest edge of the selected object, as shown in Figure
10-22.

*The result will depend on the original positions of the text and the
object, as well as the shape of the nearest edge. You may have to
experiment a bit to get the effect you want.*

Removing the Curvature from Text

To remove the curved effect from a text block, select the block,
then Text➤Curved Text. The dialog box will open. Select the
Remove Effect button, then OK.

FIGURE 10-22. The text block shown here has been fitted to the edge of an arc.

USING ACCELERATOR KEYS

In Windows and in Freelance Graphics for Windows, certain frequently used selections have been implemented as one- or two-key operations. In Lotus applications such as Freelance Graphics, these are called *accelerator keys*. (In Windows, they are called *shortcut keys*. In other applications, they might be called *hotkeys* or *speed keys*.)

For example, the accelerator key for printing a presentation from within Freelance Graphics is Ctrl-P (while holding down the Ctrl key, you press the P key). Accelerator keys are listed to the right of their equivalent commands in pull-down menus.

Even if you rely mainly on the mouse, some of the accelerator keys can be handy for toggling program modes quickly as you draw. For example, Shift-F4 toggles cursor size between Big (use with rulers) and Small, Shift-F6 toggles Edit Points mode, and Shift-F7 toggles the snapping of object vertices to the grid.

Accelerator keys and their command equivalents in Freelance Graphics are presented in Table 10-1.

TABLE 10-1. Accelerator keys (continued next page)

Action or Command Equivalent	*Accelerator Key*
Arrange➤Edit Points➤Add Point	Ins
Arrange➤Edit Points➤Delete Point	Del
Arrange➤Points Mode	Shift-F6[1]
Arrange➤Priority➤Fall Back One	F8
Arrange➤Priority➤Send Forward One	Shift-F8
Close Window	Ctrl-F4
Color *or* B&W display	Alt-F9[1]
Compose Characters	Alt-F1[2] (enter special characters as sequences of keystrokes)
Control menu (active window)	Alt-Hyphen
Control menu (application)	Alt-Spacebar
Edit (toggle Text Edit mode)	F2[1]
Edit➤Clear	Del
Edit➤Copy	Ctrl-C
Edit➤Cut	Ctrl-X
Edit➤Edit Page Layouts *or* Edit➤Presentation Pages	Shift-F9[1]
Edit➤Paste	Ctrl-V
Edit➤Replicate	Ctrl-F3
Edit➤Select All	F4
Edit➤Undo	Ctrl-Z
File➤Exit (close application)	Alt-F4
File➤Print	Ctrl-P
File➤Save	Ctrl-S
Go to	F5[3]
Help (context sensitive)	F1
Import Data	F6
Menu (permit keyboard selections)	F10
Menu (activate a pull-down)	Alt-*underscored letter*
Next Application	Alt-Esc
Next Window	Ctrl-F6
Page➤Duplicate	Alt-F7

TABLE 10-1. Accelerator keys (continued)

Action or Command Equivalent	*Accelerator Key*
Page≻New	F7
Task List	Ctrl-Esc
Text (align left)	Ctrl-L[2]
Text (align center)	Ctrl-E[2]
Text (align right)	Ctrl-R[2]
Text≻Bold	Ctrl-B[1,2]
Text≻Edit	F2[1]
Text≻Italic	Ctrl-I[1,2]
Text≻Normal	Ctrl-N[1,2]
Text (strikeout)	Shift-Ctrl-S[1,2]
Text≻Underline	Ctrl-U[1,2]
Tools≻Spell Check	Ctrl-F2
View≻Redraw	F9
View≻Screen Show≻Run	Alt-F10
View≻Units & Grids≻Snap	Shift-F7[1]
View≻View Preferences≻Cursor Size	Shift-F4[1]

[1] Toggles, or switches between two program modes.

[2] Works only in Text Edit mode, when a text block is open for editing its characters. For attribute changes, press the key combination before you type the string.

[3] Works only when the Chart Data window is open for moving the highlight to a specified cell address.

CUSTOMIZING SMARTICONS AND SETS

The SmartIcons, or button shortcuts, of Freelance Graphics for Windows can be customized to suit your preferences. The default set of SmartIcons is normally positioned across the top of the drawing area in the Current Page view. You can change this position, rearrange the icons, add other icons, or hide the set.

As a further option, you can create custom sets of SmartIcons that you can retrieve by name.

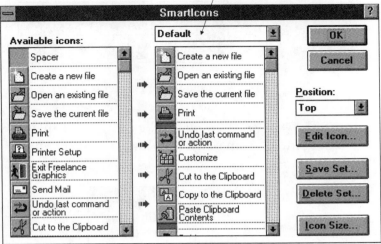

FIGURE 10-23.   Customize SmartIcon sets in this dialog box.

Changing the Display Position of the Set

To change the display position of the current SmartIcon set, select Tools≻SmartIcons. Or, click on the Customize icon:

The SmartIcons dialog box will appear, as shown in Figure 10-23. Select a screen location from the Position drop-down box. Then select OK.

If you select Floating for the position of the set, you will be able to drag the set around on the screen to any position you wish. You can also drag its borders to resize the set. Clicking on its control button will hide a floating set:

Control button

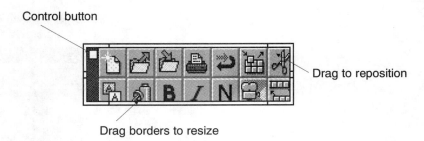

Drag to reposition

Drag borders to resize

To make the set reappear, click on the Display➤Hide SmartIcons box at the bottom of the window, and select Show:

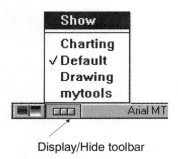

Display/Hide toolbar

Customize a SmartIcon Set

To customize icons for a set of SmartIcons, select Tools➤ Smart-Icons, or click on the Customize icon. The SmartIcons dialog box will open. (Refer again to Figure 10-23.) To add a SmartIcon to the current set, drag it from the Available Icons list on the left into the current set on the right. To change the order of icons in the current set, drag them within the list to rearrange them. To create gaps in the toolbar, segregating icons into groups, drag the Spacer icon to the point in the current set where the gap should appear. (You can also reverse this procedure to remove gaps from the set.)

To create a new, named set, select the Save Set button. The Save SmartIcon Set dialog box will open, as shown in Figure 10-24. Enter the name by which the set will labeled in the program, and also a

FIGURE 10-24. Specify a filename for the new SmartIcon set in this dialog box.

filename (which can be the same, but no more than eight characters without the extension).

The name of the new set will appear among the drop-down box
selections in the SmartIcons dialog box. It will also be available
whenever you select the Display➤Hide SmartIcons box.

To delete a previously named, custom set of SmartIcons, select
the Delete Set button. The Delete Sets dialog box will open:

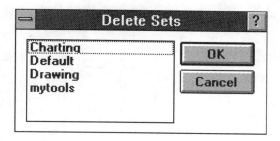

Select the name of the set to be deleted, then OK.

Selecting the Icon Size button permits you to change the displayed size of SmartIcons. Three options are available, depending
on the type of video display on your system: Small (EGA), Medium
(VGA), and Large (Super VGA).

When you are finished customizing SmartIcon sets, select OK to
close the dialog box.

Customizing Individual SmartIcons

You can edit any of the SmartIcons or create new ones that cause actions you specify. Select Tools➤SmartIcons or click on the Customize icon to open the SmartIcons dialog box.

Modifying an Existing Icon Image

From the Available Icons list, select the icon that you want to modify or use as a basis for a new icon. Then select the Edit Icon button.

You cannot modify a standard icon, but you can use it as a basis for creating a new one. If you select one of the standard icons, you will be prompted for a new filename.

The icon you selected will appear as a magnified bitmap image in the Edit SmartIcon dialog box, as shown in Figure 10-25.

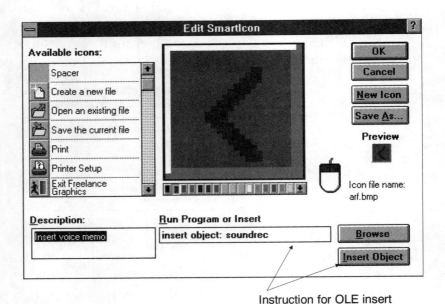

Instruction for OLE insert

FIGURE 10-25. This dialog box appears when you select the Edit Icon button in the SmartIcons dialog box.

To edit the bitmap image of the icon, click on a color from the row of colors just below it. To see more colors, click on the palette drop-down button at the right end of the row. Then, drag the pointer over the pixels in the image that you want to recolor. As you draw, your changes will be shown in actual size in the Preview area.

Optionally, you can add a text description for the new icon. This description will appear in the Available Icons list.

Selecting the icon must trigger a program action. In the Run Program or Insert box, type the *command line*, or program instruction, that will be run when the icon is clicked. Be sure to include the full path (including device and directories), as well as the filename of the program or routine. (The requirements for the path and filename are the same as for any command line you would enter when selecting File➤Run in Windows Program Manager.) To navigate the directory system to find a particular executable file, select the Browse button and make your selection in the File Run dialog box.

To save a new icon, select the New Icon button. To rename and save a modified icon, select Save As. A dialog box will open. Type a filename and select OK. Select OK again to close the Edit Smart-Icon dialog box.

The icon you created or modified will be added to the list of available icons in the SmartIcons dialog box. For the icon to be used, you must now add it to one of the named sets. Select any named set from the drop-down box. Its icons will appear in the list on the right. Drag the new icon from the list on the left to the desired position in the list on the right, and select OK.

Embedding an Object as a SmartIcon

As an alternative to entering a command line for the new SmartIcon, you can choose to embed a Windows object. Select the Insert Object button in the SmartIcons dialog box. The Insert Object dialog box will open. Select the object type to be embedded from the list of Windows applications and objects. Then select OK. This selection will appear as an Insert instruction in the Run Program or Insert text box. Proceed to save the icon as described above, and add it to one of the available sets.

When you click on the new icon, the Windows application you selected will open, permitting you to access a document within it. For more information about object linking and embedding, see Chapter 14.

Change to a Different SmartIcon Set

To switch among predefined sets of SmartIcons, select the Display/Hide SmartIcons box at the bottom of the window. The names of available sets will appear in the pop-up menu. Select the name of the SmartIcon set you want to use. The standard set is named Default. Any other sets you create by the procedure described above will also appear.

As an alternative, click on the Next Icon Set icon in the toolbar:

Clicking on the icon causes the display to cycle among the available sets.

CREATING A BUILDUP SEQUENCE

A buildup sequence, or *build,* is a series of pages in a slide show or screen show in which information is revealed progressively, or built up in stages.

Using the Autobuild Feature for Bulleted Lists

For any page that contains a bulleted list, Freelance Graphics for Windows can create a buildup sequence automatically.

Start by creating the last page in the buildup sequence—a bulleted list that contains all the items to be shown. This master list is called the *parent page.* With the parent page shown in the Current Page view or selected in the Page Sorter, select Page➤Create Build. Or, click on the Create Page Build icon:

The program will generate a new page automatically for each preceding stage of the buildup. That is, one *child page* will be generated for each item in the bulleted list. On each child page, the current bulleted item will be shown in highlight color, with the preceding items dimmed, or subdued. The child pages will be inserted in the correct order in the presentation sequence, preceding the parent page.

 Remember that a separate page will be created for each item in the bulleted list, including subordinate (indented) items. To create a build in which only first-level items are added—along with their subordinates—select the itemized child pages you want to exclude from the build in the Page Sorter and then perform Page➤Remove. You will then have to reopen the text blocks in the Current Page view and recolor any dimmed items that you want to highlight.

 You can perform Page➤Create Build in any view. But if you are in the Page Sorter or the Outliner, the selected page cannot be part of another build.

To delete a buildup sequence, move the parent page into the Current Page view (or select it in the Page Sorter) and perform Page➤Delete Build. Or, click on the Delete Page Build icon:

Creating Buildups of Other Chart Types

Buildups of other chart types can be done by creating the parent page first, performing Page➤Duplicate to create copies of it for each of the child pages, and then deleting items selectively in those pages in the Current Page view. A recommended approach is to create the sequence in reverse order, deleting more items from each of the preceding pages.

If you create a buildup this way, be careful that none of your deletions cause the program to recompose the page. If this happens, objects might shift in position, and the buildup effect will be destroyed—*registration,* or page-to-page matching of object position, will be lost.

Such recomposition will be likely if you are deleting elements such as data series from graphs or boxes from organization charts. To avoid this and maintain registration between pages, do not delete buildup items at all. Instead, hide the items by recoloring them to match the background of the graph or page.

When recoloring buildup items, beware of the consequences of changing palettes later—this could cause the colors to change. To make sure that the items stay hidden even if you change palettes, use the background color in the palette (usually the first color in the second row) that is assigned to the surrounding area. (See Figure 10-26.)

TIP *When creating a buildup sequence of X-Y charts by deleting data sets, you may have to set explicit minimum and maximum axis values in Chart➤Scale to prevent the scales from being recalculated for each page. This will not be necessary if you simply recolor the data sets to match the chart background.*

CREATING SPECIAL EFFECTS

The following special effects are usually done with text but also can be applied to other types of objects, such as rectangles or circles:

Be sure to select color from this row
when hiding objects

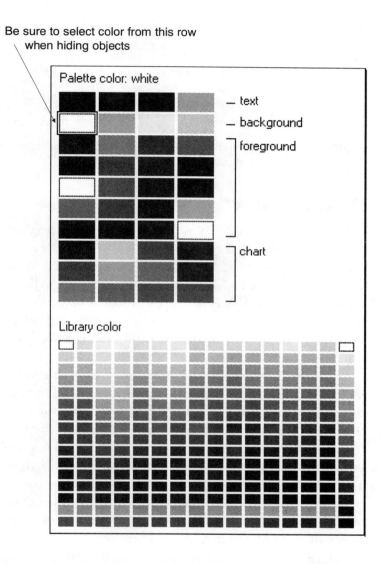

FIGURE 10-26.   To hide objects in buildup sequences, recolor them by using one
of the background colors in the palette.

- Drop shadow
- Floating drop shadow
- Multiple drop shadow and sweep

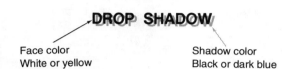

Background
Medium blue

Face color
White or yellow

Shadow color
Black or dark blue

FIGURE 10-27. Text with drop shadow is most effective in large-point type, such as that used for titles.

Drop Shadow

Freelance Graphics for Windows Release 2 has no feature for generating drop-shadowed text automatically. Shadow is an option, however, for graphic objects such as rectangles and text frames.

You can create drop-shadowed text with a little patience. As shown in Figure 10-27, a drop shadow is a second instance of the text, usually just behind it, slightly down and to the right. The shadow gives the text a dimensional effect and often helps it stand out from the background.

Use the Edit➤Replicate command to create a second text object. Zoom the view in the drawing area to magnify the text and drag the copy (the shadow) precisely where you want it. To retain the exact position of the original object, select the copy (which is in front) and perform Arrange➤Priority➤Fall Back One so that the copy is obscured by the original text. Select Style➤Attributes or Text➤Font to change the color of the shadow so that it contrasts both with the face color and the background. Finally, select both text objects and perform Arrange➤Group to combine them so that they will always be manipulated together.

Here are some general rules of thumb for selecting color combinations that work with drop-shadowed text:

- Drop shadow is most effective on text in the larger point sizes, such as titles, for which the default size is 48. In general, avoid drop shadows if text size is less than 24. An exception might be when you must place text over a background or fill that is similar to the text face color. The shadow could make the text more legible.

- For slides and screen shows with black backgrounds, select yellow for the text face color and gold or yellow-orange for the shadow.

- For dark-colored backgrounds, such as dark blue, violet, crimson, or dark green, make the shadow color black.

- Drop-shadowed titles don't necessarily read well on light backgrounds. Black or blue text with a gray drop shadow might work, depending on the value (lightness or darkness) of the background color.

Floating Drop Shadow

An even bolder title, a *floating drop shadow,* can be constructed with a little more effort, as shown in Figure 10-28. Create a third (back-most) shadow first. This effect works best on dark-colored (not black) backgrounds. Make the text color black. Then, perform Edit➤Replicate twice to create two other copies of the text. Recolor the top object yellow and the middle object gold (yellow-orange). Then adjust the positions of all three shadows. The back (black) shadow should be offset more than the gold shadow, but not so much as to affect the readability of the title. Finish by grouping the three objects.

Save the floating drop shadow as a symbol for adding to other pages, or save it in position in a custom page layout for use as a title chart by itself.

Multiple Drop Shadow and Sweep

By making multiple copies of a text block, you can create a *multiple drop shadow,* as shown in Figure 10-29.

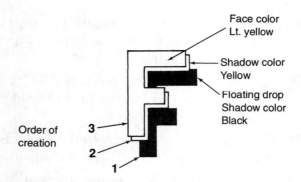

FIGURE 10-28. Text with floating drop shadow can be saved as a symbol.

The objects in a multiple drop shadow can change incrementally in size, color, and rotation. When the transitions are smooth, the effect is called a *sweep.*

With Release 2 of the program, multiple drop shadows and sweeps must be created one object at a time, using the Edit➤Replicate command. Incremental changes can be made as each new copy is created. For example, when the copy appears, you can select Arrange➤Rotate to rotate it slightly. When you perform Edit➤Replicate again, the program will increment the rotation further in the next copy, as shown in Figure 10-30.

Once you have created such an effect, combine the objects as a group and save it as a symbol so that it can be reused in other presentations. The text will remain editable, but you will have to ungroup the blocks first, and they must be edited separately.

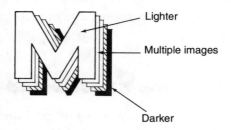

FIGURE 10-29. A multiple drop shadow is also called a *sweep.*

FIGURE 10-30. This multiple drop-shadow effect was produced by using a combination of Replicate and Rotate operations.

Use sweep and multiple drop-shadow effects sparingly. Some output devices cannot reproduce them at all; others might render them poorly. Furthermore, creating a large number of object copies will greatly increase the complexity of a page, especially if the original object is text. Slides with such effects can be impressive but may require very long output times on devices such as color-film recorders.

CREATING CUSTOM PAGES AND SMARTMASTER SETS

A SmartMaster is a template, or guide, for the layout of a page. A SmartMaster set typically contains one layout for each type of chart.

To save production time, you can customize page layouts so that presentations conform automatically to your own design preferences. You can also customize entire sets of SmartMasters—without the effort of starting from scratch—by modifying one of the supplied sets.

Creating custom SmartMasters will be particularly helpful if you must create presentations for different clients. Each client's design preferences can be included in one or more separate, customized sets of layouts.

Creating Custom Pages in a Presentation File

To create a page that departs from the corresponding page layout in the current SmartMaster set, with the page in the Current Page view, select Page➤Unlink Page Layout. Then select OK to confirm the link cancellation. You can now edit the page and the page layout independently of one another.

Making Global Changes to Text Appearance

Among the most apparent design elements of a presentation are text attributes. As an alternative to creating a new SmartMaster set with different text attributes, you can change text globally throughout a presentation. Your changes will apply to the current presentation only, and the SmartMaster set and any other presentations you create from it will remain unchanged. Sometimes, this is the fastest and easiest way to change the appearance of an entire presentation.

To change text attributes globally when you are working in the Current Page view, double-click on any of the "Click here..." text blocks. The Paragraph Styles dialog box will open. Reset the options to change the appearance of the text, then select OK.

Your changes will affect the corresponding text block in every presentation page that uses the current page layout. For example, if you change the bullet items in a page that uses the Bulleted List page layout, the bullet items in all other pages that use this layout will also be changed.

Changing the Basic Layout of a Presentation

Another way to make changes globally in a presentation involves editing the Basic Layout in the current SmartMaster set. Unlike the procedure just described for changing text attributes globally, this approach involves changes to the SmartMaster itself.

The Basic Layout in any SmartMaster set controls common design elements of all other page layouts in the set, except the Title layout. These common elements include background color, page-title position and attributes, symbols, borders, and so on.

To edit the Basic Layout of a SmartMaster set in the Current Page view, select Page➤Choose Page Layout and then Basic Layout. Select OK to close the Choose Page Layout dialog box. The Basic Layout will appear in the drawing area. Then, select Edit➤Edit Page Layouts. Or, select the Edit Page Layouts icon:

A hatched pattern will appear at the edges of the drawing area, indicating that you are in SmartMaster Edit mode. In this mode, changes you make in the drawing area affect the underlying page layout rather than the presentation page.

Edit the Basic Layout as you would a presentation page, perhaps adding symbols. Remember that any changes you make will appear on all presentation pages except those that use the Title page layout.

To make your changes to the SmartMaster permanent, select File➤Save As. Select SmartMaster Set (.MAS) for the file type. Be sure that you are logged on to the FLW\MASTERS directory. Use the name of the existing set to update it, or type a new filename to create a separate, customized version. Select OK to close the Save As dialog box and save the file.

After you have edited the Basic Layout and updated the Smart-Master set, select Edit➤Edit Presentation Pages to resume working on the presentation.

Creating a New SmartMaster Set

To customize an existing SmartMaster set, follow the procedure described above for editing the Basic Layout, but also edit each of the predefined layouts for the chart types. Switch among page layouts in SmartMaster Edit mode by selecting Page➤Choose Page Layout.

You can often change the appearance of a presentation dramatically simply by changing to another color palette or editing the current palette. To change palettes, select Style➤Choose Palette. To edit the current palette, select Style➤Edit Palette. If you make these changes in SmartMaster Edit mode and save them to an .MAS file, all new presentations you create with that SmartMaster set will be affected. There's more information on changing palettes and colors in Chapter 12.

Creating New "Click here..." Blocks

When you are working in SmartMaster Edit mode, you can create new "Click here..." areas for text blocks and for graphic objects such as charts and symbols.

Creating a New "Click here..." Text Block

To create a new "Click here..." block for text when you are editing a SmartMaster, select the Text tool. In the drawing area, drag a rectangle to define the position and size of the new text block.

 Dragging the rectangle in this procedure creates a text block in which word wrap will operate. Text entries that overflow a line will automatically start the next line. To create a text block in which word wrap does not operate, click once on the starting point of the block instead of dragging the rectangle. That is, after selecting the Text tool, move the pointer to the left corner of the text location and click just once. A text block that is just a single character wide will open. It will grow in width as you type, but the lines will not wrap. In such a block, you must press Enter to force a line break.

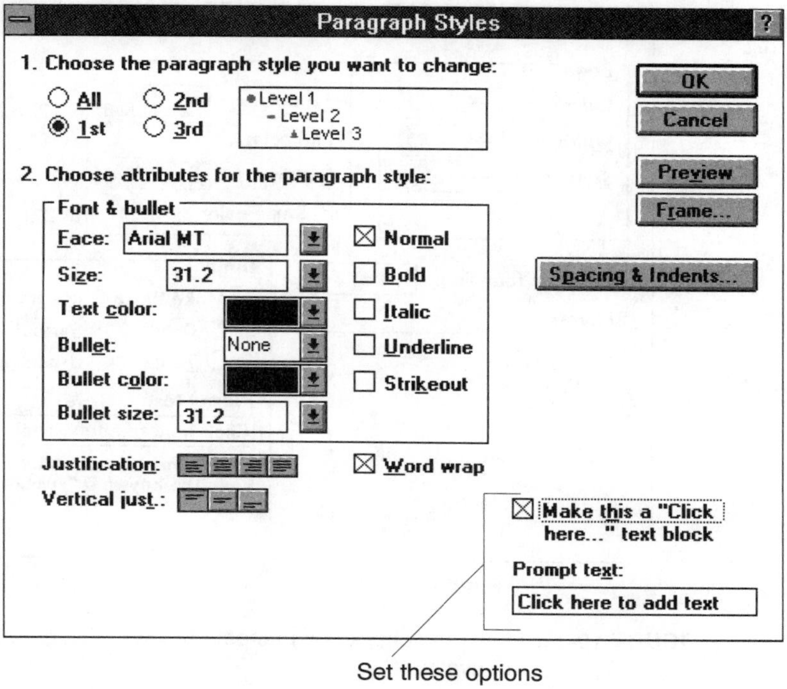

FIGURE 10-31. Mark this check box to create a new "Click here..." text block.

With the text block open, select Text➤Paragraph Styles. The Paragraph Styles dialog box will open, as shown in Figure 10-31. Reset the options that will apply to text in the new block. Then, mark the check box Make This a "Click Here..." Text Block. When you do this, the Prompt Text option will become available. You can accept the prompt already shown ("Click here to add text"), or you can type any other prompt in the text box. Select OK to close the dialog box.

The prompt text will appear in the open text block in the drawing area. Select OK to close the block. If you have no other changes to make to the block, click a blank area of the page to release it.

For this change to be permanent, you must select File➤Save As and save the revised SmartMaster set as an .MAS file.

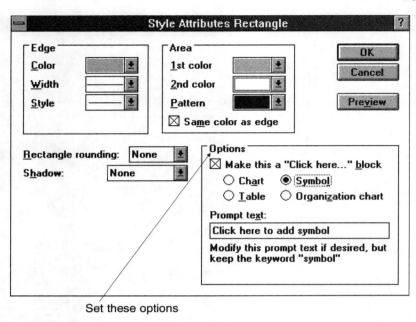

Set these options

FIGURE 10-32.   Mark the check box to create a new "Click here..." area for a chart or symbol.

Creating a New "Click here..." Area for Graphics

To create a new "Click here..." area for charts or symbols when editing a SmartMaster, select the Rectangle tool. In the drawing area, drag a rectangle to define the position and size of the new area.

A rectangle will appear, surrounded by handles. Double-click on the rectangle to open the Style Attributes Rectangle dialog box shown in Figure 10-32. Mark the check box Make This a "Click Here..." Block. When you do this, option buttons for chart type and the Prompt Text option will become available. Select one of the option buttons for the chart type or symbol that will later be inserted in the area you are creating. You can accept the prompt already shown ("Click here to add *chart type*"), or you can type any other prompt in the text box. (But make sure that the chart type is included.) Select OK to close the dialog box.

SmartMaster Edit mode

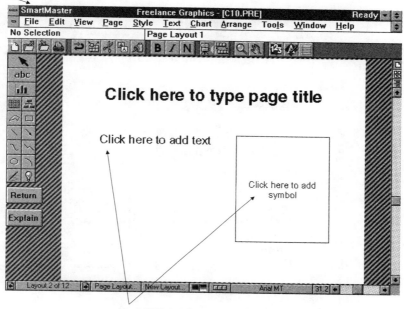

New "Click here . . ." blocks

FIGURE 10-33. This custom page layout has new "Click here..." areas for both text and a symbol.

The prompt text will appear in the rectangle in the drawing area. If you have no other changes to make to the block, click a blank area of the page to release it. The result is shown in Figure 10-33.

For this change to be permanent, you must select File➤Save As and save the revised SmartMaster set as an .MAS file.

Adding a New Page Layout

To add a new page layout to the current SmartMaster set, select Edit➤Edit Page Layouts to start SmartMaster Edit mode. Select Page➤New (or the New Layout button at the bottom of the win-

Enter descriptive name

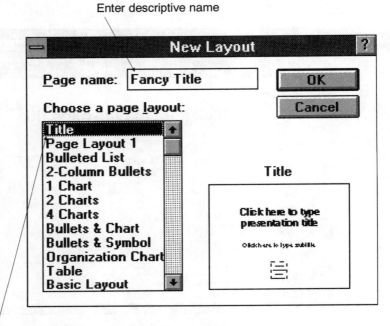

This layout will be used as basis for new one

FIGURE 10-34. The New Layout dialog box appears when you select Page≻New in SmartMaster Edit mode.

dow). The New Layout dialog box will appear, as shown in Figure 10-34. To start a new layout from scratch, select Blank Page. Select one of the other layouts to modify it or to use it as a basis for the new layout. In the Page Name text box, you can accept the default name (Page Layout #), or you can type a more descriptive name, such as FANCY TITLE. Then, select OK to close the dialog box.

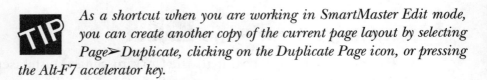

As a shortcut when you are working in SmartMaster Edit mode, you can create another copy of the current page layout by selecting Page≻Duplicate, clicking on the Duplicate Page icon, or pressing the Alt-F7 accelerator key.

The layout you chose will appear in the drawing area. Note that this is another copy of the SmartMaster. Changes that you make to it will be saved as a separate version of that chart type and will not affect the original. Edit it as you would a presentation page. When you have finished making changes to the SmartMaster set, select File➤Save As to update the .MAS file. Select Edit➤Edit Presentation Pages to resume working on a presentation.

Gaining the
Professional Edge

C hapters 11 through 15 provide a professional perspective on using business graphics as an essential part of your regular work. Topics include the technical side of computer graphics systems, color as a design tool, procedures for putting together presentations and shows, corporate networking, and graphic-arts production management.

P
A
R
T

I
I
I

BEHIND THE SCENES: COMPUTERS AND GRAPHICS

T his chapter presents a technical overview of the inner workings of business graphics systems. These issues become important when you begin to test the limits of tools like Freelance Graphics for Windows and when you attempt to use it in conjunction with other types of computer graphics systems.

COMPUTER GRAPHICS AND THE CARTESIAN COORDINATE SYSTEM

Computer graphics systems represent and manipulate images with reference to a spatial grid, or *Cartesian coordinate system* (Figure 11-1). In concept, this is essentially the same scheme used to plot X-Y graphs. However, in computer graphics this grid underlies *all* images, not just graphs, and is the reference system within which all calculations are made.

In the Cartesian system (named for the French mathematician René Descartes), any point is determined by two coordinates, or distances from a central point called an *origin*. That is, a point is located *x* numeric units horizontally and *y* units vertically from the origin. A line (or line segment) is defined by four numbers—two for each of its endpoints. So the Cartesian coordinate system pro-

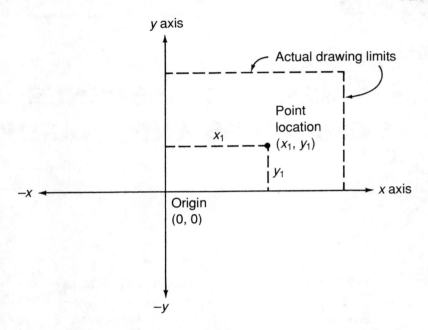

FIGURE 11-1. Cartesian coordinate system: Note that Freelance Graphics for Windows Release 2 places the origin at the top left, not as shown here.

vides a means of translating images into arrays of numbers, and vice versa.

You can actually see a form of this spatial array in Freelance Graphics for Windows. In the Current Page view, select View≻Units & Grids, and mark the check box Display Grid. The unit of measure that will apply to the numeric horizontal and vertical space values (spacing between grid points) can be set among the Units option buttons. Selecting OK will cause a grid to appear in the drawing area as an array of dots.

Then select View≻View Preferences, mark the check box Display Coordinates, and select OK. The resulting display in the page view is shown in Figure 11-2, where the x and y values corresponding to the current pointer location are reported at the top right of the screen. The numeric readings correspond to the unit of measure you selected in View≻Units & Grids. (In the figure shown

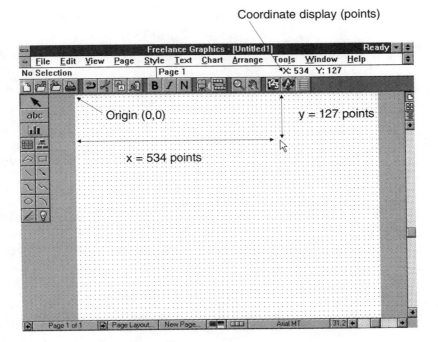

FIGURE 11-2.   Freelance Graphics page: View➤Units & Grids➤Display Grid is on, as is View➤View Preferences➤Display Coordinates. Note the X and Y readouts in the top right corner of the screen. Coordinates reported for *x* and *y* will have the greatest number of significant digits (three) if Points is selected as the unit of measure (shown here), corresponding to typographic point size (about 72 points to the inch).

here, the option Points is selected as the unit of measure. It will display as many as three digits for each coordinate value.)

With these options turned on, you can move the pointer among the dots of the grid and observe the readings of the equivalent numeric *x,y* coordinates. Note that in Freelance Graphics, the origin—location (0,0)—is at the top-left corner of the page—*not* at the bottom-left, as you might expect.

Within the computer, points in a chart or drawing are referenced the same way, only there are many thousands of points in each dimension and the numeric values are not expressed in physical distances such as inches.

The maximum *resolution,* or fineness of detail, of a computer graphic image is a picture composed of a $w \times h$ array, or w points wide by h points high. This is a practical limit on the complexity of the image. The system is usually designed so that this numeric representation greatly exceeds that of any of the output devices it must support. In effect, you are always working in finer detail than you can see in the finished product.

 The term points *here refers to* x,y *coordinate locations, not to the typographic unit of measure.*

Specifically, the $w \times h$ measurement refers to *spatial resolution,* or the fineness of detail in the image area. Another factor is *chromatic resolution,* or the number of colors or shades of gray that can be displayed in a picture.

For example, the numeric representation within a program like Freelance Graphics might be an array of about $26,000 \times 20,000$ possible coordinate locations. (These dimensions refer not to dots in a picture, but to the decimal precision by which point coordinates can be specified.) The resolution of a typical laser printer is 300 dots per inch (dpi), so a printed output on $11 \times 8\frac{1}{2}$-inch letter paper (referring to Landscape orientation) has a maximum resolution of $3,300 \times 2,550$ dots. That's also about the resolution of a 35mm color slide. The computer screen renders far less detail: A standard VGA monitor has a spatial resolution of 640×480 dots. (A Super VGA monitor can display either 800×600 or $1,024 \times 768$ dots, depending on the amount of video memory available.)

A drawing in the X-Y Cartesian system is two-dimensional (2-D), or *planar.* To add depth to "flat" 2-D images, a third dimension, or z axis, is required, as shown in Figure 11-3. In such a system, a point in space is defined by three coordinates—x, y, and z. Large-scale computer graphics systems, including some CAD systems, allow the user to work in all three dimensions, if desired. However, applications in business graphics generally do not require full 3-D imagery.

Particularly in CAD systems, the z axis more often is used not to add visual depth to the picture, but to hold multiple 2-D layers, or

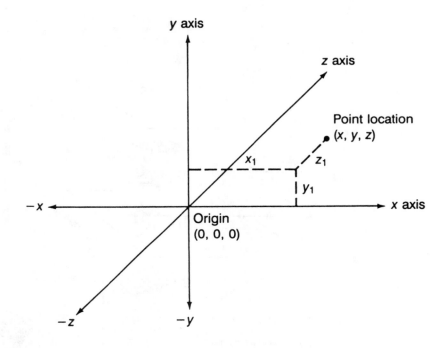

FIGURE 11-3. XYZ plotting scheme (3-D)

overlays. This scheme, called *2½-D representation,* is composed of several drawing planes, as shown in Figure 11-4. In 2½-D, the z-axis value can correspond to the *visual priority* of objects or drawing planes that intersect the z axis at that point. Objects in planes with high visual priority may be assumed to be in the foreground of the composite picture that is formed by combining the layers. Objects with high visual priority obscure the objects on the layers beneath.

Manipulating objects in separate, layered planes is particularly useful in engineering drawings. For example, over a floor plan of an office, there might be separate layers corresponding to electrical wiring, heating and air conditioning, plumbing, and so on.

Freelance Graphics for Windows uses a scheme of visual priority to determine which objects in an image overlay those beneath. However, these aren't separate and distinct drawing planes. Rather, the program simply assigns a priority to objects in the order in

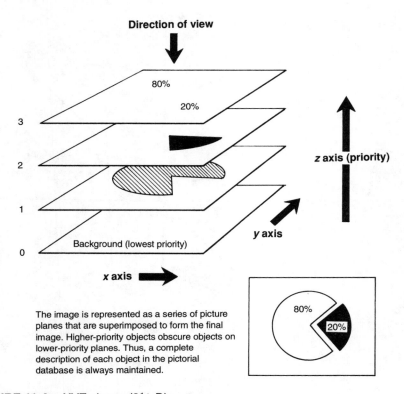

FIGURE 11-4.   XYZ planes (2½-D)

which they were created. An object that overlays another object is said to be "forward" or "on top." The other object is "in back" or "on the bottom." The commands in the Arrange➤Priority submenu of the Current Page view permit you to change these attributes and so manipulate the object's visual priorities. (There is also a set of optional SmartIcons for this purpose: Bring to Front, Send to Back, Forward One, and Back One.)

These distinctions can be important when you attempt to import 2½- or 3-D images generated on other systems to Freelance Graphics. In general, most of the z-axis information (depth, layers, or object priority) will be lost. Object priorities, in effect, will be frozen. Converting such a picture (containing depth information) to

Freelance Graphics for Windows can be like running over a basket-ball with a steamroller. You've still got a basketball, but its structure has collapsed—and cannot be easily restored.

OBJECT REPRESENTATION

In computer graphics, there are different ways of describing images mathematically so that they can be processed by computer hardware. An *object* may be thought of as any graphic entity or group of related *geometric primitives,* such as lines and shapes. Examples of objects would include a line of text, a single slice of a pie graph, an axis label, and so on. The internal number crunching done by graphics software (called *computational geometry*), has to do with the ways in which objects are defined and how, once defined, they may be manipulated (edited).

Within computer systems, there are two basic types of image representation schemes:

- Vector graphics
- Raster images

Freelance Graphics for Windows actually uses both of these techniques for different phases of image input, generation, manipulation, and output.

Vector Graphics

Freelance Graphics for Windows builds and manipulates charts and drawings as vector graphics. In mathematics, a *vector* is a line segment that has both direction from a particular point of origin and a specific length. A vector representation of a graphic object is actually a series of linked points and line segments—a *concatenated vector.* A connect-the-dots drawing is a set of concatenated vectors.

So, vector graphics are, at basis, line drawings. When you output a drawing to a pen plotter, you are sending it vector information.

Vector representations of objects become problematic when shading, or filling an area with color or tone, is required. Plotters and some types of printers do shading as textures, or patterns. Large, areas are usually rendered with patterned fill because these devices render solids very slowly—one thin line at a time.

A key advantage to graphics built from vectors is that they are essentially hardware-independent in terms of resolution. Recall that the data array, or numeric representation of a drawing, will greatly exceed the resolution of the film that will record it. Therefore, a graphics program that generates drawings as vectors can produce the sharpest possible picture from each type of output device.

Raster Images

Raster images are directly analogous to video pictures. A raster image, or picture composed of individual scan lines, represents a given object as a series of color-dot values on successive scan lines.

 In the jargon of computer graphics, the term graphic *usually refers to objects composed of vectors and the term* image *is used to describe pictures composed of rasters.*

A raster image may be thought of as a matrix of dots, or *pixels* (picture elements). A raster image usually is stored in a computer's memory space as an array of pixel values. This area is called a *display buffer* and the array of data values is called a bitmap.

The display buffer is a memory area that is dedicated to graphic output. In the case of a video display, its display buffer is called *video memory*. On some personal computers, the video memory is located physically on a separate video interface card. On other machines, the video interface may be built into the main computer board, or *motherboard*. In such cases, the entire video interface may have been integrated in a single computer chip.

For color images, three values are stored for each pixel. These values represent the primary color components of red, green, and blue (RGB). The combination of these colors, as reproduced by the red-, green-, and blue-color electron guns of an RGB video monitor, produces a full-color screen display. (With all three color components at maximum setting, or fully on, the result is white; if all are off, the result is black.)

A computer graphics system generates screen displays as raster images. Vector graphics such as Freelance Graphics charts and drawings are converted by a video graphics interface within the machine to raster images. In Freelance Graphics for Windows, various kinds of bitmap picture files can be incorporated in presentation pages—as backgrounds, as inset photos or video sequences, and as a type of patterned object fill—as well as presented as full screens in screen shows.

Raster pictures, unlike vector graphics, are ideal for showing areas of solid color. However, raster images are difficult to edit, have fixed (device-dependent) resolution and become jagged when increased in size, and take up lots of computer memory and disk storage area. Also, once the pixel values have been overwritten, as when editing the picture, it may not be possible to restore the original picture. This problem is particularly evident in the task of *hidden line removal,* in which one object must obscure, or overlay, another.

For business graphics, raster imagery is useful primarily as an output format. The output of fax machines and video scanner/digitizers is also in raster (bitmap) format. For most applications in business graphics, it is very cumbersome to work with these raster images. However, raster input can be merged readily as bitmap pictures with some Windows applications, including Freelance Graphics. The distinction between vector and raster imagery becomes important when you begin to use other computer graphic devices and systems in conjunction with Freelance Graphics.

For example, art containing solid color or shading that will be output to video or to film is typically produced with *paint software.* Most paint systems, such as Windows Paintbrush, work with bitmaps as raster images. Art for television broadcast that also contains text may be produced on a *character generator,* which also produces raster images. Scientific systems for medical diagnosis, analysis of satellite photos, and so on are *image-processing* systems that work with raster data. Video or film art that moves requires animation software that can generate the "in-between" positions among artist-drawn key frames. Animation commonly is drawn in vector form and then rendered with a separate software program that fills and shades the drawings as color raster output. *Desktop-publishing* systems usually are based on vector graphics but may have the capability for merging bitmaps, such as scanned photography to be used as illustrations in documents such as newsletters. Computer-aided design systems generate engineering drawings, which are vector graphics.

One of the real benefits of the Windows environment is that it establishes rules for exchange of data among applications. Those data can include vector graphics, bitmaps, digital video, and sound, as well as text and numbers. Freelance Graphics for Windows supports a variety of these graphic- and image-data formats.

IMAGE GENERATION IN FREELANCE GRAPHICS

Freelance Graphics generates and manipulates images through a process called *vector draw/polygon fill*. If you're going to do business graphics (rather than backgrounds for animated cartoons or television weather maps with wispy cloud formations), this is by far the best way to make pictures. Recall that, in vector drawing, a graphic object is described by the software to the display device as a series of concatenated vectors—an outline. (Curves may be described by mathematical formulas, such as Bézier curves or cubic splines.) Polygon fill means that, once the outline of the object has been described, the *intelligent* display device is instructed to fill the area bounded by the outline. (An intelligent computer device has its own processor and memory.)

Freelance Graphics for Windows translates output to the specific requirements of output devices through auxiliary programs called *device drivers*. When you install Windows and specify printers and other output devices, you are installing a device driver for each.

WINDOWS DEVICE DRIVERS

Windows applications differ significantly from their DOS counterparts in the controlling of devices such as displays and printers. In the DOS environment, each application is largely in business for itself. Each application must have its own set of device drivers, or subprograms that translate input and output (I/O) into the hardware-control instructions for specific models of displays and printers. By contrast, Windows interposes itself between the application and the devices, acting as both translator and traffic cop. All applications share the same set of Windows device drivers.

The driver software typically is developed by the manufacturer of the device. Device drivers can be found in the WINDOWS\SYSTEM directory and use the file extension .DRV.

Device drivers must adhere to the standards that Windows imposes. This standardization enhances *interoperability,* or the ability of applications to work in coordination with one another. Windows applications may seem to have similar capabilities because they are required to share the same I/O devices in the same ways.

From the standpoint of creating graphics, device drivers become important because they—not Freelance Graphics—handle the translation, or mapping, of graphics data to the specific colors and textures that can be reproduced on output devices such as printers, plotters, and film recorders.

Reproduction capabilities differ widely among output devices. This becomes apparent, for example, when you compare a computer-generated color slide to the screen display of the same graphic. The colors probably won't match exactly, and the slide will be much sharper. Even more dramatic differences will be noted when you send slide data to a monochrome laser printer, where areas of solid color will be translated into textured shades of gray.

To have better control over this translation, you need to understand the constraints of each type of device.

VIDEO DISPLAYS

Video displays are raster devices. Perhaps the most commonly used video display device on computers that run Windows is the *Video Graphics Array* (VGA). Standard models of this device are capable of displaying 16 colors—and other models can display 256 colors or more. Or, in monochrome mode, 64 shades of gray can be generated.

Video Memory and Resolution

For any video display device, spatial and chromatic resolution represent a trade-off. That is, if you increase the spatial resolution, you will lose chromatic resolution, and vice versa. The reason for the loss is the finite size of the video memory, or display buffer.

The total required buffer size is $w \times h \times c$, where c is the number of data bits stored for each pixel, representing its color or shade. You can see the relationship between video memory and resolution in Table 11-1.

TABLE 11-1. Relationship of Video Memory Size to Spatial and Chromatic Resolution. Note that video memory sizes are typically given in *bytes,* even though the other requirements in the table are expressed in *bits.*

Memory Size	Spatial Resolution	Data Bits per Pixel	Chromatic Resolution (Colors)
256KB	640 × 480	4	16
512KB	640 × 480	8	256
512KB	1024 × 768	4	16
1MB	1024 × 768	8	256
4MB	1024 × 768	24	16.7 million

Higher-Resolution Displays

Video interfaces that offer higher resolution are extended VGA (sometimes called Super VGA or SVGA), XGA (an IBM Microchannel device), and special interfaces termed collectively High Color and True Color.

Higher-resolution video cards require high-frequency (measured in megahertz, or MHz) color monitors. Monitors that can handle multiple video interfaces, from VGA through higher resolutions, have wide bandwidths, or frequency ranges, and are called multifrequency monitors.

Table 11-2 shows how these devices compare in the number of displayable colors produced. Note how the chromatic resolution increases dramatically with the number of data bits that can be stored for each pixel.

Do not confuse a 16-color display with one that has 16 data bits per pixel. As shown in the table, a 16-bit display can generate 65,536 colors.

TABLE 11-2. Categories of Video Displays according to Pixel Bit-Depth

Data Bits/Pixel	Display Type	Total Colors
4	Standard VGA	16
8	Super VGA	256
16	XGA and High Color*	65,536
24	True Color	16.7 million

*Some High Color displays store 15 bits per pixel, for a total of 32,768 colors.

Dithering

On 16-color displays, multicolored groups of pixels can approximate a range of 256 colors. However, this *dithering* technique reduces the spatial resolution of the display. In other words, dithered pictures look "grainy."

Dithering juxtaposes patterns of small dots of two different colors to produce the appearance of a third color. The third color is perceived as a mixture of the first two. Varying the density of each dot pattern controls the amount of each color in the mixture.

In Freelance Graphics for Windows, you will see much less dithering on 256-color displays, which can show many more of the colors generated by the program as solid, continuous tones. In technical terms, the program contains a 24-bit internal color model. This makes it possible for each Library Color to have three settings ranging from 0–255 for red, green, and blue. The result is that you can build your palettes from a selection of 16.7 million possible colors. But, on most video monitors, you will not be able to see the difference between similar settings. Even using a 256-color card with an SVGA monitor, you may see some dithering, especially in shaded backgrounds. The differences can become apparent, however, when you send the output to a high-resolution film recorder.

Recall that video displays have far lower resolutions than most color film recorders. This is true for both spatial and chromatic resolution. Dithering is an approximation, on a comparatively low-resolution device, of an RGB color value that will be produced as a continuous tone on a film recorder. The following discussion should clarify why screen displays often differ in appearance from slide output.

PRINTERS AND COLOR MAPPING

In computer graphics, the conversion of solid colors to monochrome textures (hatches and patterns) is called *color mapping*. Windows device drivers automatically translate screen colors to textures for output to monochrome output devices such as dot-matrix and laser printers. For color dot-matrix and ink-jet printers, which have just a few primary colors, the areas are shown in color and dithered. For color plotters, which also have just a few pen colors, areas may be converted to solid primary colors or to various colored hatches, or patterns of lines.

In Freelance Graphics for Windows, it is important to understand that the conversion process normally is handled *outside* the program—in the Windows environment. That is, an area with a specific RGB color setting is sent to the Windows driver that controls the selected output device. The driver renders the color according to a mapping scheme that is predefined for that device.

This is different from DOS-based graphics programs, which typically have their own unique internal schemes for converting colors to patterns. (In DOS, each application must have its own set of device drivers.)

Within Freelance Graphics for Windows, patterns also can be manipulated separately from colors—as attributes to be assigned explicitly to graphic objects, regardless of color. After selecting an object, choose Style➤Attributes, then set the Area Pattern option. Or, select Style➤Default Attributes and reset the option globally for specific types of new objects. These patterns have no relation to the color mapping performed by the Windows drivers and will be rendered just as you see them on the screen (provided that the printer or plotter can reproduce them).

 On color output devices, areas within objects can be rendered both in color and with a pattern.

Controlling the Color Map

One way to control the appearance of monochrome output is to change the on-screen colors of objects. That is, you can control the Windows printer driver indirectly—by changing the color you've selected for specific objects.

However, Freelance Graphics for Windows provides a more convenient means of previewing the conversion of colors to patterns. Each full-color palette supplied with the program has a counterpart monochrome palette. When you select the Color/BW button in the status bar at the bottom of the Current Page view, the page display will toggle between color and gray-scale monochrome.

Equivalent commands in the Style menu are Style➤Use Black & White Palette and Style➤Use Color Palette.

As an alternative, you can disable the internal monochrome palettes of Freelance Graphics and accept the default color-to-texture mapping as it is handled by the Windows printer driver. This can produce better results on some printers and may be necessary for plotters. In any view select Tools➤User Setup, mark the check box Disable Black & White Palettes, and select OK. This dialog box is shown in Figure 11-5. (For more information about colors and palettes in Freelance Graphics for Windows, see Chapter 12.)

Using Alternate Palettes

Color mapping becomes a concern when you want a presentation to serve a dual purpose: You want to be able to show it in color as a screen show or on slides, and you also want to print paper hard copies that might be bound in handouts or reports. In many cases, you can simply compose the presentation in color and rely on Freelance Graphics to use its internal monochrome palettes to handle the conversion for a monochrome printer.

In some cases, you may want to design in monochrome. Some of the SmartMaster sets, such as BLANK.MAS, use monochrome palettes by default. But regardless of the default, each of the supplied SmartMaster sets has one full-color palette and one monochrome palette. Again, you can switch between them in the Current Page

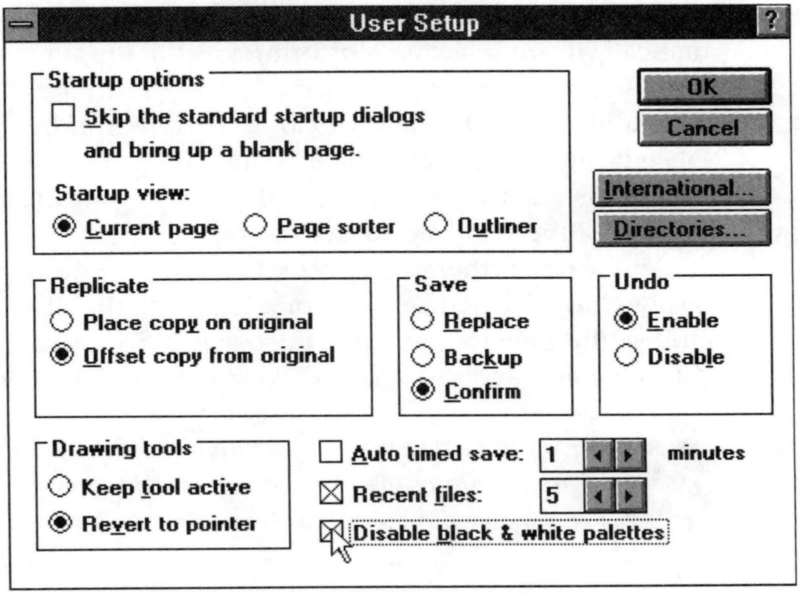

FIGURE 11-5. Mark the Disable Black & White Palettes check box to use the color mapping of the Windows printer driver instead of the internal monochrome palettes in Freelance Graphics.

view by selecting the Color/BW button or the Style➤Use Black & White Palette or Style➤Use Color Palette commands.

You can perform Style➤Choose Palette to select a different palette file. Remember that only the filenames of full-color palettes will appear if you have been working in color. To see the names of monochrome palettes when you execute this command, you must first switch to monochrome viewing mode.

Freelance Graphics for Windows also provides an alternate palette (CPRINTER.PAL) that has been designed specifically for limited-color devices such as pen plotters and four-color dot-matrix printers. This alternate palette will be found in the FLW directory, not in the FLW\MASTERS directory with the conventional palettes.

The palette CPRINTER.PAL is used by Freelance Graphics automatically if you select a color printer as the output device. After you have selected the printer through File➤Printer Setup, the check box Adjust Color Library for Color Printing will be set to on in the File➤Print dialog box. Turning this option off will cause the current color palette to be rendered according to the color-mapping scheme of the Windows device driver.

You can further customize this palette, if necessary. Select Style➤Choose Palette➤Directory, log on to the FLW directory, and choose the palette filename. Then select Style➤Edit Palette, make your changes, and save the revised palette under its default name.

If you save the edited palette under its default name, first make a backup copy of the file in a separate directory or disk so that you can restore the original version later.

COLOR FILM RECORDERS

Color film—any color film—is not directly compatible with the RGB colors produced on your video display. Again, the display is an array of red, green, and blue dots. But color film is a collection of grains of magenta, blue, and cyan dyes. Producers of computer graphics presentations can attest that there is not always a good color match between RGB displays and color-film output—even with the best color adapters, monitors, and film recorders.

Film recorders typically use a black-and-white *cathode ray tube* (CRT), a type of video picture tube, by which an image is built in three separate exposures while the film remains stationary in the camera (Figure 11-6). A color-filter wheel in front of the CRT is rotated to the corresponding color filter—red, green, or blue—for each of the exposures.

Film recorders are of two basic types: computer camera and intelligent film recorder.

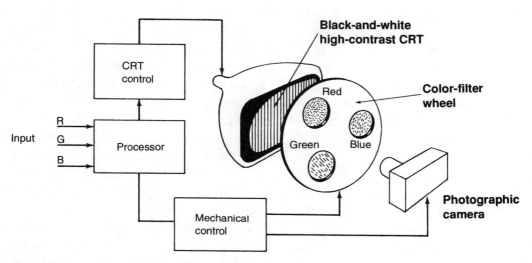

FIGURE 11-6.   The film recording process uses three exposures.

Computer Cameras

A computer camera is connected directly to the RGB color signals generated by the video interface card in the computer. The device contains a miniature color CRT that has much the same resolution and characteristics as the video monitor. Thus, the film copy is a record of the screen display, with its colors, fonts, and resolution.

Intelligent Film Recorders

An intelligent film recorder is driven by a parallel data interface (such as Centronics or SCSI) to one of the computer's printer ports (such as LPT1). Through Windows driver software, the recorder accepts instructions in high-level command language. Examples of high-level languages used with film recorders are color PostScript, Encapsulated PostScript, SCODL, and Binary Lasergraphics Language.

These instructions constitute a *display list,* a description of a vector graphic that is processed within the film recorder to produce a high-resolution color bitmap. The display list can be processed to drive the recorder to the limits of its resolution, which is typically 2,048 × 2,048 or 4,096 × 4,096 pixels. (The lower resolution usually is sufficient for 35mm film; the higher is needed for 4 × 5-inch and 8 × 10-inch formats.) Film recorders generally have resident fonts, which may resemble (but not necessarily match exactly) the software fonts in Freelance Graphics for Windows. (Recall that you can manipulate hardware fonts in Freelance Graphics. If you have installed hardware fonts, they will appear in program menus with bullets preceding the font names.)

Film recorders typically handle images with 24-bit pixel depth, yielding 16.7 million colors. Thus, the closest match between screen display and slides will be seen with a True Color video card and compatible analog monitor. However, there might still be some visible differences, since the two display technologies are not the same. There's more on this subject in Chapter 13.

SETTING UP FOR FILM RECORDING

Before you can send output to a film recorder, you must perform some setup procedures in Windows and in Freelance Graphics. The basic steps are:

1. Install the required printer driver through the Windows Control Panel.
2. Perform File➤Printer Setup in Freelance Graphics.
3. Perform File➤Page Setup.

Printer Drivers for Film Recording

In Windows, film recorders, as well as plotters and printers, are installed as printers through the Control Panel, which can be found in the program group Main.

Slide output usually is a two-step process, involving printing a presentation to disk, then submitting the file to a postprocessing program supplied by the film-recorder manufacturer. (Some plotters may require a similar output procedure of first printing the presentation to disk, then postprocessing the file.) Here are descriptions of some film recorders:

Autographix

Some film recorders are handled in Windows as PostScript printers and require that you first convert presentations to color PostScript (.CPS) or Encapsulated PostScript (.EPS) files. The Autographix Overnight Slide Service uses these file types. You can print to a PostScript file even if you do not have a PostScript printer, by installing the appropriate printer driver in the Windows Control Panel and assigning the device to the FILE port (rather than LPT1 or LPT2).

Autographix provides its own PostScript driver definition. Its device name (which should appear in the Printer Setup dialog box) is AUTOGRAPHIX, which is contained in the PostScript Printer options of the Control Panel. The driver (PSCRIPT.DRV) requires the Windows printer definition file AGX41.WPD, which is found among the distribution disks shipped with Freelance Graphics for Windows, Release 2. The PostScript driver actually contains printer definitions for a variety of makes and models of printer. The AGX41.WPD file will appear as the device name AUTOGRAPHIX in the listing when you install or update the driver through Windows Control Panel➤Printers.

In general, each make and model of film recorder requires its own Windows printer driver and a unique type of disk file for postprocessing by the recorder software. For example, special drivers must be obtained for Lasergraphics and Agfa Matrix film recorders.

Procedures for installing film-recorder drivers vary for each make and model, as well as for Windows 3.0 and 3.1. The dialog boxes for PostScript printer setup in Windows 3.1 are shown in Figure 11-7.

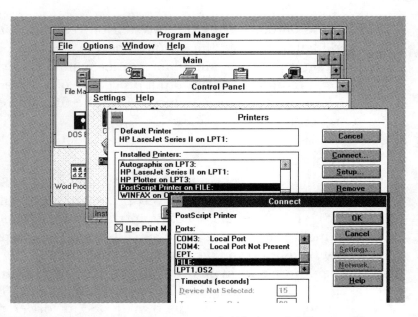

FIGURE 11-7. These dialog boxes appear in Windows 3.1 Program Manager when you select Main➤Control Panel➤Printers➤Connect. Shown here are settings for a color PostScript printer for which output will be redirected to a disk file.

Setup Options for Autographix

After you have installed the Autographix printer drivers through the Windows Control Panel, you must make sure that the printer and page settings in Freelance Graphics are correct for the type of output you want.

Printer Setup options selected within Freelance Graphics become Windows system settings, affecting all presentations until you reset them. By contrast, Page Setup options are specific to the current presentation and are saved with it. Furthermore, Printer Setup and Page Setup options must match. For example, if the printer is set for Landscape orientation, the Page Setup should be the same. (However, if you are using Windows 3.1 or a later version, the Page settings will override the Printer Setup, if they are different.)

Printer Setup for Autographix

The Autographix PostScript printer driver can be set up within Freelance Graphics when you select File➤Printer Setup. Table 11-3 shows the required option settings.

TABLE 11-3. Printer Setup Options for Autographix Slide Output

Dialog Box	Option	Setting
File Printer Setup	Printer	Autographix
	Port	FILE (set in Control Panel)
	Set Margins for Slides	On
PostScript Printer	Paper Size	Note 8.5 × 11 in.
	Orientation	Landscape (recommended) Portrait (optional)
	Copies	1 (specify quantity in To AGX instructions)
Options	Print	File (name and extension)*
	Margins	Default
	Scaling	100 percent
	Color	On
	Send Header with Each Job	On
Advanced	Halftone Frequency	60 (reset from 0)
	Halftone Angle	45 (reset from 0)
	TrueType Fonts Send to Printer As	Adobe Type 1
	Use Substitution Table	On (with defaults)
	Compress Bitmaps	On
	Print PostScript Error Information	On
	All other check boxes	Off

* You can omit the filename if you have assigned FILE as the port. Windows will then prompt you for a filename when you select File➤Print. Be sure to include the .CPS extension.

Page Setup for Autographix

After you have made the systemwide printer settings, perform File➤Page Setup in Freelance Graphics to set or recheck the options, which must match the printer settings. The correct Page Setup options for Autographix slide output are shown in Table 11-4. Remember, Printer Options apply to the system; Page Options apply to the presentation and are saved in its .PRE file.

Margins   The unit of measure for margins is set in View➤Units & Grids, as shown in Figure 11-8. The settings in Table 11-4 are shown in millimeters, the default. If you use a different unit of measure, such as inches, reset View➤Units & Grids to Millimeters, make these settings in File➤Page Setup, then reset View➤Units & Grids to Inches and save the presentation file. If you perform File➤Page Setup again, you will see that the Margins settings in the dialog box have been converted automatically to inches.

Aspect Ratio   The *aspect ratio* of an output is the proportion of its width to its height. Slides usually have an aspect ratio of 3:2, or three units wide by two units high.

A quick way of assuring the correct aspect ratio for slides is to mark the Set Margins for Slides check box in File➤Page Setup or in File➤Printer Setup. When you mark this option in either dialog

TABLE 11-4. Page Setup Options for Autographix Slide Output

Dialog Box	*Options*	*Setting*	
File Page Setup	Orientation	Landscape (recommended)	
		Portrait (optional)	
	Margins (mm)*	Landscape:	
		Top: 14.9	Bottom: 14.7
		Left: 12.7	Right: 12.7
		Portrait:	
		Top: 12.7	Bottom: 12.7
		Left: 14.7	Right: 14.9

* Unit of measure for margins is set in View➤Units & Grids.

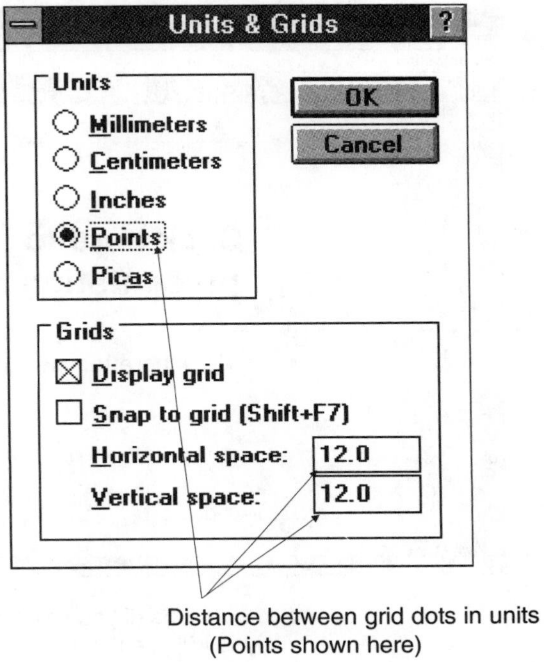

Distance between grid dots in units
(Points shown here)

FIGURE 11-8. The View➤Units & Grids dialog box is set initially to display units of measure in millimeters, which also affect page-margin settings.

box, the Margins settings will become dimmed and the program will set them automatically for 35 mm slides.

As an alternative, you can leave the check box unmarked and set slide margins manually, particularly if you need a custom aperture. For your reference, the margin settings in Table 11-4 show the correct ratio for 35mm double-frame slides—*provided that you also set Paper Size to Note.* (Within Freelance Graphics, set Paper Size in File➤Printer Setup➤Setup.) To display these margin settings in the Current Page view of Freelance Graphics, select View➤View Preferences➤Printable Area. As shown in Figure 11-9, this setting causes the printable area of the page to be displayed with a dotted line around its border. Objects that fall outside the border will not appear on the slide. (The printable-area border will appear automatically if you select Set Margins for Slides.)

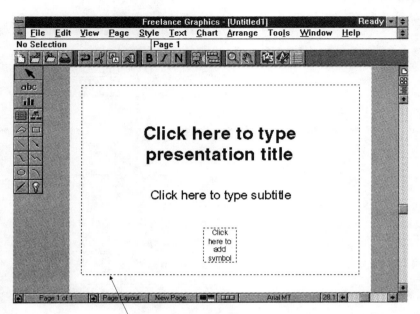

Slide margins (if you select Printable Area instead,
you will see the limits of the PostScript printer driver,
not slide margins)

FIGURE 11-9. The printable area *or* margins can be shown in the Current Page
view as a dotted-line border. Shown here are correct margin settings for Autographix color-slide output in Landscape orientation.

RECORDING PROCEDURE FOR COLOR SLIDES

Once you have set Printer Setup and Page Setup options as
described above, the basic steps for recording color slides are:

1. Print the presentation to a disk file.
2. Process the file according to the film recorder manufacturer's instructions.

Procedures vary by make and model of recorder. The following
specific instructions are included for Autographix:

Printing to a Color PostScript File

To print a presentation to a color PostScript file, start or restore Freelance Graphics. Open the presentation file to be output, and then select File➤Print. The Print dialog box will appear.

In the File Print dialog box, set the options according to Table 11-5, then select the Print button. (If you did not previously enter a name for the PostScript file in the File➤Printer Setup procedure and you are printing to the port named FILE, Windows will prompt you for a filename.) The presentation will be translated to color PostScript instructions, saved in the disk file you specified.

 If you wish, you can print only a portion of the presentation to disk by entering the starting and ending page numbers in the File Print dialog box. If you select the check box Current Presentation Page Only, the print file will contain a single slide.

Submitting an Order to Autographix

Included with Freelance Graphics for Windows Release 2 are all the facilities needed to submit presentation files to the Autographix

TABLE 11-5. Settings in the File Print Dialog Box for Autographix Output

Option	Setting
Number of Copies	1 (specify quantity in ToAGX instructions)
From Page	1 to 999 (the default, prints the entire presentation)
Format	Full Page
Adjust Color Library for Color Printing	Off*

* If this check box is on, the palette CPRINT.PAL will be used instead of the palette with which you designed your presentation.

FIGURE 11-10. ToAGX application icon

Overnight Slide Service, a service bureau that can provide computer film recording and photographic processing.

After you have completed the Freelance Graphics installation procedure, the ToAGX application icon should appear in the same program group. (Figure 11-10). By selecting this application, you can prepare orders for batches of slides. Orders can be transmitted by modem using a communications program that is built into ToAGX, or an order disk can be prepared and shipped to an Autographix Imaging Center. Again, presentations sent to Autographix must first be converted to color PostScript (.CPS) format. (This format is not the same as Encapsulated PostScript [.EPS].)

Order Submission Procedure

To submit one or more presentations for film recording, first write the presentation to disk by selecting File➤Print to a .CPS file, as described above, and exit Freelance Graphics. Then, open the program group in Windows Program Manager that contains Freelance Graphics. Select the ToAGX application icon.

The ToAGX-Windows application window will open, as shown in Figure 11-11. If necessary, change to the directory that holds the converted .CPS files by selecting Switch Directories from its File menu. (You can also choose Switch File Types to specify *.CPS, or only files with color PostScript extensions.)

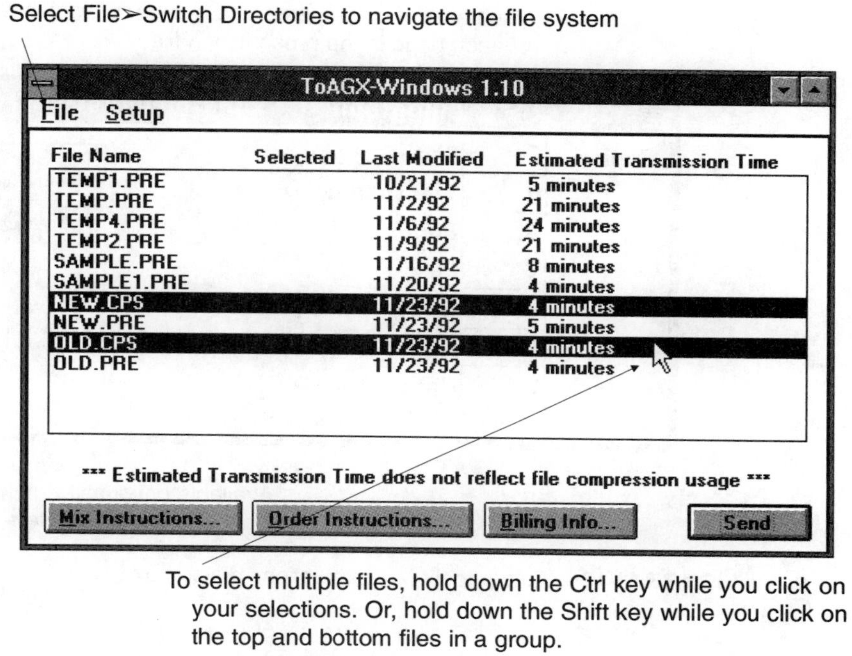

Select File➤Switch Directories to navigate the file system

To select multiple files, hold down the Ctrl key while you click on
your selections. Or, hold down the Shift key while you click on
the top and bottom files in a group.

FIGURE 11-11. ToAGX-Windows application window

Files in the selected directory should appear in the top portion
of the window in the File Name list box. From the listing, click on a
.CPS file to be submitted. Or, move the highlight to the desired file
using the arrow keys. You can select multiple files if you hold down
the Ctrl key as you click on each of them. Then, select the Mix
Instructions button at the bottom of the window.

In the Autographix Mix Instructions dialog box (Figure 11-12),
type the number of copies desired of each type of output: 35mm
slides, overhead transparencies, photographic color prints, and
lasers (color laser output on paper). (Other custom options, which
vary by local service center, are numbered 1–3.) Then, select OK.
Repeat this procedure for each file to be submitted.

Select the Order Instructions button. Select submission by
either modem or diskette. Enter the rest of the required information in the dialog box and then select OK.

For each type of output, enter the number of copies desired
of each page in the presentation file

Autographix Mix Instructions

Copies		
2	Slides	
0	Transparencies	
0	Prints	
1	Lasers	
2	Option 1	
0	Option 2	
0	Option 3	

OK

Cancel

Available options vary
among service centers

FIGURE 11-12. Autographix Mix Instructions dialog box

*In the Order Instructions dialog box, glass mounts should be spec-
ified if precise slide-to-slide registration is required, as in multi-
image projection, or when high-heat projection lamps will be used.*

Select the Send button. If you selected Modem, the program
handles the details of transmission automatically. If you selected
Diskette, insert a formatted disk in the drive, enter the device and
path in the Output Directory dialog box, and then select OK.

Before any order can be submitted, you must have completed
the information requested when you select the Billing Information
button. If you are submitting your order by modem, you must also
select File➤Communications Setup. Modem transmissions and disk
files are compressed automatically by the utility PKZIP.EXE. The
command File➤Compression permits you to turn off this feature or
to enter a specific path on your hard disk for use as a temporary
work area for the compression program.

Slides that contain large bitmaps, backgrounds built from bitmaps, or both can generate large film-recorder files. For example, a complex slide that also contains a large bitmap easily could exceed 1MB as a .CPS file. The PKZIP compression utility that comes with the Autographix software will shrink such a file to about 200K, which will still require approximately 15 minutes to transmit at 2,400 bits per second (bps). (Higher transmission speeds, such as 9,600 or 14.4K bps, might be used as they become available at processing centers.) For a large presentation, it may be more practical to send a disk by an express shipping service and then use the modem to transmit those inevitable last-minute revisions.

The next chapter covers the topic of color, first on a more subjective level as an element of design, and then from the technical viewpoint involving use of color palettes in Freelance Graphics. Differences among media—particularly in their reproduction characteristics—are covered further in Chapter 13.

ALL ABOUT COLOR

Effective use of color in visual presentations depends on knowing your audience and the context within which the presentation will be viewed, as well as the capabilities and technical constraints of computer graphic systems and output media. This chapter presents an overview of the alternatives in applying color to business presentations, and attempts to convey a sense of the numerous variables involved in this complex subject. The discussion then moves on to the ways in which color can be manipulated in Freelance Graphics for Windows. Characteristics of output media are covered further in the next chapter.

Colors in Freelance Graphics for Windows are assigned primarily by the preselected schemes within SmartMaster sets, or presentation "looks," so you can create entire presentations that have well-coordinated colors without having to make specific color selections. However, the program gives you the ability to change the color composition of an entire presentation, as well as the colors of specific objects, with a single command.

To please yourself or your clients, you may find it necessary to create custom colors—perhaps even to maintain separate sets of colors and presentation styles for each project or client. The guidelines in this chapter aim at providing you with a subjective basis for judgment, before getting into the technical aspects of selecting and editing colors in Freelance Graphics for Windows.

COLOR TERMINOLOGY

Because the term *color* can have a wide variety of meanings, graphic artists have developed more precise terminology for dealing with this subject. Here are some basic definitions. (Refer to Figure 12-1.)

Hue

Hue describes the primary colors from which a specific color blend, or tone, is derived. Basic hues for computer graphic systems might include red, red-orange, orange, yellow-orange, yellow, yellow-green, green, blue-green, blue, blue-violet, violet, and red-violet.

Tint

The *tint* of a color refers to the amount of white that is mixed with it. Thus, light tints appear washed out. In some computer graphic systems, tint corresponds to *chroma,* or color purity. In others, this parameter is called *saturation.*

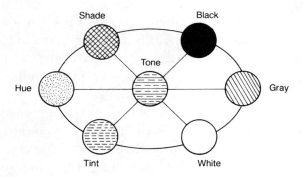

FIGURE 12-1. Relationship of color terms

Shade

Shade refers to the amount of black in, or darkness of, a color tone. Essentially equivalent terms for shade are *value, lightness,* and *intensity.*

Tone

A specific color *tone* is the composite of hue, saturation (tint), and value (shade).

Note that in popular speech, many of these terms are used interchangeably. However, in graphic design, as well as in computer graphics, each has its own precise, technical meaning.

Within Freelance Graphics for Windows, colors are defined as composites of red, green, and blue. These are the same primary colors of the RGB electron guns of a color cathode ray tube (CRT) and the red, green, and blue color filters inside a computer film recorder.

THE PSYCHOLOGY OF COLOR

It might seem to be a matter of common sense that people have an intuitive understanding of color. But graphic designers who handle business presentations for many different types of clients and audiences will tell you otherwise. Differences among audiences are not just matters of taste: The meaning and purpose of using color can change significantly from one type of audience to another.

Consider how the visual connotations of some basic color hues differ, depending on the audience. A survey of American movie audiences reveals one set of perceptions, as shown in the second column of Table 12-1. In fact, similar tables are used by professional cinematographers to choose the correct *color balance* for film prints to suit the moods of specific scenes. (The overall color balance of a film print is a matter of tint rather than intense color, but this only means that the movie audience's reaction may be more subtle.)

TABLE 12-1. Subjective Interpretations of Color by Different Audiences

	Interpretation			
Color Hue	*Movie Audience*	*Financial Managers*	*Health Care Professionals*	*Control Engineers*
Blue	Tender	Corporate, reliable	Dead	Cold, water
Cyan	Leisurely	Cool, subdued	Cyanotic, deprived of oxygen	Steam
Green	Playful	Profitable	Infected, bilious	Nominal, safe
Yellow	Happy	Highlighted item, important	Jaundiced	Caution
Red	Exciting	Unprofitable	Healthy	Danger
Magenta	Sad	Wealthy	Cause for concern	Hot, radioactive

Based on the colors preferred by financial managers in slide presentations, possible interpretations of the hues are shown in the third column of the table.

However, the reactions of doctors and other health care professionals to these same colors might come as something of a surprise, as shown in the fourth column.

Finally, think about the perceptions of a group of control engineers with responsibility for monitoring a nuclear reactor (fifth column in the table).

Despite the color preferences of specific professions or groups, the interpretation of colors can change with the situation. People make these mental shifts frequently and without conscious effort, usually depending on their understanding of the purpose of a visual message. For example, in some circumstances, it will be natural for movie audiences to react more like control engineers. When the moviegoers exit the theater parking lot in their cars and approach the first traffic signal, their situation will be much closer to that of the control engineers in a power plant: Very quickly, they must interpret a limited set of color codes. In this simplified context, a red light always means *stop,* regardless of how that color might be interpreted elsewhere.

Conversely, people with specialized biases, like the control engineers, do not necessarily carry them into other aspects of their lives: A control engineer's reactions to colors in the movie theater are not necessarily any different from those of doctors, accountants, or the public at large.

What does this mean to you as a graphic designer? Again, you must tailor the presentation to the biases of the audience. Doctors like red blood and accountants hate red ink. And individual tastes vary considerably, for all kinds of subjective reasons.

COLOR AND MEANING

Related to the viewing context is the function of color in communicating information. Depending on the context, color may be used for

- Coding
- Rendering nature and for artistic expression
- Design elements

Color as Coding

In the example of the control engineers in the nuclear plant, color is used as coding. Computer displays that monitor conditions within the reactor may use specific colors to signal the status of each of the plant's subsystems.

The power of any coding scheme is its simplicity. When colors are used as distinct codes, the range of colors must be restricted to the *fewest colors needed* to represent each condition or status within the scheme of codes. The greater the number of colors, the higher the likelihood of confusion. For example, consider how confusing it would be to interpret traffic signals that displayed six or seven colors. Instead of GO, CAUTION, and STOP, you might be confronted with color codes for

GO
NO RIGHT TURN
NO LEFT TURN
NO U TURN
CAUTION
WAIT FOR PEDESTRIANS . . .

A need to restrict the range of colors means that computer displays for applications such as monitoring and control can be limited in color range without any sacrifice of functionality. For example, color displays in CAD or process control need not be able to render more than a few basic colors. Further, the precise shades or tints of those color hues will not be critical, as long as the colors can be readily distinguished from one another. (Possible color blindness of some viewers can be a factor here.) So, for control applications, a computer graphics system capable of displaying four, or perhaps eight, colors simultaneously might be acceptable.

Color in Rendering Nature and in Artistic Expression

In the field of computer graphics, the use of color to render scenes in nature is one type of image processing. The number of colors required in a single scene can run into the thousands—from a possible range that might number in the millions. To simulate natural scenes or to create completely synthetic imagery also require an exceptionally wide range of colors. Use of color in artistic expression would require the widest possible range of colors (Figure 12-2). Notice that simply reproducing the original picture here as a monochrome photograph not only sacrifices the richness of full color, but also makes the scene lack depth.

FIGURE 12-2.   Picture requiring wide color range for accurate rendering

   This need for richness and flexibility puts these applications at
the opposite extreme from applications that use color as coding.
Rather than restricting the number of colors, the objective would be
to render all possible subtleties of hue, shading, and tint.

   Computer graphic systems for this type of work are among the
most expensive. Color range, in computer terms, translates to the
variability of pixel values. Hardware factors that result in higher cost
include relatively large memory areas and fast processors. Software
must be highly sophisticated, often using parallel processing techniques to achieve acceptable speed of manipulating large areas of
memory.

Color as a Design Element

Systems for generating business presentations fall between the
extremes of color used as coding and as color rendering. The 16

displayable colors of standard VGA certainly will be sufficient for applications in which color is used primarily as coding. For business presentations, this color selection is a bit more constraining. If you attempt to use electronic imagery that was generated on other computer graphic systems as bitmaps in your drawings, you may face the challenge of trying to render a wide range of shades in just a few colors.

Business presentations that show charts and graphs use color essentially as a design element. Other such applications include advertising collateral materials, television graphics such as weather maps, training media, and so on.

These types of applications may use color both as coding and as an element of composition. Although less literal than control codes, a type of color coding might be used to distinguish among company divisions or product lines. Also, plots that show profit and loss may be distinguished by some type of color coding. If such a thematic approach is used, the guideline for restricting color range still applies. That is, using too many color themes, or codes, will confuse the audience. However, when color is also used as a design element, there may be many different shades of color within the same hue, or theme.

The objective of using color as a design element is to achieve an effective composition and clarity of content. In this context, color is used along with type font, line weight, spatial composition, and other elements to produce a visual composition that is readable, understandable, and aesthetically pleasing.

COLOR RANGE IN BUSINESS PRESENTATIONS

Since using too many color codes or color themes can confuse the audience of a business presentation, there is no obvious need for a wide range of colors. The problem arises in having a sufficiently wide range of colors from which to select a *few* that work well together. When requirements move beyond coding to include pleas-

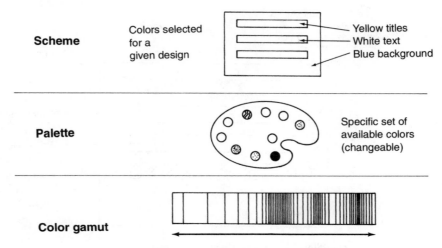

FIGURE 12-3.   Visual representation of color scheme, palette, and gamut

ing and effective color composition, the range needed actually becomes quite large. To understand why this is so, you have to consider some of the factors that determine color range.

The designer's color choices for a given visual composition make up the *color scheme* of the composition. Recall that, within a computer graphic system, the set of specific colors available is the *color palette.* The range of colors that may be reproduced by a given color-display device or output medium is called its *color gamut.* (See Figure 12-3.)

Thus, a color scheme is an abstract concept, a notion of the graphic designer. A color palette is a tool for implementing a color scheme. In turn, the color gamuts of the computer devices and output media are physical, technical constraints that determine what colors can be chosen for the palette. In choosing a palette, designers should consider the ideal objectives of effective color schemes as well as the color-gamut constraints of devices and output media.

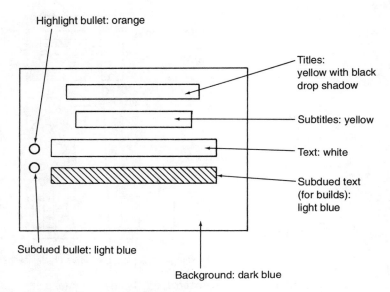

FIGURE 12-4.   Elements of a color scheme for business graphics

COLOR SELECTION

Preliminary decisions about color scheme include color selections for background, main title and subtitles, text (body copy and labels), buildup highlight, and buildup dim (subdued text). (Refer to Figure 12-4.)

Background color is the single most important factor in determining a color scheme and corresponding color palette. Considerations in choosing a color palette include the nature of the output medium, lighting conditions under which the final image will be viewed, the mood or bias inherent in the visual content, and compatibility with other output media or duplication processes.

The value of a color refers to its degree of darkness. The value of the background in a given color scheme is a major factor in determining the *contrast range* of the entire image, or the value range between the lightest and the darkest colors. The greatest contrast generally should be between the background and titles or text. This contrast promotes readability. To achieve this result, a color palette

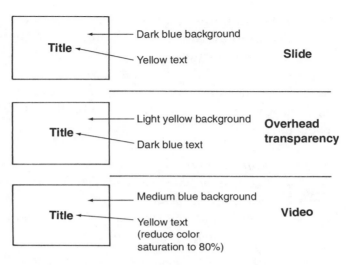

FIGURE 12-5. Rules of thumb for selecting colors for different presentation media

must be selected that is within a contrast range that is determined by the output medium, lighting conditions, and requirements for reproduction quality.

Typical output media include color slides, overhead transparencies, paper hard copies, and video. The most effective color slides have relatively dark backgrounds. However, the value of the background must be increased in proportion to the brightness of the ambient light in the viewing room. Brighter room lights require lighter background colors and a narrower contrast range. The colors chosen for titles and text should be among the lightest colors. Dimmed, or subdued, colors are used for toning down or de-emphasizing selected text or areas of the picture. An appropriate subdued color for slides would be a lighter shade of the background. Highlight color is used to draw attention to specific elements or objects. This color should be the brightest of the colors in the chosen color palette. Examples of the same chart executed for different media are shown in Figure 12-5.

For overhead transparencies, the opposite is true. The most effective overheads have light-colored backgrounds. While slides usually are viewed in darkened rooms, overheads often are preferred when the room lights must be bright, as in training sessions or demonstrations. For this medium, the brighter the lights in the room, the brighter must be the color of the background. Titles and text usually are rendered in dark colors, to provide sufficient contrast. Subduing and highlighting are less common for overheads, since the range of colors that may be distinguished easily is relatively narrow.

TIP *Build-and-subdue techniques usually are not done for overheads, since this might involve possible fumbling of the multiple frames when just one will do. Instead, the presenter can cover portions of text with a blank card and slide the card downward as the discussion progresses to reveal each line or section of text.*

Returning to the topic of contrast, graphics produced for video require relatively narrow contrast ranges, due to the response characteristics of video systems. In general, slides that project well in dark rooms have too much contrast for successful transfer to video.

The mood or content of the presentation is another factor in choosing a background color. By far the most popular color for the backgrounds of business slides is a deep blue. There are two reasons for this:

- Blue objects tend to recede, or appear in the background, in relation to other colors; blue contrasts well and does not detract from other elements of the composition.

- Blue is the most popular color for corporate logos. This is a content issue: The audience is likely to be biased in favor of this color as an overall theme for all slides in the presentation. Yellow and white for titles and text provide good contrast with blue.

Other effective background colors for slides are green and dark gray. Both of these colors are easy on the eyes and compose well with the colors of other elements.

Pastel colors often are used for the backgrounds of overhead transparencies. Yellow, pink (or light magenta), light green, and light blue are good choices. Titles and text might be dark blue or black.

Backgrounds for video graphics must be chosen to decrease the overall contrast range of the image. The guidelines are much the same as for color slides, but the combined intensities of the value and chroma, or saturation, of video backgrounds should not exceed 80 percent of primary, or fully saturated, colors.

Compatibility with other output media is a final consideration in choosing a color palette. Converting slides to video or slides to paper hard copies, for example, usually involves some redesign for reproduction in a different medium. For conversion to video, the contrast range and color saturations of images designed for projection will have to be reduced. When converting to paper hard copy, keep in mind that many of the available output devices, such as ink-jet printers, have relatively narrow color ranges. To get around these limitations, textures such as hatches or patterns might have to be substituted. (As discussed in the previous chapter, this conversion can be a built-in function of the device driver.)

If you plan to duplicate your visual materials, bear in mind that most forms of duplication (copying) add contrast with each reproduction step (generation). For example, slide originals designed for duplication must have narrower contrast ranges than slides intended for projection.

The color gamut of computer graphic systems and output media will determine which specific hues, tints, and shades will be available to you. From this brief discussion, it becomes apparent that a handful of color choices is just not sufficient for designing effective business presentations.

COLOR CAPABILITIES OF
BUSINESS GRAPHICS SYSTEMS

You would think that people could agree on how many colors are enough. As I pointed out in the previous discussion, process-control engineers who design displays for monitoring nuclear reactors might tell you that four colors may be too few—and eight, too many!

Their assumption is that, for coding, a scheme of too many colors is apt to be confusing. Indeed, some accountants feel this way about business slides: A scheme of too many colors is distracting and even somehow dishonest, an attempt to obscure the underlying meaning with dazzle. However, in my experience the typical business executive expects color to be used liberally. Even if you take the conservative position that boardroom graphics should be restricted to, say, eight colors, that begs the question: *Which* eight?

Evaluating the color capability of graphics systems, both software and hardware, is not a simple task. If you want to be able to discriminate among four shades of corporate blue, for example, you must also have that degree of discrimination among the other basic colors. Already, you're way beyond eight colors.

Color capability of graphics systems results from two technical considerations:

- How many levels of intensity can be produced by the color electron guns (or other light-generation method) in the display device?
- How many data bits are associated with each picture element (pixel) in the image?

Both factors have hardware and software components, but their net effect is to limit the color variations that can be produced by the display. In the case of color monitors, the variations are among red, green, and blue electron guns of a color CRT. In the case of plotters or ink-jet printers, it is the number of pens or inks that can be controlled and the combinations in which they can be laid down on paper.

Again, color as a design consideration is subjective. The only valid generalization, even among the comparatively narrow ranks of business graphics users, is that you will always end up needing more than you thought when you acquired your system or set up your color palettes.

These requirements become important when you are evaluating computer systems for graphic applications. Color capability of displays is usually referred to as a subset of simultaneously displayable colors of some total set, or palette, of colors. Color ranges also depend on the processing capabilities (word length in bits) and memory capacities (bytes) of video cards or intelligent output devices.

One good criterion for the use of color is to categorize the application according to the meaning ascribed to colors. For example, colors may be used arbitrarily, in an almost random fashion, to discriminate between various plots on a single chart, as in converting a black-and-white drawing to color. To add one more level of meaning, color may be used, as in the process-control application just cited, to code for certain conditions—a red-coded circuit in a steam-piping diagram, for example.

Finally, the most demanding use of color in business applications combines meaningful coding with good graphic design. Variety of color, consistency with corporate colors, and executive color preferences—all enter into the complex evaluation of color requirements and capabilities.

COLORS IN FREELANCE GRAPHICS

If you let SmartMasters control the design of your presentations, you might have no reason to learn any more about the program's color capabilities. However, just as soon as a supervisor or client requests a color change in a chart you've made or wants a different color scheme, you need to be concerned about details such as color-palette definition, order of color assignment, changing of color attributes, correspondence between colors and monochrome textures, and so on.

There are two basic ways of selecting colors in Freelance Graphics for Windows:

- Select a SmartMaster set and its predefined color scheme. The color scheme is controlled by the order of colors in the current color palette, which is associated with the SmartMaster set.

- In the Current Page view, change the color of an object or the page background explicitly by resetting its attributes, such as its edge color or its area fill color.

Color Palettes

Each SmartMaster set of Freelance Graphics for Windows Release 2 is associated with two palette files, one (.PAL extension) for full-color output and the other (.BW extension) for black-and-white output. The shades of gray in the black-and-white palette are designed to match the values of colors in the full-color palette so that output on black-and-white media will be an accurate monochrome rendering of the full-color version.

 Clicking the Color/BW button at the bottom of the Current Page view toggles the display between the full-color and the black-and-white palettes in the current SmartMaster set.

Color/BW button

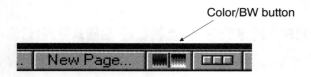

The program comes with a variety of these palettes, which are designed to produce pleasing color compositions when used with specific SmartMaster sets and output media, such as film or paper. For example, the set BLOCKS.MAS uses the palette BLOCKS.PAL, which has a blue background and light-colored text—suitable for screen shows and color slides. The SKETCH.MAS set uses SKETCH.PAL, which has a white background and dark-colored text—primarily for color output on paper or overhead transparency film.

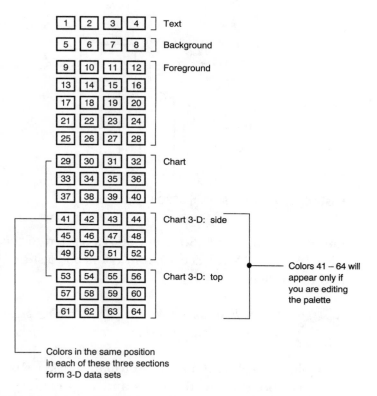

FIGURE 12-6. Color-palette organization

A palette is an ordered arrangement of 64 colors or shades of gray, as shown in Figure 12-6. Note in the illustration that the positions of colors in a palette are numbered 1–64. This numbered order is the sequence in which the program assigns colors to the different types of graphic objects that you create. In general, colors 1–4 are used for text objects, colors 5–8 for page and chart backgrounds (including shading), and colors 9–28 are used for objects in the foreground.

Colors 29–40 are assigned sequentially to the data sets A–L of graphs. Then the order of assignment repeats, using color 29 for data set M, color 30 for N, and so on. In a pie chart, colors 29–40 are assigned to pie slices 1–12. Then the order repeats, but skips color 29, which would normally be used only for the most impor-

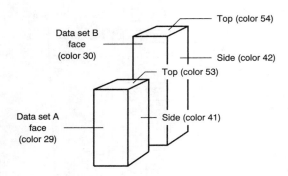

FIGURE 12-7. Coordination of 3D Chart colors

tant data item, slice 1. So, color 30 is assigned to slice 13, color 31 to slice 14, color 32 to slice 15, and color 33 to slice 16. (Pies are limited to 16 slices.)

 You will see only colors 1–40 in dialog boxes unless you select Style➤Edit Palette to change the palette colors.

Colors 41–52 and 53–64 are usually darker shades of colors 29–40, corresponding to the sides and tops of graph data sets when they are plotted in 3-D. The order of assignment is the same (from A–L), then repeating, starting with data set M. The order of assignment for 3-D pie slices follows the same sequence used for the face colors.

In any type of 3-D graph, the palette colors fall into sets of three shades of the same color: the face color (29), the side (41), and the top (53) of the 3-D bar, area, or line. (Refer to Figure 12-7.)

Specific assignments of palette color numbers to types of chart objects are shown in Table 12-2.

In effect, chart objects are colorless. Instead, each object has a color number—although you will not normally see these numbers. The object will take on the color or shade of gray found at that position in the current palette. So, simply by selecting another palette for use with a presentation, you can change its entire color scheme. Each object in the presentation will take on the color found at the

TABLE 12-2. Assignment of Palette Color Numbers to Object Types

Palette Number	Object Type
Text	
1	Title
2	Subtitles, bulleted text, and added text*
3	Data chart text
4	Autobuild gray (subdued text)
Background	
5	Solid background, main color
6	Patterned background, secondary color
7	Alternate background, main color
8	Alternate background, secondary color
Foreground	
9–14	Drawn objects
15	Area and edge of drawn object
16	Chart frame edge
17	Chart frame area (graph background)
18	Organization chart, box area
	Table background
	Cell background
19	3-D organization chart, box side
20	3-D organization chart, box bottom
21	Shadow
22	Bullet, line, and area
23	Organization chart line
24	3-D data chart floor
25	Chart and graph grid
26	Edge (outline in charts)
27	Table border and cell border
28	3-D chart wall
Charts	
29–40	Data sets 1–12, A–L
Chart 3-D: Side	
41–52	Data sets 1–12, A–L
Chart 3-D: Top	
53–64	Data sets 1–12, A–L

* Exceptions are NOTEBOOK.MAS and BRASS.MAS.

same numbered position in the new palette. The command for this purpose is Style➤Choose Palette (or the Choose Palette icon).

You can also edit the colors in a palette by selecting Style➤Edit Palette. (See "Editing Colors" in this chapter.) When you do this, the change will affect all objects that have the same color number. For example, color 1 in any palette is always used for the main titles, or headings, of pages. If the titles in your presentation were yellow, you could change them all to white by changing color 1 from yellow to white in the current palette.

Color Palettes in Data Files

Color palettes are actually stored in three types of data files:

- Palettes (.PAL and .BW files)
- SmartMaster sets (.MAS files)
- Presentations (.PRE files)

Color-Palette Files

Palettes that can be selected for any presentation with the Style➤ Choose Palette command are stored separately as .PAL (color) and .BW (black-and-white) palette files. Choosing another palette file will reset the colors (or gray-scale tones) in a presentation globally, or for all chart objects on all its pages.

Palettes in SmartMaster Sets

Palettes that are associated with SmartMaster sets have been customized for that set and are stored within its .MAS file. You cannot access these palettes directly through the Style➤Choose Palette command. Instead, you must use the Style➤Choose SmartMaster Set command to apply the style to the presentation, then perform Style➤Edit Palette. Optionally, after editing the palette colors, you can select the Save button in the Edit Palette dialog box to save the revised palette as a .PAL or .BW file (stored separately from the .MAS file).

To save the revised palette with the SmartMaster set, select File➤Save As and choose SmartMaster Set (MAS) in the File Types drop-down box. Use a new filename if you want to be able to use the previous version of the set, as well.

Palettes in Presentation Files

Whether the palette came from a SmartMaster set, from a separate .PAL file, or from editing either of these, the current palette used to create a presentation is always saved in the .PRE document file. Therefore, if you edit a palette *but do not save it as a separate .PAL or .BW file,* your changes will affect the current presentation only and will be saved in its .PRE file. That is, the palette in the source .MAS or .PAL file will remain unchanged unless you explicitly save the edited palette with the original filename.

The Color Library

It might be best to think of color palettes as sets of 64 color *assignments,* since the colors need not be all different. For example, for design purposes, you might want color 1, used for titles, to be the same as subtitles (color 2), frame edges (color 16), bullets (color 22), and table borders (color 27). (Again, you do not work with color numbers directly. You control color assignments by the positions of colors in the palette.)

A color palette is actually a subset of a much larger variety of colors found in the *color library.* The color library contains 256 different colors. All these color selections appear when you perform Style➤Edit Palette and then select the Edit Library button, or whenever you select any of the color drop-down boxes in performing Style➤Attributes, Style➤Default Attributes, or the Attributes command in a pop-up menu.

Names of Colors

For ease of reference, colors in Freelance Graphics for Windows have names. When you make a selection from a color menu, its name is also displayed in that dialog box. You can tell which colors from the library have been chosen for the palette by noting the names. When you mix new colors in the library, as described below, you can edit their names, as well.

Uses of the Color Library

The color library has three main uses in Freelance Graphics for Windows. Colors in the library can be:

- Selected as substitutions for predefined palette colors to create custom palettes
- Assigned as explicit, or permanent, colors of objects in drawings
- Used as a basis for mixing a much wider variety of color tones—as many as 16.7 million

Each of these options is discussed further in this chapter under "Editing Colors."

You might think of palette colors as relative and library colors as absolute. Objects, such as chart elements, that take their colors from the current palette will change color when you change palettes. Objects, such as drawings, to which you have assigned colors from the library will stay the same even if you change color palettes.

Every color palette has a color library. Initially, or when you literally take Freelance Graphics for Windows out of the box for the first time, these color libraries are all the same. Hence, you see references in the manuals and in this book to *the* color library, as if there were only one. But, in fact, each color palette can have its own, custom-mixed color library.

In practice, you might never need to edit the library colors. However, if you edit a library color, the change will affect the current presentation only. With respect to the current palette, the edited library colors will be permanent only if you save the revised

.PAL file. In any case, the libraries in other palettes will retain their default settings. So, you can mix custom colors for a presentation without being concerned that the default color assignments of other presentations will be affected. This will become particularly important if you need to create custom palettes that are designed to match the color reproduction characteristics of specific printers or film recorders.

CHANGING THE APPEARANCE OF PRESENTATIONS

SmartMasters can be regarded as collections of parameters that describe graphic compositions. These parameters include page layouts, as well as object attributes such as colors and styles. When you create a new presentation, the parameters in the SmartMaster set you choose are copied into it. Subsequently, styles and palettes from external files can be applied to the presentation to reset many options at, literally, a stroke. The parameters are copied into the presentation file, becoming an integral part of the page data. In other words, a presentation file has all the information in it that is necessary to render the pages. Once a style or palette has been applied to the presentation, the external file has no further relation to it. This is different from some word processing programs that use style sheets, which must always be available for the corresponding data files to be interpreted properly.

Changing the Appearance of an Entire Presentation

In general, to change the appearance of an entire presentation—including its color scheme—choose a different set of SmartMasters. With the presentation open in the Current Page view, select Style≻Choose SmartMaster Set or click the Choose SmartMaster Set icon.

The Choose SmartMaster Set dialog box will appear, as shown in Figure 12-8.

 If the SmartMaster With Blank Background check box in the Choose SmartMaster Set dialog box is reset to on, the presentation will use the BLANK.MAS set, which has a plain white background.

Select a new presentation style (.MAS file) by selecting the filename from the list box, then OK. Or, simply double-click the filename.

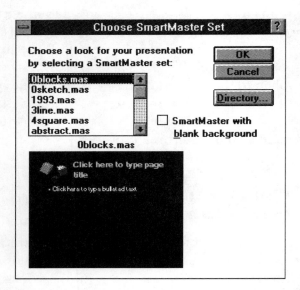

FIGURE 12-8.   The Choose SmartMaster Set dialog box lists all .MAS files in the FLW\MASTERS directory.

Using Predefined Styles

SmartMaster sets are designed around a variety of graphic themes, some including fancy backgrounds, borders, or both. Variations include text font, color palette, page layout, and output medium.

In the procedure just described, you can inspect a style before you apply it to the current presentation. The preview box in the lower portion of the Choose SmartMaster Set dialog box shows a sample layout of the set that is highlighted in the list box above it. The sample page layout shown is Bulleted List.

Creating New SmartMasters

To create a new presentation style, you can modify the templates, or page layouts, in an existing SmartMaster set.

There are two ways to access a SmartMaster set for editing:

- When you are working on a presentation in the Current Page view, select Edit➤Edit Page Layouts or the Edit Page Layouts icon:

- Load the SmartMaster file into the Current Page view by selecting File➤Open and selecting SmartMaster Set (MAS) in the File Types drop-down list box:

File types:

| SmartMaster Set (MAS) |
| Presentation (PRE) |
| SmartMaster Set (MAS) |
| Symbol Library (SYM) |

(Making this selection should change the Directories setting automatically to FLW\MASTERS, where the .MAS files are stored.)

Hatched display indicates SmartMaster is being edited

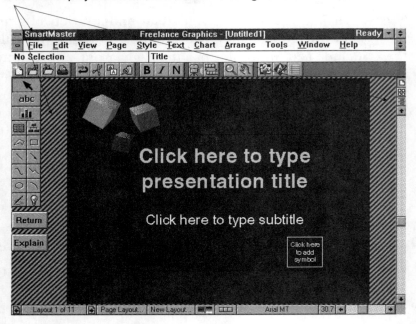

FIGURE 12-9.   When a hatch pattern appears at the sides of the screen, you are
editing the SmartMaster page layouts that control the appearance
of pages in the presentation.

Either of these procedures has the same effect—permitting you
to work on the 11 predefined page layouts in the SmartMaster set
just as you would pages in a presentation. You can work on a layout
in the Current Page view, or you can see all the layouts in the Page
Sorter. (The Outline view is not available when you are working on
SmartMasters.) When you are working on a page layout in either
view, the program window displays a distinctive hatch pattern, as
shown in Figure 12-9. This special display lets you know positively
that you are editing a template that will affect all presentation pages
of a particular chart type.

*If you make a change to the Basic Layout template, all pages in
your presentation will show that change, with the exception of the
title page. Use this feature, for example, to add logos or borders to*

every page. This technique not only reduces the amount of time required to change the pages, it also assures consistency of composition from page to page.

As a further aid to editing SmartMasters, two buttons appear at the left of the Current Page window: Return and Explain.

Selecting the Return button simply returns you to working on the presentation itself. (If you loaded the SmartMaster file, this is the same as executing File➤New to begin a new presentation.) Selecting the Return button is also the same as executing the Edit➤Edit Presentation Pages command.

Selecting the Explain button activates the Help system, displaying instructions for the Edit➤Edit Page Layouts command. (To resume work, select File➤Exit in the Help window.)

Edit templates in the set as you would pages in a presentation. Use the color palette and designs you prefer. Just remember that modifying any of the 11 predefined page layouts will affect all charts of that type when you apply the SmartMaster with the Style➤ Choose SmartMaster Set command.

When working on the SmartMasters, you can also add new, custom templates by selecting Page➤New or clicking the New Layout button in the status bar. Subsequently, when you are working on a presentation that uses the same SmartMasters, any templates you have added will be available when you select Page➤Choose Page Layout or the Page Layout button in the status bar.

To store your changes to the SmartMasters, select File➢Save As. The Save As dialog box will appear. Select SmartMaster Set (MAS) in the File Types drop-down list box. To update the original set, accept the name shown in the Filename text box. To create an alternate version of the set, enter a new filename. Select OK to save the file to disk.

Finding SmartMaster Sets You Use Frequently

When you start Freelance Graphics for Windows, the SmartMaster selection defaults to the set that was current when you ended the previous work session (provided that you used the File➢Exit command to quit).

A handy way of identifying a SmartMaster set that you use often is to place it at the top of the file listing. For example, the first time you use the program, the set 0BLOCKS.MAS is selected by default. Note that the set is actually a copy of BLOCKS.MAS with the *0* prefix in the name, which causes it to be listed first (numbers precede letters in computer sorting). To place a different set at the top of the list and so make it easier to find, save another copy of the set with a new name that will precede the others in alphabetical order. For example, you could make any filename precede 0BLOCKS.MAS in the list by giving it a prefix of *00*, since the second *0* in the new name will be sorted to precede the *B* in 0BLOCKS.

Choosing Another Color Palette

Recall that SmartMasters affect the appearance of presentation pages in all aspects of design, including color. For most people, if a suitable style is available, applying it will be the most efficient way to control the color scheme. This is also good practice, since color should be an integral part of the presentation design.

However, there will be times when you wish to change the color scheme without affecting the other aspects of presentation design.

In such cases, you can simply select Style➤Choose Palette (or the Choose Palette icon) and select another .PAL or .BW file from the Palettes list box.

Select the Directory button in this dialog box if you need to access the CPRINTER.PAL file, which is in the FLW directory, not in FLW\MASTERS with the other palettes. Edit this palette only if you need to customize color printing for specific output devices. There is more on this topic in Chapter 13.

To see how the new palette will look with your presentation, select the Preview button. (You may want to drag the dialog box by its title bar to another part of the screen to see the full effect on the current page.)

To accept the new palette, select OK to close the dialog box. If you select Cancel, the presentation will revert to the colors in the current SmartMaster.

EDITING COLORS

Changing the colors of objects in Freelance Graphics for Windows can be done by

- Editing the current color palette
- Changing the color attributes of specific objects

Editing the Current Color Palette

The purpose of editing the current color palette is to change the color of all objects of a certain type throughout a presentation. For example, if you change color 1 in the palette, the change will affect all the titles on all the pages.

To edit the current color palette, select Style➤Edit Palette in either the Current Page or Page Sorter views. All 64 color assignments in the current palette will appear in the Edit Palette dialog

Currently selected color

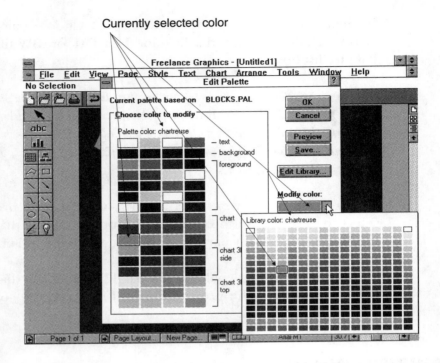

FIGURE 12-10. The Edit Palette dialog box shows all 64 colors in the current palette.

box (Figure 12-10). Among the color patches in the Choose Color to Modify box, select the color *position* that corresponds to the type of object you want to change. Refer again to the color assignments in Table 12-2.

When you have made your selection, a box will surround the color patch to be edited. Then, select the Modify Color drop-down box. The 256 tones in the color library associated with the palette will appear. Double-click the replacement color. Or, move the arrow keys to highlight the color you want, then press Enter.

 If you cannot find the exact color tone you want in the library, click outside its pop-up window to close it, then select the Edit Library button and follow the instructions below, under "Editing Library Colors."

Repeat the color-selection procedure for any other assignment in the palette that you wish to change. Remember that your changes will affect all objects of a given type in your presentation. To accept your changes, select OK to close the dialog box.

If you simply save the presentation, the original SmartMaster or palette file will remain unchanged. The revised palette will be stored in the presentation file and will affect that presentation only. To save the revised palette so that you can use it with other presentations, select the Save button in the Edit Palette dialog box before you close it. Enter a unique filename if you don't want to modify the original palette. Select OK to save the file and close the Save As dialog box, and OK again to close the Edit Palette dialog box.

Changing the Color Attributes of Specific Objects

To change the color of an object in the Current Page view, first select the object. Handles should appear around it, confirming your selection. Refer to Figure 12-11.

Select Style➤Attributes. Or, click the *right* mouse button and select Attributes from the pop-up menu; if the object is a text block, the selection in the pop-up is Font. Yet another alternative is simply to double-click on the object.

A dialog box will appear, containing attribute options for that object type. One of the options will be a drop-down box labeled Color:

When you select the drop-down button, colors 1–40 of the current palette and the entire library will appear in a pop-up menu, as shown in Figure 12-12. Select the color you want, and the pop-up menu will close. Then select OK to close the dialog box.

As an alternative, select Style➤Attributes

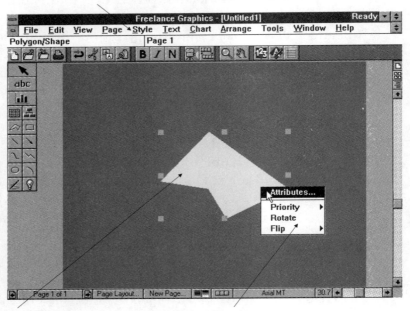

Or, simply double-click on the object

Pop-up menu appears when you select the object and click the *right* mouse button

FIGURE 12-11. To change the color of an object individually, you have three ways of accessing its attribute options.

If you have selected a solid object, such as a rectangle, separate color options will appear for Edge (its outline) and Area (its fill). However, if the check box Same Color As Edge is set to on, the Edge selection will control both the outline and the fill, and the Area selection will be ignored.

Choosing Palette Colors for Objects

In the procedure just described, if you select a palette color, the object will take on whatever color is found in that position in the current palette. So, if you change palettes, the object will change

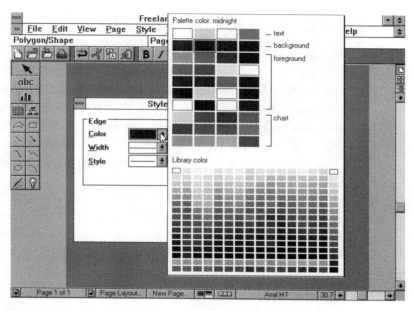

FIGURE 12-12. Color Palette pop-up menu, showing color 5 selected (solid background color)

color. This is a good way to ensure that the object is color-coordi-
nated with whatever SmartMaster set you select.

Choosing Library Colors for Objects

If you make your selection from the library colors instead, the
assignment will be permanent. The color of the object will not
change if you change palettes or SmartMaster sets. Use this technique if the object is a symbol, such as a company logo, that must
always be the same color.

 *In technical terms, objects that have library-color attributes are
assigned explicit RGB values rather than color-palette numbers.*

Any library colors you assign to objects in the Current Page view
will be saved with the object attributes in the presentation file,
regardless of whether you also save the revised palette.

Display of Library Colors

If you are using a standard 16-color VGA video card, 16 of the palette colors (including black and white) will be shown as solid colors. The others will be reproduced by dithering. (Dithering creates a dot pattern that uses two colors to produce the impression of a third.) On 256-color displays, all the library colors will appear solid.

Even if colors appear dithered on the screen, they will normally be reproduced as solid tones in slide output from high-resolution color film recorders.

Especially when you are designing full-color presentations for screen shows, you may wish to avoid dithering by using only the solid, or pure, VGA colors. These colors are listed by name in Table 12-3.

TABLE 12-3. Pure Colors on 16-Color VGA Displays

Color Name	RGB Values
	Red-Green-Blue
Red	255-000-000
Yellow	255-255-000
Olive	129-129-000
Neon Green	000-255-000
Dark Green	000-128-000
Turquoise	000-255-255
Aztec Blue	000-130-128
Blue (or Flag Blue)	000-000-255
Midnight	000-000-128
Hot Pink	255-000-255
Plum Red	128-000-128
Scarlet	129-000-000
White	255-255-255
25% Gray	192-192-192
50% Gray	128-128-128
Black	000-000-000

Editing Library Colors

In full-color palettes (.PAL extensions), any library color can be mixed to create a new color tone. If you edit a library color that also happens to be in the palette, the change will affect all occurrences of that color in the palette and in your presentation. You can verify which library colors are in the palette by matching their names.

The library colors of monochrome palettes (.BW extensions) cannot be edited.

Freelance Graphics for Windows uses the RGB method of color mixing. That is, you mix a custom color by making separate adjustments to its red, green, and blue components.

To make subjective color selections, it usually will be easier just to select among the library colors. The best use of the RGB method is to adjust numeric settings to match values in published tables for film recorders and other output devices.

To edit library-color settings, or to mix custom colors, select Style➤Edit Palette. The Edit Palette dialog box will appear.

Select the Edit Library button. The Edit Library dialog box will appear, as shown in Figure 12-13.

Separate sliders appear in the lower portion of the dialog box for Red, Green, and Blue. Adjust the slider for each color component to a value from 0 through 255. Use the left-right sliders to make the adjustments by dragging the indicator on the scale. Or, click repeatedly on an arrow button at either end to make fine adjustments in that direction.

Another way of working with color is to adjust components of hue (position in the color spectrum), saturation (intensity), and value (darkness or lightness).

Adjusting Hue   To change hues, add one or two of the component colors. For example, adding some red and some green will add

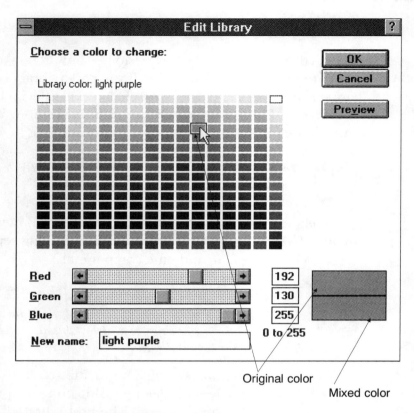

Original color

Mixed color

FIGURE 12-13.　The Edit Library dialog box permits you to mix custom colors by the RGB method and to change the names assigned to colors in the library.

yellow; adding green and blue will add blue-green; adding blue and red will add violet.

Adjusting Saturation and Value　　To adjust the saturation, or tint, of a color, increase Red, Green, and Blue equally. To adjust the value, or shade, of a color, decrease all components equally.

Optionally, you can rename the color by typing in the New Name text box. Select OK to accept your changes and close the Edit Library dialog box. As with palettes, unless you save the palette file that contains this library, your color changes will affect only the current presentation.

Even on a 256-color display, you will not be able to see the differences between some of the library colors on the screen. However, the differences become apparent when color slides are output on high-resolution film recorders.

BACKGROUNDS

In Freelance Graphics for Windows, a page background can include all the graphic elements, including color, over which charts and drawings can be built. The background can be a solid color, a pattern or blend of two colors, or even bitmap pictures. You can also include graphic objects such as borders, symbols, and logos. Examples can be found in the color plates.

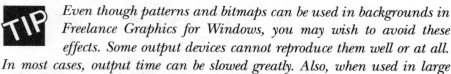 *Even though patterns and bitmaps can be used in backgrounds in Freelance Graphics for Windows, you may wish to avoid these effects. Some output devices cannot reproduce them well or at all. In most cases, output time can be slowed greatly. Also, when used in large areas, these effects add significantly to the size of presentation files.*

Creating and Editing a Background

To change the background of an entire presentation in the Current Page view, first select Page➤Choose Page Layout (or the Page Layout button in the status bar). Then select Basic Layout. Basic Layout affects all pages in a presentation, except the title page.

With the Basic Layout page displayed, select Edit➤Edit Page Layouts. Then edit the objects in the layout as you would any page, adding symbols, adjusting title position or attributes, and so on.

To change the background color, pattern, or both, select Page➤Background. The Page Background dialog box will appear, as shown in Figure 12-14. To change the color of a solid background, select the 1st Color drop-down box and choose a color.

Normally, you would pick colors from the second row of the palette (colors 5–8) for the background. This way, if you change palettes, the background will still be well coordinated with the color scheme.

To select a background that uses a two-color pattern, make selections from all three drop-down boxes: 1st Color, 2nd Color, and Pattern. The two colors you select will compose the two-color pattern.

 For best results, the first and second colors should be contrasting values of the same color hue, such as light blue and dark blue.

When you are editing the Basic Layout, the Scope option should be set to Entire Presentation. Select OK to close the Page Background dialog box, then select Edit➤Edit Presentation pages (or click the Return button) to resume work on your presentation.

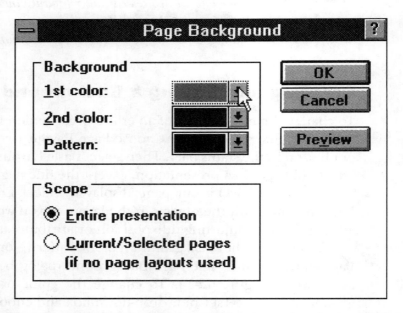

FIGURE 12-14.   The Page Background dialog box has options for resetting background colors and pattern for selected pages or for the entire presentation.

Changing the Background Color and Pattern Only

If you need to change only the color or pattern of a background without editing its other elements, you can select Page➤Background at any time you are working on a presentation in the Current Page or Page Sorter views.

Another way of changing background color globally is to edit the current palette (Style➤Edit Palette). To change a solid background, edit color 5 (the first color in the second row). To change a patterned background, edit colors 5 and 6.

Using Different Backgrounds in the Same Presentation

Normally, a presentation will have a single, consistent background, as controlled by the Basic Layout of the SmartMaster set. However, you can change the background color or pattern of some pages selectively.

For the background of a page to differ from the rest of the presentation, it must be built from the page layout None (Blank Page). To change its background in either the Current Page or Page Sorter views, select that page and perform Page➤Background. For the Scope option, select Current/Selected Pages, then OK.

You can do this same operation on multiple pages in the Page Sorter, provided that their page layouts are all set to None or Blank Page. To make a multiple selection, hold down the Shift key while you click each page to be changed. Then select Page➤Background, choose colors and pattern, select Current/Selected Pages, and select OK.

Changing the Background of a SmartMaster Set

To change the background of a SmartMaster set, you can do either of the following:

- Perform Edit➤Edit Page Layouts, select Basic Layout, and use Page➤Background to reset the background. You should do the same with the Title layout. Then use File➤Save to store the revised set.

- Perform Edit➤Edit Page Layouts, and use Style➤Edit Palette to change the colors in the second row of the palette. Then save the set.

USING BITMAPS

Bitmaps are pictures built as arrays of pixels, as opposed to the collections of vector objects in charts and drawings. Bitmaps can be imported to presentation pages as objects.

To add a bitmap image to a page in the Current Page view, select File➤Import, make a selection in the File Types drop-down box for the file format, and then navigate the directory system to select a file. Import procedures are covered in Chapter 14.

The program places the bitmap on the page, surrounded by handles. You can drag or resize it as you would any object. (Hold down the Shift key while dragging a corner, if you want to avoid distorting the image.)

The bitmap will be rendered in Freelance Graphics in closest-match library colors from the current palette. To adjust the contrast, brightness, or sharpness of the bitmap, select Style➤Attributes. Adjust the sliders for these parameters in the Style Attributes Bitmap dialog box, as shown in Figure 12-15.

You cannot change the colors of the bitmap in Freelance Graphics. Before importing it, either edit the bitmap in the application that created it, or load it into a paint program (such as Windows Paintbrush) to make the changes.

DESIGNING FOR MONOCHROME OUTPUT

A straightforward way to design presentations for black-and-white or monochrome (gray-scale) output is to switch to the alternate color palette in the current SmartMaster set. The program does this

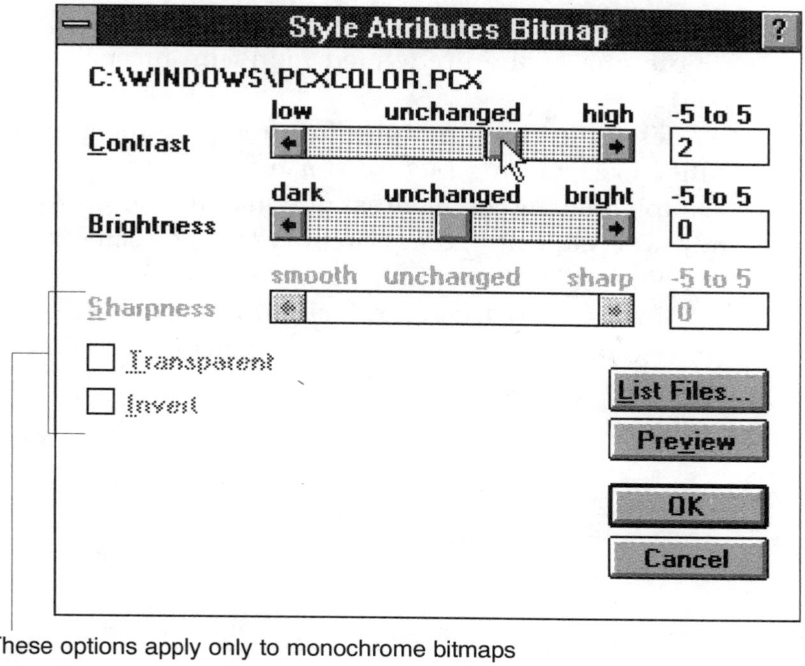

These options apply only to monochrome bitmaps

FIGURE 12-15. The only attributes of imported bitmaps that can be changed within Freelance Graphics are Contrast, Brightness, and Sharpness, depending on the bitmap file type.

automatically when you select a monochrome-output device for printing.

A real convenience feature of Freelance Graphics for Windows Release 2 is the ability to preview monochrome output literally at the touch of a button. Simply click the Color/BW button in the status bar, or select Style➤Use Black & White Palette.

When you are in black-and-white mode, you can adjust any of the gray-scale tones by selecting Style➤Edit Palette, just as you would for colors. Any changes you make will not affect the full-color palette, so you can adjust the grays for the most attractive output on the printer without fear of changing the colors in screen shows or slides.

If you are not satisfied with the black-and-white version of the palette in the SmartMaster set, you can select another palette file.

While in black-and-white mode, select Style➤Choose Palette and choose one of the predefined monochrome palettes (.BW extension).

Designing charts in color for monochrome gray-scale output is rather like painting pictures for a person who is color-blind. For example, red and green areas of equal RGB intensity have the same gray-scale value and, therefore, will look the same in monochrome. The blue component will be almost entirely ignored.

Differences in the reproduction characteristics of output media, which can require alternate color palettes, are among the topics covered in the next chapter.

CHAPTER 13

PREPARING A PRESENTATION

T he discussion so far has focused on the making of individual presentation charts and pages. This chapter moves on to explain how you can:

- Organize a sequence of screens or slides for a presentation
- Produce pages for a specific presentation medium and method of display

THE PRESENTATION OPPORTUNITY

Before you write the first line of your speech or sketch the first chart, you should give some thought to the business situation that is propelling you into the limelight. The wisdom of this approach should be amply demonstrated by the story in Chapter 1 about the plant manager who didn't correctly assess his presentation opportunity until it was almost too late. Your considerations at the outset should include:

- Objective
- Audience
- Organizational level
- Location

- Equipment
- Rehearsal

Objective

You should have a clear idea of what the successful outcome of the presentation should be, even if you're not the presenter. The outcome can be a management decision, an instructional objective, an information update, the launch of a project, and so on.

If you don't know the purpose of the meeting, you don't need a presentation. Taking a canned presentation into an uncertain situation invites disaster. You're going to be mighty embarrassed if you go in prepared to sell hard and find out that they've already bought or have their own agenda for selling you!

You can produce some spectacular charts and drawings with Freelance Graphics for Windows. But you want to avoid overkill: You're in big trouble if the *only* thing they want to talk about afterward is how you did the graphics.

Audience

Knowing the objective of the presentation should help identify the audience. Who are they? What is the degree of formality? How will they be dressed? What will they expect? How many in the audience? How far will they sit from the charts? Do they generally take notes during presentations? Are they prone to interrupt with questions? Do they expect to take paper copies of charts from the meeting?

Organizational Level

As covered in Chapter 1, different rules apply to peer, presentation, and publication levels in an organization. Identifying the organizational level helps determine the appropriate display medium. (Refer to Figure 13-1.)

FIGURE 13-1. Peer, presentation, and publication levels with corresponding media

Peer Level

Meetings at *peer level* involve a few members of the same work group, who gather for things such as an informal brainstorming or investigative session. Appropriate media may be flip charts or overhead transparencies. Often, displaying graphs on the computer stimulates a discussion of alternatives. A peer-level presentation might be done as a screen show on a computer monitor or video projector.

Presentation Level

Meetings at the *presentation level* usually involve reporting to management. Slides and paper handouts are the most common media, although video projection might also be appropriate. As discussed later in this chapter, beware of interactive display techniques when presenting to decision makers.

Publication Level

Showing information at the *publication level* means that you are taking an organizational or corporate message to the public, such as sales prospects or stockholders. Media can include glossy color brochures, broadcast and recorded video, multi-image slide shows, and computer multimedia.

Location

Getting information in advance is crucial. The presentation site and facilities determine room size, audience seating plan, viewing distances, screen size, available display equipment, room lighting conditions (*very* important), projection and setup support staff, and other technical details that contribute to your choice of output medium and display method.

 According to the Society of Motion Picture and Television Engineers, the optimum viewing distance is four times the height of the screen. (See Figure 13-2.)

Equipment

Do not make possibly unwarranted assumptions about the type and availability of display equipment that may be at the meeting site. Yes, it's not uncommon to find a 35mm Kodak Carousel slide projector, a VCR in VHS format, or a personal computer that can run a screen show (but not necessarily with the color display adapter you

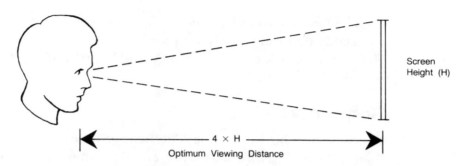

Screen
Height (H)

4 × H
Optimum Viewing Distance

FIGURE 13-2.   Optimum viewing distance. Calculate this to determine the correct
screen size for a room.

need). Even if the required equipment is in place, will it be available the day and time of your presentation? Will it be in good repair?

Of course, you should control the situation as much as possible. If you're taking a major show on the road, you have little choice but to take your own equipment—as well as a professional projectionist, and perhaps also a sound technician.

As a rule, don't rely on obtaining audiovisual equipment from a hotel, even if you're assured that it is available. Instead, rent equipment locally from a reputable audiovisual service, especially if its own setup staff can also be hired. For large meetings at hotels and conference facilities, in-house public-address systems are notoriously unreliable. Take your own equipment and staff. Think of the extra expense as insurance.

Transporting computer equipment for electronic shows can be both cumbersome and risky. Besides being bulky, PCs are delicate instruments that don't travel well. Hard disks are especially prone to failure from the physical shocks of handling, which can also cause printed circuit boards to shift in their slots and connectors to fail. If you must take an electronic show on the road, choose a portable computer that has a VGA color-interface board and connect it to a monitor or video-projection system that's in place or that was shipped—and checked out—in advance. Also verify monitor compatibility in advance.

The best all-around solution might be to choose a VGA card for a portable that can provide outputs in a variety of modes, including Hercules monochrome, EGA, VGA, and Super VGA (SVGA).

Rehearsal

The old show-biz saying goes, "Rehearse, rehearse, rehearse—and then, rehearse!" For a major presentation, there are actually three different phases of rehearsal:

- Speech rehearsal
- Technical rehearsal
- Dress rehearsal

Speech Rehearsal

The presenter should rehearse the speech, while looking at the slides. Watch the positioning of visual cues—or the exact point in the text at which a slide should appear. Revisions to the speech text or graphics may be necessary, especially when the elements of speech and visuals are seen together for the first time. This type of rehearsal need not be done at the meeting site.

Technical Rehearsal

This is a *run-through* for purposes of setting projector focus, lights, and sound levels, as well as for positioning and practicing visual cues and rehearsing entrances and exits of presenters.

This type of rehearsal is always done at the meeting site—preferably after all changes have been made to speeches and visuals. This is not the time to worry about content, but last-minute changes may be necessary. The technicians are in charge, and because of frequent interruptions, it may actually be preferable for someone to stand in for the presenter.

Dress Rehearsal

Just as in the theater, major business presentations must have a full run-through with presenters, visuals, and all technical effects. To add realism, the dress rehearsal is rarely stopped for commentary, or notes, which are saved for afterward. Changes at this point are unthinkable—but will be demanded anyway!

That's a brief overview of the planning process for a major presentation. Now consider the detailed steps of preparing a presentation—starting first with its intended message.

WRITING AND STORYBOARDING

A storyboard, or sequence of thumbnail sketches, is the time-honored tool of the presentation designer. Before the microcomputer era, storyboards were mandatory in computer-graphics production environments. Computer time was so expensive that graphics had to be laid out in detail in advance so that experimentation at the console would be minimized. This required exceptional discipline on the part of computer artists, who sometimes had to resist the understandable temptation to test the system's power and flexibility.

Today, a PC-based system that can run Freelance Graphics for Windows is so inexpensive (by comparison) that you can experiment to your heart's content. In the time it would take to sketch just the storyboards, the program makes it possible for you to produce near-final versions of charts.

But there's a chicken-or-the-egg paradox about designing presentations: Which comes first—the speech text or the graphics?

The Windows environment permits multitasking, or switching among a number of concurrently running applications. Thus, it is possible to alternate between writing speech text in a word processor and composing slides in Freelance Graphics for Windows.

The close correlation between storyboarding and speech writing is an excellent example of the need for multitasking. Neither component—text nor graphics—should take precedence over the other in the creative process.

Rather, these elements should contribute to one another. Free-lance Graphics for Windows actually improves on the multitasking capabilities of Windows by permitting multiple views of the data *within* a presentation, as you are creating it. A feature of the version for Windows, the Outliner, is a text-processing utility for organizing presentation content in outline form, as well as promoting the rapid entry of text data for title and bullet charts. The Outliner is one of three views, or document windows that display presentation data; the other two are the Current Page view and the Page Sorter. (A screen show is another method of viewing a presentation, but it is not a document window because you cannot edit the data in this mode.)

Çomposing in the Outliner

It can be a part of your regular work routine with Freelance Graphics for Windows to begin the process of speech writing by typing the main topics of your presentation in the Outliner. You can see your entries as text charts in the Current Page view. The type of layout used for each page is determined as follows:

- The program assumes that Page 1 of any presentation is a title (which can include a subtitle also).

- When you create new pages by entering text in the Outliner, those pages become bulleted list charts (a title with an indented list), unless you reset the page layout.

- If you reset the page layout in the Outliner view by selecting Page➤Choose Page Layout or the Page Layout button in the status bar, you can enter the titles and subtitles in the Outliner. For the 2-Column Bullets option, you can enter all the topics in both columns.

- The Outliner will show only the first two blocks of text, such as title and subtitle or title and bulleted list, on a page—regardless of the page layout selected. To enter text for tables, organization charts, and annotations, switch to the Current Page view.

If you create pages first in the Current Page view and then open the Outliner, the document symbols next to the page numbers will indicate the type of layout you used for each:

Title Chart	Title or bullet chart
Drawing	Drawing or mixed graphics
Data Chart	X-Y, pie, or radar
Organization Chart	Organization chart
Table	Text table

The text contained in the first two blocks on each page will appear in the Outliner, listed in page-number sequence.

 All text in the Outliner is shown there in the same typeface (Arial) and size. Attributes can be set from the Text menu in the Current Page view.

Using the Outliner

To open the Outliner, from either the Current Page view or the Page Sorter, select View➤Outliner from the menu bar. Or, select the Outliner button (third icon from the top in the upper-right corner of the document window).

To create a text outline from scratch, select File➤New, choose a SmartMaster set, then open the Outliner.

The Outliner view resembles a ruled yellow pad, with a double vertical rule at the left margin. To enter text, move the insertion point to an empty field by clicking or by using the arrow keys, and then type the characters. At the end of a text line, press Enter to drop down one line to the next entry. After you type a title, pressing Enter drops down and indents automatically so you can enter the second text block.

Again, if you are making entries for Page 1, the second entry will appear as a subtitle. Otherwise, it will be the first item in a bulleted list. Pressing Enter after typing the first item will drop down to the next item on the same level of indentation.

To indent further (up to three levels), press the Tab key before typing the line. Or, instead of pressing Tab, you can click on the Demote icon at the top of the document window:

To break, or split, a line of text within the same entry or topic, press Ctrl-Enter at the point of the break and continue typing characters.

To move the insertion point back to a higher level, press Shift-Tab or click on the Promote icon:

To begin a new page, press Shift-Tab or click the Promote icon, repeatedly if necessary, to move up through the levels of indentation, until a new document symbol and page number appear in the left margin.

Editing an Outline

You can edit text in the Outliner much as you would in any Windows word processing application, such as Notepad. You must select a string or line of text before you can perform menu operations on that text.

Selecting Text

To select a page and both its text blocks, click on its page symbol in the left margin. To select a bullet item and all its subordinate items, click its bullet.

To select any text item or group of adjacent items, start with the cursor in the left margin and drag a box around your selection.

To select a group of nonadjacent items, select the first item by one of the procedures just described, then use the *right* mouse button to click the document symbols or bullets of the other items.

To select a string, or group of adjacent characters, within a line of text, first select the line. Move the insertion point to the starting point of the string, and it will change to an I-beam pointer. Drag the I-beam over the string to highlight it. With the string highlighted, you can type a new string to replace it, or you can perform other editing operations.

Editing Operations

With a text portion selected, you can perform Edit➤Copy or Edit➤Cut (thereby placing the text on the Clipboard) and Edit➤ Paste (retrieving a copy of the text at the insertion point).

Perform Edit➤Clear to delete a selected portion of text, or select it and press Del. As with editing commands elsewhere in Freelance Graphics for Windows, you can select Edit➤Undo to reverse the previous edit, for as many as the 10 most recent changes.

Moving Pages and Entries

To move a page within the outline, simply drag its document symbol. As you do this, the pointer will change to a right triangle (the

Move Page pointer), and the point of insertion within the outline will be indicated by a moving horizontal bar.

To move a bullet item to the same level anywhere else in the outline, drag its bullet.

You cannot drag an item to a different level. Instead, move the item as just described, then change its level by promoting it (Shift-Tab or Promote icon) or demoting it (Tab or Demote icon).

Other Commands in the Outliner

The Outline menu item appears in the Outliner's menu bar. Commands in its pull-down menu include the following:

Expand

This command reveals the underlying data in an outline on which a Collapse command has been performed. Outline➤Expand affects only the currently selected page in the outline. The same action will result from selecting the Expand icon just below the toolbar:

 This icon looks much like the boldface Expand All icon, described below, which expands the whole presentation, not just the page.

Collapse

This command condenses the view of the outline without affecting the underlying data. Outline➤Collapse suppresses the display of the second text block in the selected page only. As a result, only its title is shown in the outline. An alternative for this command is the Collapse icon:

When a page entry has been collapsed, a plus sign (+) will appear to the left of its document symbol in the outline. The Collapse icon looks much like the boldface Collapse All icon, described below, which collapses the whole presentation, not just the page.

Expand All

The Outline➤Expand All command restores the full text of an outline that has been collapsed previously. Expand All icon does the same thing:

Collapse All

Selecting Outline➤Collapse All reduces the amount of text displayed for all pages in the outline so that only the titles are showing. The underlying data are unaffected. The Collapse All icon is also available:

Promote and Demote

The commands Outline➤Promote and Outline➤Demote have the same effects on a selected text item as pressing Shift-Tab and Tab, respectively.

Make Second Column

If the page layout chosen for the current page is 2-Column Bullets, the command Outline➤Make Second Column starts the second column of bulleted items after the insertion point. The start of the second-column list is marked in the outline by the Second Column indicator:

Within an existing two-column list, this command can also be used to change the starting point of the second column to the first item after the insertion point.

Alternate Methods of Entering Text

As a further convenience for working with the text of your presentation, you can bring text generated by other applications, such as word and outline-processing programs, into the Outliner through the Clipboard. (Review the discussion of the Clipboard in Chapter 4. To pass data through the Clipboard, select the data in the source application, and then from the menu bar, select Edit➤Copy or Edit➤Cut. Then select Edit➤Paste in the Outliner.)

Importing an Entire ASCII File

You can also bring in the contents of any ASCII text file even if it was created by a non-Windows program. Select File➤Import from the Outliner's menu bar to access the file. The contents of the file will be placed after the current insertion point in the outline.

The levels, or hierarchy, of the text in the external ASCII file will be translated by Freelance Graphics for Windows to become page titles and bulleted items, according to the following rules:

- Items that have no leading spaces (flush to the left margin) in the external file will be interpreted as page titles.

- Items preceded by spaces will be assigned to levels according to the number of spaces: One leading space indicates a first-level indent, two spaces a second level, and three spaces a third level.

Importing Selected Text

You can also import selected portions of an external file. In the Outliner view, press F6 (Data Import). Select the path and filename in the Import Data File dialog box, as well as the file type.

If the file you selected matches the type you specified, such as a text or worksheet file, the Import Data window will open, showing the content of the file. (See Figure 13-3.) Highlight the portion to be imported, then select OK. The selected text will be placed on the Clipboard.

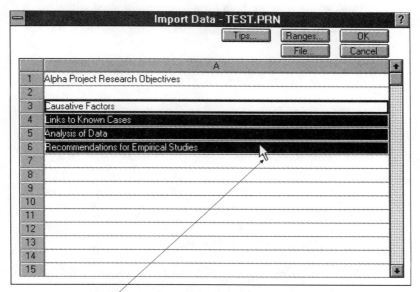

Drag pointer to highlight range of items to be imported

FIGURE 13-3. The Import Data window shows the data content of an external file so that you can select the items to be imported.

Back in the Outliner, move the insertion point to the place where the text will appear. Then perform Edit➤Paste.

Using the Completed Outline

A finished outline can be pasted into a word processing application through the Clipboard or can be written to an external file. You can then expand on the outline to develop the full text of your speech.

If Ami Pro for Windows is installed on your system, you can start this word processing application from within Freelance Graphics by selecting its application icon from the toolbar:

For other Lotus applications to start successfully from within Free-lance Graphics for Windows, references to those programs in the FLW2.INI file must include the correct devices and paths. You will have to edit this file if you installed the applications somewhere other than in the default directories C:\123W and C:\AMIPRO.

The File➤Export command is not available from the Outliner. To write the outline to a disk file as ANSI text, select the pages in the Outliner view, then perform Edit➤Copy. Open the Windows Clip-board application and then execute File➤Save As. Or, use Edit➤Paste to read the text into a word processing application.

Printing an Outline

To print a text outline of your presentation, select File➤Print in the Outliner (or select the File Print icon), then select the Outline option button in the Print File dialog box.

The outline will print as it is displayed, so any text that has been suppressed by a Collapse operation will not be printed. To print the entire outline, perform Outline>Expand All or click the Expand All icon before selecting File>Print.

VISUALIZING THE MESSAGE

Even though computer multitasking can be a very convenient way to work, many people are still more comfortable with pencil and paper, especially in the early stages of writing and visual design. Manually produced storyboards have a more practical reason for existence, however. A sketch on paper can still be the best means of interaction when you're preparing a presentation for someone else. The storyboard becomes a contract, in effect, for the work to be produced—a method of securing agreement in advance about chart design and content.

As shown in Figure 13-4, annotating a storyboard is also an excellent way of documenting changes when you will be billing your work. (Of course, this process of marking up a document also has its electronic analog, the pen-based computer. Watch for this work

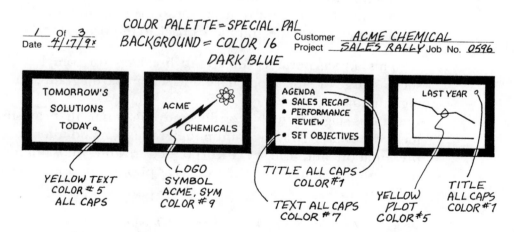

FIGURE 13-4. A storyboard on paper helps to visualize the presentation. Note that the annotations on this example assist in this process.

method to gain rapid acceptance among people who work daily with—possibly paperless—storyboards.)

Storyboards on paper can be readily photocopied along with scripts. An effective format during the intermediate stages of production has the speech text, or narration, on the same page as the storyboard frames.

When developing a storyboard, you're an image engineer, in the sense described in Chapter 2. Your task is to literally make ideas visible. Don't put the speech on the screen: Find a way to show its essential ideas.

For conceptualizing a presentation visually, professionals in graphic arts recommend that you take a page from the comic books:

Notice how they use overall views to establish the setting of a scene. Then note how they use medium views and close-up views to show pertinent details. If you can find an instruction-oriented comic, note also how the illustrator presents graphic material such as charts, graphs, or schematic drawings. Study not only the composition of this graphic material, but also the way the illustrator introduced it into the strip and how he or she moves from the graphic art back to the visual story.

This advice pertains directly to breaking up complex charts, such as large organization charts and schematic diagrams, and adding buildup sequences.

At this stage, plan also for illustrative materials that can supplement the charts. Drawings and photographs can add interest to the presentation and can be incorporated readily into multimedia screen shows or added to slide shows as photocomposites, as shown in Figure 13-5.

Creating a paper record of your production work is an excellent use of the Handouts feature of Freelance Graphics for Windows. See "Producing Output" later in this chapter.

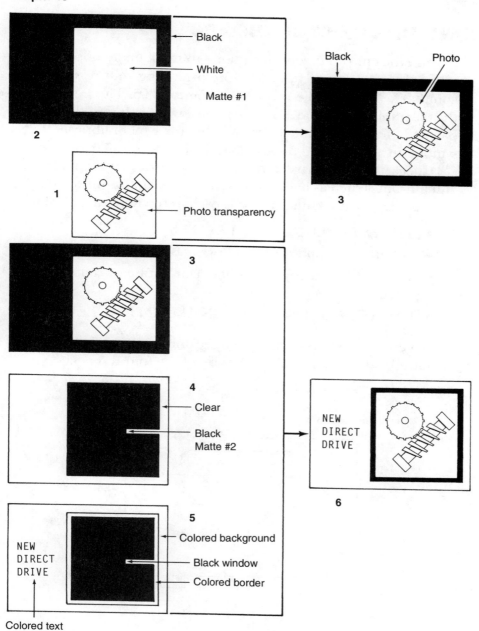

FIGURE 13-5. Basic steps in building a photocomposite using 35mm slides. Mattes must be used to block out areas that will be exposed in other steps. The objective is to expose each area of the film just once.

MARKING UP THE STORYBOARD

It's an efficient production technique to mark up an approved storyboard for colors and effects before beginning your session at the computer. (An example is shown in Figure 13-6. The numbers on the diagram correspond to the positions of the colors in the current palette.) If a printed catalog is available for symbol libraries, select symbols in advance and be sure that the files are available.

Check the storyboard for consistency of design. Capitalization and attributes such as italics should be consistent for titles, subtitles, text, and labels. A commonly used style has the following attributes:

- TITLES IN ALL CAPITAL LETTERS
- Subtitles in Uppercase and Lowercase Letters
- Text in lowercase with first letter of phrase or sentence capitalized
- LABELS AND FOOTNOTES IN ALL CAPITAL LETTERS

In general, text in mixed uppercase and lowercase letters will be the most readable, especially if the size of the font is small.

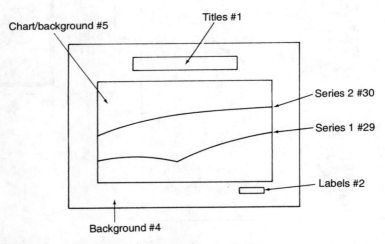

FIGURE 13-6.   Color assignments (palette color numbers) on a production storyboard for a data chart

COLOR-PALETTE DESIGN

Select or design a color palette for the presentation. Keep a consistent color scheme for the entire presentation or for major segments of it, perhaps a different scheme for each presenter.

Important factors in selecting a color palette include:

- Projection method
- Room lighting
- Duplication requirements

Projection Method

As a rule of thumb, slides should have dark backgrounds and light text. Overhead transparencies should have light, pastel backgrounds and dark text.

Room Lighting

Overhead transparencies are preferred for brightly lit rooms. You might choose this presentation method in a classroom situation where the audience must see to take notes.

 Rooms can seldom be made totally dark unless specifically designed for projection. The amount of ambient light in the room will affect the apparent color saturation of your slides. If the room is semilit, dark backgrounds of any color will appear black. If the room is very dark, brightly colored backgrounds will make text difficult to read and may cause eyestrain. Black backgrounds can be a good compromise because the frame border on the screen disappears and text appears to float. However, there can be a distracting illusion in which the chart appears three-dimensional: Objects in cool colors such as blues and greens will appear to recede into the background.

Slides designed for transfer to video should be limited in contrast and color saturation. Otherwise, video noise will be generated at the edges of contrasting objects, making them look blurred.

Duplication Requirements

If your presentation needs to be reproduced in quantity, the color palette must be modified accordingly. Film duplication causes an increase in contrast: Darks get darker and lights get lighter. A deep blue background on an original slide might reproduce as black. Video duplication on tape causes buildup in both contrast and noise, or blurring.

Slides that will be used as masters for making color photocopies on paper should be composed in the same colors you would use for overhead transparencies—light backgrounds with dark text. Technical considerations for duplicating processes are covered later in this chapter.

POWER PRODUCTION TECHNIQUES

Freelance Graphics for Windows includes capabilities for manipulating slide sequences as presentations and for helping you manage the production process. These features include:

- Predefined page layouts
- Page Sorter
- Spelling Checker
- Macros

PREDEFINED PAGE LAYOUTS

Chapter 11 covers the use of SmartMaster sets, or presentation styles, which contain predefined page layouts for different chart types. Each layout is a template for a page that has preselected object attributes and positions. In effect, a SmartMaster set is a presentation that is empty of data, and a page layout is an empty page of a specific chart type (such as Bulleted List).

You can modify SmartMaster layouts in the Current Page view by selecting Edit➤Edit Page Layouts. This places the program in SmartMaster mode, which permits you to edit the layouts as though they were pages. Besides editing the supplied layouts, you can also create new ones for special types of charts that you use frequently. To begin a new layout when you are in SmartMaster mode, select Page➤New or click the New Layout button in the status bar.

New layouts will be added to the list in the New Layout dialog box, as shown in Figure 13-7. The default name is Page Layout N, where N is a sequential number. Or, you can enter any unique name by typing it in the Page Name text box. The list of SmartMasters will appear each time you start a new page. Remember, though:

- To be able to use the new layouts later, you must save the revised SmartMaster set with the File➤Save As command, using the SmartMaster Set file type (.MAS).

- Any new layouts will be available only when you apply that particular set to a presentation.

Predefining charts that you use often as SmartMaster layouts can save you work, speed the creation process, and assure consistent results. These benefits will be particularly important to you if you do volume production work or regularly prepare presentations for others. SmartMaster files are a way of organizing a collection of these templates around a consistent design scheme that can apply throughout a presentation.

If you must prepare presentations regularly for others, consider creating a separate customized set of SmartMasters for each presenter. Develop custom templates for recurring chart designs.

A problem in designing templates is that you must be able to anticipate changes. For example, a simple update should not throw the layout of a slide off balance. Here are some guidelines:

Name of new layout based on
this template

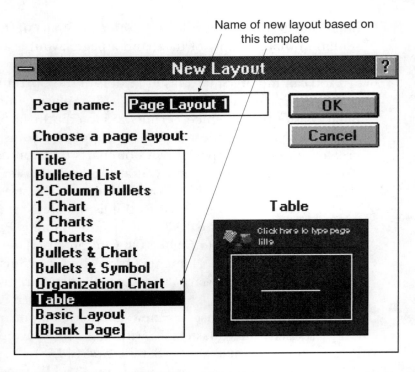

FIGURE 13-7. The New Layouts dialog box permits you to name a custom template that will be added to the SmartMaster set.

- If a text string is longer in the update, will it still fit in the selected text size?

- In layouts for data charts, have you provided for a sufficient number of data sets?

- Particularly if there might be many data sets, should their default colors, patterns, or line-style assignments be changed?

- Should an X-Y graph template include a second y (2Y) axis?

ORGANIZING PRESENTATIONS WITH THE PAGE SORTER

You can get an overview of an entire presentation with the Page Sorter. In this view of a presentation file, pages are shown in sequence as thumbnail, or miniaturized, images.

The primary use of the Page Sorter is to edit a presentation by rearranging, duplicating, or deleting the pages in a presentation. (In SmartMaster mode, you can do the same operations on page layouts. Although the sequence of layouts usually is unimportant, the Page Sorter is a handy way of duplicating layouts that you want to customize.)

The Page Sorter is an electronic analog of the light table, a large flat surface of white glass that is lit from beneath that you can use to inspect and arrange a collection of slides. Use the Page Sorter to:

- Place pages in presentation sequence, including all buildup sequences and repetitions.

- Put slides in a production queue, or batch, for submission to output devices such as printers, plotters, film recorders, and outside recording services.

- Create the sequence for a screen show, an electronic slide show on the computer monitor.

Using the Page Sorter

You can access the Page Sorter from any other view after you have created or opened a presentation. Select View➤Page Sorter from the menu, or select the Page Sorter icon (second button from the top in the top right corner of the current window).

Separate miniaturized images for each page in the presentation will appear in numbered order in the Page Sorter window. To change the order, simply drag a page to a new position in the sequence.

In the Page Sorter, selecting Page≻New from the menu or the New Page button from the status bar brings up the New Page dialog box, from which you must select a page layout. When you have done this, the new page will be inserted after the current one (shown by a box drawn around its thumbnail view). To highlight a different page, simply click on it.

To insert a duplicate page in the order, select the page and execute Page≻Duplicate. (Or, you can perform Edit≻Copy or Cut and Edit≻Paste.) A copy of the page will appear. Drag the copy to the desired position in the sequence.

To delete a page, select it and perform Page≻Remove. Or, you can press the Del key or select Edit≻Clear.

One way to move a page into the Current Page view quickly is to highlight it in the Page Sorter and then press Enter.

SPELLING CHECKER

Freelance Graphics for Windows has a built-in spelling-checker program for catching typographical errors in pages that contain text, as well as in any speaker notes that might also be in the presentation file. Spelling may be checked for selected text blocks within the current page, for the entire current page, or for an entire presentation. A personal dictionary can be edited to include exceptions, such as technical terms and proper names, that appear frequently in your presentations. English-language options include the choice of American or British spelling.

Dictionary files are installed in the \LOTUSAPP\SPELL subdirectory, which is shared among Lotus applications. The main dictionary for English is contained in the file LOTUSEN1.DIC. It has a proprietary, compressed format and cannot be edited directly by word processing applications. However, you can choose to include the user's dictionary LTSUSER1.DIC. This file is in ANSI format and can be edited either within the Spell Check operation or by loading it into a file editor such as Windows Notepad.

Performing a Spelling Check

To check spelling, create or open a presentation. Checking can be performed in any view—Current Page, Page Sorter, or Outliner. If you wish to check a single page only, select that page. To check selected words only, open the text block that contains the word and highlight it. To start checking, select Tools➤Spell Check, click the Spell Check SmartIcon, or press Ctrl-F2.

 The spelling-check process will not check for selected words unless the text block is open as shown in Figure 13-8.

A Spell Check dialog box will appear (Figure 13-9). Select an option button to indicate whether checking will be applied to selected words, the current page, or the entire presentation.

Select any of the check boxes to include data charts, organization charts, or speaker notes in the checking.

Another set of check boxes will appear if you select the Options button. Select any combination of these: Check for Repeated Words (the the), Check Words with Numbers (FILE1), Check Words with Initial Caps (otherwise, excludes proper names and other capitalized words), and Include User Dictionary Alternatives (permit words in LTSUSER1.DIC).

TIP   Omitting types of pages or classes of words from the spelling check can make it go faster, particularly within a large presentation. For example, you would not ordinarily want to include organization charts, since they contain mainly proper names that would otherwise be flagged as errors.

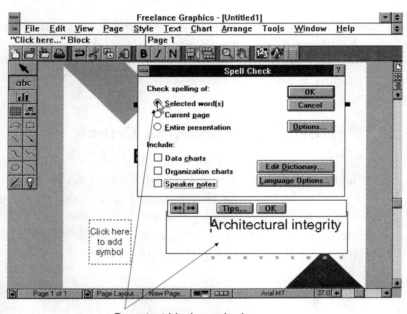

Open text block required

FIGURE 13-8.   A text block must be open for a spell check to be performed on
selected words only.

The checking process will start. Each time the program finds an
exception—an unrecognized word or other error—the Spell Check
exception dialog box will appear, as shown in Figure 13-10. The
exception is flagged and shown in the top left text box beneath the
page number in which it appears. (Words that contain internal capitalization are flagged also.)

If a questionable item is acceptable to you, select the Skip button. Or, if you want to accept all occurrences of the word, select
Skip All. If the spelling is correct and you wish to make a note of it
for future sessions, select Add to Dictionary instead.

If the item is incorrect and you wish to make a change, retype
the entry in the Replace with text box, then select the Replace button. Or, highlight an alternative item in the Alternatives list box and
select Replace. If you want to correct all occurrences that were mis-
spelled exactly the same (including capitalization), select Replace

Types of items to exclude

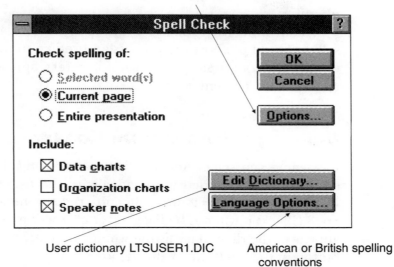

User dictionary LTSUSER1.DIC   American or British spelling
                                       conventions

FIGURE 13-9.   The Spell Check dialog box is accessed by selecting Tools➤Spell
Check.

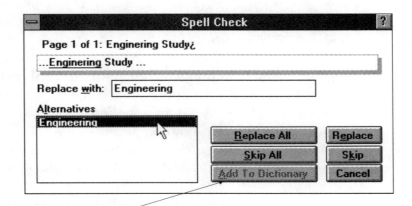

This button will be available only if
replacement is not in dictionary

FIGURE 13-10.   Exceptions appear in this dialog box when the program flags a
word for verification or correction.

All instead. Repeat this procedure for each word that the program identifies.

At any time when you are in the Spell Check dialog box, you can select Cancel to abort the process and return to the prior view. Or, when the prompt `Spelling Check Complete` appears, select OK to return to the current view.

Building a Personal Dictionary

Each time you select Add to Dictionary during the checking process, the item is added automatically to the user's dictionary file. Consequently, if the item is encountered the next time you select Spell Check, it will not be flagged for correction. Also, the item will appear in the dictionary listing when you select the Edit Dictionary button in the Spell Check dialog box.

TIP *If you must prepare presentations for others, you may wish to create a separate personal dictionary for each presenter. Include technical terms, jargon, and abbreviations that are unique to that client. (To select one of the dictionaries, use File Manager or another utility to rename it LTSUSER1.DIC.)*

Again, the default user's dictionary is an ANSI text file that can be loaded and edited in applications such as Windows Notepad. This feature could be useful for appending a lengthy custom dictionary generated by a non-Lotus application.

You can also make entries to the user's dictionary when you are running a spelling check. In the Spell Check dialog box, select Edit Dictionary.

The Spell Check User's Dictionary dialog box will appear. Type a new item in the New Word text box, then select Add. The new item will appear in the Current Words list box, which displays the contents of the personal dictionary file. To remove an item from the list, highlight it, then select the Delete button.

To change an item already in the dictionary, highlight the item in the list box and select the Delete button. Then type the new spelling in the the New Word box and select Add.

When you have finished adding or editing items in the user's dictionary, select OK.

MACROS

A *macro* is a sequence of prerecorded keystrokes and mouse actions that perform a specific task and that can be executed with a single action. Macros are useful for automating routine production tasks, such as performing updates to charts, printing batches of presentations, and so on.

There is no internal macro language for the Windows versions of Freelance Graphics. However, you can use the Windows Recorder application to record any sequence of mouse selections and keystrokes when you are working in Freelance Graphics.

 For more information about macros, see the section "Recorder" in the Microsoft Windows User's Guide.

Recording a Macro

To record a macro, double-click on the Recorder icon in the Accessories window. The Recorder window will open; minimize this application. The Recorder will shrink to an icon.

Start Freelance Graphics for Windows. Advance to the point in the program at which you want to begin recording, and move the cursor to the exact location on the screen at which the macro will begin. Press Ctrl-Esc to bring up the Windows Task List, then double-click on Recorder to restore the Recorder application.

Enter name (omit extension)

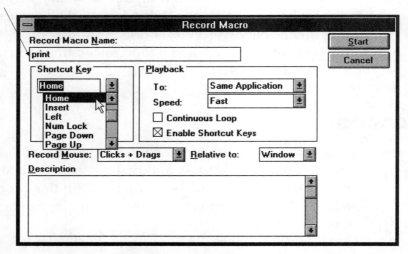

FIGURE 13-11. Open the Record Macro window in Windows before starting Free-lance Graphics for Windows.

The Recorder window will reopen. Choose Macro➤Record to bring up the Record Macro dialog box (see Figure 13-11). Enter a name (up to 40 characters long) for the macro in the Record Macro Name text box.

Assign the key that will trigger the macro by making a selection from the Shortcut Key drop-down list box. Then, select Start.

Macro recording will begin. Perform all mouse operations and keystrokes in Freelance Graphics that you want to automate. Then, press Ctrl-Break to stop the macro from recording. A dialog box will appear. Select Save Macro, then click on OK.

 Recording keystrokes is likely to produce a more reliable macro than recording mouse clicks.

Playing Back a Macro

To play back a macro, start the Recorder application in Windows, then minimize it. Start Freelance Graphics, and advance to the point at which you want macro playback to begin.

Restore the Recorder window. In the Recorder window, select the desired macro name.

Switch to Freelance Graphics, move the cursor to the macro starting point (such as the command selection that will start the task), and press the shortcut key you assigned when recording the macro. To stop the macro before it completes its task, simply press Ctrl-Break.

ORGANIZING PRODUCTION WORK

You might organize presentations prepared for different projects or presenters in separate disk directories. For each recurring project, create custom SmartMaster sets that include typical page layouts, design choices, and company or product logos.

TIP   *Back up each directory or project from a hard disk to floppy disk (or to a separate directory on a tape drive or file server). Update presentations* in place, *by writing over the old files on the hard disk, but back up to a* new floppy-disk file *each time. This leaves you with a set of disks containing all prior versions. You may need these files for restoring prior versions if the client didn't like your changes or for documenting chargeable changes.*

Working with custom SmartMasters in different presentation-data directories can help you access your tools quickly, segregate work for different projects and presenters, and reduce repetitive work by helping you retrieve and reuse chart formats and designs.

SCREEN SHOWS

In Freelance Graphics, a Screen Show is a slide show that is presented on a computer monitor or video projector. Pages are displayed in the sequence of their appearance in the presentation file.

Running a Screen Show

Any presentation can be viewed as a Screen Show. Simply open the presentation file and then select View➤Screen Show➤Run from the menu in any view (or press Alt-F10).

Prior to running a Screen Show, select File➤Printer Setup and choose Optimize for Screen Show, which adjusts margins and colors for the screen.

- Click the *left* mouse button, or press PgDn or Enter to advance to the next page.

- Click the *right* mouse button or press PgUp to back up to the previous page.

- Press the Spacebar to pause the show, and press it again to continue.

- Press Esc to select a page out of sequence (jump to a specific page number) or to quit the show and return to the prior view.

- To draw on the screen during a show, hold down the left mouse button and drag. The color and width of the drawn line can be set with the command View➤Screen Show➤Edit Effects➤Options, as described below under "Screen Show Options."

The presentation sequence can also be changed if user selections are built into the show. Such a SmartShow is a Screen Show that provides for *branches,* or alternative sequences. Selections can be made by viewers, as in an interactive training session, or by the presenter, as when adapting a presentation to a specific situation in the meeting room.

Branching is triggered by selecting special objects within pages called *Buttons.* These "hot spots" cause specific actions when the viewer clicks on them with the mouse, usually in response to a direction on the screen to do so. There is more about Buttons and SmartShows in Chapter 19.

Buttons in Freelance Graphics Screen Shows have the same purpose as the on-screen buttons in Windows: They can be selected to trigger program actions. However, in Freelance Graphics, "Button" can be an attribute of any object, not just rectangles that are shaped like pushbuttons.

Creating a Screen Show with Effects

Freelance Graphics for Windows provides a selection of effects, such as wipes and dissolves, that can be used for transitions between slides viewed on a computer display. A Screen Show is a presentation to which such effects have been added.

To create a Screen Show, first create or open a presentation that has all required pages in show sequence, including any repetitions. (If necessary, use the Page Sorter to duplicate and arrange pages in sequence.)

Specifying Transition Effects and Durations

In any view, select View➤Screen Show➤Edit Effects. The Edit Screen Show dialog box will appear (Figure 13-12), with a page selection on the left and a list of effects on the right. In the Choose a Page box, select any page for which transition effects must be specified. Or, select the check box Apply Effect to All Pages.

Select an effect from the Choose an Effect list box to control the transition from the previous page. (Options for each are listed in the next subsection.) If no effect is specified, the Top option will be used, which creates the impression of a window shade being drawn downward.

To view the effect you have specified for any page, select the Preview button. You will see the effect, and then control will be returned to the Edit Screen Show dialog box.

Repeat the Edit Effects procedure for each page that requires unique transition effects.

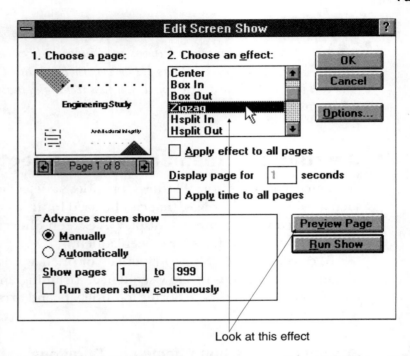

Look at this effect

FIGURE 13-12. The Edit Screen Show dialog box permits you to select a different transition effect for each page in the show.

Optionally, to cause the show to run without user selections, choose the Advance Screen Show Automatically option button. Enter a display duration (1–60 seconds) for the current page in the text box Display Page for *N* Seconds. To set this duration for all transitions in the automatic show, select the check box Apply Time to All Pages.

In an automatic show, pages will be shown for the specified length of time or until the operator clicks the left mouse button, *whichever occurs first.*

To select a consecutive sequence within a larger presentation, enter starting (*N*) and ending (*M*) page numbers as Show Pages *N* to *M*.

You can also make the show run in a loop, starting the show again after the last page is displayed, by selecting Run Screen Show Continuously. Use this feature to create automatic Screen Shows for exhibits.

If you are designing a Screen Show to be used by others, and you select specific times for page duration, include an on-screen instruction (as a text annotation), to advise users how to advance or pause the presentation manually. For example, create a Button with the text label, "Click here to continue."

Screen Show Options

Selecting the Options button in the Edit Screen Show dialog box will bring up another dialog box, Screen Show Options (Figure 13-13). If you want to permit the user to draw on the screen during the show, the color and width of the drawn line can be set in drop-down boxes here.

To draw during a Screen Show, you must click and hold the left mouse button down as you drag a freehand line on the screen. If you simply click the mouse button, the show will advance to the next page.

A handy option for controlling the flow of a show is a control panel, which will be displayed as a set of buttons on the screen during the show:

Activate the check box to turn on display of the control panel. You can also specify that the control panel be located at any of the corners of the screen.

The control panel is modeled after the buttons on a tape recorder or VCR, as are Windows multimedia players. From left to

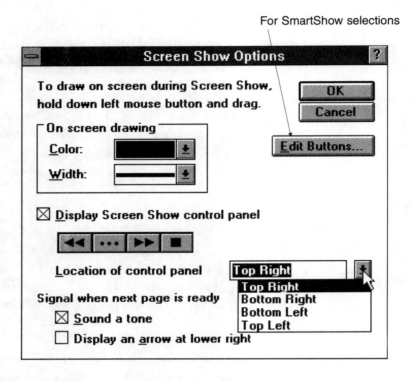

For SmartShow selections

FIGURE 13-13. The Screen Show Options dialog box has selections for on-
screen drawing and user controls.

right, the buttons are Reverse (back one page), List Pages (go to a
specific page number), Forward (advance one page), and Stop
(exit).

Even on relatively fast computers, there is always some delay
while the screen image is being calculated and loaded into video
memory. You can specify a signal that will tell the operator or presenter when this process is complete and the show can be advanced.
Select one or both of the bottom check boxes: Sound a Tone or Display an Arrow at Lower Right.

Also in this dialog box, you can select Edit Buttons to open the
Create/Edit Screen Show Buttons dialog box. Options here are covered in Chapter 19.

Select OK to close the Screen Show Options dialog box, which returns you to the Edit Screen Show dialog box. From here, select OK to accept the settings and return to the current view, or Run Show to start the show immediately.

Generating Stand-Alone Screen Shows

A special feature of Freelance Graphics for Windows makes it possible for you to create a Screen Show file that can be run directly on any DOS-based microcomputer with a VGA or EGA display. This eliminates the need to have the program installed on computers to which an electronic show will be distributed. Furthermore, the security of the show is enhanced, since the DOS version cannot be edited readily without the program.

To create a version of a presentation that can be run as a standalone Screen Show, or without the program being present, select View➤Screen Show➤Prepare Standalone. Enter a filename and select OK. A Screen Show (.SHW) file will be written to disk.

Select the Options button in this dialog box to specify VGA or EGA display format. Stand-alone Screen Shows are device- and resolution-specific, so you must have separate versions of a show for each type of display. If you select the check box Run Screen Show Directly from DOS, the program will copy the display utility program SHOW.EXE along with the .SHW file. Both of these files must be copied to a diskette that will be loaded into the computer that will run the show. To start the show from the DOS prompt on that computer, the user simply logs on to the drive that holds the diskette, then types **SHOW** followed by the name of the .SHW file. (However, the show will run faster if the files are first copied to the computer's hard disk.)

SPECIAL PRESENTATION EFFECTS

Besides transition effects and pauses, other effects that can be added to screen shows and slide shows include:

- Buildup sequences
- Pictures
- Video and audio (multimedia)

Buildup Sequences

In a buildup sequence, portions of a chart or drawing are shown as separate pages for purposes of highlighting key points of a message. The main reason for creating buildup sequences is to prevent the audience from reading ahead of the speech. The full chart is revealed progressively, or built up in stages. Examples of buildup sequences are included in the color plates.

Bullet charts can be built by bullet item, table charts by columns or rows. The basic technique for creating a buildup sequence is to create the last page in the sequence, then delete lines of text selectively, saving each page in the sequence and making sure that the composition is unchanged in each case.

Freelance Graphics for Windows Release 2 can generate buildup sequences automatically from bulleted lists (Figure 13-14).

For more information, see "Creating Buildup Sequences" in Chapter 10.

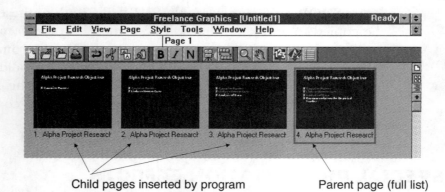

Child pages inserted by program　　　　　　　Parent page (full list)

FIGURE 13-14. The Page➤Create Build command generates multiple child pages from the last, or parent, page in a bulleted-list sequence.

Adding Picture Files

Picture files, containing bitmap (raster) images can be included in Screen Shows. In the Current Page view, select File➤Import to bring the bitmap into a page.

Picture files are generated by paint programs and image scanners. Also, any computer-screen display, regardless of its method of generation, can be written to a bitmap file by graphics utility programs such as Tiffany, TGL Grab, and Collage Plus.

Multimedia

Any Windows multimedia file, such as a movie clip or a sound recording, can be played during a Screen Show. To do this, you must create a Button on the page that is linked to the multimedia object. When the user clicks the Button, the media file will be played. There's more about this in Chapter 19.

To play media files, you must install Lotus Multimedia Applications. Lotus Media Manager and Lotus Sound Recorder are provided with Release 2 of Freelance Graphics for Windows.

PRODUCING OUTPUT

Output methods available in Freelance Graphics for Windows include:

- Printing and plotting
- Film recording

All these types of output are handled in Windows as if they were being done on printers. A printing job can be queued, or run concurrently with applications and other printing jobs, if you mark the Use Print Manager check box in Windows Control Panel➤Printers.

To override printer settings in Windows Control Panel➤Printers for the current presentation, change the settings in File➤Page

Setup and File➤Printer Setup in Freelance Graphics before you initiate the File➤Print command. Page and printer setup options are saved in the presentation file.

 Be aware that changing printer settings may affect the appearance of all pages in a presentation.

Printing and Plotting

To produce printouts from presentation files, first install the required printer in Windows Control Panel➤Printers, including configuration options. Then start Freelance Graphics, and create or open a presentation. In any view, select File➤Print, click the Print icon, or press Ctrl-P.

The Print File dialog box will appear, as shown in Figure 13-15. The name of the currently selected printer will appear at the top. Specify the number of copies of each page or handout, and optionally a range of pages in From *page number* To *page number.* Or, to print the currently selected page only, select the Current Page Only check box.

From the set of option buttons, select the output format: Full Page (for presentation-quality output), Speaker Notes, Audience Notes, Handouts, or Outline.

If you select Handouts, output layout options appear to the right, arranged two, four, or six presentation pages to a single page of printout.

To use the alternate color palette CPRINTER.PAL, select the check box Adjust Color Library for Color Printing. (This option will be available only if you have selected a color output device.)

Primarily for monochrome outputs, select the check boxes that control conversion of colors (grayscale or all black) and fills (render or omit). (See "Output Options" in the next subsection.) Select OK to start printing.

To enter speaker notes for the current page, select Page➤ Speaker Notes and type the text. Speaker notes will be printed in

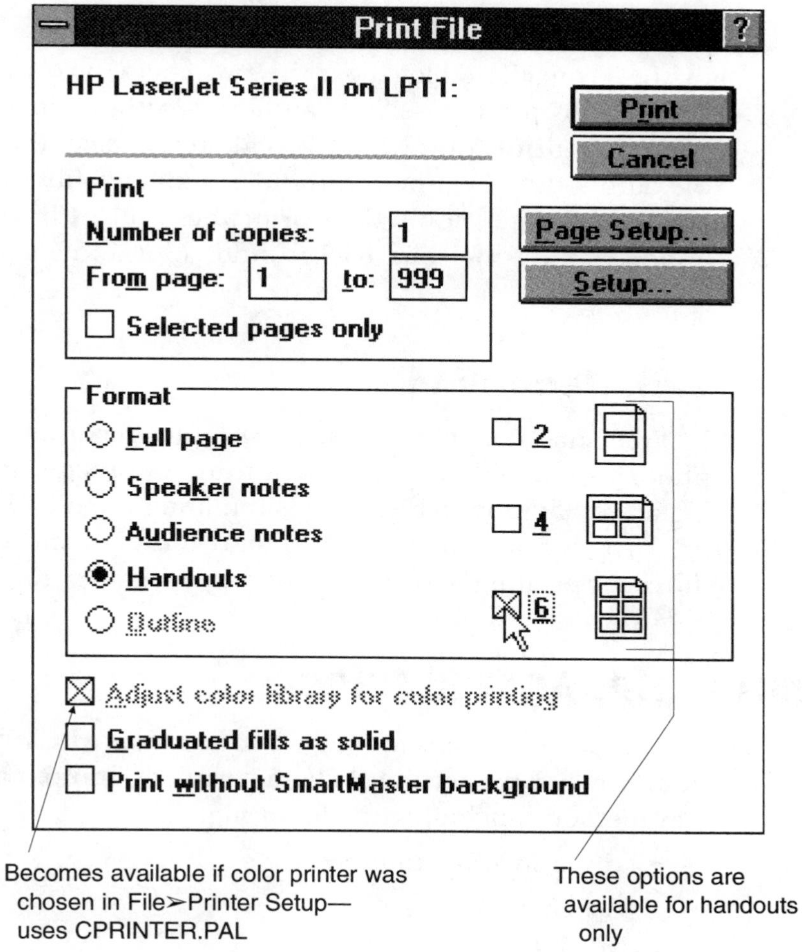

Becomes available if color printer was
chosen in File➤Printer Setup—
uses CPRINTER.PAL

These options are
available for handouts
only

FIGURE 13-15. Use the Print File dialog box to produce printouts of pages, notes,
handouts, or outlines.

portrait orientation with a miniature view of the presentation page
on the top and the note text on the bottom. Audience notes are
printed in a similar format, but with blank ruled lines at the bottom
for the audience to write notes during a presentation.

Output Options

In the Print File dialog box, the two check boxes at the bottom, Print Graduated Fills as Solid and Print Without SmartMaster Background, control conversion of solid areas. Select the first option if the output device cannot reproduce graduated fills or to reduce the amount of time required to print these fills. Choose the second option to omit the solid background color and any design for the same reasons.

Film Recording

In Freelance Graphics for Windows, film recording, or output of photographic slides, typically is a two-step process, involving printing a presentation to disk, then submitting the file to a postprocessing program supplied by the film-recorder manufacturer. Procedures for printing to disk are covered in Chapter 11.

MEDIA CHARACTERISTICS

In producing and assembling a presentation, you will want to consider some of the technical characteristics of output media and display methods, including the following:

- Color incompatibilities
- Aspect ratios
- Slide duplication

Color Incompatibilities

Major incompatibilities exist between the color rendering and resolution of the RGB video technology used in computer graphics systems and reproduction systems for other media, including:

- Television
- Photographic film
- Four-color printing

Television

The RGB video output of computer graphics systems is very different from the video standard for broadcast or cable television and for video recording. The origin of this divergence can be traced to the early 1950s, when the National Television Standards Committee (NTSC) was charged with the task of finding a way to make color-television transmissions fully compatible with existing black-and-white sets.

The result, the NTSC standard in use today throughout the United States, is a scheme for encoding color in three components: luminance (Y) and two components of chrominance (I, Q). Black-and-white sets are sensitive only to the luminance, or Y, component, which contains information about light and dark areas. Color information is carried in the chrominance signals. Color receivers handle all three components (I, Q, Y) to produce signals that control the color guns in the picture tube.

As in computer video, the color guns of video cameras and picture tubes are red (R), green (G), and blue (B), but television pictures typically lack the color saturation and resolution of RGB video displays. The reason is that some picture quality is lost in the translation from RGB in the camera to IQY broadcast and back to RGB in the receiver's picture tube. Also, some of the signal gets lost in transmission. So, the resolution, or image quality, of television is generally lower than that of most computer graphics systems.

To convert an RGB display signal for recording on a VCR or for television broadcast, the four components of the signal from the computer must be fed through an electronic device called an *NTSC encoder.* Encoders typically have four coaxial input connectors (BNC type) for R, G, B, and Sync signals, and a single output connector (either BNC or RCA) for NTSC video, as shown in Figure 13-16. Some RGB devices put Sync on the Green signal and so have only three output lines.

Some computer video-interface boards have NTSC output connectors. This means that there is a built-in encoder on the board.

Video output from the encoder will not match the RGB display because the IQY transformation is designed to fit color video infor-

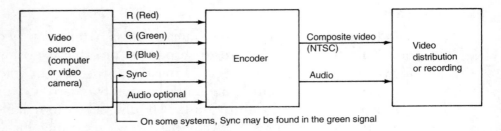

FIGURE 13-16.   Video encoder connections

mation in a television transmission signal of relatively narrow bandwidth, or message-carrying capacity (4.2 MHz). Again, significant color and contrast information is lost in the process, and in transmission. The effective resolution of many television home receivers is about 335 lines, or noticeably less than the resolution of the VGA color video interface.

Another potential difficulty with encoding computer graphics for television is that encoders tend to generate video noise when processing graphics. Noise will be most evident on the video picture as blurring at the edges of text and graphic objects. The noise is caused by abrupt transitions between light and dark areas along the video scan line, or raster. (Most of the video equipment used for television is designed primarily to respond to live scenes, which have relatively gradual transitions between light and dark areas.)

Character generators and computer graphics systems that are designed specifically for broadcast video applications have specially designed fonts that minimize these effects. Most other presentation-graphics systems, including Freelance Graphics for Windows, do not provide such fonts, since they are not intended primarily for broadcast applications.

Ways of reducing video noise include the following:

- Select a color palette for the original graphic in which no colors exceed 80 percent saturation, or ⅘ of maximum intensity.

- If a slide graphic has a dark background and light text, increase the value of the background for conversion of the slide to television.

- Insert a *comb filter,* a video noise-reducing device, in each RGB line between the computer and the encoder.

Incompatibilities between RGB and NTSC video can also affect your choice of video-projection equipment for presenting screen shows in conference rooms. Whenever possible, use a video projector that accepts RGB input. Video projectors designed for the consumer market, although perhaps less expensive, may accept only NTSC input and, therefore, may not give satisfactory results.

Video standards in other countries differ from both NTSC and RGB. These include the British PAL and French SECAM systems. Both of these standards present similar problems for RGB video encoding.

Photographic Film

As discussed in Chapter 11, the characteristics of photographic film, including the colors of dyes that compose the image, do not match those of RGB monitors.

Another important factor is *contrast range,* or the difference between the lightest and the darkest areas of an image. Computer film recorders can produce images of exceptionally wide contrast range. That is, the saturation ratio between the lightest and the darkest areas of a slide can be on the order of 1,000 to 1. This is wonderful for producing sharp original slides for projection. But high contrast can present problems when you attempt to duplicate slides photographically or when you attempt to convert slides to other media, such as paper or video.

Video graphics—even on high-resolution color monitors—are very flat by comparison, having contrast ranges on the order of 100 to 1. Slides designed for projection that have greater contrast ranges will exceed the capabilities of video equipment, producing noise. This is why I recommend an 80-percent saturation guideline for slides or RGB images that will be converted to NTSC video. This guideline does not apply for RGB video projection, which is driven by the computer video interface.

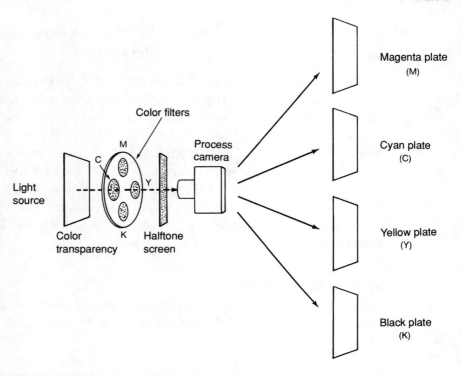

FIGURE 13-17. Four-color printing separations

Four-Color Printing

Glossy color brochures, catalogs, and magazines generally are produced by color offset lithography, which uses a four-color printing process. Four separate impressions are made on the paper, each with a different color of printing ink: magenta, blue, yellow, and black. These colors don't necessarily accurately render pictures that were created in red, green, and blue.

The preferred original medium for color photography for print media is a positive color transparency—ideally in 4-by-5-inch format, although 35mm slides can be acceptable, depending on the size of reproduction. From the transparency, *color separations* are made for each printing plate, as shown in Figure 13-17.

The traditional method has been to photograph the original transparency through screens (for rendering in halftone—a series of tiny dots) and colored filters, exposing the image on *orthographic film,* which produces high-contrast black-and-white images, with no shading. In recent years, computer techniques have been developed for scanning images digitally and generating the color separations. Some computer graphics systems can produce color separations directly from digital-image files, thus bypassing the photographic steps entirely.

Color rendering can differ considerably between the transparency and the four-color printed version. Not only are the component dyes different, but there is also an essential difference between the *transmissive* colors of the transparency and the *reflective* colors of the print. Photographic slide film renders an image by *subtracting* film dyes from a celluloid base in proportion to the colors passing through it. In print, an image is formed by the addition of component printing dyes as light is reflected back to the eye by the white paper underneath.

In designing graphics for print, remember that contrast builds each time an image is copied photographically. Since conventional color-separation methods use photographic techniques, master slides should appear flat, or have less contrast, than the desired result.

A widely used color standard for printing is the Pantone Matching System, known throughout the industry simply as PMS colors. PMS colors, which are available as numbered swatches in a catalog, are designed to match both Pantone coated art papers and the colors that are reproducible by the four-color process. If you are creating color slides as masters for printing, the manufacturer of your film recorder may be able to assist you in finding nearest-match RGB palette settings for PMS colors.

Aspect Ratios

Another important difference among video and film media is the *aspect ratio* of the image (Figure 13-18). This is the shape of the pro-

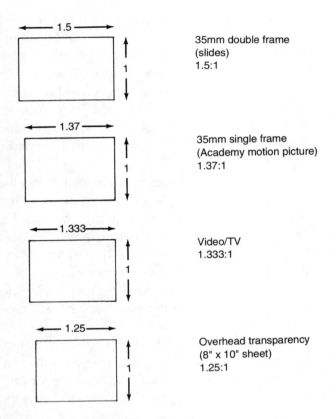

FIGURE 13-18. Aspect ratios for different media

jection or viewing aperture, expressed as a ratio between its height and its width. Since aspect ratios vary considerably, you need to take the characteristics of the output medium into consideration when designing charts with Freelance Graphics.

Be aware also that computer-screen displays are not in quite the same aspect ratio as video and television, and are not displayed the same way. In a screen show, a black border always surrounds the picture so that it appears to "float" on the screen. On a video monitor or on television, the image extends to the edges of the screen.

The drawing area of the Current Page view will display the correct aspect ratio for the Margins settings in File➤Page Setup and the Paper Size setting selected in File➤Printer Setup➤Setup. To view the margins as dotted lines in the drawing area, select View➤View Preferences and Margins or Printable Area.

 The printable area extends as far as possible to the edges of the print medium. The margins are those you set explicitly. Freelance Graphics for Windows permits you to draw outside both, thereby permitting objects to bleed off the edge of an image.

To set margins properly for color-slide output on 35mm double-frame film, turn on the check box Set Margins for Slides in File➤ Page Setup or in File➤Printer Setup (if you set one, the other will be reset automatically). Also, Paper Size should be reset from Letter to Note, which has no margins of its own.

TIP *To fill the monitor screen as much as possible for screen shows, select File➤Printer Setup and the option button Optimize for Screen Show.*

If you are converting RGB output to NTSC video, you'll notice that the preview display does not fill the frame on your monitor, which may be undesirable. A way to overcome this "window" effect is to use charts with black backgrounds. If you do, to avoid contrast, you may have to adjust the color palette so that the colors of text and other objects are considerably less than 80 percent saturated.

Professional projectionists recommend that images fill a screen completely. However, many large screens in theaters and conference rooms are in Academy format, which refers to the old 35mm single-frame aspect ratio established by the Academy of Motion Picture Arts and Sciences (see Figure 13-19). To fit a 35mm double-frame image onto such a screen, you can buy slide mounts that mask the image to this aspect ratio so that the screen is filled properly. Just be sure to compose the image within this area.

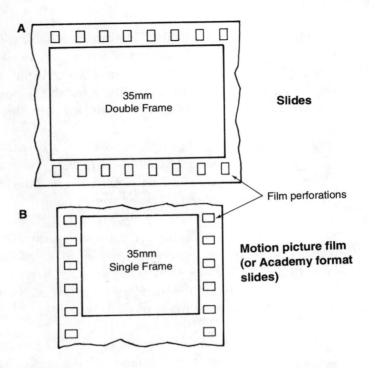

FIGURE 13-19. Projection formats for 35mm projection: A. double frame (slides), B. single frame (motion pictures)

Slide Duplication

You will also need to adjust your color palette if you are designing a slide show that must be duplicated in quantity.

As previously stated, any photographic copying of an image increases its contrast. In general, masters for duplication should appear flatter than slides that are intended primarily for projection.

Other considerations center around film types and duplication methods. Film types include reversal and negative films:

Reversal Film   Original slide film is called *reversal* film because a positive image forms on the same piece of film that is exposed in the camera or film recorder. Such a slide can be projected directly or can serve as a master for duplication. Kodak Ektachrome, Polaroid Polachrome, and other film brand names ending in *–chrome* are reversal films.

Negative Film Film types with names ending in *–color*, such as Ektacolor, are negative films. To produce a positive image, a negative must be printed either to paper (as a print) or to *positive* film (as a slide, filmstrip, or motion picture).

There are two basic methods of slide duplication, one using reversal-type stocks, and the other using negative-to-positive film printing:

- Reversal dupes
- Prints from negative

Each has its trade-offs of quality and expense.

Reversal Dupes

If you order multiple copies of slides from an outside film-recording service, you may receive either multiple originals or one original from the film recorder and duplicate copies (*dupes*) on reversal film. The dupes are made by photographing the original slide onto a type of reversal film that is made especially for copying slide positives. Dupes generally cost less than originals because computer film-recorder time is more expensive.

Reversal dupes of slides are the most faithful to the original because the dyes and photographic response of reversal copying film are balanced especially for the original film stock. Among professional photographers and laboratories, Ektachrome (a reversal film) is the accepted stock for slide originals.

If you are ordering only one or two extra copies of a slide show, the reversal copying process can be perfectly acceptable. However, slide-show sets usually must be collated by hand into stacks or projector trays. If you order 10 reversal duplicates, the technician in the photo lab will shoot 10 photographic copies of slide one, then 10 of slide two, and so on, until all the slides have been copied. When the

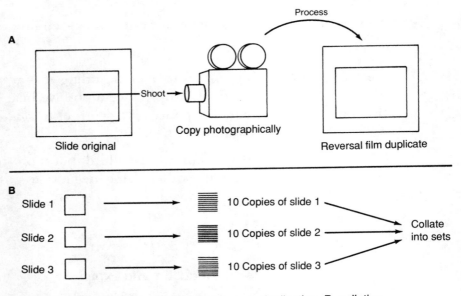

FIGURE 13-20. Reversal dupe procedure: A. duplication, B. collation

film comes out of chemical processing, it is fed to a slide-mounting machine. The result is a stack of slide-one copies, a stack of slide-two copies, and so on. These stacks must then be collated—usually by hand—into slide-show sets (Figure 13-20).

Duplicating with Negative Film

A more economical and efficient technique for duplicating slides is to photograph a slide show in sequence onto negative film. This is called *animating* the slide show because, in the days of conventional art production, negatives were shot from art boards on large animation stands, as is still done for conventional animated movies. Professional film laboratories that specialize in volume slide duplication use this technique. The negative, which has the presentation slides in sequence, is then spliced head-to-tail to form a continuous loop. This loop is placed on a high-speed film printer that exposes strips of positive film, as shown in Figure 13-21.

Each strip of positive film coming off the printer is an entire slide show, already collated in sequence. The strip can be fed to a

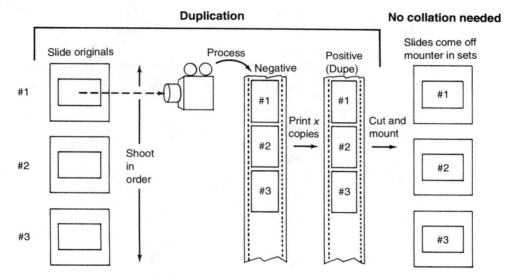

FIGURE 13-21. Printing from a film negative

slide-mounting machine, which adds slide numbers to the mounts automatically, accumulating them in numbered sets. The sets can be boxed or placed in projector trays.

For slide duplication in volume, negative-to-positive printing generally is more economical than reversal printing. The cost of animating the negative is more than offset by the savings in time and money resulting from automatic collation. Color reproduction may not be as accurate, however.

Making Changes to a Slide Show

You will encounter major differences between these methods if you attempt to incorporate changes in a slide show after the initial quantity has been run. In the case of reversal printing, changes must be hand-collated into the existing sets. If you're adding or deleting slides, that means shuffling all the slides in all the projector trays, especially if there are insertions or deletions.

In a negative-printing process, changes are animated on a separate negative strip. The original negative is retained as an *A-roll.* The

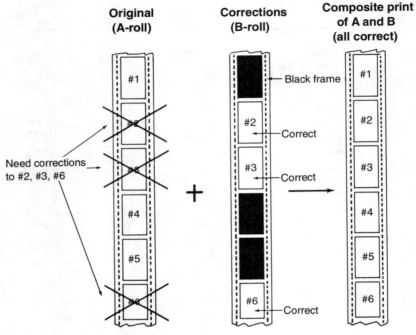

FIGURE 13-22. A- and B-roll printing to make changes in an existing slide show

strip with the changes on it is a *B-roll*. (See Figure 13-22.) To save the time and expense of manual collation, it can be practical to reprint the entire show. When the A-roll goes through the printer, it is stopped at the first frame to be changed, and the B-roll image is printed. This process repeats, alternating between A and B negatives, until a fully correct positive has been printed. This positive has all originals and changes in the proper sequence and is ready for automated slide mounting and loading into boxes or trays.

Matching Computer Colors: A Case History

Manual collation, as well as the difficulty of managing last-minute changes, argue against slide duplication by the reversal process when you must produce more than a few sets.

However, with negative printing, differences in color between originals and copies can be especially troublesome because adjustment of *print timing* (color balance) will always affect the entire presentation. (Since reversal copies are collated individually, different color timings and film stocks can be intermixed, if necessary.) In theory, the color balance of film prints can be adjusted for the best match between computer graphics output and slide copies. In practice, other factors mitigate against this.

This point was brought home to me vividly when I produced a slide show for an audiovisual agency in Detroit. The agency's client was an automobile manufacturer. The slide presentation included word slides, charts, and, of course, photographs (beauty shots) of automobiles.

For the computer-generated slide graphics, the client had chosen backgrounds of deep burgundy. When the original slides were projected, they were gorgeous.

The agency, which had contracted elsewhere for the car photos, made the decision to handle its own slide duplication through one of the professional film laboratories.

When the slide dupes came back, I received an angry call from the agency. The beautiful burgundy backgrounds had turned an unattractive brown—and the film laboratory insisted there was nothing to be done!

I had a look at the duplicates, then I paid a visit to the film laboratory. I knew that the timing of the film prints could be adjusted to more closely match the computer-generated colors. I had a long and heated conversation with the technical chief, who explained, "People in this town look at three things in a film print—people, sky, and cars. When we do the timings on a print, we go first for the faces. And auto paint is very difficult to render, especially the metallics. We have to get the paint job to look right without turning the people green. The graphics just aren't a consideration. Who else but you knows what color they were to start with?"

The situation had been made worse by the selection of the exceptionally dark burgundy background color, which was nice for projection but could not be rendered properly by the negative film—at least not without sacrificing some other color range in the rest of the presentation. So, if we were to adjust the color balance of the prints to enhance the background color, we'd ruin the live photography, including the color of the client's product!

The solution in this case was to make a special set of slide masters—with lighter backgrounds in the same hue—for duplication.

So, consider that a single photograph of a client's product in a slide show could well dictate the color balance of the entire presentation. Therefore, choose colors with medium contrast that will hold up well in duplication.

WAR-ROOM GRAPHICS

I'll conclude this chapter with some thoughts—and warnings—about screen shows. The discussion bears directly on decisions to use the Screen Show and SmartShow techniques of Freelance Graphics for presentations to management.

Some observers of the computer graphics industry have speculated that electronic presentation media will soon replace film. This trend should accelerate with the introduction of high-definition television (HDTV), which rivals 35mm film in resolution. (Film is still sharper, but the apparent resolution at a typical viewing distance is comparable.) An HDTV projector connected to a computer-based decision support system might, therefore, become standard equipment in business conference rooms. The term *war-room graphics* has been coined to describe such interactive projection systems.

A top executive of one of the film-recorder companies disagrees strongly with this view of the future. He once remarked to me that on-line video might never replace slide media. His rationale went something like this: Middle managers use slides to make presentations to senior managers. These formal presentations differ from peer reviews, which are primarily investigative and may use all types of display media—from chalkboards to interactive computer displays. Formal presentations are more structured and rehearsed, usually involving reviews of performance. The presenters' budgets—and their jobs—are on the line.

Slides have been preferred in such situations—not only for their high image quality, but also because a slide presentation can be designed, sequenced, rehearsed—and then frozen in content. The finished presentation adheres to the presenter's point of view and agenda and has the best chance of achieving a well-defined result. The slide medium lends itself to modularity, so that sequences can be rearranged—but not necessarily changed in content—in rehearsal. Flexibility is possible only to a degree, and with some advance planning; once sequence and content have been fixed and the meeting starts, possibilities for interaction with the audience are limited. The objective is to deliver the message as planned, solicit the anticipated response, and, after a minimum amount of interrogation, get out of the room.

Electronic media, including the Screen Shows and SmartShows of Freelance Graphics for Windows, require a link to a computer to retrieve and to generate the images. Although it is possible to run a canned screen show without interaction, the audience will no doubt be aware that the graphics are being generated on the spot. There may be a strong temptation for managers to request alternative views of the data—much to the chagrin of the presenter. What presenter wants to play real-time what-if games with a group of managers?

Thus, it has been asserted that war-room graphics will never be popular for management reviews. In view of the exceptional cost-effectiveness of slide-projection equipment, there might seem to be no other compelling reason for electronic media to predominate.

This set of assumptions might change as HDTV becomes a universal output medium. Recall the plant manager in the case study in Chapter 1 who was informed that a printed report would have to be redone as color slides—simply because the board of directors expected to see slides. When every pro football game is broadcast in HDTV with stereo sound, animated graphics, and real-time, computer-tabulated statistical recaps, what then will be the expectations of those same executives?

The fundamental answers may come from another direction. After all, who makes the decisions? Who decides to commit corporate resources to telecommunication networks and computer systems? Here's an analogous situation from political history:

Lyndon Johnson reportedly told his staff that, to get key middle managers in government on the telephone, he didn't wish to follow protocol or go through channels or talk to their bosses. Instead, he just wanted to "mash a button" on his phone. Perhaps against the better judgment of the staff, such a system was installed, and Johnson routinely used this form of skip-level communication. Nobody liked the system—least of all the middle managers—except the President. The man who made the decisions loved it.

The more formal the presentation—and the higher the stakes— the more reason to use slides in a more permanent medium such as film. Adhere to your own agenda. If you present a screen show, be aware that the audience might just want to see the charts adjusted on the spot!

CHAPTER 14

SHARING INFORMATION

T his chapter is about what computer professionals call *systems integration,* which encompasses the techniques and tools for exchanging and sharing data among computer devices, programs, and users.

You will inevitably deal with integration issues if you use a microcomputer within a larger business organization. As a user of Freelance Graphics for Windows, you will encounter these issues when you:

- Submit presentations to an outside service bureau for film recording

- Access an on-line database for stock market prices or currency exchange rates for input to a chart

- Extract data from a mainframe database for input to a PC-based spreadsheet

- Import data from a spreadsheet for conversion to charts

- Send graphics files to other workstations in a corporate network for review and approval, or for discussion

- Use electronic clip art from a commercial library

- Share styles, symbols, and picture files with other users of Freelance Graphics

- Import drawings and scanned photographs from other computer graphics systems for use in your presentation
- Export charts and drawings from Freelance Graphics to desktop publishing systems for production of newsletters and reports
- Transport a Screen Show to another computer graphics system for display at another location
- Include multimedia sound and movies in your screen shows
- Link and embed objects with other Windows applications

THE WINDOWS ENVIRONMENT

The Windows environment itself takes care of many of the otherwise troublesome aspects of systems integration. Windows not only allows you to interact with applications graphically, but it also enforces a set of rules by which applications interact. Some of these rules, for example, apply to the ways in which data of many different types can be exchanged among programs.

The Windows Family

Microsoft Windows is now an interconnected family of operating systems, consisting of:

- Windows desktop version
- Windows for Workgroups
- Windows NT

Windows Desktop Version

The desktop version is the graphic operating environment for stand-alone microcomputers, and its capabilities are discussed both in Chapter 4 and in this chapter.

Windows for Workgroups

Windows for Workgroups adds file-sharing capabilities for groups of workstations that are connected by a network. The system makes it possible to annotate files and to exchange other types of messages over the network. (Some of its file-exchange features are similar to those of Lotus Notes.)

Windows NT

Windows desktop version and Windows for Workgroups are built around the 16-bit MS-DOS microcomputer operating system. Windows NT includes not only the Windows graphical environment but also its own 32-bit operating system. It is designed to support larger-scale systems such as engineering workstations, file servers, and minicomputers.

These three operating environments are compatible with one another and support all types of Windows data exchange.

Data Exchange in Windows

As discussed in Chapter 4, one of the primary means of data exchange in Windows is the Clipboard. The Clipboard is a scratch-pad memory area that is accessible by most Windows applications. One of the rules of the Windows environment is that, in any application, you should be able to select a data item, then select Edit➤Copy or Edit➤Cut to copy or move it to the Clipboard. You should then be able to select Edit➤Paste to retrieve that data in any application (including the one you took the data from). The Clipboard, therefore, serves as a buffer through which data can be passed.

The Windows Clipboard can handle a variety of data types, including text (character data), graphics, pictures (bitmaps), digital video sequences (movie files), and digital sound recordings.

Another level of integration in Windows that uses the Clipboard is Dynamic Data Exchange (DDE), also covered in Chapter 4. Among applications that support DDE, pasted data can be linked so that an update in one application (the source) will trigger the same change in any other application (the destination) that uses the linked data. In many applications, you create a link automatically when you paste data from the Clipboard with the Edit➤Paste Link command. In Freelance Graphics for Windows, the equivalent command is Edit➤Paste Special➤Link.

An enhancement of DDE that appeared in Windows version 3.1 is object linking and embedding (OLE). In Windows terminology, an object is any piece of information that has been generated by one of its application programs and that can be integrated into a document in another application. Examples of objects are documents containing text or alphanumeric data, vector graphics, bitmap pictures, sound recordings, and video animation (movie files). Options for achieving this integration are:

- Linking
- Embedding
- Packaging

Linking

In effect, a DDE link is the *L* in *OLE*. When you perform DDE with a link, a reference to an object within an external source file is copied into the destination document. As long as the link is maintained, there is only one copy of the data—in the source file. Each time a destination document is opened, the object is read from the source.

Use linking if you want all applications that show an object to be updated automatically when you change the source file. For example, you might have a database application that holds current stock prices. You might also have a spreadsheet application that analyzes these data, as well as a graphics application, such as Freelance Graphics for Windows, that plots the data for presentation. With object linking (DDE), the spreadsheet and the presentation graphs will be updated automatically whenever new stock prices are loaded into the database.

Linking can be done only to an existing disk file, because the path and filename are part of the link reference. That is, programs must have a specific source for the data, even when the source application and its file are closed. If you open a linked file that was closed when an update was made in another application, a prompt will inform you that the file content has changed and will ask whether you wish the update to be processed for that file also. If you move the location of the source file on disk, the link will be severed, because the destination application will not be able to find it.

Embedding

Unlike object linking, embedding inserts a copy of an object in the destination document, along with a reference to the program that created it. Note that the reference is to the source application, not to its data file. Whenever you select (double-click on) the object in the destination document, the source application will open, permitting you to edit the object. When you do this, you are accessing the source application from within the destination, and you are changing only the local, or destination, copy of the data. The source file will be unaffected.

In Freelance Graphics for Windows, you can use object embedding to include picture, sound, and movie files within Screen Shows. The presentation file will hold a complete copy of each object so that it can be reproduced or played even on systems that do not have the source application. (However, any required multimedia drivers would have to be present.) Also, you will have the convenience of being able to edit and customize the objects from within Freelance Graphics.

Packaging

As a way of accessing objects, they can be shown within destination documents as custom icons. Windows 3.1 offers a utility program called Object Packager for creating these custom icons, or *packages*. If you are running a Screen Show and you select a package that contains a sound recording, for example, the recording is played. If you select a package that contains a picture, it is displayed.

Object packages can be created to show or play information on request. So, in a database application that stores personnel records, clicking on a special icon might cause the picture of the person to appear. Or, in a SmartShow, clicking on a package that holds a sound recording might give audio prompts or reinforcement, such as, "You have successfully completed Part One of the lesson."

Use of OLE in all its forms with Freelance Graphics for Windows is covered in greater depth under "Inserting an Embedded Object" in this chapter.

Importing and Exporting Files

Windows also supports an even wider variety of file types for exchanging data among programs. Importing and exporting are especially useful when you are working with non-Windows applications, including DOS programs that have a relatively limited selection of data formats for output (and even Macintosh PICTure format). Importing and exporting can also be the means of accessing application programs that do not reside on your computer system or network.

The processes of importing data to, and exporting data from, Freelance Graphics for Windows are covered in this chapter. In general, if one of the supported file types is involved, Windows handles the conversion automatically, sparing you from knowing about the technical requirements.

However, if Windows always handled these conversions seamlessly, there would be no need for much of this chapter. Furthermore, knowledge of these technical issues becomes essential when you attempt to share data with non-Windows systems and applications.

FILE TYPES

A particular difficulty with computer graphics is that its file structures are complex and varied. There are at least a dozen file formats for computer graphics and source data that are potentially useful with Freelance Graphics for Windows. And when you consider other graphics systems, there are many, many more.

Even within the family of Freelance Graphics products, the file types of the versions for DOS differ from the types for Windows. Examples of the DOS formats include charts (.CH1), drawings (.DRW), and portfolios (.PFL), to name just a few. When you also consider other applications that support graphics, not to mention all their auxiliary fonts and add-in programs, the differences are compounded.

The sharing of data and charts is an important goal of systems integration. With the advent of Windows and other operating systems, multitasking and multiuser computer graphics applications have become practical on PCs. And as workstations are being connected to corporate networks—particularly through departmental local area networks (LANs)—system *connectivity* becomes a topic of urgent interest.

Computer professionals have coined a term for this new hodgepodge of machines and programs—*advanced office systems* (AOS). Essentially, this chapter is about using Freelance Graphics for Windows in the multifaceted—and potentially confusing—environment of AOS.

But before getting immersed in technical details of file sharing, consider the business setting in which it all takes place.

INTEGRATION: THE CHINESE DID IT FIRST

The ancient Chinese were perhaps the world's first systems integrators. Taoism holds that all things, no matter how apparently disassociated, are one with a single, integrated whole of creation, the One, in whose obliterating unity all seemingly opposed conditions of time and space are indistinguishably blended. According to this view, it is a shortcoming of human nature to subdivide and categorize the world into discrete concepts, or words. In subdividing experience, the unifying relationships are lost.

Analysts and planners who work with AOS must deal with this same handicap. A basic problem is that many office workers—including managers and professionals—really don't have a clear sense of how their work fits in with the rest of the organization.

A reasonable question might be: Why should I care what a user of some other workstation is doing?

Here's an example of a kind of interdependence in computer networks. Functionally, there is a clear relationship between calculating the aging of accounts receivable and writing collection letters. However, the secretary in the sales department who composes collection letters probably couldn't care less about the clerk in accounting who works with spreadsheets to derive a list of delinquent accounts. The relationships are shown as *data flows* in Figure 14-1.

In short, there's a functional relationship, but it isn't visible. If the same people were working on an assembly line, it would be more obvious that one group of workers assembles the engine before another group drops it into the car chassis.

Corporate-level systems integration provides electronic links among these invisible functions. A new picture emerges when, linked by workstations on a network, the secretary and the clerk can share information files. The secretary, then, accesses the list of delinquent accounts from the clerk's file and inputs it directly to a word processing mail-merge program for automated production of collection letters. Just to get at the right information, the secretary has to understand his or her relationship to the accounting function.

What does all this have to do with the graphs being generated for the marketing department? Well, the underlying data for sales performance in those graphs must have been generated at some point by the accounting department. The sales data cannot be reliable unless the collection function is in operation. Otherwise, a sig-

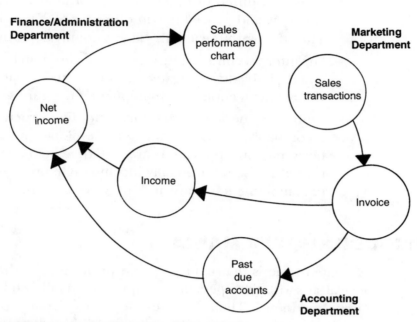

FIGURE 14-1.   Data flows among company departments

nificant portion of the sales must be discounted because the transactions have not been closed.

OBSTACLES TO INTEGRATION

So in a business, as in the Chinese version of the universe, everything is functionally connected to everything else. The ideal, then,
might be to have an all-encompassing information system that is
seamless with respect to work groups, functions, and departments.

In practice, there are several barriers to achieving such a perfect
system:

- People may not perceive the relationships among different
  job functions.

- People in different functions are not familiar with the work concepts and procedures in other parts of the organization. Thus the typical reaction: "That's not my department!"

- For internal control and security reasons, it may be necessary and desirable to segregate work functions so that no one individual knows enough to manipulate the entire system.

- Computer devices, programs, and file structures may be incompatible because they were developed initially for relatively narrow application areas. Other incompatibilities are rooted in the intentionally incompatible proprietary designs of competing hardware and software vendors.

MICROCOMPUTER MANIA

A related issue is that managers and professionals who are having love affairs with their personal computers can fall victim to a kind of "love blindness." Their fondness for a particular application or problem can prevent them from looking at broader functional relationships. There can be a strong tendency to focus on immediate tasks and relatively narrow job descriptions.

For example, consider a case in which a financial analyst has trouble finding a forest because there are so many trees in it. The situation is illustrated in Figure 14-2.

The analyst has the responsibility of preparing monthly summaries for top management from several departmental reports. The analyst, weary of performing this task with cumbersome manual spreadsheets and a burned-out calculator, buys a microcomputer with a popular spreadsheet package. The immediate problem is solved and the analyst is in bliss: No more broken pencils, no more litter of eraser dust. The software recalculates the entire spreadsheet on demand, and the analyst can make an unlimited number of changes with very little effort.

In time, however, it will occur to the analyst that this joy is only a foretaste. There should be no need to work with manual reports for

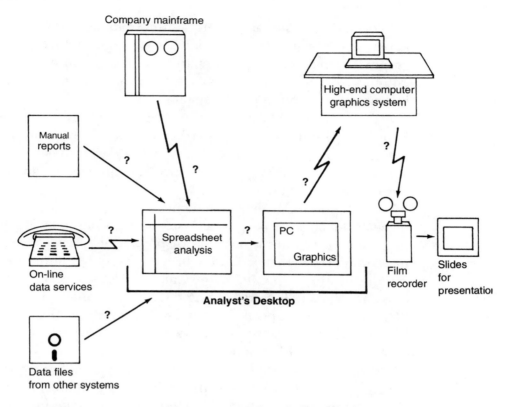

FIGURE 14-2. Compatibility and connectivity come into play at each link marked "?".

the source data! The manual departmental reports are printouts from the corporate mainframe system. It should be possible to access the report files directly and input the data to the microcomputer spreadsheet program.

And there's another opportunity for automation: Eliminate the tedium of preparing graphs of the results for review by management. The board of directors prefers to look at slides with graphs and charts rather than to pore over printouts. The analyst's enthusiasm builds further: It should be possible to generate graphs directly from the microcomputer-based spreadsheets.

Formerly, the spreadsheet totals were plotted on manual graph paper, and the marked-up originals were given to the in-house graphics department. The department has a sophisticated slide graphics computer, but turnaround is one or two weeks, at best, because of contention for the system.

When the crunch comes, the analyst can't afford to wait. To have timely information for board meetings usually means generating the report no earlier than the previous day. If the analyst could generate presentation-quality graphs, the process would be both more secure and more reliable.

At this point, the analyst runs smack up against all the commonplace headaches of corporate systems integration. Although the microcomputer does a neat job of preparing spreadsheets, it was not configured with any of these broader issues in mind. Communication with the corporate mainframe requires a special *protocol* (set of technical rules for exchanging data) not normally supported on PCs. The analyst suspects there is a way to solve the incompatibility, but the in-house systems people with the necessary expertise apparently have other things to do.

Also, the corporate database is handled by a third-party database management system (DBMS) that is incompatible with the file formats on the microcomputer. There isn't even a clue how to translate one to the other. Again, the systems people have other priorities and are not available to help.

How about automated input to the computer system in the graphics department? Well, the computer artists there aren't systems integrators. When the analyst raises the problem with the mainframe group, they roll their eyes heavenward. They want to know nothing about the proprietary software on the graphics machine.

This scenario is fairly typical of some applications in financial analysis. And, until recently, there were no straightforward solutions.

WINDOWS OPEN ON THE SOLUTION!

As stated previously, many of the tools for resolving these issues are now built into the Windows environment. And spurred on by the needs identified here, Windows applications like Freelance Graphics further enhance those capabilities.

For example, Lotus 1-2-3 for Windows includes a feature called DataLens, which supports on-line connection from the program to an external database. The database can reside on a LAN, and its data files need not be in a format supported on your PC. You can initiate queries in the database and extract data, all from within the 1-2-3 application.

To bring all this home, you can then establish a DDE link between a worksheet in Lotus 1-2-3 for Windows and the input form of a data chart in Freelance Graphics for Windows. Through DDE, whenever the worksheet changes in 1-2-3 as a result of accessing the database, the chart will also be updated.

Thus, within the Windows environment, there can be relatively seamless links between a corporate DBMS system, a worksheet application, and charts in Freelance Graphics.

If you don't think this is real progress over the world of barely compatible DOS applications, just put yourself in the place of that financial analyst.

COMPROMISE AND CORPORATE STANDARDS

Many large corporations, in an effort to avoid microcomputer-driven anarchy, have established standards and guidelines for acquisition of PCs by individuals or departments. In effect, the standards comprise approved shopping lists of hardware and software products that have been proven to work well with existing or planned information networks.

Specifications often include communication standards (especially for LANs), operating systems, and database management systems or file structures. For business charting, Freelance Graphics (perhaps in all its versions) will be found on many of those lists.

Drawbacks are that corporate standards either don't fit many applications (especially graphics) or are poorly enforced. Often, the standards are a de facto extension of the mainframe environment, which was not originally designed to support microcomputer or LAN access, would be costly to modify, and can't withstand an onslaught of new on-line users anyway.

The real difficulty is that the entire field of advanced office systems is undergoing rapid change. Standards that can provide the glue for discrete, previously incompatible, system components are just emerging—and Windows is an outstanding example. But no one can forecast with confidence how some of the more difficult integration problems will be resolved.

The integration tools in Windows and in Freelance Graphics for Windows represent significant steps forward, but the world of computing remains a sometimes maddeningly heterogeneous place.

COMPETING PRODUCTS WILL CONTEND FOR YOUR MIND!

As a user of Freelance Graphics, you are on the forefront of the phenomenon of *user-driven computing*. The temptation to expand your information sources to other workstations and systems is a natural one, part of the underlying interdependence of your business. In venturing out, however, you are likely to cross some territorial boundaries, which are guarded by the proprietary interests of competing computer vendors and the time-honored turf-protection instincts of corporate middle management.

In seeking permission to cross these boundaries, be guided by a fundamental ethic of information access—your need to know. You must exercise careful judgment here. Don't go barging in without authorization: You don't enter other people's houses just because they might leave the door unlocked. You should accord the same

respect to their computer-maintained information. With this pro-
viso, press on and fear not—you are the future!

Nowhere are these issues more apparent than in the contention
between Microsoft Windows and IBM OS/2 for the domination of
corporate microcomputer environments. As you venture into the
corporate-computing realm in search of electronic information, be
aware that these two product families and the divergent interests
they represent will be contending for control of your personal computer—which is nothing less than an extension of your mind!

The Windows product is a result of user-driven computing.
Based initially on Microsoft MS-DOS, it builds on the demands of
individual users, all in business essentially for themselves, who are
looking for very individualized solutions to practical problems. In
the corporate world, users of DOS and Windows represent a kind of
pressure from the bottom up—from the level of end users upward
to the level of corporate information systems. The development of
Windows for Workgroups and Windows NT has been an effort to
"grow" the successful desktop product into that larger environment.

On the other hand, OS/2 represents a kind of pressure from
the top downward. OS/2 applications are designed around IBM's
Systems Application Architecture, a standard by which microcomputers and mainframes are supposed to coexist comfortably, but
according to a relatively uniform corporate plan.

In a practical sense, OS/2 can be viewed as an effort by corporate information managers to reimpose control on the perceived
chaos of user-driven computing. There's nothing inherently wrong
in this; it holds the potential for functional systems integration on at
least a companywide scale.

At issue here are the fundamental concepts of *distributed* versus
centralized information systems. There are some very good reasons
for centralized control of information systems, not the least of them
having to do with security. However, now that the genie of user-
driven computing is out of the bottle, the forces of centralization
may never be able to shove it back in!

If you are working at your computer and never wish to communicate with anybody, none of these issues apply. The problems arise when you attempt to share data, as when you exchange disks or plug into a network.

NETWORK ACCESS

Common types of access to computer networks by microcomputers include:

- Local area networks (LANs)
- Time-sharing

Local Area Networks

A LAN is a way of establishing some centralized control over distributed microcomputer workstations, as shown in Figure 14-3. A LAN is a data-communications system of connections and switching capabilities that links devices within a small geographic area—usually within a building or suite of offices. The primary goal of a LAN is to

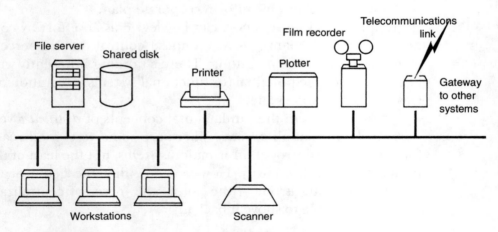

FIGURE 14-3. One type of local area network (LAN)

enable users at individual workstations to share data and such devices as disks, printers, scanners, and plotters.

At the hardware level, a LAN is connected by wire (either telephone-style twisted-pair or coaxial cable), fiber-optic cable, or wireless cellular radio. In some types of networks, one of the processors must act as traffic cop for communications flow. This processor can be called the *controller*. If it is also the shared file device, the controller is the file server (or simply, the server). In other types of LANs, the PCs are more autonomous and take turns controlling network devices (including servers) according to certain access rules in the communications software provided with the LAN.

At the software level, devices, users, and files on the network have names. Access among them is controlled by a system of authorization that matches name identification (ID) with access codes, or passwords. For example, a particular group of users might be prevented for security reasons from working with specific devices or files. The LAN also handles contention for devices when two or more users (or programs) request access at the same time. The LAN solves the problem by assigning users to a queue to wait their turn. But in practice, you might not even notice the delay.

Using Freelance Graphics for Windows on a LAN

The package for installing Freelance Graphics in a file server is called the Server Edition. The workstation package is called the Node Edition.

When Freelance Graphics for Windows is installed on the server (Figure 14-4), portions of the program are copied (or *swapped*) to each workstation as required during a session. For the most part, you won't notice the swapping any more than you notice other shared network operations.

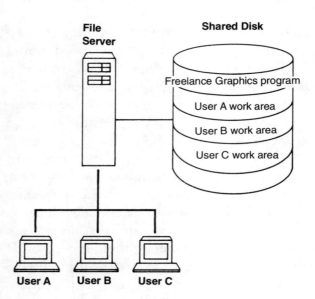

FIGURE 14-4. Freelance Graphics LAN installation

An alternative is to install the Standard Edition (for stand-alone computers) locally on the workstation and use the file server for sharing of data files.

File Locking

Within networks, a crucial control that assures security and privacy of data is called *file locking*. Applications that run on LANs do not necessarily place controls on file access. However, Freelance Graphics for Windows does include a *file reservation* system designed to prevent potentially conflicting updates to a shared file.

Network-Level Controls

If your data files reside on the server, you should also take precautions *at the network level* to prevent unauthorized access, including reading of files while you are working on them. You can do this by

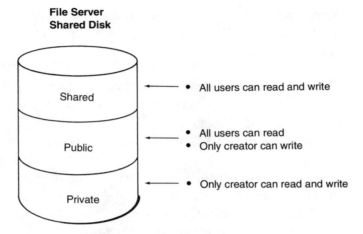

File Server
Shared Disk

Shared — All users can read and write

Public — • All users can read
• Only creator can write

Private — • Only creator can read and write

FIGURE 14-5.   Types of shared-disk access

keeping your presentation files in a directory that belongs exclu-
sively to you. You would then rely on the controls in the network
software to prevent other users from accessing this directory.

A recommended scheme of file locking is diagrammed in Figure
14-5. Depending on the type of network, access controls may be
applied at the level of devices, storage *volumes* (collections of related
files), directories, files, or records. It is not uncommon to find controls applied only at the level of volumes. A volume (or other unit of
storage such as a file) usually can be flagged for one of three types
of access:

- Public
- Shared
- Private

Public Access   A public volume is flagged read-only for all users
except its creator. That is, other users can view its files but cannot
modify them. For example, public data might include daily stock-
market quotations.

Shared Access   A shared volume allows any user to both read and write to its files. Note that, in this technical sense, shared data are more accessible than public data.

Private Access   Only the creator of a private volume can read or write to that volume. When not in use by its creator, a private volume is flagged as locked.

In some networks, it is possible to restrict sharing to a specific list of users. If you are updating a shared file, it is good practice to change it to a private file before doing the update. If you don't, other users could access the file—and perhaps change it—while you're working with it. In that case, one of the updates will be obliterated when the other is written over it.

File-Level Controls in Freelance Graphics

The file reservation system used by Freelance Graphics for Windows provides another level of protection at the level of individual files.

Network Options   Whenever you begin working on a presentation with the File➤Open command, the Network Options command becomes available on the File menu. Selecting File➤Network Options permits you to control whether you or some other user who also has access to the volume or device can make changes to that file.

In Freelance Graphics for Windows, all presentation files are regarded as public. That is, unless you implement other controls at the network level, any number of users on the network can look at (read) your presentation files. And they can all be reading the file at the same time. (In technical terms, a copy of the file is downloaded to the local cache in each workstation.)

Although virtually anyone can look at a presentation, the ability to write changes to that file is limited to just one person *at a time*. Note that this is not the same as private access. Rather, if you have the reservation, this control simply assures that no one can update the file while you are working on it. That way, one person's changes can never accidentally overwrite another's.

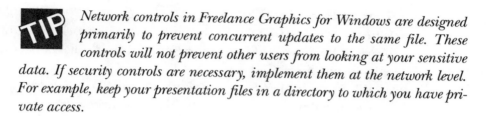

Network controls in Freelance Graphics for Windows are designed primarily to prevent concurrent updates to the same file. These controls will not prevent other users from looking at your sensitive data. If security controls are necessary, implement them at the network level. For example, keep your presentation files in a directory to which you have private access.

If you leave the network setting at Automatic (the default), you have the reservation automatically when you open a file, unless someone else is already working on the same file. If the setting is Manual, you must select Get to obtain the reservation before you can save your work. In any case, you can select Release at any time to permit reservation by some other user. When you select Release, your copy of the file becomes read-only, as indicated by the *RO* display in the program title bar:

Freelance Graphics - [MYFILE.PRE {RO}]

If someone else is working on the file when you attempt to open it, you will be able to do so, but for reading only. You will see an error message if you select Get in an attempt to secure the reservation. Furthermore, if someone else has updated a file since you opened it for read-only access, you have not been working with a current copy and you will not be able to perform Get.

If you modify a read-only copy of a presentation file and then attempt to exit the program without saving it, a warning message will appear. Remember that RO access prevents you only from updating the original file. There is nothing to prevent you from creating your own version of the file with a new name, which you can do by performing File➤Save As. If the original file was updated by someone else during your work session, you might then open and get the reservation for the original file, open your changed version as well, copy your changes into the original file, and than save it under the original name.

Sharing Files That Contain Linked or Embedded Objects

When you share files with other users on a network, some of the differences between linking and or embedding objects become especially important.

When multiple files are linked through DDE, there is only one copy of the data. The file that holds the source data is controlled by the source application, or server. Therefore, the user who has write access to the server will control all instances of the data in all the files to which the data are linked.

By contrast, when an object is embedded, there are self-contained copies of the data in both the source and destination files. An update to the source file will not affect the data in the destination file. So, if you need to have a private file, embed a local copy of the shared data rather than creating an ongoing link to an external file that you cannot control.

Mainframe Access by LANs

Access to a mainframe computer system and even to worldwide networks may be provided through a LAN, as though the larger network were just another set of local devices. The link to the mainframe is a hardware/software unit called a *gateway*, which, in effect, acts as both traffic cop and interpreter (Figure 14-6). However, the fact that this type of access is available is no guarantee that you can actually retrieve data from the mainframe in a form that will be usable by your PC. There's more about this in the following discussion on time-sharing systems.

Time-Sharing

Many corporate mainframe networks are set up as time-sharing systems, in which remote terminals share access to a large central computer, or *host*. Time-sharing is a highly centralized form of access, because all communications must be routed through a central point (the host). Remote access usually is provided over telephone lines that can be connected to a terminal or PC through a modem.

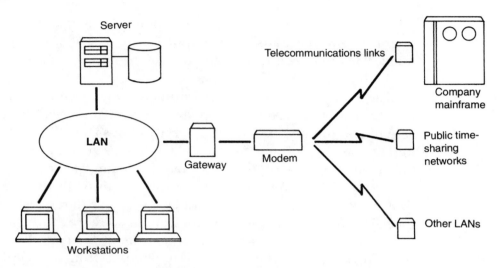

FIGURE 14-6. LAN access to mainframe and on-line services through a gateway

National information networks, such as Dow Jones News Retrieval Service, Lexis/Nexis, CompuServe, Prodigy, and Dialog, have local telephone-access numbers in most major cities. In some cases, services are linked to local phone exchanges by common-carrier networks such as Tymnet and Telenet. If your PC is connected to a LAN gateway, the gateway usually handles all connections to outside services.

Such large-scale networks actually may comprise many mainframe computers at dispersed locations. Each large computer may support one type of specialized database or service. You do not have to be concerned with switching among the computers. The information service has its own system of gateways, which makes the connections for you. You simply select from a menu of services displayed on your computer screen.

When preparing presentations in Freelance Graphics for Windows, you may need to communicate with mainframe systems to extract up-to-the-minute data from corporate or public databases, including quotations from the financial markets. When properly formatted as explained below, these data may be imported directly into Freelance Graphics to generate charts.

For these purposes, your interaction with a mainframe host might involve file transfer to download the data to your PC. Less often, you may need to run an application program on the mainframe to produce the data you need.

Particularly in corporate environments, mainframe systems are not compatible with microcomputer software. You usually won't be able to run the host's programs directly unless your PC is set up to function as a mainframe terminal. Mainframes generally transmit a full screen, or *page*, of data at a time. For many of these large systems, your PC can be made to work this way through IBM 3270 or IBM SNA terminal emulation, which usually requires installing a special hardware card and communications software in your PC.

Even if you can access host programs directly, you may have difficulty working with the results. Data output from a mainframe database system may be in a format that is not usable by PC software. You might therefore have to download the data, then use a utility program to handle translation into the proper format.

Increasingly, mainframe systems are being modified to serve users of microcomputers. Such systems often support communications protocols such as Kermit or XMODEM to facilitate file transfers to remote PCs. To use these communication protocols, you need one of the many popular microcomputer communications software programs.

On many of these large systems, including information services that are intended primarily to serve PCs, data output is translated into formats that can be imported directly into programs like Freelance Graphics for Windows.

UPLOADING FILES TO AUTOGRAPHIX: TOAGX

For the purpose of uploading presentation files for remote film recording, Freelance Graphics for Windows includes the utility program ToAGX-Windows, which is designed specifically for asynchronous file transfers to Autographix service centers. The communication software is built in, so you don't need any other program to establish the link if your computer is equipped with a modem.

To send a presentation to Autographix, you must first print the presentation to a color PostScript file, as described in Chapter 11. You then open the Autographix Slide Service application (which contains ToAGX), found in the same program group as Freelance Graphics.

You must then select .CPS files and enter processing, delivery, and billing instructions before you can select File➤Send to transmit the files. (An alternative to transmitting the files is to physically send a disk that contains the files and the required instructions to an Autographix service center.)

CHARACTER AND BINARY DATA FORMATS

One purpose of importing data from external files is to avoid the tedium of entering the data manually through the keyboard. This can also help prevent errors that might occur in retyping the data. Some types of files, such as pictures, must be imported electronically because it would be impractical to enter them otherwise. (Files not created by the application you are working in are referred to as *foreign*.)

In general, there are two types of external data-coding schemes:

- Character data
- Binary data

Character Data

There are various schemes of coding character data, or text. The specific method used by Freelance Graphics for Windows can be set up in the Tools➤User Setup➤International dialog box.

The File Translation (Code Page) setting specifies the coding scheme used to translate character data to and from external files. Selections in the drop-down box include Code Pages (translation tables) for different languages. ANSI, the extended ASCII character set used by Windows, is the default. Other common settings are U.S./DOS (Code Page 437) and Multilingual (Code Page 850). In general, the setting in Freelance Graphics should match any KEYB (keyboard) statement in the AUTOEXEC.BAT or CONFIG.SYS files of your computer or workstation. The DOS KEYB setup command controls the tables by which keystrokes are translated into binary signals.

 Changing code pages in DOS can be tricky. If you need to switch languages and keyboard layouts on a regular basis, consider installing a macro utility to handle the KEYB settings. Such macros are available from Key Tronic Corporation (Spokane, Washington) for their line of programmable keyboards.

You may need to reset the File Translation option temporarily if you are performing File➤Import on a text file that was written in a format that differs from your system setting. For example, if you are importing Italian text into an English document, you might have to reset the code page temporarily to Multilingual (Code Page 850).

Here are some further notes about the coding of character data, particularly as it applies when transferring files over telecommunications lines.

ASCII Code

Data in the American Standard Code for Information Interchange (ASCII) are strings of characters, or text. Files produced by word processing and database software often are in ASCII format or can at least be converted to it.

Decimal ASCII codes are numbers ranging from 0 to 255. The first 128 characters (0–127) are standardized among computer systems and represent upper- and lowercase alphabetic letters, Arabic numerals, punctuation marks, and special characters. The interpretation of characters 128–255 varies considerably among machines of different computer manufacturers. The set used on most IBM PC and compatible models is called the *IBM Extended Character Set* and includes graphic symbols and international characters, as well as lines and patterns for simulating graphics on older-style video terminals that can show only character data.

 To specify a special or nonprintable character, hold down the Alt key while entering its decimal ASCII code (up to three digits) on the numeric keypad.

In data transmission, variations on this format are ASCII-7 (seven data bits per character) and ASCII-8 (eight data bits per character).

In general, either coding scheme may be used as long as both the terminal and remote computer have the same settings.

To download an ASCII file over an asynchronous telecommunications link, set your terminal for 8 data bits, parity None, and 1 stop bit (8/N/1). In an ASCII transfer with parity set to None, the eighth data bit is ignored by both sender and receiver. The alternative is 7 data bits, Even parity, and 1 or 2 stop bits (7/E/2). In this case, the eighth bit is used in error checking. This setting may be more effective over noisy telephone lines.

ANSI Code

Another standard for character data has been established by the American National Standards Institute (ANSI). It extends the ASCII character set so that there is less variation among computers. Specifically, characters ASCII 127–255 have been standardized internationally. Again, Windows adheres to the ANSI standard.

Binary Data

Data transmissions in binary format are composed of digital sequences, or *bit streams,* composed of ones and zeros, which don't necessarily represent characters. Binary format is used mainly for program files, bitmaps, video, and audio.

580

GAINING THE PROFESSIONAL EDGE
• •
Part III

Binary files can be transmitted in either asynchronous or synchronous (batch) modes. Most high-speed links to mainframe systems are done in synchronous mode, and even character data can be sent in binary form.

 To transfer binary files over an asynchronous telecommunications link, your terminal must be set to 8/N/1. Transmissions at speeds from 300 to 2400 bps typically are done in asynchronous mode. Higher speeds are possible with more sophisticated error-checking modems. At these higher speeds, the limitation on transmission time usually is not the speed of the modem but the quality of the telephone connection.

Picture files can be very large, perhaps a megabyte or more, because each pixel in the image must be represented. Files may be made smaller for archival or transmission purposes through *data compression*. Compressed, or *packed*, picture or program files may have the extensions .ARC or .ZIP and must be decompressed with a file-extraction program such as ARC-E or PKUNZIP (widely available utility programs for working with compressed binary-data files).

 If possible, always compress large files before transmitting them over a modem. The time savings can be considerable.

Types of Character-Data Files

Special formatted character-data files generated by other applications that can be imported to Freelance Graphics for Windows include:

- Printer files
- Delimited ASCII files
- Spreadsheet files

Printer Files

A *printer file* contains ASCII text that has been generated by an application by redirecting its printer output to a disk file. The text is the character data that would be sent to the printer but has instead been written to a file on disk. Typical file extensions are .PRN and .TXT.

For example, in DOS versions of WordStar, an ASCII text file can be generated by selecting the printer driver named ASCII and then using the redirection symbol (>) in the command line to redirect the output to a disk file:

Name of printer? ASCII > MYFILE.PRN

Techniques for importing text files to Freelance Graphics for Windows are covered under "Importing Text from ASCII Files" in this chapter.

Delimited ASCII Files

This file format is typical of the report-writing functions of database programs. For example, a .DBF file generated by dBASE software with *delimited* options can be written as an ASCII file with delimiters as described below. (A delimiter is a special character used to separate data items.) A sample listing of a delimited file is shown in Figure 14-7. These files typically have a structure that is marked, or delimited, by three special characters:

• String separator
• Field separator
• End-of-record delimiter

String Separator The *string separator* ("), sometimes called a quote character, marks the boundaries of each text field, or comment. (A string is group of adjacent text characters.) The quote character should be omitted around numeric data items. For example, the string "SALES" uses the quote character to delimit the data

```
"ONE",1999,0506,M,1,132.98<CR/LF>
"TWO",1999,0417,F,2,93.24<CR/LF>
"THREE",1999,0303,F,0,433.00<CR/LF>
"FOUR",1999,0812,M,2,199.90<CR/LF>
```

FIGURE 14-7. Sample ASCII data file in delimited format

item SALES. Optionally, the ' character might be used, or any other special character. One or a combination of two characters can represent the quote character.

Field Separator The *field separator,* or end-of-field delimiter, is a special character used to separate data items in a series. Typical examples are commas, tabs, or blank spaces. Be sure that the character you specify is not used also as the decimal separator within data fields.

A special type of ASCII file generated by dBASE systems separates fields with blank spaces at specific column positions. Such a file actually contains no delimiters and is called *system data format* (SDF). Note that SDF is not the file extension, which typically is .DBF. An example is shown in Figure 14-8.

SDF is sometimes called space delimited format. *However, fixed column positions rather than spaces delimit the data, and this is therefore a somewhat misleading term.*

End-of-Record Delimiter This special character marks the end of a data record. In database terminology, a *record* is a set of data items that pertains to one entity. In the case of Freelance Graphics, a record normally would correspond to one data set, or column, in a Chart Data window.

```
ONE     1999    0506    M       1       132.98
TWO     1999    0417    F       2        93.24
THREE   1999    0303    F       0       433.00
FOUR    1999    0812    M       2       199.90
```

FIGURE 14-8. Sample ASCII data file in SDF format

The usual end-of-record delimiter for database files is a carriage-return and line-feed combination. The ASCII decimal codes for these are 13 and 10.

The source file might not be interpreted properly if a different delimiter is used. For example, in some applications, the form-feed code Ctrl-L marks the end of a record. Note that mainframe database systems in particular use other end-of-record codes.

Spreadsheet Files

An electronic spreadsheet (also called a worksheet or simply a sheet) is simply a matrix of data arranged in columns and rows, as shown in Figure 14-9. Each column may be designated by a letter (labeled A through Z, then AA, AB, AC, and so on, from left to right), and each row has a number, starting at the top of the form (1 through 99, say). Each juncture of a row and a column within the spreadsheet is called a cell and is designated by a cell address. A cell address consists of the letter of the column and the number of the

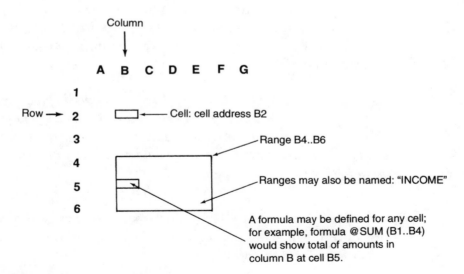

FIGURE 14-9. Spreadsheet format and terminology

row that intersect at the cell location. For example, the cell C10 would be found in the tenth row of the third column (C).

Associated with each cell address may be a mathematical formula that defines how the data value at that location is to be calculated, using input from other cells. For example, the formula @SUM(C2..C10) means the sum of the second through the tenth items in the third column. (In some spreadsheet programs, such as Microsoft Excel, the same formula would be written =SUM(C2:C10).)

Freelance Graphics for Windows does not support the use of formulas within the cells of its spreadsheet-style data forms. The spreadsheet will be imported into a Chart Data window just as it appears in the source application. That is, the data value generated by a formula will be imported, even if the result is 0. If an error message appears in a spreadsheet cell, it will be omitted, and the destination cell will be blank. (Error messages are labels, in effect, and Freelance Graphics will not insert labels in numeric data cells.)

Spreadsheet files contain character data arranged by columns and rows. This arrangement can make a convenient fit with the Chart Data window in Freelance Graphics for Windows. Each column (or row) of the spreadsheet can be imported as a data set of the current chart.

Although the columns and rows of Lotus Improv worksheets are not labeled, they are imported into a Chart Data form as though they had lettered columns and numbered rows. Once imported to Freelance Graphics, column and row data cannot be transposed as they can be in Improv.

Detailed procedures for importing various kinds of spreadsheets are covered in this chapter under "Pasting or Importing Spreadsheet Data" and also in Chapter 20.

Notes on Using Picture Files

Picture files, or bitmaps, are perhaps most useful in Freelance Graphics for Windows as illustrations in Screen Shows and SmartShows. Bitmaps can also be used in backgrounds. A variety of file types is supported. Since most picture files are resolution-specific, you must use the same display type (such as 16-color VGA) that was used to create the picture. Bitmaps will be imported in the explicit RGB colors used to create them (or the closest match that can be reproduced by the display), regardless of any color-palette settings within Freelance Graphics for Windows.

An example of a device- and resolution-specific bitmap is the Targa bitmap (.TGA), which is constructed specifically for display on AT&T Targa high-resolution video displays.

An exception is the *device-independent bitmap*, a data type supported by the Windows Clipboard, which is used internally to exchange pictures among Windows applications. As the term implies, device-independent bitmaps can be exchanged among dissimilar devices, such as between EGA- and VGA-equipped systems or between a VGA display and a graphics printer that can reproduce bitmaps. An example is the Windows bitmap (.BMP) file type, which is also compatible with systems that run OS/2 Presentation Manager.

THE GRAPHICAL KERNEL SYSTEM AND THE VIRTUAL DEVICE INTERFACE

Over the years, there have been attempts in the computer graphics industry to standardize device interfaces and drivers. Of particular interest for business-graphics users is the Graphical Kernel System (GKS). An implementation of the GKS standard is the Virtual Device Interface (VDI).

Freelance Graphics for Windows supports this standard by permitting the reading and writing of GKS data files, called Computer Graphics Metafiles, which have the .CGM file extension.

The principal method of achieving device-independent picture description (and, hence, storage) is through the use of a display list. The display list is the way the GKS standard is set up. Rather than holding a value for each pixel in a large frame buffer, a display list is a series of high-level instructions on how to make a picture. The display list describes the geometry of vectors and fill areas, and predefined shapes and their positions, as well as text and its color, justification, and position. The display list is built from a graphic language that's much like computer program instructions. The computational work of translating the display list to the requirements of a given display device is the job of intelligence residing in the output device. An intelligent graphic device accepts high-level software commands, calculates the picture, and translates it into the machine actions required to generate and record it on a particular medium, such as paper or photographic film.

One of the goals of the GKS standard is to provide uniformly applied interfaces to graphics input and output devices. Such interfaces are then provided as machine-specific software or *firmware* (programs on a chip) integrated with the device and provided by the manufacturer. These machine-specific programs are the device drivers. GKS-based application software issues a standard set of commands, or display list, to the intelligent output device. So, processing a display list results in a vector-graphic image.

As shown in Figure 14-10, the GKS description of the interface is known as the Virtual Device Interface, and output from the system, structured as a display list, is the Computer Graphics Metafile. The GKS standard also applies to desktop-publishing and engineering-graphics systems and serves to unify the requirements of graphics devices in many different application areas.

 Implementations of GKS differ, and .CGM has yet to become the universal standard for which it was intended. The implementation used in Freelance Graphics for Windows is commonly called Lotus CGM.

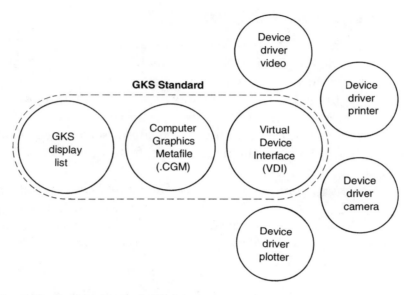

FIGURE 14-10.   Graphical Kernel System

Windows has its own object-oriented file type called the Windows metafile, extension .WMF.

READING DATA INTO FREELANCE GRAPHICS FOR WINDOWS

There are four basic methods of bringing data into Freelance Graphics for Windows. Data types can include text, alphanumeric data for charting, ready-made charts and vector graphics, pictures, sound recordings, and movie files. The methods are:

- Windows Clipboard
- File➤Import command
- File➤Import Chart command
- Import Data File (F6)

Windows Clipboard

By far, the most convenient way to move data or pictures into and out of Windows applications such as Freelance Graphics is to pass them through the Clipboard.

In the source application, select the data item, then perform Edit➤Copy (or Edit➤Cut to remove and copy the item). Then, switch to the destination application, select the document or area that will receive the data, and perform Edit➤Paste.

You can also perform Edit➤Insert Object to put an OLE package (button) on a page. When you select the button, the source application and file will open. This is not the same as the Button attribute in Freelance Graphics. (See "Inserting an Embedded Object" later in this chapter.)

If the destination is Freelance Graphics, open a text block or Chart Data & Titles window to receive the pasted item. Refer to Table 14-1 to select the appropriate destinations for different data types.

The data and file types described in this chapter were supported by Freelance Graphics for Windows Release 2 at the time of product introduction. Additional file types supported by subsequent releases are listed in the text file READ.ME in the FLW directory.

Copying Pages between Presentations

Freelance Graphics for Windows allows multiple document windows, or presentations, to be open at the same time. You can use this feature to copy pages or sequence of pages between presentations.

Select File➤Open to retrieve each presentation from its disk file. Select Window➤Tile to arrange the document windows side-by-side on your computer screen. Select the Page Sorter view in each presentation window.

TABLE 14-1. Clipboard Data Types and Permissible Freelance Graphics Destinations

Clipboard Data Type	Freelance Graphics Destination
OLE object	
metafile	page
table	page
text	page
Windows metafile	page
bitmap	page
device-independent bitmap	page
text	text block, data form, Outliner
formatted table	page
unformatted table	text block, data form
sound	page
movie	page

In the source presentation, select the page or pages to be copied. To select a page, click on its icon or move the highlight to it with the arrow keys. To select multiple pages, hold down the Shift key while you click on each page. Or, to select all the pages in a presentation, perform Edit➤Select➤All. When you are in the Page Sorter, you can press F4 to select all the pages.

Perform Edit➤Copy to copy the selected pages to the Clipboard. Then, select the page icon inside the window of the destination presentation after which you want the new pages inserted. Perform Edit➤Paste to retrieve the pages.

When you paste pages into a presentation, they will assume the attributes of the SmartMaster set that currently applies to the destination presentation.

To link as well as paste individual pages, see the following section.

Pasting an Object with a DDE Link

To create a DDE link along with a pasting operation into Freelance Graphics for Windows, select Edit➤Paste Special. The Paste Special

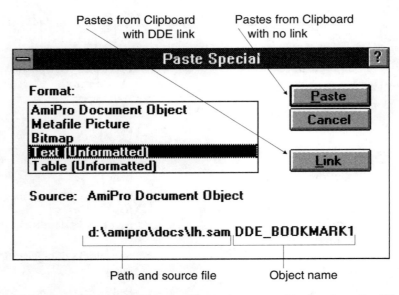

Pastes from Clipboard with DDE link

Pastes from Clipboard with no link

Path and source file

Object name

FIGURE 14-11. Use the Paste Special dialog box to read in data from the Clipboard, optionally establishing a DDE link with the Link button.

dialog box will appear, as shown in Figure 14-11. Select the data format that applied to the type of object you are pasting. Then, select Link.

In some other Windows applications that support DDE, the command to retrieve the copy and create the link is Edit➤Paste Link.

Requirements for Linking

The following requirements apply to DDE links:

- The source data must have been copied or cut to the Clipboard from a previously saved (named) file.

- The source application must support DDE as a server.

- In DDE, Freelance Graphics for Windows can be either a server or a client.

- The data format selected in the Paste Special dialog box should match the intended use of the object in the destination application.

Linking Presentation Pages

Pages can be linked as well as copied if you copy them one page at a time from the Page Sorter, and use Edit➤Paste Special➤Link to paste them separately into a new page in the Current Page view. The Clipboard format selected during this operation should be Metafile Pictures.

The linked page will be pasted into the Current Page view as a grouped object. To resize it to fill the page, drag its handles. Note that you do not have access to the underlying data for charts within the destination application, nor can you edit the objects of any such linked metafile picture. To edit a linked page, you must change it in the source presentation.

Inspecting and Editing DDE Link References

Links to external data files can be listed and edited by selecting Edit➤Links in either the Current Page or Page Sorter views. A listing of all active links in the current file will appear in the Links dialog box, as shown in Figure 14-12.

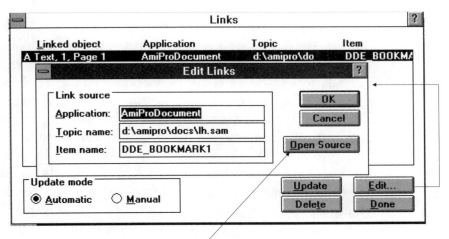

View contents of source file

FIGURE 14-12. The Links dialog box lists the all the active DDE links to the current file.

In practice, you will rarely need to edit data links this way. More often, you will delete the linked item in the destination file and then paste a different linked object into the file. One use of the Edit➤Links command is to edit a link reference after you have moved the source file to a different device or directory.

Selecting a list item and then the Edit button will bring up the Edit Links dialog box, where the link reference can be edited by typing in any of three text boxes. The *syntax,* or written form, of a link has three elements:

- Application
- Topic
- Item

Application   The application is the name of the program that holds the source data.

Topic   The topic is a complete reference for the source file, including its device, path, and filename.

Item   The item is a data set within the source file. For example, an item reference might be a page number or a worksheet range.

The Open Source button in the Edit Links dialog box can be used to reopen the source application and data file, if necessary.

The Update Mode option buttons in the Links dialog box permit you to select whether changes in the source file will be made automatically (Automatic) in the destination document or only on demand (Manual). To cause a manual update, highlight the link reference and then select the Update button in this dialog box. To sever a link, highlight it and select Delete. When you are finished editing or updating links, select Done.

Inserting an Embedded Object

To embed an object in a presentation page through OLE, select Edit➤Insert Object in the Current Page view.

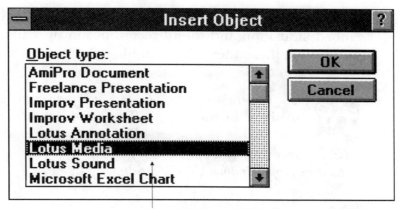

Select to insert prebuilt animation (movie) files

FIGURE 14-13.   Selecting Edit➤Insert Object brings up this dialog box, by which
objects can be embedded in presentation pages.

The Insert Object dialog box will open, as shown in Figure 14-13. Select the source application and type of object from the Object Type list box. Then, select OK.

The Windows application you selected will open. You can create a new object in its document window, or you can perform File➤Open to open an existing file and select an object from it.

When you have finished creating or retrieving the object, select File➤Exit & Return in the source application. The application will close, and you will be returned to the Current Page view. The object (or in some cases an icon that represents it) will appear in the page.

When the object appears on the page, it is surrounded by handles. Drag it to a new location on the page or resize it, if necessary.

Double-click on the object to reopen the source application and edit the object.

Some source applications, such as Lotus Media, use prebuilt objects, such as sound and movie files. If you select such an application for OLE, you will simply be prompted to select the file to be inserted at the destination.

Remember that an embedded object is a complete copy that will be saved in your presentation file.

A good use of OLE with Freelance Graphics for Windows is to embed animation and sound recordings in presentations. There's more about this under "Using Multimedia" in this chapter.

The Object Packager application of Windows can be used to create a button, or package, for Windows documents and objects. The package can then be embedded in any application that supports OLE. For more information, see "Integrating Your Windows Applications" in the Microsoft Windows User's Guide.

File➤Import Command

The file types listed in Table 14-2 can be imported into the Current Page view by the File➤Import command. Also, ASCII text files (.PRN extension) can be imported to the Outliner. This command is not available in the Page Sorter.

To import an external file to the current page, select File➤Import and select the File Type and File Name settings in the Import File dialog box (Figure 14-14). If appropriate for the file type, mark one of the check-box options (described in the next section), then select OK.

Import Options

If you are importing a bitmap, mark the check box Include Image With File to save the bitmap with the presentation. This will be necessary if you will be using the presentation on another system that does not hold the bitmap file, if you will be sending it via e-mail, or if you will be submitting it for film recording.

Saving bitmaps within a presentation can add significantly to the size of the file.

TABLE 14-2. File Types Supported for File➢Import

Extension	Data Type	Application
.AI	PostScript	Adobe Illustrator
.BMP	bitmap	Windows, Presentation Manager
.CHT	vector graphic	Harvard Graphics 2.3 (DOS)
.CH3	vector graphic	Harvard Graphics 3.0 (DOS)
.CGM	metafile (ANSI)	Computer Graphics Metafile
.DDF	metafile	Digital Document (DEC systems)
.DRW	vector graphic	Freelance Graphics (DOS)
.DRW	vector graphic	Micrografx Drawing
.DXF	vector graphic/layers	AutoCAD Drawing Exchange
.EPS	PostScript	Encapsulated PostScript*
.GAL	vector graphic	Hewlett-Packard Graphics Gallery
.GEM	bitmap	Digital Research picture
.GIF	vector graphic (compressed)	CompuServe Graphics Interchange Format
.HGL	vector (plotter)	Hewlett-Packard Graphics Language (HPGL)
.MET	metafile	IBM OS/2 Presentation Manager
.PCX	bitmap	ZSoft PC Paintbrush
.PCT	bitmap	Apple Macintosh PICTure
.PIC†	vector graphic	Lotus 1-2-3, Release 2 (DOS)
.PFL	vector graphic (multiple drawings)	Freelance Graphics Portfolio (DOS)
.PRN	text	ASCII print file
.RND	bitmap rendering (converted CAD vectors)	AutoShade/AutoCAD
.SYM	vector graphic (symbols)	Harvard Graphics 2.3 (DOS)
.SY3	vector graphic (symbols)	Harvard Graphics 3.0 (DOS)
.TIF	bitmap	Tag Image File (Aldus)
.TGA	bitmap	AT&T Targa video board
.WMF	metafile	Windows system standard
.WPG	vector graphic (symbol)	WordPerfect (DOS)

* An Encapsulated PostScript file can also contain a TIFF bitmap preview of the image.

† This is *not* the same file type as the PC Paint bitmap (also .PIC extension).

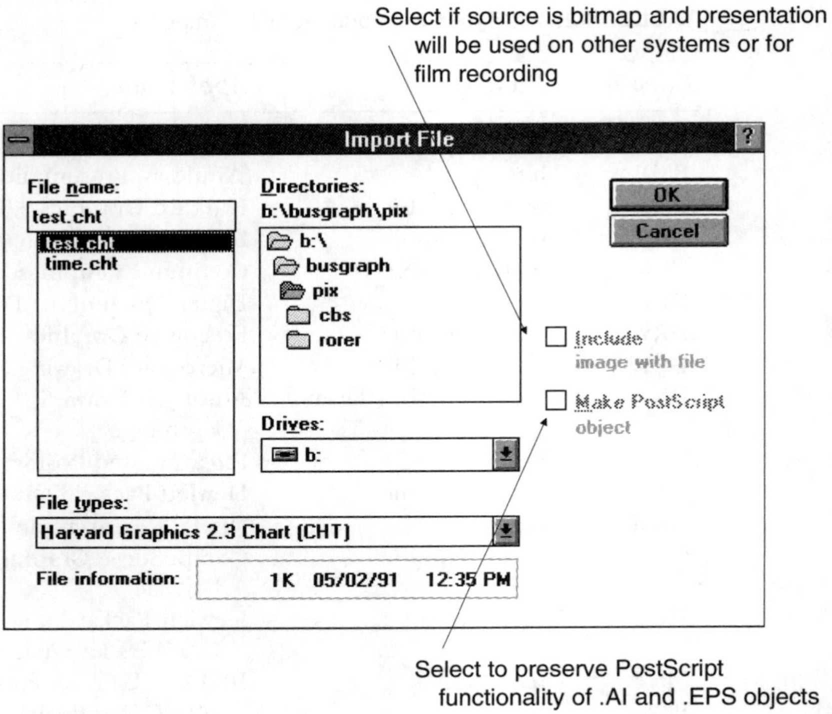

Select if source is bitmap and presentation
will be used on other systems or for
film recording

Select to preserve PostScript
functionality of .AI and .EPS objects

FIGURE 14-14.   The Import Data File dialog box permits you to select an external
file that will be imported to the current presentation.

If you are importing an Encapsulated PostScript file, mark the
check box Make PostScript Object to prevent the translation of the
file into a Freelance object. Do this if you will be exporting the file
back to .EPS or .CPS formats for use with PostScript applications.

Translation of Imported Objects

In general, a file that is read into a page by the File➤Import command is translated into a grouped collection of Freelance objects. If
the file is a chart, you will not be able to access the underlying data.
To be able to work with chart data in Freelance Graphics, use the
File➤Import Chart command instead.

File➤Import Chart Command

In the Current Page view, the File➤Import Chart command reads the data values in an external file and uses them to generate a Free-lance Graphics data chart. You can therefore edit such charts just as though they had been entered through the Chart Data & Titles window.

Import Chart Procedure

To import a chart, first select one of the chart layouts in the Current Page view. Then, select File➤Import Chart.

The Import Chart dialog box will appear. Select the File Type and File Name settings, then OK.

Accessing Named Charts

Charts that were created within Lotus 1-2-3 and Symphony work-sheets may be identified by name within the .WK? or .WR? files. Selecting the Named Charts button in the Import Chart dialog box will display a listing of existing chart names in a worksheet you have specified in the File Name text box. You can then select by name the chart to be imported.

In spreadsheet terminology, a chart name is the name of a range of cells in which each column or row of numeric values has been used as a chart data set.

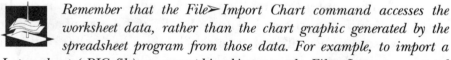 *Remember that the File➤Import Chart command accesses the worksheet data, rather than the chart graphic generated by the spreadsheet program from those data. For example, to import a Lotus chart (.PIC file) as a graphic object, use the File➤Import command instead.*

Supported File Types

The file types supported for importation as chart data are listed in Table 14-3.

TABLE 14-3. External File Types: Chart Data

Extension	File Type	Application
.CH1	chart	Freelance Graphics (DOS)
.CHT	chart	GraphWriter
.GPH	chart	Freelance Graphics for OS/2
.WK?	worksheet	Lotus 1-2-3
.WR?	worksheet	Lotus Symphony

Import Data File (F6)

In addition to the techniques just described, Freelance Graphics for Windows has a feature that permits you to view the data in an external file and select specific items that will be imported.

After you have opened the Chart Data & Titles window for any chart in the Current Page view, press F6 (Import Data File) or select the Import Data icon. Or, select the Import button that appears to the left of the data sheet. (See Figure 14-15.)

The Import Data File window will open, permitting you to select a File Type and File Name setting of an external data file. Specify the filename and select OK.

Selecting Spreadsheet Data

The content of the file you selected will appear in the Import Data window, as shown in Figure 14-16. In the case of a worksheet, a set of selections will appear as check boxes to the left of the sheet. Select the data to be used for the chart as follows, making only the choices you require:

- Highlight the sheet labels that will be used as a legend (names of data sets), and mark the Copy Legends check box.

- Highlight the sheet labels that will be used as axis labels, and mark the Copy Labels check box.

View contents of external data file
for selective import (same as F6)

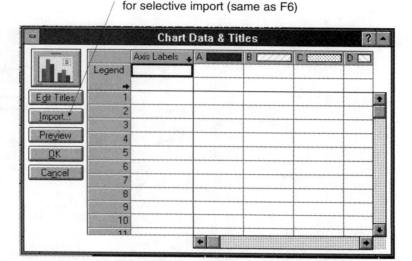

FIGURE 14-15. The Chart Data window includes an Import button. Selecting it is equivalent to pressing F6 (Import Data File).

- Highlight the sheet data values that will be used for data sets in the chart, and mark the Copy Chart Data check box. To handle the importation in a single step, the data sets should be arranged as columns in the source sheet.

If your selections from the sheet match the requirements for chart data, they will be inserted into the Chart Data & Titles window automatically when you select OK.

Import Data Options

The following options are available in the Import Data window:

Link Selections   Mark this box to create a DDE link to the source data file. When the data are inserted in the Chart Data & Titles window, they will be underscored with a cyan-colored line to indicate that they are linked. Linked items cannot be changed within Freelance Graphics as long as the link exists.

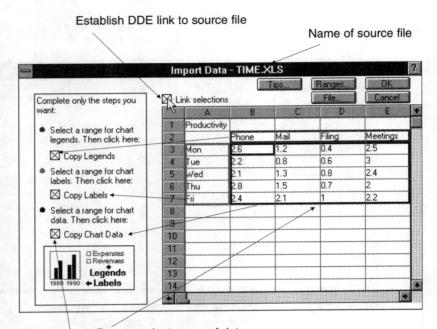

FIGURE 14-16.   When you press F6 or select the Import button, the Import Data
                    window will appear, allowing you to select specific data items to
                    be imported.

Tips   This button activates Help for the importation procedure.

Ranges   In the case of an external worksheet file, selecting this
button brings up the Go to Range dialog box. Use this control to
navigate large sheets by specifying named ranges or entering the
cells at their top-left and bottom-right corners (A1..H6).

File   If you have accessed an external data file previously in the
current work session, the file selection procedure will be skipped,
and the Import Data window will redisplay the last file you used. If

necessary, select the File button to navigate the file system and specify a different filename.

Making Selections from Text and Database Files

The Import Data File feature is a particularly convenient technique for importing .DBF files, since you don't have to be concerned with specifying delimiters. When the file content appears in the Import Data window, you simply highlight the items you want pasted into Freelance Graphics. Text and numeric data in database files can be imported to the Chart Data or Chart Titles windows, or to text blocks.

To import labels (such as headings, notes, and axis titles) to the Chart Titles window for a data chart, select the Edit Titles button in the Chart Data window and then the Import button in the Chart Titles window.

When you select data items from a text or database file, they are not copied into the destination automatically; they are copied to the Clipboard instead. You must then open the text box or Chart Data window that will receive the data, and perform Edit➤Paste or Edit➤Paste Special➤Link (for DDE).

File types that can be accessed for selective importation of data are listed in Table 14-4.

TABLE 14-4. Import Data File (F6): Supported File Types

Extension	File Type	Application or Use
.DBF	ASCII text (Delimited or SDF)	dBASE-compatible
.PRN	ASCII numbers	chart data
.PRN	ASCII text	text/label import
.SLK	symbolic link data	SYLK
.WK?	worksheet	Lotus 1-2-3
.WR?	worksheet	Lotus Symphony
.XLS	worksheet	Microsoft Excel

NOTES ON PASTING AND IMPORTING DIFFERENT DATA TYPES

Some special rules apply when you are pasting or importing text and tables.

Inserting Data as or into a Text Block

If you are pasting or importing lines of text into the Current Page view, normally you will want to open a text block in Freelance Graphics to receive it. If a text block is open when you perform Edit➤Paste, the text will be placed at the insertion point and will wrap within the block according to the attributes currently set for it.

If a text block is not open, the text will be inserted as a single, new block. The block will conform to the default settings for Paragraph 1 text. (See Chapter 5 for more information on styles within text blocks.)

Whether a destination text block is open, Freelance Graphics will start a new paragraph at each carriage return and will indent at each tab stop in the text item.

Importing Text from ASCII Files

When you are selecting the external file type for File➤Import or Import Data File operations, you must choose among data that will be read into a text block, chart labels, table chart (ASCII Text), or as chart data values (ASCII Numbers).

Inserting Tables

Table data passed through the Windows Clipboard may be formatted or unformatted. A formatted table typically has been created in a word processing application such as Ami Pro and can contain attributes, such as fonts and sizes, as well as graphic enhancements such as grid lines and shading of areas. Formatted tables are pasted into the Current Page view as new graphic objects, so that they appear just as in the source application. The table is grouped initially, so you will need to perform Arrange➤Ungroup to work on its contents as separate Freelance Graphics objects.

An unformatted table is simply an array of text data. It can be pasted from the Clipboard or imported from an external file. To build a table chart in Freelance Graphics, create a new page with a Table layout and then open its Chart Data & Titles window (Chart➤Edit) to receive the pasted or imported text. Select the destination range of cells in the data form and then perform Edit➤Paste (to retrieve a table previously copied to the Clipboard), or select File➤Import Chart to access an external file. To import data selectively from a file, select the Import button in the Chart Data & Titles window or press F6 (Import Data File).

A detailed example of the Import Data function is presented in Chapter 17.

Pasting or Importing Text into the Outliner

Some special rules apply when you are pasting or importing a block or file of text into the Outliner view. For example, you might copy an outline you had already created in a word processing application such as Ami Pro into the Outliner for purposes of generating a series of title and bullet charts.

The program interprets text read into the Outliner according to the indentation it finds preceding each line. If no space precedes a line of text (on the same line), it is inserted into the Outliner as a title chart on a new page. If a line is indented one space, it becomes a Paragraph 1 item (first-level bulleted item); two spaces, Paragraph 2 (second-level bulleted item); three spaces, Paragraph 3 (third-level bulleted item). Lines indented by three or more spaces will all be treated as third-level items. An example is presented in Figure 14-17.

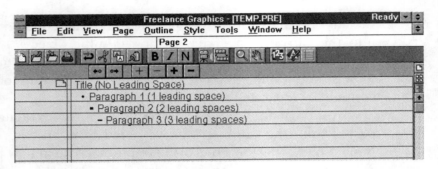

FIGURE 14-17. Leading spaces in ASCII files are translated as levels in indentation in the Outliner.

Pasting or Importing Spreadsheet Data

Some restrictions apply when you are pasting or importing data from a spreadsheet into a Chart Data & Titles window in Freelance Graphics. Cells in this window that are designated by column letters and row numbers (such as A1) can hold numeric data only. The program enforces data typing: It will not insert labels (alphanumeric text) into the numeric cells. In other words, the first two rows (legend) and the first column (axis labels) of the data form can accept either letters or numbers. *All the other cells can accept only numbers.*

 If the chart type is XY (Scatter), the first column of the data form can accept numbers only (the numeric x coordinates).

The selections in the Import Data window (described above under "Import Data File (F6)") prompt you to choose the legend and label text, as well as the numeric data. However, these options may not be available, particularly when you are pasting spreadsheet data from the Clipboard. In such cases, paste the labels and the numeric data in separate operations, as follows:

- Before pasting legends, select one or both of the Legend rows at the top of the Chart Data & Titles window.

- Before pasting x-axis labels, select the Axis Labels column.

You will also need to be selective about pasting the numeric data if the layout of the spreadsheet does not match that of the Chart Data & Titles window. For example, if data sets in the spreadsheet run row-wise (from left to right), you would want to paste them into columns in the Chart Data & Titles window. To achieve this, you will have to perform separate Edit➤Copy and Edit➤Paste operations for each data set, copying one row each time and pasting it into a column.

EXPORTING FILES FROM FREELANCE GRAPHICS

Pages and presentations can be translated by Freelance Graphics for Windows and written to the corresponding external file type. The purpose is to be able to use the presentation with other applications. Exporting can be performed in the Page Sorter or in the Current Page view. The command is not available from the Outliner.

Performing File➤Export

You initiate the export operation in either view by selecting File➤Export. The Export File dialog box will appear, as shown in Figure 14-18.

Select a file type from the drop-down box for the new external file. If you select Freelance Portfolio (.PFL), the entire presentation will be exported. For all other selections, only the current page will be exported.

 Use the View➤Screen Show➤Prepare Standalone command to export an entire presentation as a self-running show (.SHW file). To save an entire presentation for use by an OS/2 version of the program, select File➤Save As➤Freelance for OS2 (PRS).

In the Export File dialog box, the Options button will be available for some file types. Select this button to customize settings in the output filter for the specific requirements of the external appli-

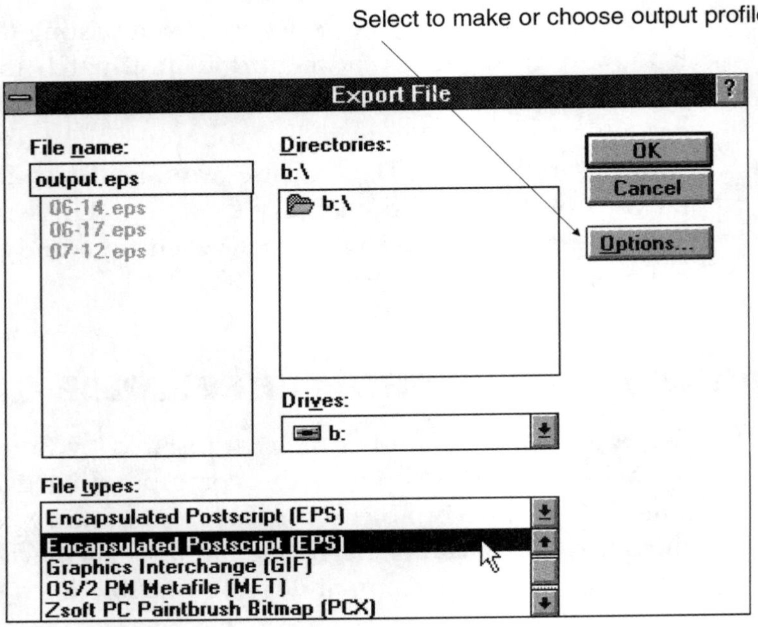

Select to make or choose output profile

FIGURE 14-18.   The Export File dialog box permits you to specify the name and type of external file to be created from the current page or presentation.

cation. Consult the documentation for the application to determine the settings you need to make in the Output Filter Setup dialog box that appears. Depending on the file type, this dialog box may have one or more of the following controls:

Profiles

This drop-down box lists sets of predefined options, or *profiles*.

New   To create a new profile, select the New button, enter a unique name, and change the setup options. After you select OK to close the Setup dialog box, the named profile will be saved for future use.

Delete   To remove a profile you have created, select its name in the Profiles drop-down box and then select the Delete button.

Defaults   After you have customized the options for a particular profile, you can restore the predefined options by selecting the Defaults button.

Edit Font Table

This button will be available if the filter has a table for converting names of fonts in applications to font names or numbers used in assigning attributes to text objects. For example, you might be able to specify that Arial fonts in the presentation be converted to the closest match, such as Helvetica, in the external application.

Printing to Disk

Other export options may be included as options for printing to disk through Windows. For example, if you print a presentation using the Autographix PostScript printer driver, you can specify output to a color PostScript (.CPS) file. When printing to disk, the conversion is handled entirely by the printer-driver software and not by Freelance Graphics.

Export File Types

Types of export filters available with Freelance Graphics for Windows Release 2 are listed in Table 14-5.

GRAPHICS CONVERSION UTILITIES

For some of the graphics and bitmap file formats that are not supported by Freelance Graphics for Windows, software utilities are available that will handle the conversion to a format that can be imported, such as .BMP, .PCX, or .TIF. Some of these utilities also

TABLE 14-5. Export Filters

Extension	File Type	Application
.AI	PostScript	Adobe Illustrator
.BMP	bitmap	Windows
.CGM	metafile (ANSI)	Computer Graphics Metafile
.DDF	metafile	Digital Document (DEC systems)
.DRW	vector graphic	Freelance Graphics (DOS)
.EPS	PostScript	Encapsulated PostScript
.GIF	vector graphic (compressed)	CompuServe Graphics Interchange Format
.MET	metafile	IBM OS/2 Presentation Manager
.PCX	bitmap	ZSoft PC Paintbrush
.PCT	bitmap	Apple Macintosh PICTure
.PFL	vector graphic (multiple)	Freelance Graphics Portfolio (DOS)
.TIF	bitmap	Tag Image File (Aldus)
.TGA	bitmap	AT&T Targa video board
.WPG	vector graphic	WordPerfect (DOS)
.WMF	metafile	Windows system standard

permit you to manipulate the gray-scale values of bitmaps, including controlling the type and amount of dithering applied.

There are a great many bitmap file formats. Electronic clip art, for example, is available in one or more of these formats. Here's a brief summary of a few of them.

.DIB This is the file version of the device-independent bitmap, another Windows internal standard. Freelance Graphics does not support it for importation (although the data can be passed through the Clipboard). It is available, however, in the Paintbrush accessory of Windows. Use the Windows Paintbrush program to create a .BMP file, then import it to Freelance Graphics for Windows.

.CUT This format is generated by Dr. Halo software.

.PIC   This format is generated by PC Paint (Mouse Systems). An entirely different format *with the same extension* is the Lotus .PIC file.

.MSP   Microsoft Windows Paint files are generated by some versions of Windows Paintbrush. Use Paintbrush to read the file, then save it as a .BMP file and import it into Freelance Graphics for Windows.

.PIX   These files are generated by programs such as INSET, which is the graphics auxiliary program used with later versions of WordStar.

.GIF   This format, which can be imported by Freelance Graphics for Windows, was specially designed for downloading picture files from the CompuServe on-line service. The files have fixed resolutions, may be in color, and are in compressed form. Without the Freelance Graphics import filter, driver software such as VGAGIF would be needed to decompress the file and present it to the display for viewing.

.RLE   Run-length encoding (RLE) is another way of compressing picture files for transmission or storage. This format is often encountered on computer bulletin boards. The images are typically monochrome.

USING MULTIMEDIA

Freelance Graphics for Windows Release 2 includes the applications Lotus Sound Recorder:

and Lotus Media Manager:

for creating and inserting multimedia effects in Screen Shows. (These icons can be found in the Lotus Applications program group, as well as in the default toolbar of Freelance Graphics.)

 Some SmartMaster sets include prebuilt multimedia effects. For example, MMGLOBE.MAS incorporates the rotating-globe movie file MMGLOBE.LSM, and MMLASER.MAS has the laser effect found in MMLASER.LSM.

Lotus Sound Recorder

This application is an enhancement of Microsoft Windows Sound Recorder, which enables digital audio recording on computer systems that are equipped with a sound card and a microphone. Selecting this application brings up a control panel that resembles a conventional audio recorder:

You can use the control panel to capture your own voice narratives into Wave (.WAV) files for insertion into Screen Shows. (Microsoft Windows Sound Recorder also records in Wave format.)

Lotus Media Manager

This application permits you to list filenames, preview (play), and copy multimedia files, including:

- Wave sound recordings made with Lotus Sound Recorder or Windows Sound Recorder (.WAV)
- MIDI sound recordings (.MID)
- Movie files, or digital video animation (.MMM, .LSM, or .AVS)

When you start this application from the Lotus Applications program group, the Lotus Media Manager window will open, listing filenames of the selected file type (Figure 14-19). Multimedia files that can be shared among Lotus Windows applications are held not in the FLW directory but in LOTUSAPP/MULTIMED.

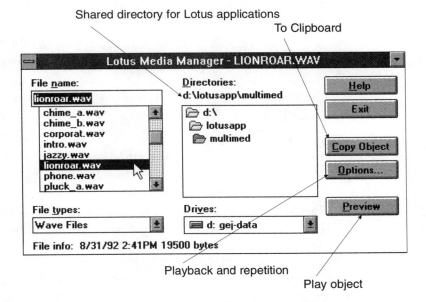

FIGURE 14-19. Access sound recordings and movie files through the Lotus Media Manager dialog box.

Select the Preview button in this dialog box to see or hear the movie or sound recording played. Set options for number of repetitions and embedding (inclusion in the presentation file) by selecting the Options button. Select Copy Object to move the object to the Clipboard in preparation for pasting it into a presentation page in Freelance Graphics.

Inserting Multimedia Objects in Presentations

There are three basic ways to insert a multimedia object into a page in the Current Page view:

- Open the Lotus Media Manager application as just described, select an object and play options, and then select the Copy Object button to copy it to the Clipboard. Switch to Freelance Graphics and perform Edit➤Paste Special➤Lotus Multimedia Object to read the object into the page.

- In the Current Page view, select Edit➤Insert Object and then Lotus Media. The Lotus Media Manager application window will open, and you can specify a filename. Instead of copying the object to the Clipboard, select OK to insert the object on the page.

- If your system is equipped for making sound recordings, select Edit➤Insert Object and then Lotus Sound or Sound (Windows Sound Recorder). Make your recording and select Edit➤Copy Sound as an Object to copy it to the Clipboard. Then, select File➤Exit and Return to FLW. In the Current Page view, select Edit➤Paste Special➤Lotus Sound Object.

When you use Edit➤Insert Object, you are embedding the object in the Freelance Graphics presentation. A sound recording will appear as a button that can be clicked by the operator during a Screen Show. A movie will appear as a metafile picture that will become animated according to the options you select in Edit➤ Lotus Multimedia Object.

Editing Multimedia Effects

When a sound-recording button or a movie metafile picture are selected in the Current Page view, handles surround it so that it can be resized or moved on the page.

Depending on the type of object that is currently selected, the commands Edit➤Lotus Sound Object or Edit➤Lotus Media Object will appear in the Edit pull-down menu. When you choose this command, a submenu will appear with the following options:

Play

This selection plays, or previews, the object in a control panel window so that you can start, pause, and reverse it.

Edit

Select this command to substitute another multimedia file for the selected object. A file selection dialog box will appear.

Play Without Controls

For sound recordings only, this option omits the display of the control panel during playback so that the recording is played just once, automatically.

Print Options

Selecting this command displays the check box Include This Object When Printing to control whether the button or metafile picture of the multimedia object will be reproduced on printouts or slides. (You will probably want to omit buttons from printouts but include pictures.)

Play Options

This command brings up the Play Options dialog box in Figure 14-20, by which you can control the behavior of the object during a show. Pick an option button for Play Object When Clicked or Play

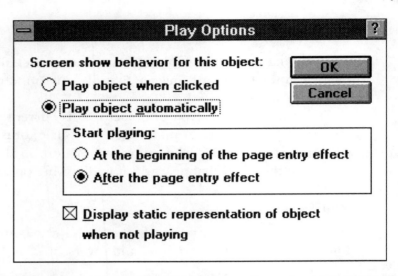

FIGURE 14-20.   The Play Options dialog box permits you to control the behavior of multimedia objects in Screen Shows

Object Automatically. You can also specify when to start playing by selecting either the At the Beginning of the Page Entry Effect (as the screen is being "painted") or After the Page Entry Effect (when the entire page is visible) setting.

A check box here controls whether the operator can actually see the object as a button or picture when it is not being played: Display Static Representation of Object When Not Playing. For example, you might want to suppress the display of a sound button if the recording plays automatically.

INSERTING NOTES IN PRESENTATIONS

You can embed comments and other types of objects in presentations with the Lotus Annotator application. To embed a note in the current presentation page, click on the Lotus Annotator icon in the toolbar:

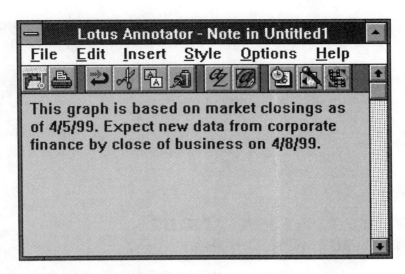

FIGURE 14-21.   The Lotus Annotator Window

Or, perform Edit➤Insert Object➤Lotus Annotator Note and select OK.

The Lotus Annotator window will open, as shown in Figure 14-21. Type the text of your annotation in the window. When you are finished, select File➤Update and Exit to Freelance from the menu bar of this window, or press F4.

The embedded note will appear on the page in the drawing area as a Note icon:

You can select and drag the icon anywhere within the page. Whenever you double-click it, the Lotus Annotator window and the text of the note will be displayed. Select File➤Exit to Freelance or press Alt-F4 to close the window.

The Note icon will appear in Screen Shows, but the annotation can be opened only in the Current Page view.

You have a variety of options when the Lotus Annotator window is open. You can insert the current date, time, and an optional name automatically in the annotation by using the command Insert➤Info Stamp. You control the content of the information stamp by the command Options➤Info Stamp.

You can insert multimedia and other application objects as annotations by the commands Insert➤New Sound, Insert➤Media File, or Insert➤Object.

Particularly if you insert an object other than text, you can change the Note icon to match the object type by using the command Style➤Note Icon.

SENDING PRESENTATIONS VIA ELECTRONIC MAIL

If your computer system or network is installed with either cc:Mail or Lotus Notes, you can append Freelance Graphics presentation files to your electronic mail (e-mail) messages. If you have ever manually collated last-minute changes to a slide show into trays for a waiting courier, you will find that this method of distributing presentations is a real labor-saver.

E-Mail Installation

The Lotus Notes icon appears in the default toolbar to the right of the Ami Pro application:

You will not be able to access Lotus Notes unless the application is installed and the following entry appears in your systems FLW2.INI file (found in the WINDOWS directory):

Notes = Lotus Notes, C:\NOTES\NOTES.EXE

The device and path must be correct for your installation. If you use Freelance Graphics on a network, the device in particular probably will be different.

The optional SmartIcon for cc:Mail looks like this:

The required syntax in FLW2.INI file is:

ccMail = cc:Mail for Windows, C:\CCMAIL\WMAIL.EXE

Appending a Presentation

To send a presentation over an e-mail network, select File➤Send Mail, or click the Send Mail icon:

The Send Mail dialog box will appear. Selecting the check box Attach appends the current presentation file to your next e-mail transmission. When you select OK, the Notes or cc:Mail dialog box will open for you to compose an accompanying text message and for routing.

GRAPHICS TELECONFERENCING

Consider the impact of being able to share presentation files over a network. If you combine the concepts of a screen show and a LAN, the result is *graphics teleconferencing*, which can permit people at workstations on a network to distribute and view their presentations electronically.

Distribution of presentations via e-mail eliminates the drawback of having to transmit extensive picture files during an on-line session, which is the major expense of a similar technology—*video-conferencing*. (Special-purpose videoconferencing cards are available for PCs.) The narrative portion of the presentation can be embedded as sound files, or a live *conference bridge* can be set up over the telephone system. A bridge combines multiple voice lines through the telephone-utility switching center or through the company PBX (private branch exchange).

In graphics teleconferencing, batches of slides can be downloaded as presentation files in a single transmission just prior to the session. Compared to the video images exchanged in traditional videoconferencing, vector-graphic files are relatively compact and require much less transmission time.

There's nothing technically difficult about any of this. It's the kind of gee-whiz electronic showmanship that's touted by the phone companies as the wave of the future when they begin to convert to high-bandwidth digital phone service. But there's no reason why it can't be done right now, starting with the tools that are included with Freelance Graphics for Windows, and running it on a network equipped with cc:Mail or Lotus Notes.

MANAGING GRAPHICS PRODUCTION

I t is a relatively new phenomenon that virtually anyone with tools like Freelance Graphics for Windows can prepare a professional-looking presentation. Much of the published material about business graphics software assumes that you, the reader, are also the presenter, or the principal end user of your graphic outputs. However, it has been the tradition in the graphic arts field that specialists did this work to order, whether in an internal graphic-arts department or an outside production house. Such an organization is diagrammed in Figure 15-1.

This chapter focuses mainly on the issues that arise when you must prepare graphic presentations for others. In this capacity, you might be:

- A member of staff preparing a report that your manager will deliver

- A member of a work group that is collaborating over an electronic network to create or share a presentation

- A staff member in an internal graphic-arts department that serves many departments in a company

- A graphic artist employed by an outside production house, or *service bureau*

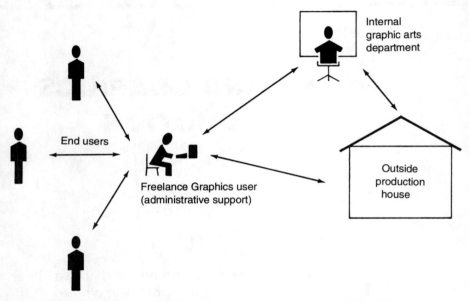

FIGURE 15-1.   Relationship of graphics service groups and end users

This chapter explores how larger production assignments from clients can be managed when using Freelance Graphics for Windows.

PREPARING PRESENTATIONS FOR OTHERS

Today, even though we now have tools and computers that are inexpensive enough to be called "personal," the tradition of delegating this work persists. Managers typically have their presentations prepared by staff. Staff members, especially middle-level managers, in turn may contract with professional show producers.

As soon as you begin to prepare graphics for others to present, you encounter a whole range of issues not often discussed in the software texts. For example, your own personal preferences about graphic design are no longer the only guide. You need to have ways of keeping track of styles, palettes, and designs for perhaps a variety of different client groups. Another challenge is the matter of sheer volume. You might need to generate—and keep track of—literally hundreds of slides in a typical work week. For this level of production, you need to find ways of ensuring that the work is efficient, consistent, and correct.

You may also have to be concerned about supervising the work of others when producing separate segments of a large presentation against a pressing deadline.

There's also the issue of charging for your services. It may just be a matter of internal billing—charging your time to a code or project number on your time sheet. Or, you may actually have to track costs and bill them to your client. What's more, graphic design can be very subjective. You need to develop techniques for managing client changes and revisions. In what circumstances are changes chargeable to your client? How can you keep adequate records to justify your charges?

Of course, you'll rarely have to do it all yourself. That is, you can delegate much of the work if you know how. For major presentations, it's likely that you'll be working with some type of graphic-arts service organization. Again, this may be an internal graphic-arts department or an outside production house.

Much of this chapter focuses on dealing with service bureaus for computer graphics. This should be helpful information whether you:

- Contract with service bureaus for film recording or custom art services

- Serve client organizations as a member of a service bureau

- Manage or perform the function of a service bureau as an internal department

A link to service bureaus is actually built into the Freelance Graphics for Windows package. The communication utility ToAGX in the Autographix application provides for transmission of presentation files to Autographix service centers for film recording. As the discussion here points out, film recording is only one aspect of service-bureau operations.

WHAT IS A SERVICE BUREAU?

The term *service bureau* originally described a kind of batch data processing in the 1950s. A client company would send stacks of punched cards containing payroll data to an outside computer service, which would deliver a stack of printed paychecks, usually overnight. This use of outside sources entered the graphics market when data-processing installations began to send archival magnetic tapes to service centers that operated specialized computer-output-microfilm recording.

For the purposes of this discussion, you can regard any graphic-arts production organization—internal or external—as a service bureau. From your vantage point as a user of Freelance Graphics, you are the proprietor of your own operation. As explained in Chapter 14, you have the option of exchanging data and output files with other users and systems. You are, in the show-business sense, a producer. You can contract with these resources for a wide variety of presentation elements. To do this effectively, you should appreciate how the management of graphic-arts production has changed with the introduction of electronic work methods like Freelance Graphics for Windows.

TECHNOSHOCK: MOVING BEYOND MANUAL ART PRODUCTION

Both the suppliers and the users of computer-generated art services are finding their work roles and business relationships changed by the impact of technology. Because electronic graphics can be generated very quickly, graphic artists often suffer from what might be called the Red Adair Syndrome: You get called in only on the really big fires and, once you've done your job, you slip back into obscurity and no one wants to pay your bill! When clients know that you can turn a job around quickly, the lead time collapses. Computer graphics producers are well acquainted with the saying, "If I had wanted it tomorrow, I would have given it to you tomorrow!"

On the other side—from the client or contracting producer's viewpoint—dealing with service bureaus can seem a risky business. It used to be that a client could derive some comfort from reviewing intermediate steps, such as pencil sketches and art boards. Today, traditional mechanical-production functions—along with their comfortable approval steps—have been merged into a bewildering, computerized *zap!* that transforms ideas into finished images. Be aware that, to many of your clients, the process within that brief transformation is still about as understandable, and as fearful, as the most arcane magic.

In short, technology has created, as it often does, a communications gap. The gap exists because participants on both sides have expectations rooted in conventional, manual-production methods. Adapting to new tools means that older notions, rules of thumb—and even what seems like common sense—must be redefined.

THE MARKET FOR SERVICE BUREAUS

Market segments for computer-graphics service bureaus have formed around different communication media, including color slides and overhead transparencies, video, and motion pictures. A specialized area also exists in prepress production for print media, including color separations, page makeup, and platemaking.

Economic incentives for using computer graphics stem from the speed and flexibility provided by digital technology. This flexibility also brings with it a kind of creative freedom. Consistent image quality also means that the haste of production needn't show in the finished product. Rush jobs—even if lacking in art direction—don't have to suffer from mechanical flaws.

Why Use a Service Bureau?

Reasons for turning to outside sources for computer graphics production and support include the following:

Lack of In-House Production Capability

Client companies or small art houses may not have staff or equipment in place for routine production. Contracting with outside sources helps contain costs by isolating expenses for specific jobs.

Short Turnaround and High Volume

Particularly in the slide business, the typical rush job is the annual management meeting for which there may be a dozen presenters and hundreds of slides. The need to present current data and the general difficulty and procrastination of executive speechwriting usually result in extremely compressed production schedules.

For a major meeting, the problem now is not one of production. Computer-graphics techniques are capable of generating these volumes within a few days. Rather, the challenge shifts to *keeping track of changes and revisions.* The ease and flexibility of generating the show on a computer can actually delay the job start, while encouraging last-minute changes. Tracking multiple versions through the production and billing cycles can be a major chore.

In-House Production Overload

Many large companies maintain in-house graphic-arts departments, including computer-graphics services. Quite naturally, their management presses for maximum utilization of equipment and staff. This means that client facilities often are operating at near-peak capacities. An unscheduled job or a rush priority can easily cause an overload that can't be resolved merely by shuffling production schedules. The outside service bureau, then, serves as buffer for this overflow.

In these situations, compatible equipment and procedures can be important in allowing the outside service to pick up in-process work on short notice, and at almost any phase in the production cycle. All the compatibility factors covered in Chapter 14 apply here. If there is no compatibility between your operation and theirs, entire jobs or self-contained job modules must be assigned. For example, each speaker's slides might be a separate module. If modules of a larger presentation are contracted out as individual jobs, costs can be easier to monitor. But some continuity, or consistency in the appearance of the modules, might be sacrificed.

Unique Computer-Generated Effects

There will be times when clients seek computer graphics specifically for unique creative effects. Certainly, this motivation can lead to good use of the medium. However, a pitfall exists in attempting to isolate "computer-suitable" pieces or modules from other project components. One of the advantages of maintaining ongoing style, presentation, and symbol files is the ability to use and reuse art elements and formats. For reasons of economy, then, elements specially created for a given project should be used liberally and spread among as many components as possible. Custom art elements that are not used to their full potential (that is, used in future jobs or allocated among other job costs) can seem unjustifiably expensive. For example, it makes little sense to take the time to draw something as complex as an automobile on the computer if you have no opportunity to reuse it. This is the function of symbols in Freelance Graphics for Windows and one of its main benefits for creating custom artwork inexpensively: The cost-effectiveness of creating these elements increases as you find opportunities to reuse them.

Update Capability or Creative Flexibility

Another valid reason for seeking outside help is the flexibility of maintaining ongoing files that contain predefined styles and reusable images. Graphic-arts professionals can assist in the design of computer-graphics formats, such as Freelance Graphics SmartMaster sets. Designs should adhere to corporate standards for presentations and can be set up well in advance of volume and rush production demands.

Consider that the financial department of a large corporation might be responsible for weekly or monthly presentations to the board of directors. Such a presentation might contain about 20 slides that update key performance criteria. Chart formats can be prepared in advance as pages within fully designed presentations that are simply empty of graph data (or that contain placeholder data). Production becomes a matter of entering data—perhaps directly from spreadsheet files into these presentations. With this scheme, production can adhere to a tight, but easily anticipated, schedule—perhaps between market closings on Friday and the presentation on Monday morning. Creating the presentation in advance eliminates repetitive production work and assures that the presentation can be delivered reliably and consistently.

Art elements, once entered into the system, can be transformed endlessly to support creative experimentation and visualization.

User Training and Support

As increasing numbers of client companies are installing business graphics software, the role of the service bureau is beginning to shift from supplier to support resource. Service bureaus can offer expert training, substitute personnel, and backup equipment and services in case of overflow or emergency, as well as capital-intensive services such as film processing, mass duplication, and custom production effects such as photographic enhancements and opticals.

Market Trends

There was a time, particularly back in the early 1970s, when computer-graphics service bureaus enjoyed a seller's market. The high cost of operating specialized equipment and maintaining round-the-clock staffing seemed prohibitive to client companies. The choice of suppliers remained relatively small, dominated primarily by minicomputer-based systems from Genigraphics and Dicomed. Few entrepreneurs had both the intestinal fortitude and the capital to take what seemed like a major business risk. Company-owned stores and franchises, quite understandably, did not set up competition for themselves in major metropolitan markets.

In the mid-1970s, the appearance of satellite workstations equipped with data-communication capabilities for remote film recording marked the first major shift in the service-bureau business. Although slowly at first, end users began to take greater control of the creation and input processes.

Today, tools like Freelance Graphics for Windows are in widespread use at client companies. Tremendous capability is in the hands of the people who actually use slides. However, as early chapters of this book emphasize, designing effective charts is not just a matter of entering data into a computer. At minimum, there's a learning curve to be traversed. Just as users often need professional support for computer hardware and software problems, they must also be able to call on professional artists and graphic designers. Service bureaus are also beginning to see such support as a way of maintaining ongoing relationships when their customers move toward in-house computer-graphics production.

Increasingly, desktop film recorders can generate slide images that approach the output of larger systems in resolution and quality. Reasons to turn to a service bureau today can have more to do with high-volume production requirements and creative support. However, no matter how inexpensive computer systems become, by far the most significant cost will always be the skilled labor of people. So, as businesses attempt to control human-resource costs, they have further motivation for contracting out graphic-arts production.

These trends are most visible in the market for business slides. But similar trends toward desktop systems can be seen in the video and motion-picture market segments, as well.

In response to these trends, service organizations should renew their emphasis on such time-honored values as creativity and customer service.

INSIDE THE SERVICE BUREAU

Consider how the perspective shifts when you look at the service bureau from the inside. Its internal organization bears directly on the crucial issue of customer service.

Project Managers and Clients

Service-bureau organization centers around the key relationship between the client and the project manager. The project manager is the person who takes responsibility for the job—both its creative qualities and its performance. The project manager directs the activities of creative and production staff. The project-management function may be served by an account executive, a creative director, or some other senior member of creative staff. Not all these job combinations are ideal, but it is important to realize that *someone* involved with the job always serves that function, whether or not it is assigned explicitly.

It might seem obvious who the client is—the person who initiates and assigns a production job. However, people involved in the production process often make incorrect assumptions about the role and the identity of the client. It is important to distinguish between clients and users. A client is the one to whom a bill will be rendered. Clients often are acting as agents for end users. In turn, users have audiences that may represent many different needs, tastes, and preferences.

Confusion often results from assuming that there is a single, all-knowing client whose decisions are unequivocal and final. To the contrary, client directives most often are developed by consensus and are subject to change at any time. This distinction is critical in computer graphics because new work methods are needed for managing changes. Project managers should attempt to secure commitment about all production details from a designated client representative. However, computer-graphics methods, by themselves, *stimulate* change.

Client representatives should be forthright with their suppliers about what specific job-approval steps will be needed in their own organizations. If there are any questions, the representative's scope of authority should be clarified before the job is begun. This is a necessary first step in the job-preparation process.

Clients and project managers also need to develop ways of managing the uncertain elements in the production process. By com-

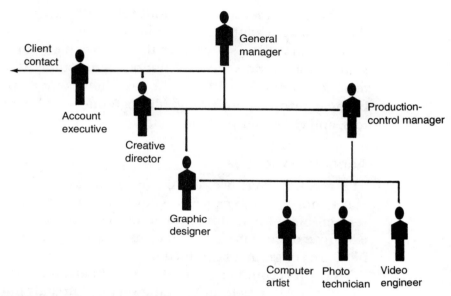

FIGURE 15-2. Common service-bureau organization

pressing time schedules and eliminating manual steps, computer-graphics methods can contribute to a sense of uncertainty. The primary tool for dealing with uncertainty is organization.

Key Players and Functions

Although organizations within service bureaus can differ considerably, the following job functions can be found in most shops (refer to Figure 15-2):

- Account executive
- Creative director
- Graphic designer
- Computer artist
- Production-control manager
- Photographic laboratory technician
- Video-systems engineer

These are the most commonly encountered job categories on the permanent staff. Some combination of these functions will be found in most shops—whether the creative medium is color slides, print graphics, videotape, or motion-picture film. According to the technical requirements of the medium, other specialists may become involved, including photographers, video-systems operators, and computer programmers.

Account Executive

The account executive, or AE, functions as the client's agent. In many shops, this person is a sales representative with bottom-line responsibility for multiple accounts. The expertise of an account executive often is in the client's business area rather than in a technical area of graphics production.

A good account executive has a split personality: In front of the client, the AE tries to uphold the service bureau's interests. When dealing with internal staff, however, the AE is the client's representative. Performed properly, these are extremely difficult roles; the AE risks being everyone's antagonist.

Too often, however, some AEs have the roles exactly reversed. That is, whether you are a client or a member of a production staff, they tell you only what you want to hear. You should develop a healthy caution for this approach. Clients and staff members alike can be deceived: If an AE consistently tells you that the other party is being unfair or is inefficient, you have to wonder what picture is being painted to that person of you or your organization. In short, perhaps nobody is getting the truth.

In other shops, especially in small production companies, the AE function is performed by a senior member of the creative staff. Many clients prefer this relationship and feel that more direct communication is established with the people who actually do the work. Bear in mind, however, that such a relationship can cause a confusion of roles. Instead, by remaining detached from the fury of production, a good AE can be a valuable and objective client advocate.

Some shops, large and small, involve the AE as an ad hoc project manager. The rationale is that a knowledgeable AE is best qualified to manage an acceptable job on the client's behalf. However, the AE who plays the dual-advocate role described above will have trouble directing project details. A project manager needs to enlist the full support, energies, and enthusiasm of the creative staff. This crucial role often is assigned to a senior member of the production team, such as the creative director.

Creative Director

The basic functions of a creative director are conceptualization and job setup. Creative directors are senior members of the creative staff. They may once have worked as artists or other production specialists. Ideally, they have hands-on experience with computer-graphics tools and understand completely the capabilities and technical requirements of designing for these production methods. Perhaps most important, they must be expert visualizers and communicators. A creative director's real value and expertise lies in knowing how to deliver business messages effectively. All other talents and skills are secondary. This is one aspect of the process that is not affected by the use of computerized production techniques.

Creative directors, then, are advocates of the client's business message—but not necessarily of the client's business relationship with the service bureau. Again, a confusion of roles can result if a creative director also has to function as the AE. Day-to-day client contact is time consuming and can focus as much on securing agreements and commitments as it does on defining project objectives. Thus, the creative director's ongoing attention to the project itself can suffer if primary client-contact responsibilities also are assumed.

Graphic Designer

As a senior member of the creative staff, the graphic designer translates creative concepts into sketches, or storyboards, to be executed by production staff. The importance of storyboards in job setup is discussed later in this chapter.

To design computer-generated art and effects, a graphic designer should have both hands-on and technical experience with digital production tools. The designer must be able to visualize accurately the fully executed version of the preliminary storyboard or sketch. Major production difficulties, cost overruns, and client misunderstandings can result if it is found that the design as conceived is not feasible or practical for rendering by computer. On the other hand, a thorough familiarity with the computer-graphics medium is needed to take full advantage of its unique effects.

Designers should have this technical knowledge so that they can code their storyboards correctly for specific colors and effects. Each computer-graphics production system has its own coding schemes for documenting production work. In the case of Freelance Graphics for Windows, this means a thorough familiarity with a wide variety of color palettes and styles.

Accurate previsualization of computer-generated charts and images promotes efficient production and is a primary means of cost control. In some shops, most of the responsibility rests with the graphic designer. Computer artists must execute the designs exactly. In other situations, production staff has some latitude to modify or enhance the design.

Computer Artist

The computer artist is a specialist in operating systems like Freelance Graphics for Windows. Like the graphic designer, the computer artist must understand the medium thoroughly. There are both creative and technical aspects to this job. Also, the skills needed to control the computer system itself vary from one type of production to another. At one extreme, the computer is a sophisticated electronic sketchpad. At the other, it is a geometric-modeling tool that needs high-level programming. Most computer artists have conventional art and design backgrounds, and some have had training in engineering drafting. Artists and technicians who work with simulation, as for producing motion-picture effects, also may need some programming skills.

An important decision in directing the work of computer artists is knowing how much creative latitude or experimentation should be encouraged. There is a basic trade-off here between cost and innovation. On large-scale systems, experimentation can be expensive. The degree of experimentation that can be permitted with storyboards depends on both the type of project and the cost overhead of the computer installation.

There's a real opportunity here for the innovative application of Freelance Graphics for Windows. Even for major business meetings, charts can be prepared with this program on microcomputers, perhaps even by the client's office staff. Presentation files can be transferred to similar PC systems within the service bureau. Low-cost experimentation with colors, fonts, shaded effects, and symbols can be done at this stage. At this point, the files might also be imported to high-end systems for enhancement, including special effects. Final output will be on the service bureau's high-resolution, high-volume film recorder.

A related question is, What specialized capabilities are offered by service bureaus that might be difficult or expensive to provide in-house? For example, different outside producers may offer:

- High-resolution digital effects, including scanned product photography, show graphics, and electronic retouching (for accuracy of product color), for merging with color slides
- Photo-optical effects involving multiple exposures of live photography with computer-generated graphics
- Animation
- Instructional design of interactive shows (SmartShows)
- Management of large business meetings and theatrical production
- Design, management, and production of ongoing corporate training programs, in a variety of media
- Volume production and distribution, even on short notice

Especially in shops that handle high production volumes, there can be extreme pressure on computer artists to turn out the work as fast as possible, almost by rote. Some managers have tried to impose various types of production incentives—piece rates, for example. The pitfall is that it becomes difficult to classify and quantify units of production uniformly and fairly. A workable incentive system would need to measure complexity and difficulty, as well as gross volume. In practical terms, someone—either a graphic designer or a senior computer artist—is going to have to weigh each piece or job segment according to these factors before it is assigned for production. The potential friction—both creative and political—among members of production staff is usually counterproductive.

By training and by creative bent, computer artists are not assembly-line workers. The real key to a productive shop lies in maintaining high morale under demanding work schedules. For artists, this means having enough mental stimulation and creative freedom to promote interest and enthusiasm. Thus experimentation, within limits, can actually stimulate productivity.

Production-Control Manager

In large, high-volume service bureaus, a separate function assigns job segments, develops production schedules, monitors and coordinates work flow, and provides quality control. In many ways, this is as traditional a production-management function as might be found in any manufacturing plant.

Production control is not—and should not be—involved in the uncertainties of the creative process. The production-control manager, therefore, does not fulfill the function of project manager. Project management involves making creative decisions with, or on behalf of, the client. Production-control managers, on the other hand, are charged with controlling time, costs, and quality.

In relatively small operations, an account executive or a senior member of the creative staff may serve as both project and production-control manager. However, this situation is not ideal. Wherever possible, coordination should be done by people who are not directly involved in the production work. Cooperation of multiple disciplines and departments, as well as production efficiency, are best achieved if production control is a separate and autonomous job function.

Photographic Laboratory Technician

Operations that rely on film-based technology, such as color slide and motion-picture production, have to cope with the technical constraints of film processing. To handle large production volumes, having an in-house photographic-processing operation is essential. Small production houses may try to handle large-volume jobs by maintaining close working relationships with commercial laboratories, but this strategy can have a competitive disadvantage.

Potential clients should understand the importance of in-house photo processing to computer-graphics production. The reasons have to do with quality and timeliness.

Film output from computer-graphics systems is produced by digital color-film recorders. The technical characteristics of this output are quite different from that of live photography. (Recall the anecdote in Chapter 13 about the difficulty of meeting this requirement in a commercial laboratory.) Photographic processing involves complex chemistry that can vary within a relatively wide range (at least, in comparison with the precision of computer colors). Commercial photo labs adjust this chemical mix to suit the discerning eyes of their customers, who are concerned primarily with flesh tones and the color of the sky. This set of choices, or color balance, does not always produce the best rendering of synthetic, computer-generated colors.

Photo technicians in computer-graphic service bureaus therefore must be accomplished photochemists. They must know how to monitor the performance of both film-processing equipment and computer-film recorders—and to adjust one to the other, if necessary. They must know photography, photographic special effects (opticals), and not just a little about computers.

Added to these job requirements are the demands of time. Another compelling rationale for the in-house photo lab is that there usually is not enough time to send exposed film stock out of the shop for processing. One of the realities of computer-graphics production is that film-processing cycles take a fixed amount of time. In a job that involves multiple steps—such as compositing live photography with graphics—there might be some slippage of the schedule from one step to the next. If a job is running behind schedule for any reason, there are often ways of doubling up staff or stacking operations to shorten those steps. There are no shortcuts, though, for the film-recording process or film processing. Photo-optical effects, if needed, can involve multiple steps and film-processing runs, and cannot be rushed.

If there is any slippage at all during any production step, the photo lab will be subjected to additional time pressures and scheduling constraints. Photographic effects and processing usually are among the final steps in the production cycle. The result is that the photo lab is almost always operating under critical deadlines.

Everyone involved in the production cycle—clients, project managers and schedulers, and production staff—should be aware of the time constraints imposed by photographic processes.

An alternative for compositing is to scan the photo digitally and to handle the whole process within the computer. However, relatively expensive high-resolution equipment will be required to match the quality of live photography. The photo can then be incorporated as a bitmap in the presentation file. Some film recorders can handle both vector and bitmap imagery.

Video-Systems Engineer

Video-systems engineers maintain and operate the equipment used for pre- and postproduction steps for computer-generated or computer-enhanced video.

The combination of video technology with computer graphics presents some challenges. As discussed in previous chapters, computer-generated images, film images, and video images all have distinctly different technical characteristics, production constraints, and creative capabilities. Further, the three technical disciplines have developed pretty much in parallel. Each has its own standard practices, professional societies, and trade jargon. It is rare to find artists or technicians who feel totally comfortable in all three areas.

The responsibility for coordinating these disciplines rests with project managers, creative directors, and graphic designers. People who are guiding the project or job must have enough experience in each area to know the requirements and constraints of each output medium.

Service-Bureau Organization

There are two basic approaches to service-bureau organization:

- Task-force approach
- Job-shop approach

The type of organization in the service bureau will determine the pattern of work flow and also can have significant effects on costs, schedule, and quality. Also vitally important, the type of organization can determine the responsiveness of the production group to changes.

Task-Force Organization

A task-force approach (Figure 15-3) is typical of small production operations. There is no formal organization until a project is assigned. When a job comes into the house, management assigns a project team from the pool of specialists available. One of the members of the team serves as project manager.

Some large organizations also form project teams to handle specific jobs or contracts. Team members are chosen according to the specialized areas of expertise needed to guide the job through the shop. Project team members then contract with their own internal, in-place departments (such as the photo lab) for job segments. Team organization lasts only as long as the duration of the job or

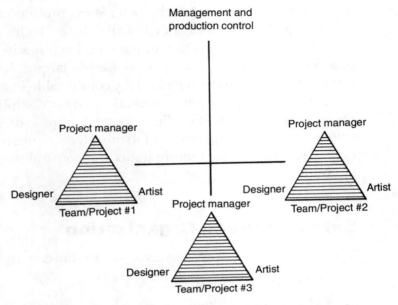

FIGURE 15-3. Task-force approach to organization within a service bureau

contract. Many aerospace companies and advertising agencies are organized this way.

An advantage of the task-force approach is flexibility. The approach is adaptive: The project team is constituted to suit the specific requirements of the job. However, flexibility can also mean lack of needed organization, especially if the team members aren't used to working with one another. A parody of the task-force approach might be, "If the boss calls, get her name."

Job-Shop Organization

By contrast, the telling comment in a job shop is, "Sorry, that's not my department." High-volume service bureaus usually are organized as job shops, as shown in Figure 15-4. In this organization, the main creative and production functions are set up as separate departments, with oversight by production control.

Work flow is triggered by a job ticket, or work order. (An example is shown in Figure 15-5.) This is a multipart form with one copy

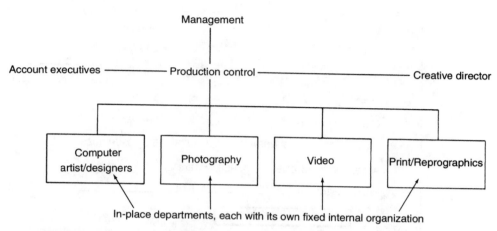

FIGURE 15-4. Job-shop approach to organization within a service bureau

for each department. The creative director or project manager, having met with the account executive and the client, records detailed job instructions on the form. The form accompanies the client's input documentation to production control. There, the parts are separated by department, and work is assigned according to a schedule that will bring major job segments or pieces together at appropriate intervals.

Control versus Creativity?

To the client, the importance of these methods of organization lies in a key trade-off between creativity and control. The task-force approach emphasizes creativity in providing for flexibility and experimentation. Work relationships and patterns are not predetermined but are assigned according to unique job requirements. Task-force organization is highly adaptable to change.

Of course, it can seem as though each job attempts to reinvent the wheel. For high-volume production, this type of approach can be chaotic. Thus, the task-force approach often is appropriate for custom jobs with special creative or technical requirements.

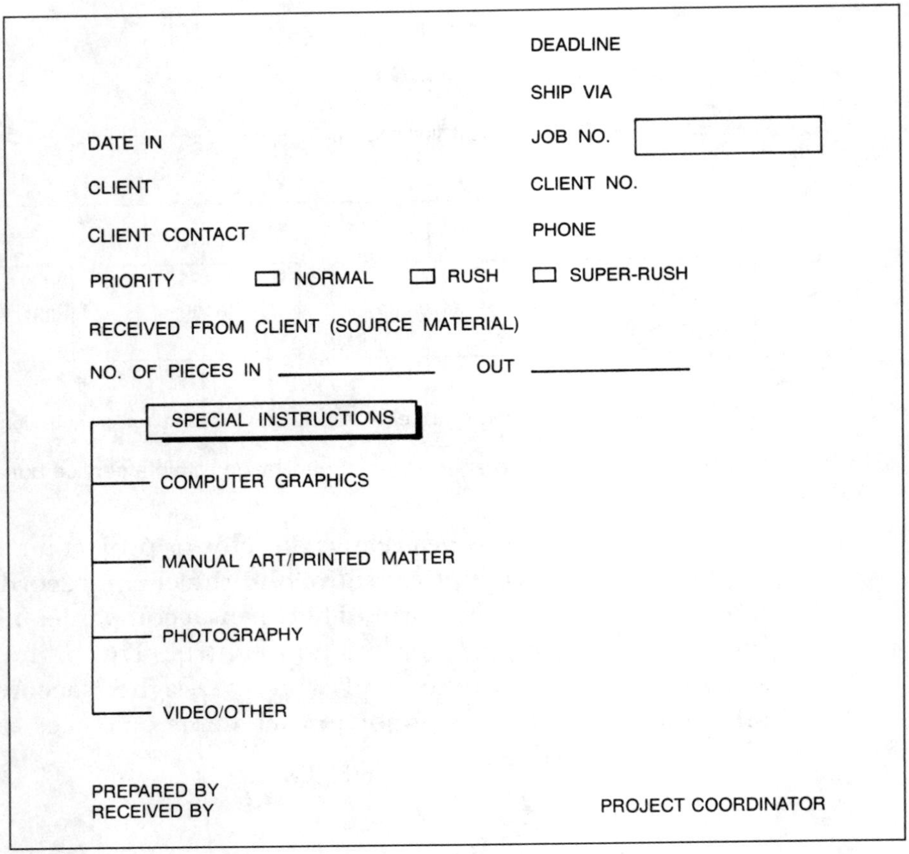
DEADLINE
SHIP VIA
DATE IN
JOB NO.
CLIENT
CLIENT NO.
CLIENT CONTACT
PHONE
PRIORITY ☐ NORMAL ☐ RUSH ☐ SUPER-RUSH
RECEIVED FROM CLIENT (SOURCE MATERIAL)
NO. OF PIECES IN ____________ OUT ____________
SPECIAL INSTRUCTIONS
COMPUTER GRAPHICS
MANUAL ART/PRINTED MATTER
PHOTOGRAPHY
VIDEO/OTHER
PREPARED BY
RECEIVED BY
PROJECT COORDINATOR

FIGURE 15-5. The job ticket is often used when a service bureau uses the job-shop approach to organization.

A job-shop approach trades flexibility for predictability. In effect, a job shop is a set of parallel assembly lines, each with a different graphic-arts specialty. With an efficient, in-place organization, costs and schedules can be tightly controlled. This process assumes that all creative elements can be predefined in job instructions and explicit designs. Accordingly, this approach tends to discourage the evaluation of alternative creative solutions during the production process. This approach resists change.

The ideal organization would provide flexibility under demanding, high-volume conditions. An emerging approach, in business in

Departments

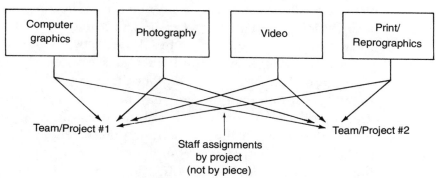

FIGURE 15-6. The task-force approach in a service bureau that is also organized as a job shop can provide both flexibility and predictability.

general as well as in computer graphics, is to organize project teams, or task forces, *within* job shops (Figure 15-6). Team members are drawn from departments based on job requirements. Departments take direction from their counterparts on the team. The project manager, the coordinating member of the team, is responsible for communication with production control, as well as with the account executive and client.

JOB PREPARATION AND SETUP

The speed and economy of using computer graphics results from the elimination of multiple, mechanical production steps. In manual production, client approvals can be sought at each step. Thus, the realization of the finished product is developed predictably, and slowly. Changes and modifications are difficult and time consuming, but this very difficulty imposes seriousness on the approvals. The most fundamental change in the client-supplier relationship in computer graphics is that the production process proceeds directly from concept to completion in a single, intangible step.

The key to controlling costs in this environment—and the paradox of computer-graphics production—is to secure detailed agreement about what is to be produced before it ever exists. Most people, especially those without art or communication backgrounds, have difficulty visualizing a finished product from verbal descriptions or even from rough sketches. Indeed, two people can imagine widely different things from identical descriptions. This situation is made more challenging by the fact that people who do not work directly in computer graphics may be unfamiliar with its unique effects. The creative director or graphic designer may be faced with the problem of describing something that the client has never seen!

The need to visualize a computer graphics project before production poses another trade-off: client- and staff-time versus computer time. One of the motivations for using a computer is to eliminate time-consuming manual labor. If the rationale of visualizing everything completely were carried to the extreme, every frame of a production would be rendered first in detailed storyboards. At some point, however, this manual process begins to erode the advantages of using the computer at all.

Also, if there's a need to experiment and to develop new effects, it can't be addressed by a conventional storyboard. The cost of system time also is a factor: The more costly the computer time, the greater the justification for manual preproduction work.

Differences among Production Media

The importance of these factors varies for each project and for each type of production. Different work patterns exist for slide, video, and motion-picture projects.

Slide Production

The cost of systems like Freelance Graphics for high-quality slide production has come down considerably in the last decade. At the same time, the salaries of creative directors and graphic designers have continued to rise. Today, the cost of a carefully executed storyboard might actually exceed the production cost with a computer. The practice in this field has been to execute rough, pencil sketches (often called thumbnails), which then are reviewed, approved, and coded for production. Much preparation effort, however, is devoted to designing and securing agreement on global production values—fonts, colors, themes, logo designs, and so on. The ability to change individual slides and slide elements selectively also means that changes and revisions after initial production can be relatively inexpensive. This represents a major difference from conventional, manual work methods.

Video Production

Video production presents a completely different set of assumptions. Video presentations rely on motion, and often on special effects. From the standpoint of production planning, for example, it may be necessary to treat a Screen Show in Freelance Graphics as a video presentation rather than a sequence of slides.

In commercial television, especially, demand is high for novelty and excitement. This result can be achieved only through experimentation. Computer-graphics techniques in this field center on limited experimentation with relatively simple test objects and motions rather than with fully rendered scenes and sequences. Once the desired effect is found, a fairly finished storyboard (called a *comp* or *semi-comp*) is prepared for client approval. This storyboard attempts to capture the digital effects as closely as possible. Upon approval of the storyboard, the scene is generated and reviewed. At this point, some fine tuning usually is required in another computer session. Postproduction steps also may merge the computer graphics with live-action scenes.

Unlike slide production, the emphasis in video is not on volume but on complexity within a relatively short running time. A more analogous situation is cartoon animation, in which digital techniques may be used to assist character drawing, *in-betweening* (generating motion), and *ink-and-paint* (coloring).

In such cases, the objective is to make efficient use of the time of skilled animators and production staff, and also to compress calendar time to finished product.

Motion Picture

The sophistication and extremely high resolution and detail of computer graphics for motion pictures (as opposed to lower-resolution video) requires considerable computing overhead. Work typically involves simulation of solids in 3-D. Accordingly, system time for motion picture work is much more expensive than the staff time needed for preparation of comprehensive storyboards. Although high-end workstations are now making it possible to automate some of the preproduction steps, the practice in this field has been to go through several iterations of storyboards before any mainframe computer time is spent. Storyboards often are executed with painstaking airbrush work to convey the effects that will be rendered. Computer tests of new effects are performed on relatively simple objects already in the computer database. Scenes are digitized first as monochrome, *wire-cage* (outline) drawings. After approval, movements are planned and executed in wire-cage form. After another approval step, full-color scenes are computed and recorded on film. (Even with the largest computers, it might take minutes to calculate a single frame—days to output just a few seconds of finished animation.) Changes at each step are approached with extreme caution, with full awareness of the cost impacts.

In the motion-picture field, work methods still follow a multistep process to conserve valuable system time. As computation of complex scenes becomes less expensive and more efficient, it can be expected that many of the manual steps in those production cycles will also disappear. For example, video animation can now be produced very cost-effectively on workstations.

Preparing a Job for Assignment to a Production House

Job setup is a responsibility shared among the client, the account executive, and the project manager. In many cases, much of the client's part of the work should be done before the job is assigned to the service bureau.

Planning and organizing a job for submission to a service bureau is strongly affected by the intention to use computer graphics. Again, assumptions based on mechanical production technology do not necessarily apply. If job preparation anticipates the actual work and approval process, the chances are much better for containing costs, adhering to production schedules, and enhancing quality.

As pointed out previously, a major reason for turning to computer graphics is lack of time. The ability to compress the production cycle through application of computers encourages the submission of high-priority, rush jobs. The client, therefore, may be under extreme time pressures before the supplier even knows that a job exists. However, clients who have become familiar with computer graphics, in anticipating short turnarounds, often forget that manual processes and approval steps remaining in the production cycle cannot be compressed proportionately. For example, regardless of the production methods used, it will still take time to gather source data, to obtain agreements on designs, to wait for photo processing, and so on. Therefore, a primary rule of planning a job should be to *schedule adequate time for tasks that are not computerized.*

Clients faced with rush jobs often make another tactical error: They choose to wait to assign the job until all source data and production parameters are obtained or known. Although the data (charting input, product prices, product configurations, and so forth) may be the most important elements from the client's point of view, these factors actually may be the least relevant from the standpoints of production planning and budgeting. This is especially true of computer graphics, in which global design parameters and formats such as chart templates can be built more or less independently of specific data content.

A project for which important data are not known presents a scheduling challenge. The client, working with the project manager, must determine the point during the production cycle at which the missing input becomes critical. Contingencies can be built in, based on anticipated data ranges or values.

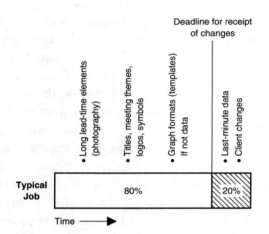

FIGURE 15-7. The 80–20 rule for production planning

In practice, most jobs conform to an 80–20 rule: Roughly 80 percent of the elements of even a last-minute job can be planned and specified in advance. Until a predetermined cutoff in the production cycle is reached, the project will have to deal with the uncertainty of the remaining 20 percent (Figure 15-7).

A basic rule of management applies equally to preparations by the client and by the supplier: *Good organization overcomes; poor organization succumbs.* Failing to deal adequately with that up-front 80 percent inevitably throws a project into crisis mode almost from the outset. The accelerated production cycles of computer graphics can actually aggravate this problem.

Another assumption that must be changed in order to make the best use of computer-based production has to do with job complexity. Common sense might argue that it will be most economical to job out only the most complex portions of a project. In today's environment, however, partitioning job segments between computer-based and manual methods can complicate the production process unnecessarily and can introduce inefficiencies, production delays, and higher costs. The complex portions of a computer-graphics project (such as the generation of company logos) need to be used as extensively as possible for best economy. Once an image exists in the database (as a symbol, for example), it is inefficient not to reuse it as often as possible. In effect, the less-complex portions of the job can come along for the ride and can benefit from the inherent efficiencies and control offered by all-electronic methods. If possible, doing a job entirely on the computer minimizes coordination of the more cumbersome mechanical operations.

The emphasis here on job preparation can be misleading. You might assume that, if it were possible to specify a job completely on input, everyone would benefit. From cost- and production-management standpoints, this might well be true. But the more that aspects of the show depend on experimentation and innovation, the less these elements can be planned. It might be best to include them in the uncertain 20 percent and to count on some midcourse corrections to the project plan.

In production planning, it is less important to know the specifics of a change than to anticipate when change might occur. It is unrealistic to assume that, even with careful planning, the job will be completely satisfactory as originally conceived. (Again, the client is not a single voice, but a consensus of many.) With computer techniques, *the content of the change often is less cost-critical than the timing of the change relative to the production cycle.* Careful planning can anticipate revision schedules, and the impact can be budgeted within the uncertain 20 percent.

Avoiding the Rush

An overwhelming reason for doing careful production planning and job setup is to avoid unnecessary rush charges. Service bureaus typically have tiered pricing structures based on turnaround time. For example, price and service options include normal service of perhaps 48 hours, rush service overnight, and super-rush service the same day. Significant surcharges apply at each level of urgency. Without proper planning for a major show, you could find yourself in perpetual super-rush mode, struggling to catch up.

Here's the main application of the 80–20 rule: Put as many elements as possible into production as early as a possible. In the case of Freelance Graphics for Windows, templates and symbols especially can be created in advance of receiving the data.

Establish intermediate deadlines with your own internal clients (data processors and other information providers) for last-minute input. Build time into the production schedule so that as much of this work as possible can be produced without paying a premium.

As a producer, your control of the situation may actually depend on how well you communicate the cost impact of client decisions. You may feel that you're at the mercy of their procrastination because you can't produce the charts if they don't give you the data. However, it becomes a strong incentive for even the most reluctant top executive when you make the point that waiting past a certain date will incur a cost premium of perhaps 100 or 200 percent. If you want to be able to justify these charges later, the point should be made before, not after, that date. If you don't have a production schedule and aren't aware of the impact of delays, it's likely that the dates will slip and the client will try to hold you accountable for the extra cost.

Assume also that there will be a fair number of revisions, for matters of taste as well as correctness. It's all very well to advise your clients that changes can't or shouldn't be made after a certain point—but they'll end up demanding some anyway. Provide a place for these changes in your very first project schedule.

Finally, rest assured that, despite your best efforts to minimize last-minute changes, they will arise anyway. Deadlines for receipt of data are subject to slippage. This is inherent in the business reason for the meeting itself: You can't present information that the audience knows is outdated. For example, if your audience follows the news and the financial markets take an unexpected turn, you can't be caught showing last week's results. The only solution is to prepare a schedule and budget that include a certain percentage of super-rush revisions. As a rule of thumb, you can expect that roughly a third of the slides in a major presentation will have to be altered at least once before the show date—and not necessarily because the people who prepared the graphics did anything wrong!

Rather, the revisions come about because the flexibility and speed of computer-based production *stimulate* change, experimentation, and innovation. It might be wiser, therefore, to anticipate, track, and direct change than to try preventing it.

Applying Freelance Graphics for Windows

P
A
R
T

I
V

C hapters 16 through 20 present case examples illustrating specific business situations. Covered are reports and newsletters, financial briefings (including spreadsheet conversion), speeches, interactive shows, and presentations for large annual meetings.

CHAPTER 16

DESIGNING FOR PRINT MEDIA

T his chapter presents some examples of Freelance Graphics for Windows applied to desktop publishing. Applications include:

- Manual forms
- Flyers
- Meeting handouts

DESIGNING A MANUAL FORM

A *manual form* is a preprinted questionnaire that can be inserted into a typewriter or filled in by hand. An example is shown in Figure 16-1.

Here are a few tips for making such a form in Freelance Graphics for Windows.

Printer and Page Setup

Select portrait orientation for your printer by performing File➤Printer Setup➤Setup. Also, be sure that the Paper Size setting matches the sheet size of the paper stock you will be using.

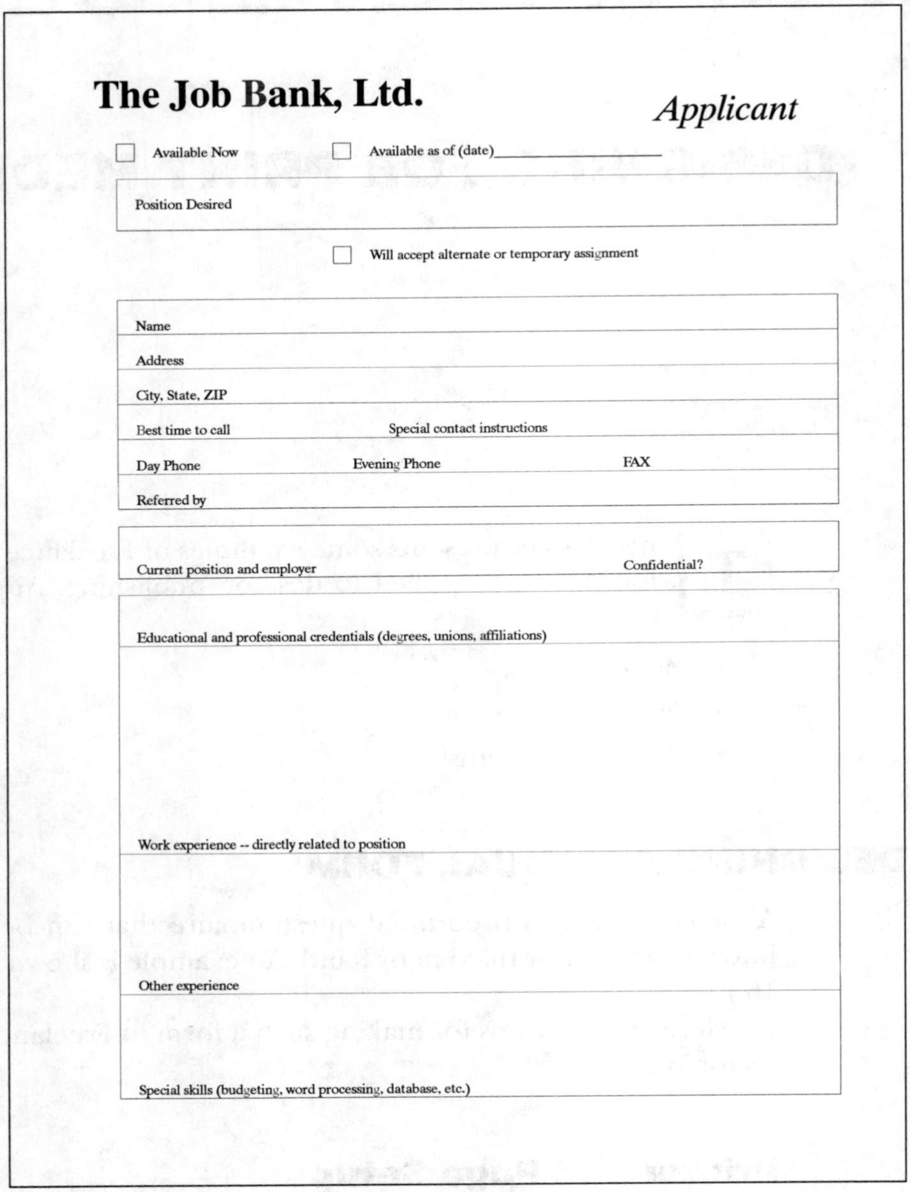

The Job Bank, Ltd.

Applicant

☐ Available Now   ☐ Available as of (date)_____

Position Desired

☐ Will accept alternate or temporary assignment

Name

Address

City, State, ZIP

Best time to call   Special contact instructions

Day Phone   Evening Phone   FAX

Referred by

Current position and employer   Confidential?

Educational and professional credentials (degrees, unions, affiliations)

Work experience -- directly related to position

Other experience

Special skills (budgeting, word processing, database, etc.)

FIGURE 16-1. This form has vertical spacing of six lines to the inch to match type-writers and computer-character printers.

Notice in Figure 16-1 that the form extends almost to the edges of the sheet. Remember, however, that the printable area can vary from one model of printer to another. For example, on some printers, you must leave a margin of at least 0.5 inch on all sides of the page. To make sure that your drawing stays within the printable area, select View➤View Preferences and set the Printable Area option button. When you select OK to close the dialog box, the printable area will be shown as a dotted line in the drawing area.

TIP *Don't confuse the printable area with page margins. The printable area for a specific printer and page size is fixed in its extent, and depends on the capabilities of the printer driver. Margin settings can be defined by you anywhere within the printable area.*

Change File➤Page Setup to portrait orientation, as well. If you want to be able to extend the drawing to the edges of the printable area, make no changes to the Margins settings in the File Page Setup dialog box.

Grid and Rulers

As an aid to laying out the form, turn the grid and rulers on in the Current Page view. Activate the grid by selecting View➤Units & Grids. The Units & Grids dialog box will open, as shown in Figure 16-2. If you will be printing on standard 8.5-inch by 11-inch letter paper, set Units to Inches. This setting controls not only the spacing of grid points but also the markings on drawing and text rulers. In the Grids section of the dialog box, select both check boxes: Display Grid and Snap To Grid.

Also in this dialog box, type the value **0.17** in both the Horizontal and Vertical Space text boxes. This value assures that the spacing of ruled lines and text on the form will be six lines to the inch, which is the usual spacing on typewriters and character printers. Setting the Horizontal Space value to the same number will make the grid square and simplify measurements.

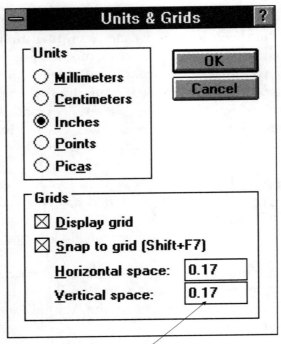

6 lines/inch typewriter spacing

FIGURE 16-2. This dialog box appears when you select View➤Units & Grids.

If you prefer to set Units to Picas, you can specify the correct spacing of six lines to the inch by setting both Horizontal and Vertical Spacing to 2.

The main reason for turning Snap on is to constrain ruled lines that you draw on the form with the Line tool. Snapping will also assist in the placement of text boxes for labels on the form.

Select OK to close the Units & Grids dialog box.

Turning the drawing rulers on also will help you lay out the form within the dimensions of the printed page. Select View➤View Preferences➤Drawing Ruler. You may also wish to select the Big

Crosshair option so that the location of the pointer in the drawing area is more clearly highlighted on each ruler. Select OK to close the dialog box.

Drawing Ruled Lines

In general, draw the lines first. Perform View≻Zoom In (or use the Zoom In tool) to work more closely on the form, as shown in Figure 16-3. It can be helpful to sketch the form first so that you know about how much space you want to allow for each item.

Units

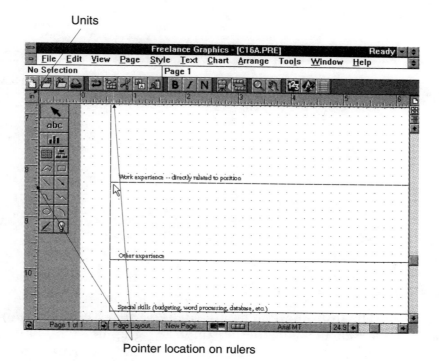

Pointer location on rulers

FIGURE 16-3. The Zoom feature has been used here in the Current Page view to magnify the form for close work.

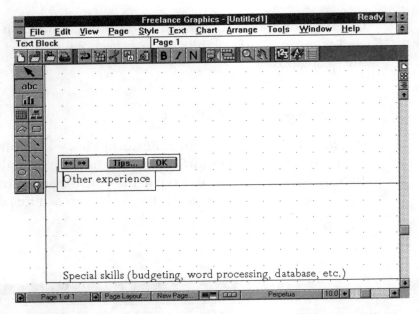

FIGURE 16-4. Box labels are created with the Text tool using Left Justification and snapping the text blocks to grid points.

Text

Use the Text tool to add item descriptions to the boxes you've drawn with the Line tool (see Figure 16-4). If Snap remains on, text blocks will be aligned on the nearest grid point. For most purposes, use Left Justification, which is the default setting.

CREATING A FLYER

The flyer shown in Figures 16-5 and 16-6 is a good example of a text layout that includes an imported graphic (the map). The procedures described here can also be used for other printed output that incorporates graphics, including title pages of reports.

Printable area   Fold

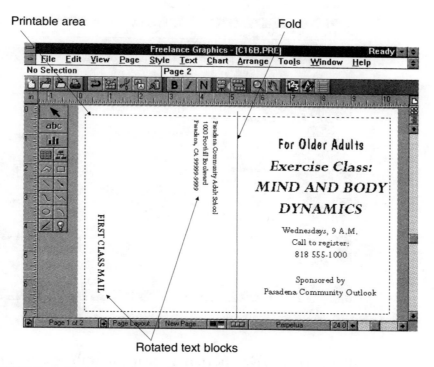

Rotated text blocks

FIGURE 16-5.   Page one of a two-sided master for a printed flyer that will be folded

Layout

The flyer was created as two pages within a presentation for which landscape orientation was specified in File➤Page Setup and File➤Printer Setup➤Setup.

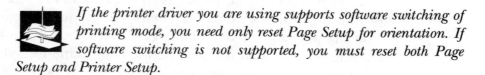

If the printer driver you are using supports software switching of printing mode, you need only reset Page Setup for orientation. If software switching is not supported, you must reset both Page Setup and Printer Setup.

Each of the pages is a master for the two-sided printing job. The flyer is designed to be folded so that the piece becomes a self-mailer.

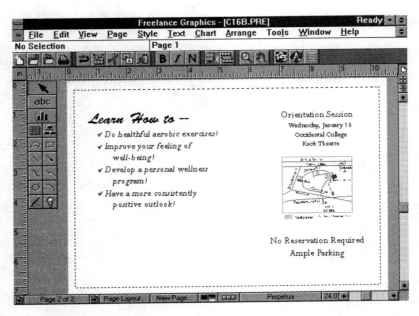

FIGURE 16-6. Page two of the master for the flyer

It is particularly important here to know the exact dimensions of the printable area. (As described previously, turn this feature on by selecting View➤View Preferences➤Printable Area.) When the piece is folded, the images should be centered on each page. To check the composition, several tests were printed, then physical measurements were made on the output for any required adjustments. Turning on the drawing rulers made it possible to match the adjustments exactly in the Current Page view.

As when designing forms, it was very helpful here to use the grid and drawing rulers so that the composition could be controlled within the printable area of the page. However, much of the time Snap had to be turned off because the composition needed to be fluid, rather than constrained to specific points on the grid. For example, Snap would have been particularly bothersome when working on the map labels. You can toggle Snap on and off while you are drawing by pressing Shift-F7.

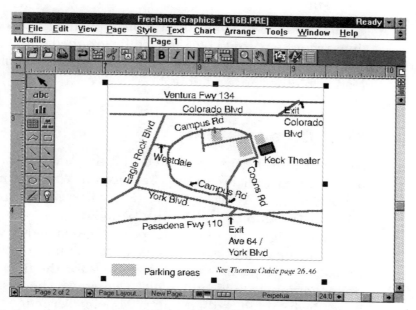

FIGURE 16-7. Zoomed view of the map graphic in the flyer

Line Art

Figure 16-7 shows a zoomed view of the flyer's line art in the Current Page view. The map was an existing piece of electronic art created in another Windows application and brought into Freelance Graphics through the Clipboard. (Perform Edit≻Copy in the source application and Edit≻Paste in Freelance Graphics.) However, a similar graphic could have been created from scratch within Freelance Graphics by using the Line, Text, and Rectangle tools. In some cases, it would necessary to use the Arrange≻Rotate command on text labels.

When the map was pasted into Freelance Graphics, it appeared as a group (metafile object) surrounded by a single set of handles. It was then sized and moved within the drawing area to adjust the page composition. If the graphic had been created in Freelance Graphics, it would have been necessary to combine the objects in a group (Arrange➤Group) prior to manipulating it this way. Another time-saving step would be to select the grouped object and perform Tools➤Add to Symbol Library so that the map could be reused readily in other presentations.

Text Composition

All the text in the flyer is created with the Adobe Type 1 fonts that are provided with Freelance Graphics for Windows in the Adobe Type Manager (ATM) package. (Freelance Graphics can also use the TrueType fonts supplied with Windows.)

On the right side of the first page, the text above and below the logo is composed of a single block with settings of 36-point Dom-Casual, Center Justification. The settings for the title block are 40-point Perpetua, Bold and Italic, Centered. The rest of the text beneath the title has the settings 24-point Perpetua, Centered. All the blocks were selected as a collection, and Arrange➤Align➤Center in a Column was done to adjust the composition so that all objects were centered on one another. Then all were grouped and moved to adjust the overall position within the print area.

On the left side, the settings for the return address are 18-point Perpetua, Left Justification. The Arrange➤Rotate command was used to rotate the block, and the Shift key was held down during the operation to constrain the rotation to 90 degrees, or vertical. The same was done separately to the FIRST CLASS MAIL block, which is in 24-point Perpetua, Bold.

On the right side of the second page, the text above the map is a single block. The top line is Paragraph 1 style: 24-point Perpetua, Centered. The next three lines are Paragraph 2 style: 18-point Perpetua, also Centered. The bottom block is also 24-point Perpetua, Centered. As was done on the first page, the three objects (two text blocks and the map) were selected as a collection, then Arrange➤Align➤Center in a Column was performed.

The bulleted list on the left has a headline in Paragraph 1 style of 36-point BrushScript, with Paragraph 2-style list items as 24-point Perpetua, Italic. The check-mark option was chosen for Bullet style.

Paper Size

This flyer was output on a laser printer on letter-size (8.5-inch by 11-inch) paper. However, the actual printing job was done by offset lithography on executive-size (7.25-inch by 10.5-inch) ivory-colored card stock. The Printer and Page setup options had to be set to this size in Freelance Graphics so that the images were composed properly for the size of the printing stock—not the size of the printing masters.

For offset lithography, the black-and-white paper masters must be photographed onto light-sensitive printing plates (usually made of cardboard or plastic). These plates are then mounted on the rotating drum of a printing press. The plates are coated with ink, which is transferred to the paper stock as it passes beneath the rotating plate.

Printing the masters on the laser printer on standard letter paper gave a properly sized image that had some extra margin around the edges to ensure that the edges would not be reproduced as lines on the printing plates. To set up the job for lithography, the masters then had to be registered when copying them photographically to printing plates so that the image was centered in the printable area of the card stock.

To set the page size in Freelance Graphics, select File➤Printer Setup➤Setup. The dialog box shown in Figure 16-8 appears. (The content of the dialog box will vary depending on the printer driver selected.) Note in the figure that the Executive sheet size has been selected. When folded, the finished product measured 7.25 inches by 5.25 inches.

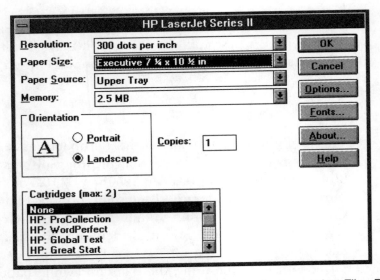

FIGURE 16-8. A printer dialog box like this appears when you select File➤Printer Setup➤Setup.

PREPARING MEETING HANDOUTS

Figure 16-9 shows printed material created using the Handouts feature of Freelance Graphics for Windows. It shows the first two pages from the tutorial presentation SAMPLE.PRE.

The File➤Print settings used to produce the sample handout are shown in Figure 16-10. The layout chosen for Handouts is 2 (two pages stacked in portrait orientation on the printout).

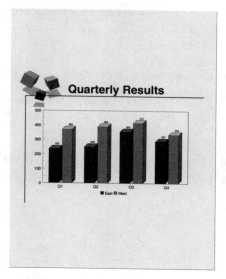

FIGURE 16-9.   Handout sample printed from a presentation file

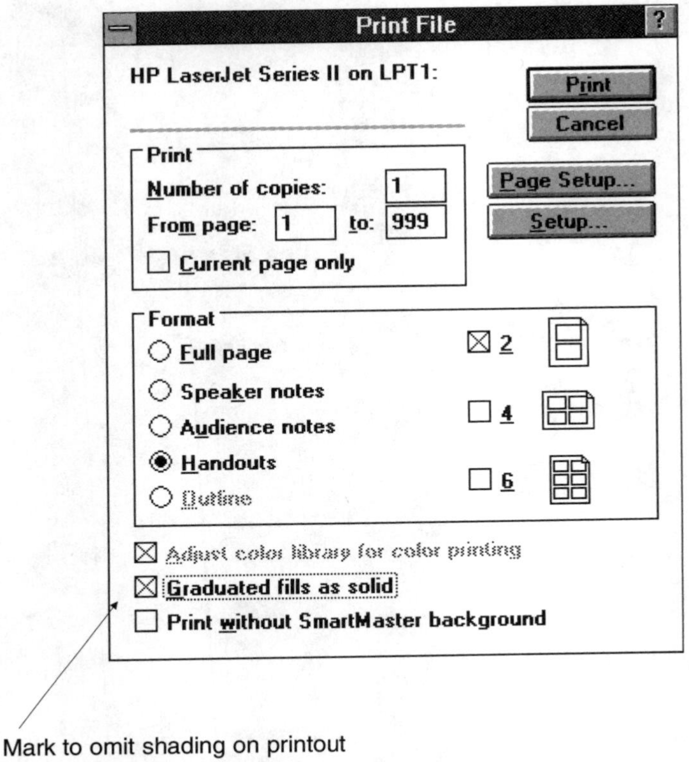

Mark to omit shading on printout

FIGURE 16-10.   The Print File dialog box shows options for composition of multiple pages on a single handout sheet.

Note also that the Graduated Fills as Solid check box has been marked to omit the shaded areas within objects.

CHAPTER 17

GRAPHING SPREADSHEET DATA

I n business, a primary tool of financial analysis is the electronic spreadsheet. And the most commonly used format for reporting results is the graph. When preparing a presentation that reports financial results, the main challenge can be deciding which portions of a spreadsheet can be converted readily into meaningful graphs.

Spreadsheet software typically supports graphing as a report format. However, your ability to alter the design of such a graph once it is generated might be somewhat limited. Particularly if you want to produce color slides, you will have greater control over the result if you import the data into a graphics program like Freelance Graphics for Windows.

The conversion will be that much easier if the applications share the Windows environment. In particular, you can set up a data link between the sheet and the graph. Whenever you change the data in the sheet, the open graph will be updated automatically (or, if closed, the graph will be updated the next time you open its file).

This chapter presents a relatively simple example involving the creation of a data link between a typical worksheet in Lotus 1-2-3 for Windows and a vertical bar graph in Freelance Graphics for Windows. The basic concepts of data transfer apply to many types of spreadsheets, or worksheets, and graphs.

A	Before Tax Yield Pct.	After Tax Yield Pct.	Annual Appreciation	Amount Invested $	Percent Invested	Before Tax Income $
Stocks	0.032	0.02272	0.095	20000	0.2	640
Taxable bonds	0.092	0.0644	0.038	20000	0.2	1840
Tax-exempt bonds	0.078	0.078	0.027	20000	0.2	1560
Money market	0.089	0.0623	0	40000	0.4	3560

FIGURE 17-1. Investment model worksheet in Lotus 1-2-3 for Windows. The cells containing the source data that will be used for graphing are highlighted.

CREATING A CHART FROM AN EXTERNAL SPREADSHEET

Figure 17-1 shows the open worksheet FILE0001.WK3 in Lotus 1-2-3 for Windows. The worksheet is a simplified personal investment model. It calculates the rates of return, before and after taxes, in an investment portfolio that totals $100,000. Alternate investment strategies can be modeled by entering different invested amounts in column E for each of the investment types in column A. Based on formulas that are embedded in the worksheet, the program calculates the income amounts and yields.

As stated previously, the main challenge in developing a graph from the worksheet can be deciding which data are meaningful for display. In making this decision, be guided by the goal of the analysis. The purpose of this model is to show which combination of investments produces the highest overall return. So it might be helpful to see a graph that compares before- and after-tax yields for each of the investment types.

The relevant range is shown in Figure 17-1. Recall that a range can be specified by naming the cells at its top left and bottom right corners. This range is A3..C6 (another valid notation used in Freelance Graphics for Windows and in Microsoft Excel is A3:C6),

which is selected by dragging the pointer from cell A3 downward
and to the right, to cell C6.

 *One of the handy features of working in a spreadsheet in Windows
is that you need not be aware of specific cell addresses or names in
order to select a range. You simply drag the pointer to indicate a
box that surrounds the desired range.*

The structure of the data in this range matches that required for
the Chart Data & Titles window of a chart in Freelance Graphics.
The first column of the worksheet holds labels that describe each
type of investment. These will become the axis labels in the first column of the Chart Data & Titles window. Column B in the worksheet
holds the data for series A (y_1 values); Column C becomes series B;
and so on.

Passing Data through the Clipboard

Once the data have been highlighted, transfer them to the Clip-
board by selecting Edit➤Copy. (The command is the same in most
Windows-based spreadsheet applications, including 1-2-3 and
Excel.)

After the data have been copied to the Clipboard, switch to
Freelance Graphics for Windows. (You can minimize 1-2-3 or activate the Control menu and make a selection from the Task List. If
you need more information on switching tasks, refer to Chapter 4.)

Open or create a presentation and add a new page. In this case,
select the 1 Chart page layout. When the layout appears in the drawing area, click on the chart box. Then select 3D Bar from the Chart
Gallery dialog box. In this example, the style button on the top
right is also selected.

When you select OK to close the Chart Gallery, an empty data
form for the new chart will appear. Notice that the pointer appears
in cell A1, which is not the same as A1 in the source worksheet.
Since the cell highlight indicates the point of data insertion, move it

to the first cell in row 1 of the Axis Labels column. (The reason for doing this is that your source data include the axis labels.)

To retrieve the data from the Clipboard and establish a DDE link, while the data form is still open perform Edit➤Paste Special➤Link.

Linking Multiple Items

The foregoing description includes only one DDE link, but there can be several between a given spreadsheet and a chart. Therefore, the data ranges used need not be contiguous within the spreadsheet. Each might be pasted separately into the appropriate columns or rows of the Chart Data form.

Data structures, including types and organization of fields, must match between the spreadsheet and the Chart Data form. If necessary, rework the spreadsheet before you attempt to import the data. Or, paste each data series into the Data Form separately.

Also, multiple applications can be linked. For example, the worksheet in the example might itself be a client of a database application. In that instance, a change in the database would trigger updates to both the source worksheet and the chart in Freelance Graphics for Windows.

Alternative Method: Using the File Import Feature

As discussed in Chapter 14, there is an alternate method of retrieving worksheet data. When the Chart Data & Titles window is open, select the Import button or press F6 (Import Data File). A file-access dialog box will appear. Specify the worksheet filename (and path) here, and select OK.

If the AUTOEXEC.BAT file of your system contains the SHARE command, only one application can have access to a file at a time. If the file you want to import is in use by another application, you will have to close that application, releasing the file lock, before you can import the file to another application.

The Import Data window will open, as shown in Figure 17-2, showing the data in the source worksheet. The procedure in this window is to highlight a range in the worksheet, then select the check box on the right indicating its data classification in the chart. This method makes it possible to be selective about the source data, even if the worksheet arrangement does not match the Chart Data form. In this example, notice that using the Import Data window makes it possible to extract a chart legend from the labels in worksheet cells B1 and C1.

Select to create ongoing data link to source file

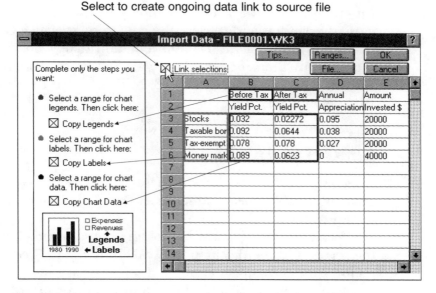

FIGURE 17-2.   This dialog box appears when the Chart Data & Titles window is open and you select the Import button or press F6 (Import Data File).

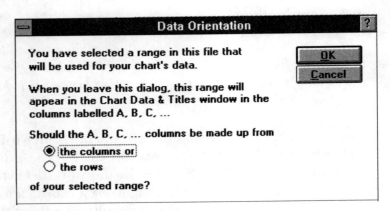

FIGURE 17-3. If the Data Orientation dialog box appears, specify whether the extraction of labels will proceed columnwise or rowwise within the source spreadsheet.

A link to the source file can be created simply by marking the Link Selections check box, as shown in the figure. Select OK to close the window and retrieve the data into Freelance Graphics.

At this point, if the Data Orientation dialog box appears, you must specify the order in which data will be read from the source spreadsheet. Refer to Figure 17-3. In this case, the Columns option (the default) is correct.

Linked Data

After you perform either of these data-retrieval procedures, the linked data will appear in the Chart Data & Titles window, as shown in Figure 17-4.

Recall that the application holding the source data is also called the server and the destination is called its client. Freelance Graphics for Windows can act either as a server or as a client. In this case, Freelance Graphics is the client, and the direction of data flow is from the spreadsheet into the Chart Data form. If a link has been specified, the data appear with a bold underscore in the data form.

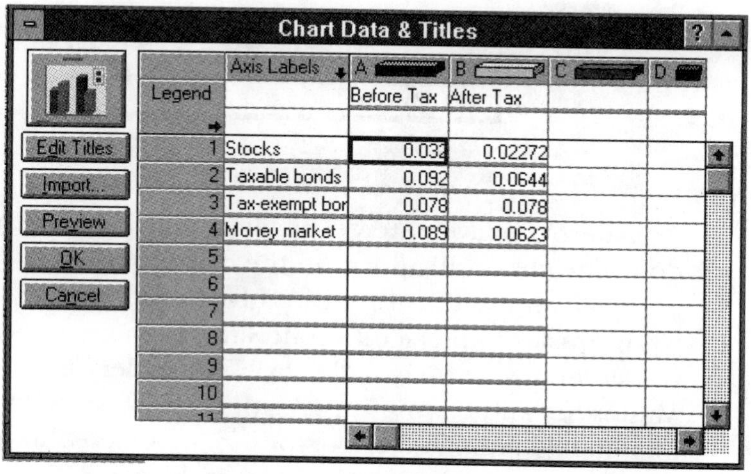

FIGURE 17-4.   Items in the data form that are highlighted with an underscore are linked to an external file.

The effects of editing linked data depend on the capabilities of the source application, as well. In this case, the source application (Lotus 1-2-3 for Windows) also can act as server or client. Therefore, if you edit the data in the Chart Data form of Freelance Graphics, the change will also appear in the source worksheet.

When data updates can be done in either direction, be careful that you don't lose track of the changes. In this example, it might be better to regard 1-2-3 only as the server and Freelance Graphics only as the client. You would then limit yourself to making data changes only in the source worksheet.

ADDING FINISHING TOUCHES TO THE CHART

Notice that the labels in the second row of the worksheet were not imported. For clarity in the chart, this information should appear not in the legend, but as the title of the *y* axis. To do this, before you close the Chart Data & Titles window, select the Edit Titles button and enter the axis title:

Axis Titles:

X

Y Yield (Percent)

2Y

After you have entered the axis title, select OK to close the window. The chart will appear in the drawing area.

Click on the title area, type **Investment Model**, and select OK.

In this example, a different SmartMaster set was selected for the presentation. To match the example, select Style➤Choose SmartMaster Set and choose the file MMLASER.MAS. (This SmartMaster includes an animated effect for use in Screen Shows.)

The completed chart is shown in Figure 17-5.

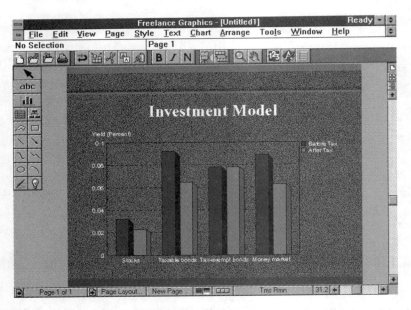

FIGURE 17-5. This graph shows a key relationship in the investment model—the comparative yields of alternative strategies. The imported data represent only a small portion of the external worksheet.

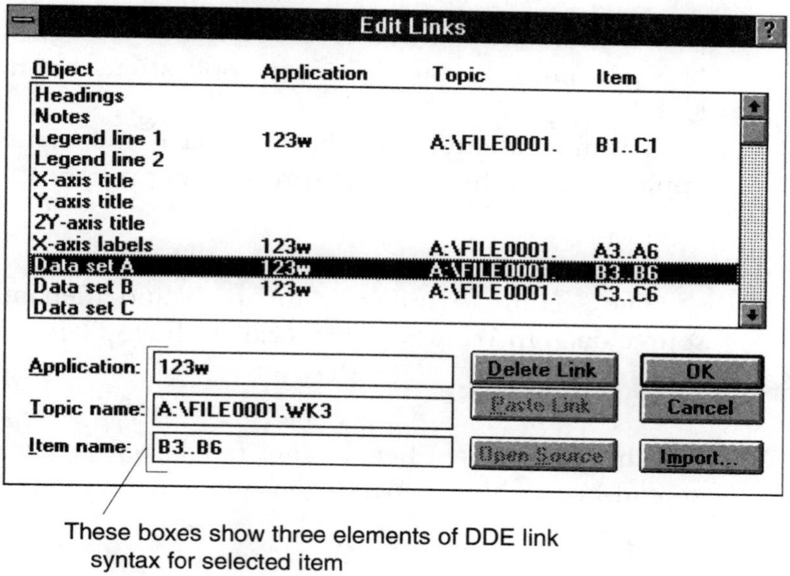

These boxes show three elements of DDE link
syntax for selected item

FIGURE 17-6. The Edit Links dialog box contains information on the source of
each linked data item.

INSPECTING DATA LINKS

You can inspect (and edit, if necessary) the data links in the chart.
Select the chart in the drawing area and perform Edit➤Links. The
Links dialog box will appear. To view the links in detail, select the
Edit button. The dialog box shown in Figure 17-6 will open.

The figure shows the link references that result from using the
File Import feature to retrieve and link the worksheet data. Selecting an object here permits you to edit its *link syntax*. The three elements of the link syntax appear in the Application, Topic Name,
and Item Name boxes. In Windows, the following special syntax is
used for DDE links:

{=123W|E:\123W\SAMPLE\FILE0001.WK3|A:A3..A:C6}

The link reference, or *triplet,* is a formula (indicated by the
equal-sign prefix) that is enclosed in curly brackets. The formula
contains a set of three identifiers, which are separated by the verti-

cal bar character. (The curly brackets, formula sign, and the vertical bars will appear in some Windows applications, but not in Freelance Graphics.)

The first identifier in the formula is the name of the server application (in this case, the spreadsheet program):

123W

The second identifier is the path and filename holding the source data. In Windows, this is called the topic name:

A:\FILE0001.WK3

The third identifier is the range reference in the source spreadsheet, which in Windows is the item name:

B3..B6

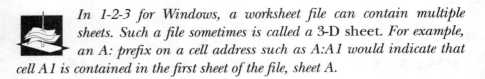

In 1-2-3 for Windows, a worksheet file can contain multiple sheets. Such a file sometimes is called a 3-D sheet. For example, an A: prefix on a cell address such as A:A1 would indicate that cell A1 is contained in the first sheet of the file, sheet A.

If the link-reference data do not appear in the Edit Links dialog box, the data have simply been pasted into the form, and no DDE link exists.

DATA UPDATE

Provided that a data link has been established, whenever the server application and Freelance Graphics for Windows are running concurrently (even if minimized), changing the data in the worksheet will trigger an automatic update in the chart. (See the previous note in this chapter about file-access restrictions imposed by the SHARE command in DOS.)

Once the files have been saved and closed, the link persists. If you attempt to reopen the presentation that contains the linked chart, Freelance Graphics will attempt to open the source file and retrieve the data. If the source file is not available, you will be prompted to provide it (by inserting the proper disk into the drive, for example).

If the source file is available, Freelance Graphics will load the data into the presentation file and display the chart. You need not be concerned with the details of opening the source application.

SUMMARY

The procedures outlined here can be used to maintain a matched set of spreadsheets and graphs for recurring financial presentations. The DDE links will be particularly useful if the data change frequently. For example, a spreadsheet containing stock quotations might be updated daily from an external database, such as a financial news service. Once the links are established, simply pasting the data into the spreadsheet from the database will cause the graphs to be updated.

PREPARING A SPEECH

T his chapter describes how you can use the Outliner feature in Freelance Graphics for Windows as you begin to conceptualize a speech. In the same process, you can both create a topic outline and generate text pages to highlight the key points of your message. You can then export this outline to a word processor so that you can write the narrative. If the word processor is also a Windows application, you will be able to switch back and forth between the tasks of writing the speech and generating the charts.

1. OUTLINE THE MAIN TOPICS

Figure 18-1 shows the main topics of a marketing presentation entered in the Outliner. Pressing Enter after you type the title of a page causes subsequent items to be treated as subtopics, or items in the body of a Bullet List chart.

The first page is shown in the Current Page view in Figure 18-2. The SmartMaster set MARBLE.MAS has been applied, and the page is displayed here in black-and-white mode.

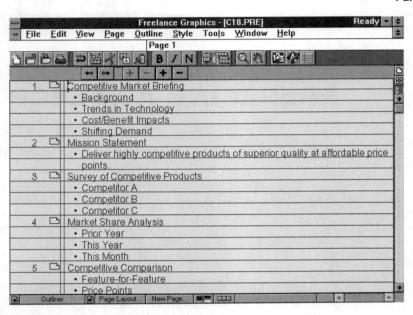

FIGURE 18-1. Main speech topics entered as list text in the Outliner

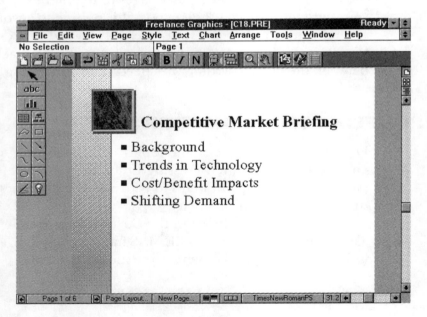

FIGURE 18-2. Bulleted list generated from the speech topics

2. COPY THE OUTLINE TO THE CLIPBOARD

When you have finished entering a topic outline in Freelance
Graphics, you can copy and paste the data into a word processing
application for purposes of drafting your speech.

Start by selecting the entire outline in the Outliner. You can
select all the pages by holding the Shift key down as you click each
of the document symbols:

Click here to select all text in page

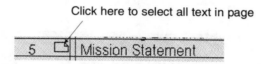

Or, starting in the top-left corner of the outline, you can select
all the text by drawing a box around all the pages.

A solid line will surround the text you have selected. Then, perform Edit➤Copy to copy the text to the Clipboard.

Switch to the word processing application. In this example, the
word processor is Windows Write. If the application is not already
open, you can switch to it by first minimizing Freelance Graphics,
then opening the Accessories program group and double-clicking
on the Write program icon:

*If the word processor is a non-Windows program, open the Clip-
board application in the Main program group. You should see the
Outline text in this window. Save the text to a file by selecting
File➤Save As. If the word processing program is listed in the Save File as
Type drop-down box, select that file type. Otherwise, select Text Files (.TXT)
to create ANSI text, which is readable by most word processing programs.*

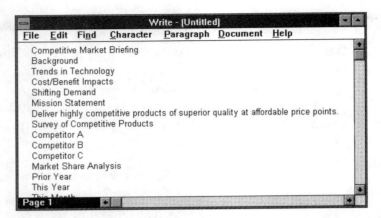

FIGURE 18-3. The text of the outline has been pasted into the Windows Write application.

3. RETRIEVE THE OUTLINE FOR WORD PROCESSING

With the outline copied to the Clipboard and the word processing application opened, retrieve the text from the Clipboard by performing Edit≻Paste. The result is shown in Figure 18-3.

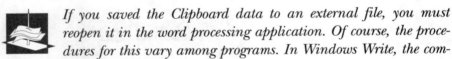

If you saved the Clipboard data to an external file, you must reopen it in the word processing application. Of course, the procedures for this vary among programs. In Windows Write, the command would be File≻Open.

4. WRITE THE NARRATIVE

Use the retrieved outline as a guide for writing the narrative. The beginning of the completed speech text is shown in Figure 18-4.

You may wish to switch frequently between the word processor and Freelance Graphics to develop your speech and its graphics in parallel. This will be particularly convenient if both applications run in Windows. If both applications remain open, press Alt-Tab to

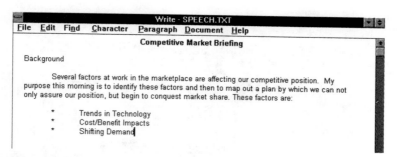

FIGURE 18-4. Speech text developed from the imported outline

switch from one to the other. (See Chapter 4 for procedures for switching tasks in Windows.)

5. MAKE BUILDUP SEQUENCES

After you have developed your speech, switch to Freelance Graphics to complete the presentation graphics. Among these might be buildup sequences, which present bulleted lists as a series of pages, usually one page for each subtopic.

Figure 18-5 shows the Page Sorter selections involved in generating a buildup sequence from Page 1. (This command can also be performed with Page 1 in the Current Page view.)

In the Page Sorter, select the parent page, or master list, for the buildup sequence. Then, perform Page➤Create Build. The result is shown in Figure 18-6. Three child pages have been inserted preceding the parent page. Each of the child pages highlights one of the subtopics in the bulleted list. The new pages are numbered Pages 1–3, and the parent page has been renamed Page 4.

6. ADD SUPPORTING CHARTS

You can intersperse the text pages with data charts that illustrate the bulleted items, or message points. For example, after Page 7 (Market Share Analysis), you might insert a pie chart that graphs the respective market shares. After Page 8 (Competitive Comparison),

Parent page

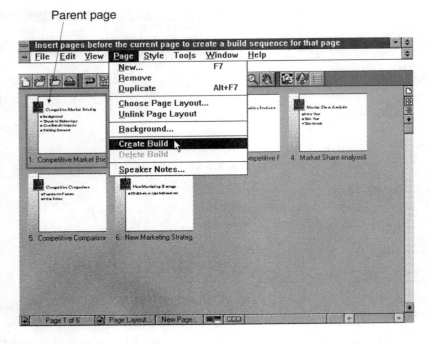

FIGURE 18-5. Perform these menu selections to create a buildup sequence from a bulleted list.

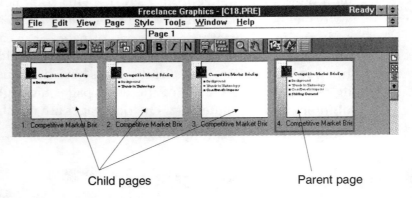

Child pages   Parent page

FIGURE 18-6. Perform the Page➤Create Build command in either the Page Sorter (shown here) or the Current Page view to generate a buildup sequence automatically from a page that uses any of the bulleted-list layouts.

you might insert a table that lists advantages and disadvantages of each product. You could even add graphs or drawings (Chart➤ New) to the bulleted-list charts to illustrate key points.

7. REARRANGE THE PRESENTATION SEQUENCE

You need not add new pages in any particular order. You can always rearrange them in the Page Sorter. Simply select a page and drag it to a different position in the sequence.

DESIGNING AN INTERACTIVE SHOW

A SmartShow is simply a Screen Show through which there can be a variety of display sequences. The sequences are controlled through user selections, triggered by clicking on objects that have been defined as Buttons and embedded in the interactive show.

The basic steps involved in building a SmartShow are:

1. Create a presentation.
2. Plan a decision tree for user interactions.
3. Add Buttons to pages for each user selection.
4. Specify a result (called a *behavior*) for each Button.
5. Optionally, edit the transition effects between pages.

CREATING A DECISION TREE

A *decision tree* is a diagram that shows the branching within an inter-active presentation on a computer display. This is not a function of Freelance Graphics for Windows, but a tool of instructional design. An example is shown in Figure 19-1.

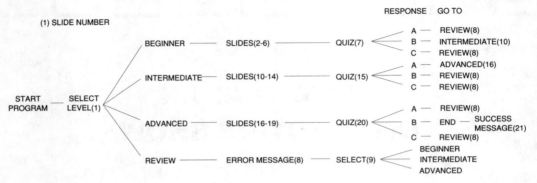

FIGURE 19-1. Sample decision tree for instructional design

As an aid to visualizing a decision tree, make an organization chart in Freelance Graphics for Windows that shows the same structure.

The purpose of creating a decision tree is to be sure that you have planned responses to all possible user selections. Each program selection adds complexity to the presentation, so even in a show that has relatively few selections, the decision tree actually can become quite extensive. Having a graphic tool for visualizing the decision tree helps assure that users will not be stumped by a computerized presentation that halts without explanation.

A branch, or set of alternative paths, proceeds from each decision, or node, on the tree. In general, you will need to create an on-screen Button for each node to provide a means of selection.

EMBEDDING BUTTONS IN PRESENTATION PAGES

In Freelance Graphics for Windows, a Button is a link between two pages, between a page and an action (such as a pause), between a page and another application program, or between a page and a multimedia object (such as a digital sound recording).

To create a Button in the Current Page view, first create the graphic object that will indicate the selection to the user (such as a stop sign symbol).

A Button should always have a text label or annotation that describes the action that will be caused by selecting it. If you want a Button (such as HELP) to appear on every page of a presentation (except the title page), draw it as part of the Basic Layout. To do this, select the Basic Layout in the Current Page View and perform Edit▸Edit Page Layouts.

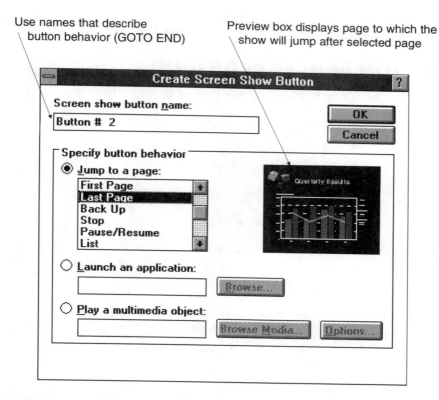

Use names that describe button behavior (GOTO END)

Preview box displays page to which the show will jump after selected page

FIGURE 19-2. In the middle section of this dialog box, you can specify the page to which the presentation will jump if the user clicks the named Button.

Select the object, then select View➤Screen Show➤Create-Edit Button.

The Create Screen Show Button dialog box will appear (Figure 19-2). Type a Button name in the text box (or accept the default button number). Then, select one of the option buttons that specify a behavior, or result of clicking that Button during a show.

> **TIP** *A collection of objects cannot be a Button, but a group can. Create the group first, then add the Button attribute. Do not create a Button object first and then group it with other objects; if any of the other objects are Buttons, the Buttons will not operate properly.*

BUTTON BEHAVIOR OPTIONS

Behavior options in the Create Screen Show Button dialog box are:

- Jump to a Page
- Launch an Application
- Play a Multimedia Object

Jumping to a Page

A *jump* is a branching of the show sequence, usually to something other than the next page. As shown previously in Figure 19-2, options in the list box are:

Next advances to the next page in the numeric page sequence. You might want to specify the next page if some other Button on the page would otherwise cause a jump to a different page.

Previous shows the preceding page.

First shows the first page, usually the presentation title.

Last shows the last page in the numbered sequence.

Page *N* displays the numbered page that you select.

Back Up   resumes the show at the page previously shown. This might not be the preceding page in the sequence if a jump has occurred.

Stop   quits the show and returns the user to the previous view of Freelance Graphics.

Pause/Resume   halts an automatically advancing show until the Button is clicked a second time. (To cause the show to advance automatically, select View➤Screen Show➤Edit Effects➤Automatically.)

List   displays all the show's page numbers, from which the user must make a selection.

In making these selections, be guided by the decision tree you built. Remember that you must include at least one Button in the show for each branch in the tree.

Launching Applications

A Button that triggers the launching of another application program from within a SmartShow is called a *hot link*.

Specifying a Hot Link

Programs triggered by hot links can be either Windows or non-Windows applications. If the program is another Windows application, it is possible that it might already be running when launched from the SmartShow. If this happens, Windows might not be able to open the program, or it might open a second instance (another copy) of the program, producing undesirable results.

To create a hot link, create a Button and select the second behavior option in the Edit Screen Show Buttons dialog box:

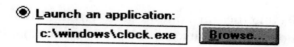

Type the application name and optional parameters in the text boxes. Or, select Browse, navigate the file system to find the application, and then select OK.

Select OK to close the Create Screen Show Button dialog box.

Requirements for Applications and Parameters

The requirements for the Application Name and Parameters settings are the same as for the Command Line setting when executing File≻Run in Windows Program Manager. The application name is the filename and extension of an executable program or batch file, including any required drive and path. Permissible extensions include .COM, .EXE, .PIF, and .BAT. An example would be:

C:\WINDOWS\CLOCK.EXE

In this case, if the user clicks on the Button during a show, the Windows Clock will be displayed.

Parameters include software switches (such as /A/1), as well as source files (or the letter of a drive that holds those files) that must be opened upon starting the program. If you use a DOS application (.COM or .EXE file), you can place parameters instead in a Windows program information file (.PIF) and omit the switch syntax.

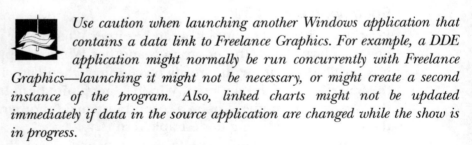 *Use caution when launching another Windows application that contains a data link to Freelance Graphics. For example, a DDE application might normally be run concurrently with Freelance Graphics—launching it might not be necessary, or might create a second instance of the program. Also, linked charts might not be updated immediately if data in the source application are changed while the show is in progress.*

Linking Buttons to Multimedia Objects

Selecting the third option button in the Create Screen Show Button dialog box permits you to specify a multimedia object that will be played if the user clicks the Button:

DESIGNING AN INTERACTIVE SHOW
■ ■
Chapter 19

693

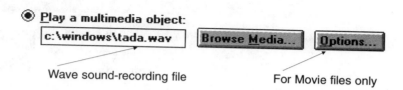

Multimedia objects can include Wave sound recordings (.WAV files), MIDI sound recordings (.MID files), and Lotus Movies (.LSM files).

The purpose of assigning a sound recording to a Button might be to reinforce the user's selection of a correct answer (perhaps with the congratulatory TADA.WAV sound). The purpose of running a movie might be to illustrate the consequences of the user's selection, as in showing an animated diagram of a chemical reaction.

Type the multimedia object's path and filename in the text box, or select the Browse Media button to navigate the file system and select a file. The Lotus Media files supplied with Freelance Graphics can be found in the directory LOTUSAPP\MULTIMED, which is shared by all Lotus applications for Windows.

When you create a Button that is linked to a multimedia object, you are actually embedding a Windows OLE package. For more information about OLE, see Chapter 14.

Some ready-made Lotus Movie (.LSM) files can be found in the LOTUSAPP\MULTIMED directory: MMGLOBE.LSM is a rotating globe of the world, and MMLASER.LSM looks like a laser beam underscoring the title of the page.

Controlling Movie Screen Location

If the multimedia object you specified is a movie file, you can select the Options button to select its screen location during the show. The Multimedia Button Options dialog box will appear, as shown in Figure 19-3. Select one of the option buttons for screen location (choose 10 to place it at the Button location), then select OK.

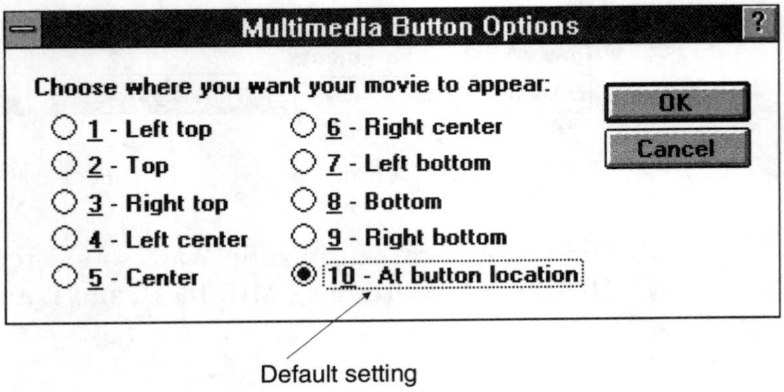

Default setting

FIGURE 19-3. Option buttons in this dialog box permit you to specify the screen location at which a multimedia movie will be displayed.

Select OK again to close the Create Screen Show Button dialog box.

Controlling Other Playback Options

Playback options, especially for sound recordings, can be controlled by selecting View➤Screen Show➤Edit Effects➤Options. The Screen Show Options dialog box will open, as shown in Figure 19-4. For more information, see Chapter 13.

EDITING SCREEN SHOW EFFECTS

In Freelance Graphics for Windows, transition effects between pages in a Screen Show are defined separately from Buttons. You can specify a different transition effect—such as Fade or Replace—for each page in a presentation. Select View➤Screen Show➤Edit Effects. The Edit Screen Show dialog box will open, as shown in Figure 19-5.

In general, you select a page number, then select the transition effect that will follow it as the show advances to the next page. For more information, see Chapter 13.

Inspect/edit all Button assignments in show

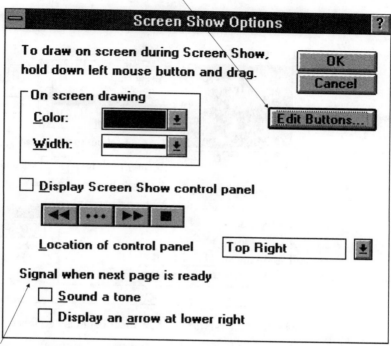

Allow time to load next page into video memory

FIGURE 19-4. This dialog box appears when you select View➤Screen Show➤Edit Effects➤Options.

INSPECTING AND EDITING BUTTON ASSIGNMENTS

After you have created all the Buttons in your interactive show, you can inspect their assignments by selecting View➤Screen Show➤Edit Effects➤Options➤Edit Buttons. The Create-Edit Screen Show Buttons dialog box will open, as shown in Figure 19-6.

Effect follows only selected page
unless check box is marked

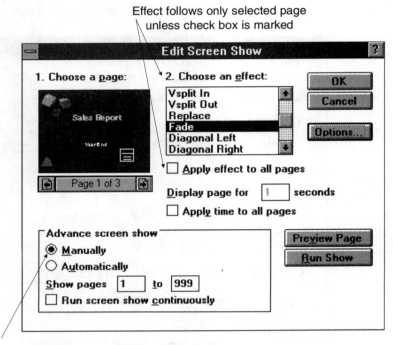

Use this setting for interactive show (user controls sequence)

FIGURE 19-5.   Settings in this dialog box control transitions between pages in a
Screen Show.

In this dialog box, select the page number and the Button number or name within that page, and the previously defined Behavior
settings will appear in the bottom section. You can reset the options
as you wish.

Or, you can remove the Button attribute from any object. Select
the page and Button, then select the Delete Link button.

When you have finished working in this dialog box, you will
need to select OK three times—once in each of the open dialog
boxes.

Names of all Buttons on selected page

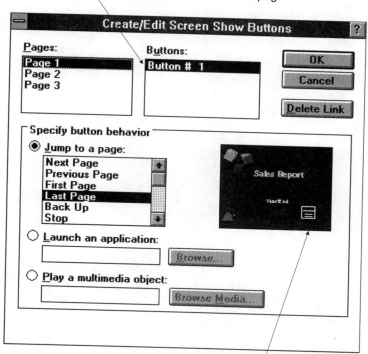

Preview of page to which
show will jump

FIGURE 19-6. Behavior settings of all Buttons in the show can be inspected and
reset in this dialog box.

PRODUCING AN ANNUAL MEETING

C hapter 15 covers all the issues that surround the production of slides in volume under challenging deadlines. Consider how all these factors come into play when producing a major business meeting.

Assume that you are an in-house producer in the marketing communications department of Arrow Motors Corporation, a large auto manufacturer. Your boss, the manager of communications, has the nominal responsibility of producing the annual management meeting, which means that actually getting the job done falls to you. You've never coordinated a large meeting before, and this is a high-visibility assignment.

Your primary client is the vice president of marketing. The VP has overall responsibility for the event, and is answerable to the CEO. Your day-to-day contact is the VP's assistant, who will obtain budget approvals and set up your meetings with individual presenters.

When you first learn of the assignment, the meeting date is two months away. The location is Hawaii—at one of the large hotels on the Kaanapali coast of Maui. Attendees at the meeting will be senior management of Arrow, its regional and district sales managers, and the primary audience: representatives from all the company's dealers, including owners of about 350 automobile franchises and their sales managers.

Presenters at the meeting will be the CEO and department heads of Arrow. Purposes of this meeting are to:

- Review sales performance for the past year
- Survey industry trends for the year ahead
- Disclose the company's new products and sales strategies
- Set sales objectives
- Motivate attendees to meet those objectives

Actual product introductions—showings of new car models—will take place at a theatrical show the evening of the business meeting. This portion of the meeting has been contracted to an outside industrial show producer, under the direction of another member of your department. The motivational aspect of product appeal, then, will be left to this portion of the program. The business meeting has to do mainly with presenting statistics—in charts. The business meeting is also motivational—in the sense that the desire of both the company executives and its dealers to be more profitable will be stimulated by the event.

The factors covered at the beginning of Chapter 13 apply here. However, in this type of situation, many of the preliminary considerations are out of your hands. That is, company management has determined factors such as meeting objectives, audience, and organizational level. This does not remove the need for you to understand these things, though. Questions of appropriateness should guide your production decisions. You need to have a fundamental understanding of the business reason for the meeting and the expectations of the primary audience. In this case, the dealers want to hear that they will have the product and sales tools to rack up a banner sales year. The company wants to establish quotas and sales rates for specific product models so that it can plan for efficient plant loading and product distribution.

Referring back to the discussion early in Chapter 13, the next items to be considered are meeting location and equipment. You

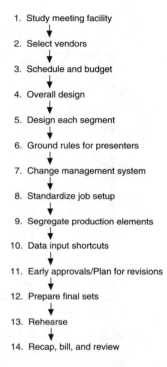

1. Study meeting facility
2. Select vendors
3. Schedule and budget
4. Overall design
5. Design each segment
6. Ground rules for presenters
7. Change management system
8. Standardize job setup
9. Segregate production elements
10. Data input shortcuts
11. Early approvals/Plan for revisions
12. Prepare final sets
13. Rehearse
14. Recap, bill, and review

FIGURE 20-1. Flow diagram for show-production steps

have been told that the expected presentation medium for the business meeting is color slides, but beyond that, the design and production recommendations must come from you. A flow diagram of the production process is shown in Figure 20-1, and details about the procedures follow.

1. STUDY THE MEETING FACILITY

Travel and accommodations are being handled by another department in the company and are not your responsibility. However, the hotel's meeting facilities are your direct concern. So, as a first step, you contact the hotel's events manager and obtain a floor plan of the auditorium in its conference center (Figure 20-2).

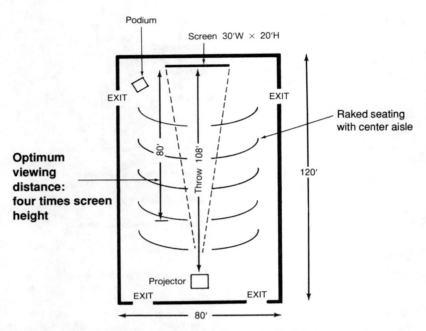

FIGURE 20-2. Auditorium floor plan, showing projection distance

Ideally, you should survey the meeting site yourself. You can learn a lot just from looking at the auditorium floor plan (you may need also to consult a professional projectionist), but, most likely, the drawing will not show all the details you need. Put questions to the hotel events manager until you have all the information, even if it means sending someone into the hall to take measurements.

The dimensions of the hall are 80 by 120 feet. It is equipped with a permanent projection booth and a screen that can be raised and lowered electrically, and is controlled from the booth. The *throw*, or distance, from the projector to the screen is 108 feet.

Remember that the optimum viewing distance is *four times* the height of the screen. So, if you pick a seating location three-fourths of the way to the back of the hall, or about 80 feet from the screen, the screen height should be at least 20 feet. If you plan to use the conventional 35mm double-frame slide aperture, the width of the screen must, therefore, be 30 feet.

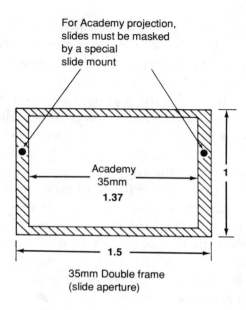

35mm Double frame
(slide aperture)

FIGURE 20-3. Slides in the Academy format can completely fill a narrower screen than that required for conventional 35mm slides.

If the meeting hall was designed properly, the screen will probably be exactly these dimensions. If the screen is considerably smaller, it is best to rent your own for the event. (Be sure that is it set up in time for rehearsals.) It will almost always be wiser to provide your own projection equipment, operated by your projectionist.

A narrower screen of the same height might be appropriate for slides in Academy format, as shown in Figure 20-3. This format is especially useful for two- and three-screen multiple projection formats, since you may be concerned about the overall width in the available space. Remember that using multiple screens requires multiple projectors. If you plan to have dissolve transitions between slides, you need at least two projectors per screen: That's four projectors for a two-screen show and six for a three-screen show. If transitions are to be rapid, simulating motion, you will need three projectors per screen to compensate for relatively slow projector slide-changing cycles (approximately two seconds between slides).

704　· APPLYING FREELANCE GRAPHICS FOR WINDOWS

Part IV

The complexity of both production and projection increases greatly with a decision to use multiple screens. For this type of meeting, don't make it fancier than necessary. In the words of architect Mies van der Rohe, "Less is more."

So, slide aperture depends on screen size and format. This is the first design requirement for the slide show. If you decide to use Academy or another custom format, a custom page layout will have to be made so that all slides can be composed with adequate margins, or *bleed,* at the edges.

The throw of 108 feet also indicates another requirement. Projectors capable of illuminating a screen at that distance use high-intensity (usually Xenon) lamps. These lamps get sufficiently hot to melt film. In the case of motion pictures, film is traveling rapidly through the projector and there usually isn't time for a frame to overheat unless the projector jams. But slides may be on the screen for 15 seconds or more. The solution is to use special high-heat glass slide mounts (Figure 20-4). These mounts sandwich the film between two thin panes of heat-resistant glass. The film is held on registration pins so that it is positioned accurately. Pin registration assures that images will not move around the screen during dissolve transitions such as those used for buildup sequences.

The slide mounts, in turn, pose other requirements for you. Film must be loaded manually into this type of mount. There's a consequence of both time and cost here. Since portions of the show are subject to change up to the last minute, it would be wasteful to have all slides mounted this way early in the process. You should instead plan for two entire show sets to be run on the film recorder and mounted a short time before the show. This assures that the slides will be free of the dust and scratches that result from handling during reviews and rehearsals. Normally, you should prepare two sets: one for projection and one for backup.

For computer-generated slides, pin registration also affects your choice of film recorder. Desktop film recorders may not have the

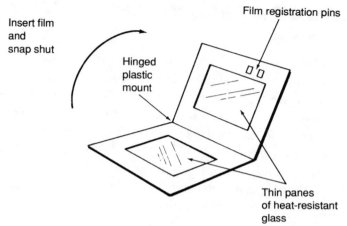

Insert film
and
snap shut

Film registration pins

Hinged
plastic
mount

Thin panes
of heat-resistant
glass

Note: Remove dust from film chip and
mount with a blast of air before closing.

FIGURE 20-4. View of a high-heat glass slide mount, shown open

frame-to-frame registration accuracy necessary for smooth dissolve transitions. High-volume film recorders, such as those used at service bureaus, typically provide frame-to-frame accuracy within 1/10,000 of an inch.

2. SELECT YOUR VENDORS

Your need for outside services will depend on which resources are not readily available to you in-house. In this case, slides will be prepared under your direction by graphic-arts staff within the marketing communications department, using Freelance Graphics. You plan to use an outside film-recording service, such as the local Autographix service center. You also have in-house desktop film recorders for producing preliminary copies of slides for rehearsals. Film processing will be handled through a local commercial film laboratory.

3. DEVELOP A PRELIMINARY SCHEDULE AND BUDGET

The basic parameters of the job can be derived from the meeting agenda, as shown in Figure 20-5. The number of slides in each presenter's segment has been estimated from the running time allocated for the speeches. A rule of thumb in this type of meeting is one slide every 15 seconds. You need to work closely with the speech writers so that, if presentations run over the allocated time, you can adjust your planning. Remember that if a morning meeting runs long and into the lunch hour (or worse, into scheduled golf games), you may get the blame.

Arrow Motors Corporation
Annual Meeting Agenda

Segment	Presenter	Minutes	Est.* No. Slides
1. Opening message	Chairman	3:00	12
2. Corporate year in review	President	5:00	20
3. Economic outlook	VP Finance	10:00	40
4. Sales performance review	VP Sales	20:00	80
5. New product overview	VP Manufacturing	20:00	80
Coffee Break		10:00	
6. Sales objectives	General Sales Manager	20:00	80
7. Merchandising plans	VP Market/Merch	12:00	48
8. Advertising plans	VP Advertising	15:00	60
9. Service outlook	VP Customer Service	15:00	60
10. Distribution forecasts	VP Distribution	10:00	40
11. Wrap-up and charge	President	5:00	20

Allow 1:30 minutes between presenters   2:25:00 → 13:30

Est. running time   2:38:30   **540 Slides in show**

*Assuming avg. of 4 slides/min.

FIGURE 20-5. Meeting agenda with estimates for running time and slide count

The number of slides is a very rough indicator of the production budget for each segment. Presentations that include extensive artwork or product photography naturally will incur a higher per-slide average. Add to this gross budget the contingencies described above for:

- Late submission of data
- Late availability of products and materials for photography
- Multistep photo compositing
- Special creative effects

When preparing a schedule, work backward from the show date. Don't forget to plan for revisions, rehearsals, and logistics like slide mounting and collating.

4. ESTABLISH THE OVERALL DESIGN

A point of creative departure is the meeting theme. In this case, the marketing department is planning the event around the theme, "Arrow Points to Tomorrow." From the theme, your staff designs a meeting logo (Figure 20-6). To your surprise, you find that the logo design must be personally approved by none other than the CEO. You go through several designs and several days before a final selection is made.

Your next concern is deciding global design parameters for the slides. Establish guidelines for fonts, capitalization styles, and color schemes. Remember that color brightness must be adjusted to the room lighting, projector-lamp intensity, and throw. In the case of Freelance Graphics for Windows, one of the predefined color palettes might be perfectly adequate, as long as all the colors (particularly, the *shades* of those colors) are usable under the meeting's lighting conditions. If necessary, create test slides and view them under actual or simulated show conditions before making final selections.

FIGURE 20-6.   Logo for the meeting's theme, "Arrow Points to Tomorrow"

Again, if the screen format requires a special aperture, create a custom SmartMaster set in which the margins have been adjusted to match the aperture.

5. SET DESIGN PARAMETERS FOR EACH SEGMENT

An excellent design approach is to keep style consistent among all presentations and to vary only the background color, pattern, or both. Recall that Freelance Graphics for Windows can generate backgrounds that include patterns and bitmaps. The controlling factor will depend on how a specific film recorder will render them.

Remember that these choices are very subjective. It may be more important to secure the presenters' approval for the background color and pattern than for other matters of content. This is a bit like picking out wallpaper: It always takes longer than you think!

Once you have established the overall and individual design rules, prepare a show design book that can be distributed to all computer artists or slide preparers.

6. ESTABLISH GROUND RULES WITH PRESENTERS

You should have a primary contact for each presenter. Each program segment is a self-contained job within the larger show and, to a large extent, can be produced and managed separately.

Determine whether speech writers will need to work with graphic-arts designers for storyboard preparation. If the presentation comprises primarily tables and graphs, this step may not be necessary.

Be sure your contacts understand the ground rules for data submission deadlines, requirements for custom artwork, provision of materials for live photography, expected turnaround, approval steps, and policies on rush service.

A final crucial area of understanding is security. If presentations include sensitive information, have a system for controlling materials and access, and be sure all parties know and follow the procedures. This applies to both internal staff and outside vendors. For the vendors, if security agreements don't already exist, they should be signed specifically for this project. Again, your understanding of the business situation informs your decisions. Any presentation of performance data in a business organization is bound to be sensitive.

7. HAVE A SYSTEM FOR MANAGING CHANGE

Financial accountability for the production also influences your planning. In this case, an internal job number is set up in your department for each program segment. Time and materials for both internal staff and external contractors will be charged to these accounts. Ultimately, each presenter will be answerable to the CEO

```
                    PROJECT CHANGE NOTICE


    CLIENT                              JOB NO.
    CLIENT CONTACT                      PHONE
    DATE
    THE FOLLOWING CHANGE REQUEST HAS BEEN RECEIVED
       (DESCRIBE):



    BUDGET IMPACT:                 SCHEDULE IMPACT:


    I HEREBY AUTHORIZE
    THIS CHANGE
    AS DESCRIBED        _____
                                    (signed)

    _____
         DATE          _____
                                    (title)
```

FIGURE 20-7. The project change notice (PCN) is a useful device for documenting requests for changes.

for the expenditures. To protect yourself, however, you need a system for managing and documenting revisions.

A very useful tool for this purpose is the project change notice (PCN), an example of which is shown in Figure 20-7. This handy little document notifies a client that a specific request for change will incur consequences in terms of time and money. The client contact is required to acknowledge and accept these consequences by signing the PCN before the work can be undertaken. This may seem like an annoying—even embarrassing—device, especially during the hectic production activity that precedes any show, but having the documentation could save you much more embarrassment later.

A coding scheme can be used to segregate chargeable changes. Keep prior versions of presentation files on disk as a way of documenting changes. Notations on individual slides can be made to indicate the responsible party: for example, *A* (for authors' alteration) or *C* (producer correction). In general, clients would not be charged for data-entry errors and misspellings. Of course, some departmental charge-back policies don't charge anything to overhead and ignore this distinction. However, client relations are improved if they believe that you are eating your mistakes.

If you keep prior versions of presentations on a set of disks, your files should be self-documenting for all revisions in the show. Later, when asked to justify your charges, you can retrieve all previous versions and even output them in draft mode for review by the client, if necessary.

8. STANDARDIZE JOB SETUP FOR PRODUCTION

Use a job ticket or work order, such as the form shown in Figure 20-8, to initiate and track each submission to production. Mark up and code rough sketches, text copy, and data sheets for style and colors. Refer to your style book and specify colors by Freelance Graphics color-library name.

Once the jobs have been set up, following them through the production process should be delegated to a production controller. This person is responsible for the details of job scheduling, including assignments given to individual computer artists and coordination with postprocessing services such as the film laboratory.

As slides are generated, or at the end of a work session, the computer artist should output a set of paper hard copies of the slides. These hard copies, along with the work order, should be returned to the controller for proofreading, including comparison of graphs with data input. (The Spell Check feature of Freelance Graphics for Windows is useful for catching errors but should not be regarded as a substitute for visual proofreading in this case.) Corrections should be made before submitting the presentation files for film recording.

9. SEGREGATE PRODUCTION ELEMENTS

In coordination with the production controller, segregate portions of jobs that require nonstandard turnaround. Special handling should be scheduled for elements with:

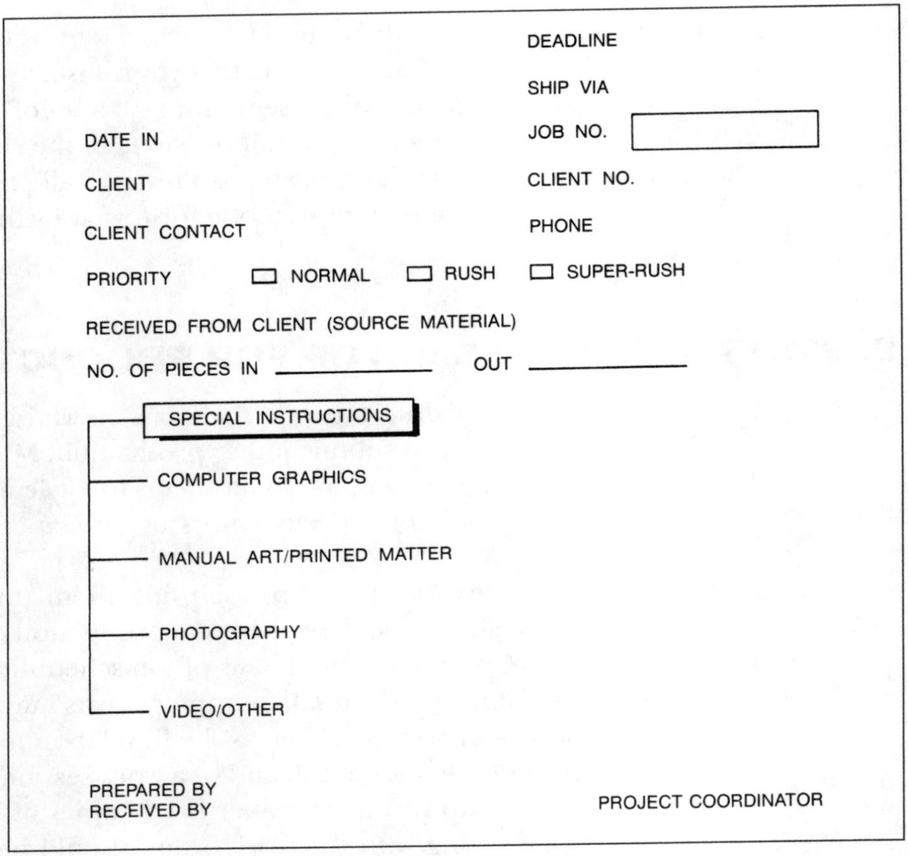
DEADLINE
SHIP VIA
DATE IN
JOB NO.
CLIENT
CLIENT NO.
CLIENT CONTACT
PHONE
PRIORITY ☐ NORMAL ☐ RUSH ☐ SUPER-RUSH
RECEIVED FROM CLIENT (SOURCE MATERIAL)
NO. OF PIECES IN ______ OUT ______
SPECIAL INSTRUCTIONS
COMPUTER GRAPHICS
MANUAL ART/PRINTED MATTER
PHOTOGRAPHY
VIDEO/OTHER
PREPARED BY
RECEIVED BY
PROJECT COORDINATOR

FIGURE 20-8. A job ticket accompanies work through a graphics department.

- Long lead time, such as photo composites
- Short lead time, such as last-minute receipt of time-sensitive data
- Repetitive formats, for which custom page layouts can be prepared even if data are not yet received

10. CONSIDER SHORTCUTS FOR DATA INPUT

There are several ways of streamlining the data-entry process for charts to speed up the production process:

- If Freelance Graphics for Windows is in use in the client departments, request that data be entered into presentation files and submitted to production either on disk or by data transmission. As a unit of storage, the presentation file itself can be a useful batch-control method.

- If the first option is not available, have staff in the client departments capture text and data with a word processing program and submit input as ASCII files for conversion to slides by the computer artists. Spreadsheet files also may be used. In either case, the charts in the presentation must lend themselves to such a highly formatted approach. Input-file formats and Freelance Graphics custom page layouts must have been designed and tested in advance.

In practice, having client staff prepare the input can be more trouble than it's worth. Certainly, this approach won't work unless your style book for the show is followed closely. Furthermore, you are likely to find that staff-prepared copy is more prone to errors. If you've never used this approach, try it on a small scale—perhaps with an early submission—before building your entire production schedule on the hope that someone else can do most of the data-entry work.

11. SOLICIT EARLY APPROVALS, BUT PLAN FOR EMERGENCY REVISIONS

Revise your schedule continually to keep it current with actual production and approvals. Seek approval of program segments as early as possible to assure that you're on the right track. Show presentations with "holes," if necessary. (Some producers have a special text slide made up as a placeholder: DATA TO COME FROM CLIENT BY [DATE].)

In this scenario, you have access to desktop film recorders for generating preliminary copies of slides. Beware of screening these slides for ultimate client approval, unless there is clear understanding that you are checking content only—not colors, patterns, or typography.

There can be noticeable differences between desktop and commercial film-recorder output, especially regarding hardware-resident fonts and patterned or shaded backgrounds.

An advantage of having paper copies of slide sets is that you can give them to presenters so that they can conduct their own speech rehearsals with their staffs. However, you can expect that the more they rehearse, the more revisions will be made to the speeches—and the slides.

A few days before the show date, block out production time for emergency revisions, even if you aren't yet aware of any. Production staff should be on standby for late shifts.

12. PREPARE FINAL SETS OF SLIDES

At the last possible moment, and as anticipated on your schedule, submit each program segment *in sequence* for final film recording and processing. Allow sufficient time for manual slide mounting, as discussed previously. Again, prepare two sets, one for projection and the other for backup. As insurance against loss or damage in transit, the backup set should travel separately to the meeting site.

13. REHEARSE

As covered early in Chapter 13, there are three stages of rehearsal:

- Presenters practice their presentations in the hall. Of course, changes are difficult to handle here. Even deleting a slide can be disruptive. Have extra copies of the meeting theme or company logo and drop them in as substitutes.

- Technicians run through the presentation to set lighting levels and cues. If possible, do this without the presenters.

- Everyone is involved in a dress rehearsal, which is not stopped for commentary.

14. AND AFTER THE SHOW . . .

Collect your job costs and bill them promptly. If you have documented revisions as described previously, you won't have any trouble justifying the charges.

Job cleanup is important because it sets the stage for presentations to come. Return original materials to clients, using signed transmittals, if necessary. Return or secure sensitive workpapers and data. Archive chart and data files. On Freelance Graphics systems, segregate styles, palettes, and symbols that can be reused to make the job easier next time.

INSTALLATION NOTES FOR FREELANCE GRAPHICS FOR WINDOWS

T his brief section is not intended as a substitute for the installation instructions in the program documentation. For more information, refer to

- *Freelance Graphics for Windows Installation Guide*
- *Freelance Graphics for Windows Network Administrator's Guide*

The discussion here covers some specific aspects of installation and system management that often raise questions.

SAMPLE HARDWARE CONFIGURATION

A sample hardware configuration for running Freelance Graphics for Windows is shown in Table A-1. This is the system I used to prepare the sample charts and drawings in this book.

TABLE A-1. Sample System Configuration

CPU	Bell Computer Systems 80386-SX 25 MHz IBM-compatible
RAM	4MB (3MB minimum)
HDD	105MB IDE-type
	At least 40MB recommended. If other applications are also being run and/or charts are being prepared for several clients, 90MB or greater is preferable.
FDD	5¼-inch high density (1.2MB) and 3½-inch high density (1.44MB)
Monitor and interface	Panasonic PanaSync C1381 with Freedom VGA-16 card 1MB video memory (256-color card)
Modem	Logicode Technology Quicktel Xeba Send/Receive FAX/Modem on COM2; external type; requires its own physical serial port. Runs at 14.4K/9600/2400/ 1200/300 bps.
Mouse	Microsoft Mouse (serial model) on COM1
Printer	Epson ActionLaser II (used in Hewlett Packard LaserJet IIP emulation); 2.5MB memory (requires 2MB upgrade module for full-page graphics)
Film recording (slides)	Autographix remote service via ToAGX
Other equipment	Proxima Power Touch Plus, model PT20 Power control module
Sound	To use multimedia extensions, you must install a sound card or a sound-card emulation driver such as PC-Speaker

PREPARING THE SYSTEM FOR INSTALLATION

Normally, you should delete the previous version of Freelance (for DOS), Freelance Plus, or Freelance Graphics for Windows before running the installation program for Windows Release 2. This will be especially important if space on your hard disk is limited.

Be sure to retain your data files, including shows, charts, and symbols, which can be read by or imported to Freelance Graphics for Windows. If you modified SmartMasters, move them to a different directory so that the installation program will not overwrite them.

After deleting old program and data files, use a defragmentation program such as Norton Speed Disk to make the free areas of the hard disk contiguous. Then proceed with the installation.

Do not defragment a disk that contains directories or programs that are copy-protected through software locking. Consult the software vendor first. It may be necessary to uninstall the protected files to prevent losing access to them!

In DOS, you cannot use the RMDIR (or RD) command to remove a directory unless you have first deleted all the files within it. As of DOS version 5, however, you can use the DEL command to delete a directory that contains files, and you will be prompted (Y/N) whether you wish to delete both the files and the directory.

Running Multiple Versions

You may wish to retain the previous version of the program for a period of time so that you can continue to use it for production while you are learning the new one, especially if you are upgrading from DOS to Windows.

In general, there will be no conflicts if you run a DOS version such as Freelance Plus and one of the Windows versions of the program on the same system. The programs will reside in different directories and have different program names and sets of support files. If you read a DOS data file into the Windows version and make a change, remember that the presentation will normally be saved to a .PRE file, which cannot be read by a DOS version of the program. If necessary, you can convert the new presentation back to a format such as .DRW when you perform File➤Save As. But be aware that

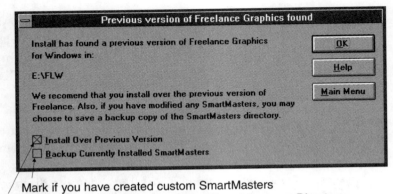

Mark if you have created custom SmartMasters
Mark to overwrite; if umarked, specify different Program Directory
for new installation

FIGURE A-1. This dialog box appears during Install if there is a previous Windows version of Freelance Graphics on your system.

the original appearance of some of the graphic elements may be changed in the translations from DOS to Windows and back to the DOS version.

Program conflicts could arise if you attempt to keep two different Windows versions, even if you put them in separate directories. *The program name FLW.EXE is the same for both Release 1 and Release 2.* However, to minimize conflicts, Release 2 creates the FLW2.INI file for program settings in the WINDOWS directory. Release 1 settings will be found in FLW.INI. Only one copy of the program—regardless of its version number—may be running at a given time under Windows Program Manager.

If you do not delete a previous Windows version of the program from your system before starting the installation, the Install program will display the dialog box shown in Figure A-1. If you select Install Over Previous Version, the new program and its support files will simply overwrite the old one. If you select Backup Currently Installed SmartMasters, your old page layouts will be saved to a different directory.

If the check box Install Over Previous Version is unmarked, the installation program will scan the hard drive(s) on your system to determine if there is sufficient space for the new version as well. If so, you will be prompted for an alternate directory name so that the versions are stored separately.

Default Directories

The installation program normally creates the directory FLW to hold the program and related files. The directory LOTUSAPP and its subdirectories are also created to hold file conversion filters, multimedia files, and spelling files that are shared among all Lotus Windows applications. Unless you specify otherwise during the installation procedure, Adobe Type Manager (ATM) will also be installed with a selection of fonts. The default directories for ATM are PSFONTS (PostScript) and PCLFONTS (Hewlett-Packard). After installation, ATM becomes a memory-resident program that is started each time Windows is loaded. ATM should improve the quality of screen displays and printed outputs in—and its fonts should be usable by—most Windows applications.

 After ATM has been installed, you can turn it off by selecting its program icon in the Windows Main program group, selecting ATM Off, then Exit. For this change to take effect, you must then restart Windows.

Disabling ATM

If ATM is already installed on your system and you wish to install the update supplied with Freelance Graphics, disable ATM and restart the computer before proceeding with installation.

PROGRAM INSTALLATION FOR A STAND-ALONE COMPUTER

The Install program handles all the details of transferring Freelance Graphics for Windows and related files from the distribution disks to your computer system. A full installation also includes an on-line tutorial, ATM and Adobe fonts, Lotus Media Manager and Lotus Sound Recorder for multimedia extensions, as well as the Autographix Slide Service. By default, all programs will be placed in the Lotus Applications program group, with the exception of ATM, which is placed in Main.

The following instructions apply to stand-alone computers rather than workstations that run the program from a network server.

DOS and Windows Requirements

Minimum system software specifications for Release 2 include MS-DOS 3.1 or later and Windows 3.0 or later versions. If you wish to use multimedia features such as sound and movies, you will want to install Windows 3.1 or later.

Main Program and Support Files

To install Freelance Graphics for Windows, first install Windows, then start it. Insert Disk 1 of the Freelance Graphics distribution disks in drive A or B of your computer.

From the Program Manager menu bar, select File➤Run. In the Command Line text box, type **a:install** if the disk is in drive A or **b:install** if the disk is in drive B.

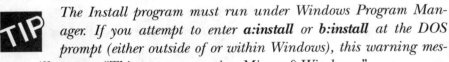 *The Install program must run under Windows Program Manager. If you attempt to enter **a:install** or **b:install** at the DOS prompt (either outside of or within Windows), this warning message will appear: "This program requires Microsoft Windows."*

The Welcome to Install dialog box, which contains copyright notices, will appear. Select OK (or press Enter) to continue with installation.

The Recording Your Name and Company Name dialog box will appear. Type your name and press Tab. Type your company name and select OK (or press Enter). The Confirm Names dialog box will appear, displaying the names you typed. Select Yes to confirm the entries. (If you select No, the previous dialog box will reopen for you to repeat the procedure.)

The Main Menu dialog box will open. To begin installation, select this icon:

 To review the READ.ME file (containing the latest product notes) select this icon:

The Type of Installation dialog box will open. Normally, select:

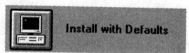

This selection will perform a full installation of the program and its supporting files. Select Install with Options instead if you want to conserve space on the hard disk by selecting specific files.

After installation, *you can run Install again and select the Change Display Type icon to choose EGA, VGA, SVGA, or IBM 8514 display. If you make no selection here, Install will set the same display type that you specified when you installed Windows.*

If you did not remove the old Windows version of the program, the dialog box shown in Figure A-1 will appear. The default selection is to overwrite the previous version. To accept this and continue, select OK.

The dialog box Specifying the Program Directory will appear. If you wish to copy the program to a different drive, select another in the Drives and Space drop-down box. To specify a different main program directory (which Install will create), type it in the Program Directory text box. Select OK to continue, then select Yes to confirm creation of the directory.

 If you choose not to overwrite a previous version of the program, you must type a different name for the default program directory.

The Install program copies files to the selected directory and displays its progress. When prompted to do so, insert another numbered disk and select OK. Repeat this step for all numbered distribution disks.

When the last of the Freelance Graphics distribution disks has been copied, the program will prompt you to insert the Adobe Type Manager disk. Insert the disk and select OK unless you already have the same version of ATM on your system. (Freelance Graphics has no fonts of its own. It uses the fonts that are supplied with ATM, as do other Lotus Windows applications.)

The programs and files on the distribution disks are in compressed format and are decompressed, or extracted, as needed by Install. Therefore, you cannot run Freelance Graphics for Windows directly from the distribution disks, nor does simply copying the disks result in a usable installation.

Autographix Installation

If you selected Install with Defaults (or selected Install with Options and marked the Autographix Slide Service check box), support programs and files for submitting presentations for outside film recording will be copied automatically. For more information, see Chapter 11.

Among these files is ToAGX, which handles transmission of presentations to the Autographix Overnight Slide Service for processing. Use of this program requires that you also install a PostScript printer driver through the Windows Control Panel. The driver software is required even if you do not have such a printer, and the required files are copied by Install. Once installed, the PostScript Printer driver must be configured for Autographix to use the supplemental printer definition AGX41.WPD.

Installation Notes

Be sure there is sufficient free space on your hard disk before you begin. A full installation, including all font, filter, symbol, and supplementary driver files, will require about 19MB. To reduce this requirement, see "Installing with Options" below.

The Install program simply creates directories and copies files. Many important system parameters are set, instead, in Windows's Main program group through Windows Setup and the Control Panel. Some other settings in Freelance Graphics are done with the Tools➤User Setup, File➤Page Setup, and File➤Printer Setup commands.

Installing with Options

If you select Install with Options, you must select which groups of files will be copied to the hard disk. By omitting files that you do not need, you can conserve disk space.

Install will scan the available drives and display the Specifying Files and Directories dialog box. Select the files to install, then OK.

Installing a Minimum File Set

To install a minimum set of operational files, select Freelance Graphics Program Files (about 7MB) and SmartMaster Files➤Selection. The Specify SmartMasters to Install dialog box will open. You can select only the sets of page layouts you will need. Each SmartMaster set requires about 15 to 60KB of disk space. You may also wish to include the Help Files (about 1.5MB).

ATM and its fonts will require another 1.2MB. (Each font takes up about 40K; these can be deleted selectively through the ATM Control Panel after installation.)

Installing Selected Files

If you have more than 10MB of free disk space but still wish to limit the size of the installation, select the file categories you require, then select OK to proceed with Install. You can save the most space by omitting the QuickStart Tutorial (about 1.2MB), Import/Export File Filters (for reading and writing data files of other applications, about 2.6MB), Multimedia Files (2.3MB), as well as selecting SmartMaster sets (saving 50K to 3.6MB).

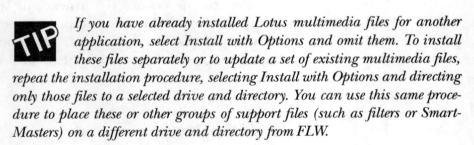

If you have already installed Lotus multimedia files for another application, select Install with Options and omit them. To install these files separately or to update a set of existing multimedia files, repeat the installation procedure, selecting Install with Options and directing only those files to a selected drive and directory. You can use this same procedure to place these or other groups of support files (such as filters or Smart-Masters) on a different drive and directory from FLW.

MOUSE OR TABLET INSTALLATION

A mouse can be installed in Program Manager by selecting Main➤Windows Setup➤Options➤Change System Settings. A digitizer tablet that takes the place of a mouse (or a mouse not found on the list) can be installed by selecting Other Mouse and installing the driver software provided by the tablet manufacturer (OEM disk). If the driver is compatible with Windows, the disk will contain a setup information file such as OEMSETUP.INF.

Mouse characteristics, such as tracking speed, can be set in Windows Control Panel➤Mouse.

For a mouse or a tablet, using a bus interface for the device is often preferable to using one of your serial ports. DOS works well with two serial ports, COM1 and COM2. On some computers, you could encounter device conflicts if you attempted to install other serial ports (COM3, COM4, and so forth). Serial devices cannot share a COM port or a device interrupt (IRQ).

If you have a modem, which is required for data transmission with the ToAGX program, it will take up one of the COM ports. If you also have a portable computer and want to transfer files from your desktop system, you might want the other COM port for that. A serial pointing device uses a driver program that has exclusive control of that port as long as Windows is running. It therefore is not practical to use that port for anything else.

MEMORY AND DISK MANAGEMENT

The memory requirement for Freelance Graphics for Windows (random access memory, or RAM) is 3MB minimum, 4MB recommended. The system described in Table A-1 ran the program successfully with 4MB, even when other Windows applications were running concurrently. More memory may be needed if you do a lot of multitasking, particularly if you want to do anything else while Print Manager is running. You can increase the temporary storage capacity and performance of your system without adding RAM by using several disk-management techniques, including the SMART-Drive disk-cache utility.

The amount of available memory limits the number and complexity of applications and documents that can be open concurrently in Windows. It also potentially constrains the complexity of slides and the size of presentations. You will be more likely to encounter these constraints if your system has only the minimum RAM (2MB for Windows or 3MB for Freelance Graphics).

Both Windows and Freelance Graphics for Windows use the system driver HIMEM.SYS to manage extended memory. The SMART-Drive utility is used to manage virtual (disk) memory. Normally, the Windows Install program installs these drivers. If the drivers are installed, the following device-assignment statements will be found in your system's CONFIG.SYS file (device and path can vary):

```
DEVICE=C:\HIMEM.SYS
DEVICE=C:\WINDOWS\SMARTDRV.SYS AvgCache MinCache
```

AvgCache is the amount of memory, in kilobytes, for the normal cache size (try 2048 for Freelance Graphics). *MinCache* is the minimum cache size (try 256). You may need to adjust these settings for best system performance.

Some non-Windows applications can use only *expanded* memory (EMS) and require a different driver. An expanded-memory driver that is compatible with Windows is EMM386.SYS. If you install this driver, you must observe the following points for Freelance Graphics to operate properly:

- Do not install this driver unless you have an application (usually a DOS program) that requires it.

- The device-assignment command for this driver must appear in the CONFIG.SYS file *after* the assignment statement for HIMEM.SYS. The statement must include a numeric parameter specifying a limit (*MemSize*) on the amount of *extended* memory, in kilobytes, that HIMEM.SYS will allocate to this driver:

```
DEVICE=C:\WINDOWS\EMM386.SYS MemSize
```

- In Standard or 386 enhanced modes, Windows may be incompatible with some versions of other expanded-memory drivers, such as 386-Max, CEMM, or QEMM.

Increasing System Performance

To increase the performance of your computer system for the purpose of running Freelance Graphics for Windows, try the following:

- Add a device-assignment statement for SMARTDrive to the CONFIG.SYS file.

- Periodically, compact (defragment) your hard disk using a disk-reorganization program. Do this to improve system performance and also immediately prior to setting up a permanent swap file, as described below.

- If you can run Windows in 386 enhanced mode, set up a permanent swap file on the hard disk.

- Set up a TEMP directory for Windows by including the following statements in the AUTOEXEC.BAT file (device and path can vary):

```
SET TEMP=C:\WINDOWS\TEMP
DEL C:\WINDOWS\TEMP\*.TMP
DEL C:\WINDOWS\TEMP\~*.*
```

- Periodically, repair lost clusters on your hard disk by running the following DOS command:

```
CHKDSK/F
```

Any lost clusters found by this routine will be converted to files with the names FILE*NNNN*.CHK, where *N* is a consecutive number. Inspect these files and delete them unless they contain data you need to recover.

Setting Up a Permanent Swap File

Different procedures are required for setting up permanent swap files in Windows 3.0 and 3.1.

TIP *A swap file requires a portion of* contiguous *empty disk space. Therefore, always defragment (compact) your hard disk before attempting to change swap-file settings. Also, some types of file compression (done by programs that conserve disk space) should not be done in the swap-file area.*

Procedure for Windows 3.0

To set up a permanent swap file in Windows 3.0, first select File➤Exit to quit Windows.

At the DOS prompt, enter **win/r.** (This command starts Windows in Real mode). In Windows, close all applications except Program Manager. Then, select File➤Run. In the Run dialog box, enter **swapfile** and select OK.

The Swapfile dialog box appears, showing the recommended swap-file size on the current drive (for use with Freelance Graphics, you will probably need 4MB or more). To accept this setting, select Create and confirm it when prompted by selecting OK.

Select File➤Exit to quit Windows. When you restart Windows in 386 enhanced mode, Freelance Graphics will be able to use the new permanent swap file.

Procedure for Windows 3.1

A permanent swap file can be created when you install Windows 3.1 for the first time. After that, to check its status or to change the swap-file settings, select 386 Enhanced in Windows Control Panel. The 386 Enhanced dialog box will appear. Select the button labeled *Virtual Memory.*

The Virtual Memory dialog box will appear (Figure A-2). The status of the swap file is displayed in the Current Settings box. If the Type setting is Permanent and the Size setting is larger than 4MB, there are no changes to make. Select OK.

Or, to change the settings, select the Change button. Select the letter of the drive that will contain the swap file. For Type, select

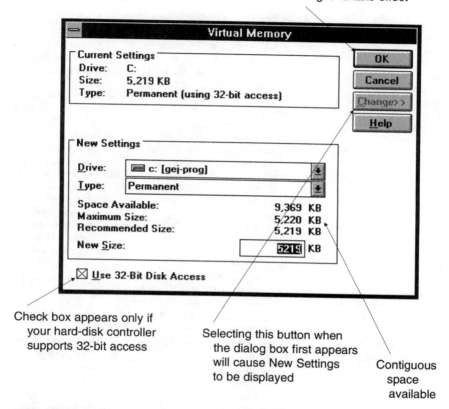

After you select OK, you must restart Windows for your changes to take effect

Check box appears only if your hard-disk controller supports 32-bit access

Selecting this button when the dialog box first appears will cause New Settings to be displayed

Contiguous space available

FIGURE A-2.   Settings in this dialog box define a permanent swap file for extending the memory area available to Windows.

Permanent. Enter a size in kilobytes for the file in the New Size box (or press Enter to accept the program's recommended size). A dialog box will appear with a warning message. Select OK twice, once to close each of the open dialog boxes. When it appears, select the Restart button. (Do not restart by pressing Ctrl-Alt-Del.)

Index

■■■